ALAN JUDD's n...   ...y
of Literature's Win...   ...a
BBC television drama. His biography *Ford Madox Ford* won
the Heinemann award and his novella *The Devil's Own Work*
the *Guardian* Fiction Prize.

He is the author of three other novels and has recently retired
from the Foreign Office.

More from the reviews:

'A fascinating book... It illuminates why Cumming is still
revered within the service. For without his personal courage,
ingenuity, persistence and determination, MI6 would surely
have died in infancy.'   DAVID STAFFORD, *Daily Mail*

'Although there are plenty of comic moments in this excellent
book, in the final analysis, it is a serious testament to the bravery
and determination of the Secret Services during the Great War
... Judd has quested for the real "C" and he has found him.'
                                ANDREW ROBERTS, *Spectator*

'Cummings was the stuff of which fictional spymasters are
made.'   PIERS BRENDON, *Independent*

'Exciting stuff with truly interesting sidetracks: the history of
pigeons in warfare, for instance, or the use of semen in invisible
ink... Judd has done an admirable job.'
                              CRAIG BROWN, *Mail on Sunday*

'An endearing portrait.'   JOHN CROSLAND, *Sunday Times*

THE
QUEST FOR C

Sir Mansfield Cumming and the
Founding of the British Secret Service

ALAN JUDD

Harper
Press

HarperCollins*Publishers*
77–85 Fulham Palace Road,
Hammersmith, London W6 8JB

This paperback edition 2000
1

First published in Great Britain by
HarperCollins*Publishers* 1999

Copyright © Alan Judd 1999

Alan Judd asserts the moral right to
be identified as the author of this work

ISBN 978-0-00-653025-1

Set in PostScript Linotype Sabon by
Rowland Phototypesetting Ltd,
Bury St Edmunds, Suffolk

Printed and bound in Great Britain by
Clays Ltd, St Ives plc

To all who have served and remained silent.

Contents

LIST OF ILLUSTRATIONS

1. Crowther Smith's copy of an earlier portrait of Mansfield Cumming, with awards and decorations added.
2. Cumming as Sub-Lieutenant Smith, RN.
3. Cumming on the deck of the *Enchantress*.
4. A post-card of Cumming qualifying for his pilot's licence.
5. The clock made by Cumming and given to Susannah Ritchie's father.
6. Cumming featured as one of the pioneers of 'motorism'.
7. Cumming's Wolseley racer, 25th April 1903.
8. Cumming at the wheel, 2nd May 1903.
9. Cumming before the race, 9th May 1903.
10. 'Waiting for the Off', 30th May 1903.
11. Cumming's Boom Defence headquarters and home, HMS *Argo*.
12. Cumming's houseboat at Bursledon.
13. The wreckage of what is believed to have been the car in which Cumming and Alastair crashed.
14. Alastair's grave in the military cemetery near Meaux.
15. The letter to Cumming from the Director of Naval Intelligence, inviting him to start the Secret Service.
16. Cumming's successful and controversial head of Rotterdam Station, Richard Tinsley (1875–1944) by Crowther Smith.
17. Burnford House, Hampshire, which Cumming rented.
18. The modern view from the site of Cumming's wartime office in Whitehall Court.
19. Part of what may have been Cumming's workshop in Whitehall Court.

20. Photograph taken by TR/16 of the Deutsche Werft yard at Kiel, June 1916.
21. Photograph taken by TR/16 in June 1937 of a destroyer fitting out in the Germania Werft yard at Kiel.
22. Self-portrait by Crowther Smith, the cartoonist who worked for Cumming.
23. Cumming's grave.
24. The remains of HMS *Sultan*'s mast in the Hamble mud.

ACKNOWLEDGEMENTS

Among the many who have helped with this book are some whose names have to be withheld. Although they cannot be publicly thanked they may, I hope, get some satisfaction from seeing the results of their help and encouragement. I am particularly grateful to the two historians who jointly inspired the book and sustained the author.

It could not have been written as it was without the generous assistance of Cumming's family, in particular Alison Watkins and her husband, Tony, Ann Harries and Pippa Temple. Susannah Ritchie, historian of Bursledon, threw light on Cumming's little-known Bursledon years, as also did Doreen Vetcher and, in generously making available her mother's letters, Judith Buford. Mr. and Mrs. John Sneezum, owners of the house Cumming built, were informative and hospitable. Patricia O'Driscoll generously shared her knowledge of Cumming's nautical activities. Stewart and Bee Lang kindly put up with me in Cambridge. Viscount and Viscountess Mersey saved me from falling deeper into error and revived me with a memorable lunch. The advice and help of Mark Seaman of the Imperial War Museum has been more valuable than his modesty would permit him to recognise, while the wisdom of Professor Christopher Andrew has consistently proved an inspiration and a boon.

I owe much to Stuart Proffitt, my commissioning editor (now with Penguin), and to Arabella Pike and Michael Fishwick of HarperCollins. My agent, Anthony Goff, has been stalwart. Ellie Hinchey graciously found me room when room was greatly needed. Nicola Magill combined untiring efficiency with forgiving good-nature. From memories more coloured than clouded by wine I retain the strong impression of David Crane's insight and cheerful realism, while through the same atmosphere – thickened by cigar smoke – looms the concentrated sagacity and goodwill of Richard Holmes. My thanks, too, to David Wade, Steve Woods and Professor John Dancy for suggesting additions and improvements in time for the paperback edition. Finally, every book has its victims (the author apart), and in this case I owe thanks to my wife, Judy, and daughter, Katie, for their forbearance.

1

Early Years

In August 1909 a fifty-year-old naval commander, living in active semi-retirement on a houseboat near Southampton, received a handwritten letter on Admiralty paper. It was dated 10 August and marked 'private':

> My dear Mansfield Cumming,
>
> Boom defence must be getting a bit stale with you and the recent experiments with [illegible] rather discounts yours at Southampton. You may therefore perhaps like a new billet. If so I have something good I can offer you and if you would like to come and see me on Thursday about noon I will tell you what it is.
>
> Yours sincerely
> A. W. Bethell.

Rear Admiral Bethell was the Director of Naval Intelligence (DNI), a post which, in the days of Empire when a quarter of the globe was British and the Royal Navy was by policy kept at a strength double that of its two nearest rivals combined, signified no arcane or invisible Whitehall department. Although it would be years yet before the link between intelligence and operations was properly understood within the Admiralty, the DNI was a man with worldwide responsibility, considerable autonomy and direct access to the brains and heart of imperial power. For all its informality, this was not a casual invitation.

Few people start new careers at fifty and Mansfield Cumming was at first reluctant. Comfortably, if somewhat eccentrically, ensconced in Bursledon, on the River Hamble, he enjoyed devising and organising the boom defences that were his task. These were a series of wires, nets, hulks and boats intended to keep out enemy ships and submarines in the event of war. Cumming had been doing it since 1898 and it appealed to his ingenious practicality, while enabling him to go on messing about in boats and – most of the time – living on one.

The offer of a desk job in Whitehall was probably not what he looked for when the post was rowed out to him. But Admiral Bethell's 'something good' turned out to be the offer to set up and run a new organisation called the Secret Service Bureau, the progenitor of the Security Service (MI5) and the Secret Intelligence Service (MI6). It was not just a desk job, more a way of life.

Although initially reluctant to leave boom defence, Cumming became the first Chief of SIS, known as 'C' (for Cumming, not for Chief) and using green ink, traditions which his successors have continued in his honour to this day. From 1909 he was to live and die in the Secret Service, the embodiment of Hamlet's now unfashionable contention that we do know what we are, but not what we may be. Before this, the unambitious, middle-aged commander gave every sign of being content with his lot and probably would have said that in playing around with boom defences on a beautiful estuary, in reach of family and friends, he had found his métier. Yet in fulfilling this summons, he made himself more than himself, and forged a tradition and an organisation that bears his stamp still.

When he was born on All Fools Day, 1859, his name was not Cumming but Mansfield George Smith. He took the name Cumming later, on his second marriage, and was thereafter known either as that or as Smith Cumming. His branch of the family traced their ancestry back through Sir John Smyth, Knight, from 1540 to 1547 second Baron of the Exchequer to Henry VIII, to John Carrington who served Richard II and fled abroad when Richard was overthrown by Henry IV. John returned incognito in 1404 and, under the patronage of an abbot cousin, secretly adopted the name Smyth and married the granddaughter of the Mayor of London. His branch of the Carringtons, which descended from Sir Michael Carrington, standard-bearer to Richard I in the Holy Land, thus went into abeyance for several centuries until some of its nineteenth- and twentieth-century Smiths rediscovered their heritage and reverted to the less common name, a cause of some dissension in the family.

Sir John Smyth's numerous descendants proved a prosperous family who throve mainly in Essex, Nottinghamshire and Warwickshire, undistracted by sensation or unwonted distinction, solid and successful. One branch produced the grandmother of Queen Elizabeth the Queen Mother, and the former Foreign Secretary, Lord Carrington. Later, another John Smyth, a director of the East India Company, bought an estate in Cardiganshire called Foël Allt, where Cumming's father was born. The Foël Allt association must have been important because when in 1856 Cumming's father, Colonel John Thomas Smith, bought a house in Lee, South London, he named it Foëllt House, and it was here that Cumming was born three years later.

Now called Pentland House and functioning as a hall of residence for Goldsmiths College, the house is thought to be the oldest surviving domestic building in the borough. It was built in about 1685, probably around the shell of an older building, and in 1691 it was leased by another tribe of Smiths (no relation to Cumming) who subsequently bought and owned it until selling it to Cumming's father. It was a substantial building even then, before extensive later additions, perhaps larger than the handsome manor set next to it which was owned by the Baring banking family and is now a public library.

Lee was a respectable and popular area when Cumming's parents moved there, settled by retired admirals and generals. In fact, the mid-nineteenth-century tenant of Foëllt was Admiral Sir George Martin, a contemporary of Nelson's. The house still wears the white rendering put on it at that time and is dominated at the front by three striking trees, a sycamore, a plane and a rare maidenhair tree, a type thought extinct until rediscovered in China in the nineteenth century. They could have been planted by the Smiths. There is an elaborate covered walkway to the front and a large garden behind backing on to what is now Manor Park, formerly the manor's gardens. Inside there is at least one Adam fireplace and the staircase is decorated with imported carved wooden bowls of flowers, possibly by Grinling Gibbons.

The later utilitarian additions misled Pesvner into thinking it and the manor 'too close together'. Despite the marks of municipal care, the pervasive scruffiness, the French six-pounder cannon heaved off their trestles and abandoned on the lawn of the manor, it is still just possible to discern in these two buildings the rich and privileged lives of Victorian gentry. Staircases have been moved, fireplaces boarded, walls knocked through in the interests of institutional need but here and there a piece of panelling, a high mantelpiece, a chandelier, the unexpected perspective of a dining room, have survived to hint at the busy, comfortable and probably noisy household into which the young Mansfield George Smith was born, the twelfth of thirteen children.

His mother, Maria Sarah Tyser, daughter of a doctor, married in 1837 and spent over ten of her next twenty-three years pregnant, and most of the rest – unless she used wet nurses – breastfeeding. She bred five boys and eight girls, rearing all but one girl to adulthood. Ten were born before the family settled in Lee, mostly – because of her husband's career – in India.

The family tree gives John Thomas as having been born in

1808 and dying in 1884, though the *Dictionary of National Biography* has him as born in 1805 and dying in 1882. He became an engineer of some distinction, taking a commission in the Madras Royal Engineers after attending the military college of the East India Company. In Madras he designed a reciprocating light for lighthouses and translated an abstruse but important thesis on mortars and cements. In 1837, the year of his marriage, he was elected a Fellow of the Royal Society and put in charge of public works in Madras and neighbouring areas. Three years later, as Master of the Madras Mint, he replaced animal power by steam and, after a visit to South Africa, designed an innovative machine for minting and weighing which was shown at the Great Exhibition in 1851. He also designed a refracting sight for rifles and some 'ingenious inventions' which he proposed for the demolition of the fortifications at Kronstadt. In 1885 he was made Mint Master at Calcutta but some time after that returned to England with the honorary rank of colonel, bought Foëllt House and devoted himself to currency problems while retaining various Indian-related consultancy posts. He wrote many learned papers and a number of technical publications. He sold Foëllt House some time after 1874 and when he died in 1882 it was at 10 Gledhow Gardens in South Kensington. Perhaps the building site that South London became from mid-century onwards, spawning the seemingly numberless terraces that now surround Pentland and the manor, drove the family out, or perhaps the children were mostly away and the house seemed too big. 'He was', said one friend, Sir Arthur Cotton, 'one of the most talented, laborious, clear-headed and sound-judging men I have ever met with, or known by other means.' These epithets were to find resonance in the life of his twelfth child.

In that vigorous, fecund, high-achieving age, Cumming's seems to have been an almost archetypically successful family of Victoria and Empire. His eldest brother, for instance, was another military engineer who served in South Africa from 1857 to 1862, was responsible for the defences of Portland and Weymouth and, as Director of Public Works for the Admiralty, oversaw the harbour works in Malta, Gibraltar, Bermuda, Halifax and Newfoundland. He published a number of papers and his anonymously written three-volume *Notes on Building Construction* was regarded as the best book on the subject. He was twenty-one years older than Cumming and died in 1893 as an honorary major general, aged fifty-five. The other siblings seem generally to have served in or married into the church, the army or the professions. Cumming's unusual first name, Mansfield, is likely to have been taken from his eldest brother's Nottinghamshire father-in-law, Mansfield Parkyns of Woodborough Hall.

It may have been due to his eldest brother's Admiralty connections that Cumming was put down for Dartmouth, but there could have been other reasons. Lionel Dawson, who was a cadet around the end of the century and wrote about it in his autobiography, *Flotillas*, identified economy as the reason why his family chose the navy for him: 'the Navy was – and, I dare say, still is – the cheapest way of disposing of a boy from the age of 13 that exists – at least, so far as the service of the Crown is concerned.' Even so, it wasn't cheap: the four-year Dartmouth course that began early in the twentieth century cost each boy's parents about £1,000.

When the twelve-year-old Cumming went to Dartmouth in January 1872, however, it was not to the long-course shore establishment that it later became and still is. The 'college' comprised two elderly sailing ships moored in the River Dart, having previously comprised one ship moored in the predictably unhealthy Haslar Creek, Portsmouth, then at the predictably exposed Portland, before moving to Dartmouth in 1863. When Cumming arrived the two hulks were the *Britannia* (formerly the *Prince of Wales*) and the teak-built *Hindostan*. He was berthed in the *Britannia*, which was eventually broken up for her copper in 1916.

The Dartmouth course has probably always been hard but then it was positively grim, though there was sufficient competition for it to compel most boys to go to crammers in order to qualify. The courses generally lasted fifteen to eighteen months, divided into four-month periods, with discipline maintained by ship's corporals. The *Britannia*'s intended complement of 150 was crowded enough, but over the years a further 120 were crammed into her. Cadets chose their friends only from those within the same four-month age span as themselves who slept, in alphabetical order, in the same dormitories. Everything, from teeth-cleaning to praying, was done by order signalled by bell. Instant, unquestioning obedience was the central principle of the system, and independence or originality were at best frowned upon, more often punished. Beatings – sometimes by boys only a few months older than the victim – were common. A contemporary of Cumming's, Sir Seymour Fortescue, recorded his impressions in his book *Looking Back*: 'There is no period of my life that I look back upon with less pleasure than I do to the time I spent in *Britannia*. . . . I had not reckoned on the amount of elementary mathematics which I detested even more than Latin grammar, that was to be forced into me during the 15 months training in the *Britannia*.' Dawson, who was there later, stresses the physical nature of the course as well as the amount of time dedicated to obsolescent sail-training. The other principal subjects were navigation, mathematics, drawing, science and naval history, along with French which was at one time taught by a Frenchman whose technique was to dictate his own short stories. E. A. Hughes, in his history *The Royal Naval College, Dartmouth*, quotes an unnamed cadet as saying: 'I never heard a Lieutenant of a Term address his cadets on any subject but games . . . never did we have a lecture on how to be an officer, how to treat men, how to conduct oneself on duty and off.' Although by Dawson's time the food was apparently 'good and plentiful', in Cumming's time it was, according to Fortescue, 'disgracefully bad and scanty . . . it became a regular practice of the cadets when passing a bluejacket to drop a hand-kerchief with sixpence knotted in the corner, the handkerchief being surreptitiously returned in the course of a few minutes with bits of ships biscuit wrapped up in it instead of the sixpence.'

Spartan and severe it certainly was, but it was probably fair and may even have compared well with public schools of the period. Certainly, naval records and naval standards of navigation show that the officers it produced wrote clear, grammatical, properly punctuated English and knew their business when it came to sailing their ships.

There is no extant list of cadets for Cumming's course and no photographs, but he has a page to himself in the college's disciplinary book, *Conduct of naval cadets. 1869–72. HMS Britannia.* Identified as '66 No. 368', his relative standing in all four terms varies between 25 and 31, though we don't know how many were on his course. A decade later the future Admiral Beatty's course numbered 33 (in which Beatty came eighteenth), while on Dawson's course there were 64. Cumming's assessments for Study and Seamanship were 'fair' and 'satisfactory', his French is twice assessed as 'fair' and is twice illegible; his Conduct declines from 'good', to 'fair', to 'unsatisfactory', to illegible.

On 10 March 1872, two months after joining, the twelve-year-old Cumming was punished for 'Reading a Novel in Study'. Subsequent troubles during his first year comprise filling ink pots with blotting paper in French study, destroying his work and throwing it overboard, improper behaviour towards a cadet captain, throwing a glass bottle at a train, laughing, talking, loitering and disorderly behaviour. He began the following year by misbehaving and talking during morning prayers, and was later punished for 'Assisting in bullying Messrs Gristorth and Hancock, two 1st term Cadets, and making them sing songs on a Sunday'. Punishments are generally unrecorded though he had to pay damages and spend three days in the Cockpit Mess for the bottle and train offence, but bullying seems to have been taken more seriously. Under 'Remarks' it is noted that he received both second- and first-class punishments, albeit let off a proportion of the latter. The second-class punishment was probably similar to that later described by Dawson: 'The very hardened criminals were segregated from the remainder for a period and called second classmen. They wore a white band around their arms, and lived behind a screen on the orlop deck – that is, the lowest – of the *Britannia*. . . they were marched everywhere, to studies and drill, by a ship's corporal.'

Dawson never saw any of what he calls real bullying on the *Britannia*, and certainly nothing comparable to 'what was afterwards experienced in a "hot" gun room at sea'. He also believes that the careers of those on the course proceeded in inverse proportion to their relative positions on passing out: 'our subsequent careers aptly fulfilled that discouraging Biblical promise that "the last shall be first".'

Cumming's other crimes were less serious. He was punished for further improper behaviour during Divine Service, for bathing at Blackpool when on shore for afternoon recreation (presumably they had sailed up the coast) and finally, just before he left, for not obeying a sentry. It was probably a fairly average career at Dartmouth. Beatty, for instance, was rather more punished: twenty-five minor offences and three more serious, for one of which he was severely beaten. Dawson, to judge by his account, was perhaps less punished. When Cumming signed off on 19 December 1873, as fourteen-year-old Cadet Smith, he was graded second class in study and his conduct, fair.

It is also hard to judge the overall effectiveness of this method of training Royal Naval officers. In his excellent book about Jutland, *The Rules of the Game*, Andrew Gordon digs deep into the nineteenth-century navy to account for the attitudes displayed at that confused engagement, particularly those concerning adherence to rules, method and procedure. Most captains seemed to have thought that Dartmouth training was an advance on the previous haphazard system of sending boys to sea to flounder or flourish as luck and their captains would have it, but in 1871 Commodore James Goodenough (who was killed by poisonous arrows in the South Pacific four years later) deplored 'the loss of individuality which is inevitable when all young gentlemen are passed through the same course from the age of twelve years'.

Nelson's navy was disciplined in action but untidy, irregular and individualistic out of it. The Victorians sought to account, to regulate, to standardise, to measure. These habits of thought, particularly the mania for measurement, are now so deeply ingrained that we no longer see them as choices. Uniformity seems to us so much the natural way that we do not ask, as did an aggrieved rating whom Gordon quotes, why each man's ditty-bag should be the same size and pattern, why hats should be stowed in a particular way – why, indeed, uniforms should be uniform. Even saluting, for instance, was standardised only in 1889. Before that naval officers either removed their caps, took the brim between finger and thumb or simply touched the peak. Significantly, it took a German – Kaiser Wilhelm II, an honorary admiral of the Royal Navy – to complain about this unmilitary variety; his complaints led to standardisation.

Thus, at the time when Cumming was being trained and moulded, it was still possible to conceive of less regulated ways of doing things, a fact that may partly account for the iron insistence on to-the-letter obedience characteristic of the later Victorian and Edwardian days. It is worth emphasising this ethic of obedience because it helps explain some of the middle-aged Cumming's attitudes, actions and restraints when founding and running the Secret Service. His belief in obeying orders no matter what he thought of them prompted at least one of his First World War staff to comment that he was a product of the age he was born into. Understanding of this background is also essential to a true appreciation of Cumming's achievement in simultaneously exemplifying and transcending it by creating a Secret Service that, while never seeking to exceed its political control, became famed for its inventiveness, individuality, ingenuity and – in keeping with its founder – eccentricity.

The high, or low, point of the navy's initiative-crushing discipline was the notorious 1893 collision between the Mediterranean Squadron's flagship *Camperdown* and the *Victoria*. A rigid interpretation of flag signals led to the two ships manoeuvring to collide even though the officers concerned could see what was about to happen. No senior officer had the confidence to steer any course other than that which was ordered, with the result that 358 officers and men, including Vice-Admiral Sir George Tyron, perished. Even as the *Victoria* was rapidly sinking, about six hundred of the crew fell in four deep on the quarterdeck and waited, motionless and silent, for the order to move. One of those saved was the future First Sea Lord, Lord Fisher. The lessons learned did not include the big one, which perhaps required deeper soul-searching than the navy was yet prepared for. Nor were they alone in this: Queen Victoria confided to her journal: 'To say, as many did, that juniors should disobey in the event of anything dangerous taking place, would never do.'

On leaving the *Britannia* Cumming was sent to the *Duke of Wellington*, a guardship and receiving ship moored in Portsmouth harbour. Fortescue had been on her a couple of years before: 'Anything worse for the morals and discipline of a number of lads of our age than life aboard the guardships of those days, it is hard to imagine. We were nearly 100 in the mess.' It wasn't only young cadets and midshipmen who stayed aboard her between ships, but also older officers. Cumming appears on her strength several times in subsequent years.

Cadets and midshipmen – mids or snotties – were neither officers nor seamen and those who were saw it as essential to good training to make life as hard as possible for them. By long tradition, their education was supposed to continue at sea, and generally did. On larger ships the chaplain was often given the responsibility but it could be undertaken by one of the senior officers or by the captain himself. Sometimes they were sent to training ships before going properly to sea. Fortescue records that all fifty of his *Britannia* team were sent to the *Bristol* for training. It was a gruelling routine, mainly sail work, and it left Fortescue with lasting admiration for the sailors who taught them. The upper yardmen, he thought, were

> the finest specimens of humanity I have ever met . . . as active as cats and as brave as lions; for, if once a man showed, when aloft, the smallest desire to hold on with one hand and work with the other, instead of chancing everything and working with both, he was useless as an upper yardman, and was at once relegated to safer and less ambitious duties.

Ominously, in view of inadequacies later laid bare, Fortescue also shows how decades without a major action ('Intellects becalmed in the smoke of Trafalgar' was the opinion of the Admiralty expressed by the *Quarterly Review* in 1847) had corrupted a navy that ironically still thought of itself as Nelsonic: 'Anything in the shape of science was a bore . . . when it came to gun practice, which consisted in firing at a cask with a small flagstaff bobbing about in the sea, the one object was to get it over as soon as possible, as it was looked upon as distinctly uninteresting.' This practice was still extant in the early twentieth century, when warships in home waters still had black hulls with red water-lines, yellow funnels and white upper works.

In the first few days of 1874 Cadet Smith joined a new, wood-built screw corvette of fourteen guns, the *Modeste*, under Captain H. T. Thompson. This was not a training ship, but one bound for active service. On February she sailed for the Far East via Gibraltar, Malta, Suez, Aden (which took two months to reach), Bombay, Singapore, Manila, Hong Kong, the China

Strait, Nagasaki and Shanghai, where the crew spent Christmas. As with many Victorians who survived into what was recognisably the modern world, we have to remind ourselves that Cumming's earlier influences and experiences were those of another age. The punishment recorded against a crew member, E. Millers, in the *Modeste*'s log is a reminder: '24 cuts of the birch as per warrant'.

They remained at Shanghai until May 1875, then spent the rest of the year cruising in Chinese and Malay waters. The end of the year, however, brought some action: the British Resident had been murdered by natives of the Perak River region in Malaya and a punitive expedition was mounted. The *Modeste* blockaded the river mouth while officers and men from the *Fly* and the *Thistle*, which had joined her, manned native boats and headed upriver. They captured the Residency and an enemy stockade without loss, taking six guns and destroying the houses and villages of the 'offending people'. Cumming was probably still aboard the *Modeste* but in January 1876 a Naval Brigade was formed of officers and men from the *Modeste* and *Ringdove*, under Captain Buller of the *Modeste*. They co-operated with the army under Major General Colborne and advanced in tandem on neighbouring rivers with Lieutenant Colonel Hill. The evidence for Cumming's involvement in this operation is, first, that he is recorded as having served as ADC during this period and it is hard to see for whom else but Major General Colborne or his own captain, perhaps liaising between the navy and the army. Second, his naval record (PRO ADM196/20) has a not very legible reference to a brigade in this period. (The dates don't quite match but they overlap with the local campaign dates and variations are not uncommon.)

Whatever his role, it was not a comfortable operation. It lasted a month and involved poling substantial quantities of arms and ammunition upriver, then carrying heavy loads across very difficult terrain. Their diet was mainly preserved meat, supplemented by the occasional wild buffalo. They had no bread or vegetables, were wet the whole time and for much of it were waist deep in mud and water. The remarkable fact of no one going sick was attributed to the issue of one waterproof ground sheet per man. By an Admiralty order of 23 February 1880, all who served off the coast of Parak between 12 November 1875 and 20 March 1876 were awarded the Indian General Service Medal and Parak Clasp, sixteen-year-old Midshipman (as he by then was) Smith included.[1]

There were many such operations throughout the Empire, not in themselves particularly noteworthy but important because no empire could have been sustained without the will and ability to mount them. Mostly they were quiet, remote affairs, but vivid, monotonous, enjoyable, gruelling, sometimes lethal for those involved, often mounted with, as it were, the left hand. They would probably have been regarded as character-forming.

After this the *Modeste* spent a few more months in Malayan waters before sailing to Japan and from there to Hong Kong, where the crew were paid off on 10 May 1877. After another spell on the *Duke of Wellington* and in other home bases, Cumming's next significant appointment was in January 1878 to the *Bellerophon*, a modern, smart, prestigious, fully-rigged, iron flagship dating from 1866. She was then the flagship of Vice-Admiral Sir H. Cooper Key, Commander-in-Chief North America and West Indies, and her captain was John Arbuthnot Fisher, the future First Sea Lord. This must have been a great change from the intimacy of the *Modeste*; forty-six officers, eighty-three petty officers, two hundred and ninety-four seamen, forty-six boys, seventy-six marines. Her main armament was ten 9-inch and five 7-inch guns.

When Cumming joined her she was in Bermuda and the next few months were spent cruising West Indian waters – St Kitts, Antigua, St Vincent, Barbados and Trinidad. This was presumably a tolerable existence – given what life could be in the navy – even for the ever-hungry midshipmen, though there may have been a tiresome amount of 'bull'. Cumming was promoted sub-lieutenant in June 1878 just after they had sailed up to Halifax. In August they visited Newport, Rhode Island; Charlottetown, Prince Edward Island; and Quebec, before returning to Halifax for a royal visit by Princess Louise and the Marquess of Lorne. Such ceremonial sailing and flag-showing must have been either congenial or tedious, according to temperament and circumstance. For Cumming it was anyway fairly brief, for towards the end of the year he was discharged to the *Black Prince* 'for passage to England'. As a junior officer, further training forever loomed.

After the inevitable sojourn aboard the *Duke of Wellington*, Cumming was transferred to the *Excellent*, an elderly ship moored in Portsmouth harbour and used mostly for gunnery training. He seems to have spent two periods on her, the first for examinations, which he passed, and the second for a gunnery course. He also spent some time in Haslar, the shore-based naval hospital at Gosport. This is the first indication in his record of the ill-health that was to cause him to retire from the active list. Once again, Cumming was following in the footsteps of Fortescue who describes the three-month gunnery course as one during which

> besides having practically to perform all the drill of every arm carried by a man-of-war it was also necessary to learn what might be called the 'patter' of the business – pages and pages of the gunnery and small-arms drill books – the idea being that one should be able to pass on the extensive knowledge thus acquired to others.

Noses, he said, were 'kept very closely to the grind stone' and there was little amusement 'except after dinner when we became great patrons of the drama in the front row of the pit of the old Portsmouth theatre'.

Cumming passed the course and in April 1880 was appointed

to the *Hecla*, another modern warship, launched only two years earlier, iron built and of 'very economical steam', under Captain Morgan Singer. She displaced 64,000 tons and had a complement of 224. She was at Portsmouth when Cumming joined and spent the next few months in home waters conducting torpedo and submarine defence trials, and watching counter-mine trials. In August she sailed to Malta and spent the rest of that year and into the next cruising the Mediterranean, conducting further trials and visiting Corfu, Cephalonia, Zahte, Patras and Ithaca. At that time and over ensuing decades the Mediterranean fleet was what Gordon aptly calls 'the greatest display team in the world'. It was centred on Malta, which had familiar British companies, shops and banks and was a place where pay stretched farther. Admittedly, the summer heat could be uncomfortable and there was the threat of Malta fever (in fact, brucellosis, a debilitating recurring fever normally contracted from infected cattle or milk), but otherwise life afloat and ashore was agreeably social. There was a good deal of entertaining and sport, a reasonable supply of (English) prostitutes and for ambitious young officers a chance to make friendships and contacts which would serve well later. Cruises were constructed around political and social events and gradually, unconsciously, the Mediterranean came to be regarded as the navy's private pleasure lake.

Display took precedence over preparation for war, with competitive drills and a pervasive passion for order and cleanliness. For many these were halcyon days, a high-water mark of unchallenged imperial grandeur, a beautiful natural playground in which to show off, to admire and be admired. Nobody was shot at and all the while purpose remained submerged in process, with results that would show only a generation later in the somewhat greyer, very much colder waters off Jutland.

In June 1881 Cumming left the *Hecla* for passage to England. Life for the next few months was, if anything, even more ceremonial than that which he had already enjoyed, or endured. He was appointed to one of the royal yachts, the *Victoria and*

Albert, for its summer cruise. Based at Portsmouth where she had been converted from hulk to yacht, the *Victoria and Albert* actually spent the summer as the Royal Cowes ferry, before finally carrying the Crown Prince of Germany and his retinue back to Le Havre in September. There were constant social and sporting events, such as a 15 August boat race between the officers of the *Victoria and Albert* and another royal yacht, the *Osborne*, watched by the Queen. The *Victoria and Albert* won.

In September, the week before this agreeable interlude ended, Cumming was promoted to lieutenant and appointed to HMS *President*, an old frigate moored in the Thames on whose strength he was held while attending further training at the Royal Naval College, Greenwich. Fortescue, of course, had been there already on the 'very mathematical' six-month seamanship course, and he recalls a magnificent bear-fight at the end-of-course dinner which resulted in the entire course being placed under one month's close arrest in guardships. Despite the rigid discipline, or perhaps because of it, spontaneity could occasionally make itself forcefully felt.

Thereafter, it was back to the Mediterranean for nearly a year in HMS *Daring* and HMS *Ruby*, the latter supporting the operation to buttress the Khedive's position in Egypt. Although there were significant land actions in the Middle East and North Africa at the time, that at sea was inconsiderable. Nevertheless, the Egypt Medal and the Khedive Star were bestowed upon anyone in the general area, land or sea. Although the *Ruby* does not appear to have taken any part in the operations, she was geographically proximate and so Cumming, along with the rest, was awarded the medals.

His next ship was the *Sultan*, in which he spent just under a year cruising, before returning to the Royal Naval College for further study. The future King George V was also there and in a 1916 diary entry mentioning an audience with Cumming – who apparently told him some 'interesting things' – he refers to their having attended Greenwich together. The entry in his diary for 12 December 1884 records 'billiards with Smith' (as Cumming still was).

Cumming's last significant ship – perhaps his most significant – was the *Raleigh*, whither he was posted along with the *Sultan*'s captain, Sir Walter Hunt-Grubbe, who was promoted to Admiral. He took Cumming with him as his flag lieutenant, a prestigious and important post. The captain of the *Raleigh* was Captain Arthur Wilson, VC. She sailed to South Africa, anchoring at Simonstown, and it was from there that Cumming returned unexpectedly to England to become, on 21 December 1885, a retired officer on active half pay, at six shillings a day.

The reason for ascribing such significance to Cumming's time in the *Raleigh* is, admittedly, conjectural, but it is conjecture that relies on the well-established Royal Naval tradition of patronage or 'interest'. Nearly all officers who succeeded owed their success partly to having at some point in their careers discovered a patron. Cumming must have been well thought of by Hunt-Grubbe otherwise he would not have been appointed flag lieutenant, but it is possible that another and even more influential patron might have been the captain, Arthur Wilson. 'Tug' Wilson had won his Victoria Cross the year before, ashore at El Teb in Sudan, when the Square (the defensive position frequently adopted by British troops in fights with locals) in which Wilson was present 'as a loafer, just to see the fight', was breached and Wilson plugged the gap with his fists after breaking his sword in a 'cool prod at an Arab'. A ferocious disciplinarian (known also as 'Old 'ard 'art'), he was a short, stocky, tireless man with a spade beard, no concept of leisure and an indifference to the elements remarkable even by the standards of his own naval generation, one not noted for its fussiness over personal comforts. Lionel Dawson was his midshipman when Wilson later commanded the Channel Fleet and reckoned him the hardest man, physically and in every other way, he ever knew. He wore out his hard-working staff, mostly twenty years his junior, without ever showing any sign of fatigue, and seemed as indifferent to noise as he was to the elements:

> We had a fighting top not a dozen feet above our heads on the Admiral's bridge in which dwelt three venomous six-pounder guns. When they were firing his promenade directly beneath them continued unchecked, while not only the flag lieutenant and myself but the signalman on the bridge below, endeavoured to keep as far away from their ear cracking bark as possible. But the admiral continued to issue orders, which had to be interpreted as intelligently as possible through the din and racket that appeared to pass him by completely.

When he was compelled to go ashore, Wilson's clothing was plain beyond simplicity and as much like his uniform as possible. His only recreation on shore was to walk at prodigious speeds for prodigious distances, further exhausting his flag lieutenant, and he generally returned from leave early. He was an iron-nerved and very capable sailor who became the foremost torpedo expert of his day and was closely concerned with the early development of torpedo craft. Dawson believed that in rare moments of relaxation Wilson could be kindly and human and thought him essentially shy and reserved; he reputedly pleaded a former engagement when invited to dine in the Royal Yacht with Queen Victoria.

The conjectural importance of Wilson in Cumming's career is in what happened after they served together. It is still not known why Rear Admiral Bethell, DNI, offered Cumming the task of founding the Secret Service Bureau rather than asking any number of other officers on the active retired list. It would be going beyond the evidence to say that Wilson, as an admiral of the fleet, was behind the choice, but he was in a position to influence it. This is one of a number of suggestive coincidences of timing. In 1898, the year after Wilson's influential appointment as Comptroller of Navy, Cumming was invited to take charge of boom defence at Southampton. When Wilson commanded the Channel Squadron and Home and Channel Fleets, pursuing his interest in torpedoes and small craft, Cumming was similarly engaged to form the Reserve of Motor Boat Owners, for which his naval record shows he was promoted to Commander and in the course of which he was seconded to the Department of Agriculture for Scotland in order to assess the feasibility of converting sail-driven fishing boats to engine power. In April 1909 Wilson was appointed to the Committee of Imperial Defence, the body ultimately responsible for setting up the Secret Service Bureau; in August of that year Cumming received his invitation. (We should also bear in mind, though, that at the time of Cumming's appointment the First Sea Lord was his former captain of *Bellerophon*, John Arbuthnot Fisher; so, if we look for patronage, there are alternative sources. Freemasonry was sometimes a vehicle of patronage in the Royal Navy at that time, but there is no record of Cumming having been a Mason.)

Cumming's naval record (PRO ADM 196/20, p. 123) gives the reason for his apparently abrupt retirement as 'Retired 21st. Dec. 85 (unfit) on Active Half Pay.' There is no indication here as to what 'unfit' referred to although there is a further reference to 'recurrent problems with seasickness' and also a family tradition that this was the cause. This is slightly odd because he had spent most of the previous twelve years at sea with, apart from a fortnight in the naval hospital at Haslar in 1879, no suggestion of incapacitating health problems. His career, to judge by his flag lieutenancy, seems to have been going well. If it was seasickness, it may have been of the large ship rather than small boat variety, since he later owned and sailed a number of small fast craft and the one account we have by someone who took a small boat across the Channel with him makes no reference to illness.

Otherwise, his naval record describes him as 'a clever officer with great taste for electricity . . . a knowledge of photography . . . speaks French . . . draws well.' His engineering father and eldest brother would doubtless have approved.

2

COMING ASHORE

Another result of Cumming's last voyage seems to have been marriage. 'Seems' because there is no evidence as to where or when he met his wife-to-be but it was possibly while visiting the Cape.

Johanna Theodora Cloete (pronounced Clerter), known as Dora, was born on 9 January 1867 and baptised at Wynberg, the sixth of ten children born to Hardwick Cloete and Mary Duckitt. The Cloetes were, and are, a large and distinguished South African family famed for lawyers and wine and originating with Jacob Cloete of Cologne who came to the Cape in 1652. In 1778 Henry Cloete acquired the famous Constantia Wine Estate, which went on to produce wines acknowledged as among the best – at one period perhaps the best – in the world.

The Simonstown base was a popular port of call for the Royal Navy. The region offered an abundance of the usual facilities with, for the officers, shooting and other entertainments on the large hospitable estates inland. Relations had not then been complicated by the Boer War; climate and countryside were congenial. The *Raleigh*, flying her Admiral's flag, would have been a social focus, and the twenty-six-year-old flag lieutenant would have found an abundance of social duties and opportunities. Eligible daughters were eagerly sought among – and perhaps as eagerly provided by – the wealthy estate-owning families.

Nothing is known of the courtship. Cumming lived within

living memory, became an important official – if not very public – figure, was generously honoured and was part of a large and successful family, some of whom lived into modern times, yet there are long periods and large areas of his life that are traceable in outline only. His official existence is fairly well documented, as is his private life at those points where law compelled official record, but the inwardness, the emotional engagement, the generation and degeneration of personality and the interactions that forced potential into being must remain, in his case, more a matter of speculation than observation.

So we may, if we will, imagine the courtship among the high hills and vineyards of the Cape, the spacious white-walled houses and cool verandas where the young naval lieutenant and the eighteen-year-old Dora walked and talked. Whether or not it happened there, it happened fast, probably in the excitement of heady first love. She would be unlikely to have married without her parents' consent, nor he without his captain's; also, given that his father had spent some time in South Africa and his older brother five years there, it is possible that the families knew each other already. She might, of course, have visited London and they might therefore have met before Cumming went to South Africa, so that the ill-health that sent him back after a brief stay might have proved a longed-for blessing.

We do not know where the marriage took place, only that – according to *Who's Who* and other publications – it was in 1885. Unless they knew each other before he went to South Africa it would most likely have been towards the end of the year in either country.

The next thing we know of Dora, however, is her death certificate. Two years later, on 28 November 1887, she died at York Place, Baker Street, London, of septicaemia following an ovaricotomy. The poison had taken forty-eight hours to do its work. There is no electoral record of her and Cumming living at York Place but, given the registrar's different criteria at different times, that does not mean they did not. It could, alternatively, have been a clinic. The doctor in attendance was Cumming's elder brother, Walter, whose address is given as Holland Park Terrace, Kensington. That is all we know of Dora. We know nothing of her marriage, her personality, how she found London, whether she missed home, whether the early signs of the tumour were mistaken for a hoped-for pregnancy. Nor do we know how her husband was affected. Did she die with the headlights of their love full on, mutually blazing? Was Cumming numbed or distraught, did he try to put it behind him and pretend it hadn't happened, locking his heart in the deep freeze? Or was he, at a level he dared not admit even to himself, secretly relieved? Most likely he faced it with the emotional frankness and structured display that it is a pet illusion of our own age to overlook in that other. The healing rituals of mourning – drawn blinds, wearing black, calling – were commonly performed and the rituals of the Church of England, with the starkness and beauty of its Book of Common Prayer, were widely practised. We do not actually know whether Cumming was a Christian, but he was a man of his time and class, two of his sisters married clergymen, his brother Walter married the daughter of an arch-deacon, and there is a suggestion that he later taught at Sunday school in Hampshire. He very likely was.

What we do know is that sixteen months later, on Wednesday 13 March 1889, Cumming married again. His bride, Leslie Marion Valiant Cumming, a year younger than himself, was the daughter of the late Captain (RN) Lockhart Mure Valiant and of Emily Frances Cumming of Logie Castle, Forres, Morayshire. They were married not at the bride's home but at Cossington, Somerset, by Cumming's brother-in-law, the Reverend Harvey Brooks. Nine months later, almost to the day – 14 December – their son, Alastair Mansfield, was born.

After sixteen months the funereal baked meats may be allowed to be cold, though perhaps not very, but we should not assume that Dora's memory was devalued by Cumming's speedy acquisition of a successor. Just as the Victorians grieved more openly and wholesomely than we, they may have been more prepared to put things behind them and get on. Youthful death was common enough for no survivor to assume he had decades ahead of him.

Alastair was born at 9 Holland Park Terrace, next door to Cumming's doctor brother. The electoral register does not show Cumming living there until 1891, when he becomes eligible to vote by virtue of being a dweller rather than an owner. They stayed until 1894.

It was on marriage to May, as she was known, that Lieutenant Mansfield Smith, RN (retired) began the long process of becoming Captain Sir Mansfield Cumming. May's mother, Emily Cumming, had inherited the Morayshire estate from her father. The family evidently had a strong dynastic urge since on her marriage to Captain Valiant, himself a widower, he took her name and became Valiant Cumming. He died when May was six and Emily married another widower, George Battye, a Bengal judge who had fathered eleven children by his late wife. Ten of these were sons, all of whom served with sufficient distinction in India for Battye to become a household name on the sub-continent. May thus acquired ten well-known stepbrothers and one little unknown stepsister. Her stepfather also took on the name Cumming, so she was brought up as May Battye Cumming.

She in turned inherited from her mother and when she married at twenty-nine – perhaps a little late for that time – both she and her husband took the name Smith Cumming. This was Cumming's official name for the rest of his life, recognised by the navy and inscribed by May on his tombstone, though he was nearly always referred to simply as Cumming. This was apparently his choice. He seems to have developed an affection for the letter C, giving to several motor boats he later owned such names as Commander, Communicator, Competitor and Comely. It must have pleased him greatly to have become officially known as 'C'.

A descendant of the Battye tribe, Evelyn, later published a

book about the Battye sons, *The Fighting Ten*. While researching it she came across the link with May and in a magazine article about her (so far unidentified) she describes her in the following terms: 'To the next generation of Battyes, "Aunt May" was a quiet, delicate-looking woman (although she was never ill!) with small bones and tiny narrow feet. She was gentle, calm and specially kind and generous to the young, though they soon became aware of her steely morals and strong ideals if they stepped out of line.'

This was, of course, the sketch of an older May than the one who married Cumming, but the essentials probably held; she retained her soft Scottish accent throughout her life. Alastair, meanwhile, apparently became 'the apple of his mother's eye'.

Evelyn Battye also had something to say about Cumming. 'Her husband was an extrovert, bluff and charming man, a live-wire of boisterous, outgoing nature and a great tease with the children.' This is one of relatively few descriptions of Cumming's personality and is of a piece with what others say. Battye goes on to record how he used to encourage visiting nephews and nieces to poke hatpins in the wooden (possibly cork) leg he had by then acquired.

As with Dora, however, nothing is known of their courtship, nor of how and where they met. There are no letters, no divorce papers, no gossiping friends or relations keeping diaries. The only certainty is Alastair's punctual arrival.

Cumming's whereabouts and daily activities between leaving the navy in 1885 and his appointment to the boom defence at Southampton in 1898 have so far been a mystery. There have been various speculations, such as that he was running his wife's estates at Logie or doing undercover intelligence work for the Naval Intelligence Department (NID), but no evidence. Happily, we can now account for some of those years, although, as is often the case with Cumming, we have no idea how he came to do what he was doing.

We know that he was living at 9 Holland Park Terrace until

1894 and probably not beyond. There is nobody registered at the address in 1895 and in 1896 a Mr Underhill moved in. However Cumming features in a magazine article published early in the next century, part of a series entitled 'Unconventional Portraits of Leaders in Motorism'. He is by then promoted to Commander, which makes it post-1906, and the article begins by referring to his being Rear Commodore of the Motor Yacht Club (the public face, perhaps, of his Reserve of Motor Boat Owners). The article ends:

> The public knows him as the Commander of the Southampton Boom Defence, an Admiralty appointment that he has held for considerable time. Having had a naval training, subsequently he became secretary and agent to the Earl of Meath, managing his estates in Ireland, since when he has been stationed at Southampton. He is one of those individuals who holds quite a unique position in the world's affairs.

Judging by the coy understatement at the beginning and end of the paragraph, it seems likely that the article was written after 1909 when Cumming became the first 'C', and that the writer knew. It claims that he took to motoring – he was to become a great enthusiast – as a result of a 'bad spill' in the hunting field when he broke both arms. Where it is possible to corroborate statements in the article, their accuracy is borne out, so it is at least possible that this is true. Perhaps it happened while he was working for the Earl of Meath.

As for that period, the then Earl was blessed with a memory for detail and later published his lengthy *Memories of the Twentieth Century*. He says of Cumming:

> The eminent services rendered to the country during the Great War by the late Sir Mansfield Cumming are well known to the initiated. I had the privilege for several years of benefiting by his remarkable intelligence. He was at one time my private secretary,

and afterwards my agent in Ireland. His sense of humour was great, and this made him extremely popular with my tenantry, even when he had in the course of his duties to take drastic steps in support of my interests.

Upon one occasion he endeavoured to avoid an eviction by personally calling on a sister and two brothers who appeared impervious to reason, and seemed to court eviction. As he approached the tenant's house he met the sister, who did not know him, but suspected he was the agent, and when she learnt that her suspicion was correct, she cursed him. He took off his hat and went on to see her brothers, she continuing to walk in the opposite direction. After his conversation, which was carried on in a very amicable spirit, was over, he walked away from the house, and had to pass along a deeply sunk road with high banks surmounted by thick hedges. Remembering the curses of the sister, he kept his eyes open, and at length saw the flicker of a skirt on the top of one of the banks. The sister was waiting for him. She had taken off a stocking and had placed a heavy stone in it. As he passed she made a strike at him, but missing her blow she overbalanced and fell head foremost into the road. There happened to be a wire in the hedge. Her foot caught in this, and she therefore hung helpless by her foot, head downwards – *jupes retroussées*. He rushed to the rescue, but it was some time before he could release the foot, and replace the skirt – the only garment – in its proper position. He then discovered that she had twisted her knee, and he had to bind up the injured limb with a wet handkerchief, and carry the damsel to her home and put her to bed.

Some time afterwards he asked me to visit these people and see if my personal influence could bring them to reason. This I did. I expected to be received with curses, and to hear the bitterest reproaches hurled at myself and my agent; but, on the contrary, when I visited the lady, who was still in bed, she told me that I had 'a darlint of an agint,' and was never weary of recounting all he had done for her. My reply was, 'You must really tell

Cumming all you have said about him' – so I called him to the room, and when I had repeated the lady's remarks, he cried, 'Oh, Miss Byrne! Why didn't you speak sooner? Alas! I am a married man!'

Sir Mansfield Cumming once told me that when in Canada he came across a train filled by a large party of emigrants on their way to settle in Manitoba or Saskatchewan. They consisted of young men and maidens, of old men and women, accompanied by innumerable babies. They were being personally conducted by an official representative of the organisation which was responsible for this numerous transfer of population from a particular district in Eastern Europe to the vast grain-plains of Canada. The conductor seemed very proud of his selection of emigrants, and pointed out that each man and woman had been chosen for the purpose of filling some particular niche in the economic edifice of this important settlement. Seeing a very old man, nearly bent double by age, sitting with his head almost between his knees, Cumming enquired why such an old man, who was evidently past work, had been brought for thousands of miles across sea and land, and asked what possible use could such a man be to a community which would need all its energies to maintain itself in the severe struggle against nature which was evidently before it. 'Oh,' was the reply, 'a most important duty lies before him.' 'What is that?' said Cumming. 'He will have to open the cemetery.'!

There is no other reference to Cumming having travelled in Canada, but the story might date from his visit to North America aboard his second ship, the *Bellerophon*.

The Earl spent his early years in the Diplomatic Service and later formed, with his wife (a Lauderdale heiress), a conscientious, apparently tireless and possibly rather formidable duo dedicated to charitable works and, from his seat in the Lords, political improvement. They travelled the world founding hospitals, starting schools for the blind, for epileptics and for others in need. The family think it likely that Cumming was employed as the Earl's private secretary in London, attending him when he was there and seeing to affairs when he was not. His period as agent in Ireland probably followed this – perhaps after 1894 when he left Holland Park Terrace – and he presumably left the Earl's service on taking up the boom defence.

Cumming's naval record shows that he returned to the navy on the active retired list on 30 April 1898, spending a month attached to HMS *Vernon* on a training course. He spent the next few years on the strength of, variously, the *Australia*, the *Venus*, the inevitable *Duke of Wellington*, Nelson's *Victory* and her special service tender, the *Fire Queen*. Those serving away from the Admiralty on shore or home-based had to be under command of someone and were generally on the strength of permanently moored ships or shore establishments named after ships. The *Victory*, for example, was one of many old wooden warships used for stores, as receiving or school ships, or as headquarters. She was at that time flagship to Sir Michael Culme-Seymour, the Commander-in-Chief Portsmouth and first among equals of the navy's three senior 'Home Port' commanders. (She continued this sort of service until after the First World War when she was bought by the Society for Nautical Research and restoration was begun.) While on her strength Cumming would have come under C-in-C Portsmouth. The wording of his appointment has it that he was appointed to 'Superintend the working of the Boom Defence at Southampton. Appt during pleasure.'

It must have been a very congenial time to rejoin the flag. The year before, 1897, the navy had celebrated Queen Victoria's diamond jubilee by gathering 165 warships at Spithead without withdrawing a single vessel from any overseas command. With 360 major fighting ships, the strength of the Royal Navy was equal to that of the next five navies combined. All must have seemed well but other navies, particularly the German, were growing ominously, and some Britons sensed or foresaw the linked perils of economic decline and strategic overstretch. Joseph Chamberlain was one, describing England as 'a weary titan staggering beneath the too great orb of its fate'. But such views, despite their unlooked-for exemplification in the Boer War, were not popular.

There is no knowing whether Cumming was conventionally complacent or uneasily perceptive about this. Despite at the age of thirty-nine reverting to the rank at which he had left the navy (lieutenant), he obviously enjoyed being paid to mess about with boats on a big-boy's scale. He was based for the first few years in Southampton Water where his staff practised blocking off parts of the port with booms and then running destroyers against them. This no doubt encouraged the amateur engineering interest and practical ingenuity that bubbles up throughout his adult life, and it was probably fun. He based himself for at least part of the time in an old ship called the *Argo*, but the family home was by then at Burnford House in the New Forest village of Bramshaw. They rented – again, Cumming appears as dweller rather than owner-occupier – and they seem to have had it from at least 1897 to 1902 inclusive.

Despite the busy road along which it straggles, Bramshaw remains an attractive village, pleasantly encroached upon by the tall beeches and common grazing of the forest. The usual cattle and ponies roam at will with, less predictably, a number of pigs. Burnford House is large and rendered with a slate roof and was built some time before 1839. It is neither stylish and coherent nor pleasingly rambling; it has bay windows, a conservatory and a long covered porch that reaches to the road, like the house where Cumming was born. Now divided into flats, it is apparently to be 'redeveloped', with covered path and roadside wall retained. There have been moves to preserve it on the grounds – in the absence of any architectural merit – that it was used by MI5 in the Second World War and before that by Cumming as his headquarters. Whether or not it was used by MI5, MI6 or SOE – not in itself a reason for preservation – the rest of the argument, sadly, will not wash; when Cumming lived there he was not only not 'C' but had no idea that he ever would be. It was at the local church in Burnford that he is believed to have taught at Sunday school.

Meanwhile, unknown to him, far and near, events that would shape his later life were gestating. A young clerk to the House of Commons, Erskine Childers, was fitting out a small, recently acquired yacht called the *Vixen*. In August 1897 he sailed her across the North Sea on the first of six voyages through the intimate, narrow, foggy, shifting sand banks, mud banks and channels of the Friesian Islands of Northern Holland and Germany. The sturdy *Vixen* was cramped and far from beautiful, but well adapted to both shallow- and deep-water sailing. Childers later bought a larger yacht, the 15-ton *Sunbeam*, which he kept at Bursledon during the time Cumming was there. He is referred to only twice in Cumming's diary and letters, each time briefly but in terms that make it clear that Cumming knew him.

Childers had interrupted his House of Commons career to serve in the Boer War as a gunner-driver with the City Imperial Volunteers and afterwards achieved considerable success with a book based on his war diary, *In the Ranks of the CIV*. Next he turned his mind to a novel inspired by his voyages in the *Vixen*. This was to become *The Riddle of the Sands*, arguably the first modern spy story. Narrated by Carruthers of the FO, it tells how he was persuaded by his friend Davies to join him aboard the little *Dulcibella* for a voyage of discovery among the remote creeks and islands of the Ems and Weser estuaries. Gradually, Carruthers realises there is more to it than the pleasure of small-boat sailing in treacherous waters; Davies has a theory about German preparation for an invasion of eastern England, which their adventures among the shifting sands confirm.

When the book was published in 1903 it was an immense success. Childers was stunned by the public reaction but not wholly pleased. He hadn't wanted the book advertised as a novel, because he felt that would distract from the serious intention of alerting the British government to the German threat. He wrote to his friend Basil Williams:

> It's a yachting story, with a purpose, suggested by a cruise I once took in German waters. I discovered a scheme of invasion directed against England. I am finding it terribly difficult as being in the nature of a detective story. There is no sensation, only what is meant to be a convincing fact. I was weak enough to 'spatchcock' a girl into it and now find her a horrible nuisance.

In a later letter to Williams he wrote:

> As a fact I invented the whole thing, building it, though, on careful observation of my own on the German coast but I have since had most remarkable confirmation of the ideas in it. Source confidential of course and details too – but I think there is no reason to doubt that my method of invasion – in general principle – had been worked out by the Germans.

The confirmation Childers claims was most likely confirmation of the feasibility of his scheme rather than of its existence, though by 1903 there was no doubt of the German naval threat in general. In 1897 Alfred von Tirpitz had been appointed German Secretary of State for Naval Affairs and thereafter the naval race between Britain and Germany to build more, bigger and better warships became increasingly evident. Kaiser Wilhelm II envied Britain her Empire and felt that Germany, too, had her right to 'a place in the sun'. The fundamental British strategic assumption was that neither the Empire nor the home base itself could be secure unless the Royal Navy was more powerful than any combination that might come against it. The army, by contrast, was kept small and used mainly in colonial campaigns.

Although the Boer War proved a significant shock and introduced many changes, it was still assumed – and went on being assumed right up until 1914 – that the army would never play the major part in any continental campaign. Britain's war would be naval so the navy had to reign supreme. 'If the German fleet becomes superior to ours, the German Army can conquer this country,' asserted the First Sea Lord in 1902.

So far from his message not being taken seriously because it was a novel, Childers's book not only found a willing audience in government and Admiralty but was in fact all the more effective because of its fictional form. Had he written his central idea as a strategy paper, it would doubtless have suffered the fate of most such papers, good and bad, but dramatisation lent it an emotional and imaginative power beyond argument. While the first edition was in the press, as Childers's postscript acknowledges, a Committee of National Defence was set up almost as if the authorities were keen to demonstrate their agreement with him. (He was probably referring, in fact, to the Committee of Imperial Defence.)

The Riddle of the Sands book is one of the clearest examples of art influencing life and although other books influenced the political climate, Childers's had, as we shall see, particular contributions to particular historical events. Indeed, it is possible that these contributions began early and involved Cumming, in that his formation of a Reserve of Motor Boat Owners is very much of a piece with what Davies, one of the two main characters in the book, urges: 'There must be hundreds of chaps like me . . . who know our coasts like a book . . . shoals, creeks, tides, rocks . . . they ought to make some use of us as a naval reserve.'

An emotional and intelligent man, Childers was perhaps predisposed to embrace causes with more passionate partiality than judgement, seizing upon one aspect of a problem and regarding it as the whole. By 1914 he was gun-running for Irish Republicans while at the same time serving conscientiously and bravely as a lieutenant in the Royal Navy. The theme and setting of *The*

Riddle of the Sands repeated themselves then and throughout his life. He provided invaluable navigational assistance to the navy and took part in the Cuxhaven Raid, the first ever sea-launched air attack on a land target. At the outbreak of the war, when he was on (gun-running) leave from the navy, the Admiralty, at Churchill's behest, mounted a desperate search for him and commissioned him to write a paper on 'The Seizure of Borkhum and Juist', precisely the area he had logged with minute particularity in the *Vixen* nearly twenty years before. It was a good and reasoned paper and Childers was a loyal and patriotic naval officer, yet he persuaded himself that the Irish Volunteers, for whom he was gun-running, could be persuaded to serve the Crown in the looming Armageddon. He was eventually executed after the First World War by the newly independent Irish government, for his services to the IRA.

His book, however, transcends the cause that inspires it, just as it also transcends the creaky and unlikely plot. The 'spatch-cocking' into it of the girl, the implausibility of the chief villain's role and other weaknesses do not matter. The heart of the book's appeal are the shifting sands, shoals, fogs and ambiguities of the setting:

> The ground sloped down, and a rushing river glimmered before us. We struck off at a tangent and followed its course to the north, stumbling in muddy rifts, slipping on seaweed, beginning to be blinded by a fine salt spray and deafened by the thunder of the ocean's surf. The river broadened, whitened, roughened, gathered itself for the shock, was shattered and dissolved in milky gloom. We wheeled away to the right, and splashed into yeasty froth. I turned my back to the wind, scooped the brine out of my eyes, faced back and saw that our path was barred by a welter of surf. Davies's voice was in my ear and his arm was pointing seaward.

John Buchan was one of the earliest thriller writers to benefit from this book. He thought it 'the best story of adventure published in the last quarter of a century . . . the atmosphere of grey northern skies and miles of yeasty water and wet sands is as masterfully reproduced as in any story of Conrad's'. It presages the modern thriller in making technical detail (specifically, nautical matters and railway timetables) central to the progress of the story and is le Carré-esque in its use of weather and setting to reflect and enhance the menace and uncertainty of the situation. You do not need to be nautical to be engrossed and the story does not need to be plausible, nor the ending unguessed at, to be exciting.

It was certainly plausible enough for the times. No matter how much we assert its impact, we probably cannot fully appreciate the extent to which it fed the already burgeoning national perception of nautical threat, and the need for intelligence on it. Cumming was now once again living in a world intimately connected with that. His boom defence was already part of it, and what he was to go on to, very much more so. For all that the French government still, at the end of the nineteenth century, maintained theoretical plans for the invasion of England, there was no doubt where the more serious threat came from.

By no means all of Cumming's time was consumed by attempts to counter the threat of invasion. Early in 1905 he was tasked, as already briefly noted, by the Secretary for Scotland to look into the question of providing auxiliary motor power for sail-driven fishing boats. His twenty-page report was produced by 2 March 1905 and summarised in the 22 April issue of the *Fish Trades Gazette and Poultry Game and Rabbit Trades Chronicle*. This might be thought an unlikely point of emergence into the public world for a future chief of the Secret Service, but the *Chronicle* was serious reading. Cumming's report is a no-nonsense, succinct and competent piece of work. While researching it he visited eight Scottish ports as well as ports in Germany, Sweden and Denmark. He also visited Berlin. These foreign visits were for the purpose of examining existing engines, mostly 'heavy oil' (diesel, named after its German inventor) since Cumming believed that, for reasons of safety and economy, 'conditions on board the fishing fleet did not admit of the use of petrol motors'. British boats tended not to be so equipped at the time, perhaps because small-engine development in Britain lagged behind that on the Continent as a result of legal restrictions on motor vehicles. Cumming gives a technical description of each engine, ending with an assessment in laymen's terms:

> The engine is cheap, good, and very economical, but it has the serious defect of being of the 2 cycle type. In my opinion this is not to be compared with the 4 cycle type for the purpose intended. The power developed with a light load, falls away very quickly when the load is increased and the various operations are not so thoroughly performed.

He went to sea in some of the boats he examined (excursions which were presumably avoidable had seasickness been a constant and serious problem), and he offered to supervise trials with selected engines in Scottish boats. He also suggested English firms which could be invited to build engines, among which were some familiar names:

> I interviewed the representatives of several of the principal firms – the Wolsley Co. (Messrs Vickers Sons and Maxim) who build the Admiralty Submarine engines; Messrs Thorneycroft, the Torpedo boat and Motor Builders; Messrs Napier, builders of the most successful fast motorboats; Messrs Rolls; Crossley; Maudslay, and others all of whom have expressed themselves willing to take the matter up.

Detailed testing, he recommends, could be undertaken by the Marine Department of the Automobile Club (later the RAC).

These names were familiar to Cumming as a result of a private passion that had, in fact, brought him to earlier but modest public attention in a form more usually associated with the mythology of Secret Service than that suggested by the *Fish Trades Gazette and Poultry Game and Rabbit Trades Chronicle*. The inaugural meeting of the Automobile Club of Great Britain and Ireland had taken place in December 1898 after a lunch of consommé, lobster, fois gras, contrefilet, chicken, pheasant, partridge and Charlotte Russe. That and other early meetings took place in 4 Whitehall Court, a building in which Cumming was later to house his wartime headquarters. His passion for cars led him to become an enthusiastic, then a well-known and finally an influential member of the RAC.

That lunch and the perception that it was the proper way to begin an inaugural meeting, gives a taste of what the early RAC was like – Edwardian, rich, aristocratic, glamorous, hedonistic, fast. The famous Spirit of Ecstasy that still adorns Rolls-Royce cars was modelled on Nelly Thornton who worked for the club and became Lord Montague's secretary and mistress, bearing his child in secret. (She later drowned when the ship they were on was torpedoed during the First World War.) For all the opulence with which they surrounded themselves, these men were serious about cars, and the early history of the RAC is virtually the early history of British motoring.

Cumming was part of that history. Already styled as Cumming rather than Smith Cumming, he was elected to membership in 1902, proposed by the Hon. J. Scott Montague. It was Cumming's fourth club (following the Naval & Military, the Portsmouth Naval and the Royal Southern Yacht). The *Automotor Journal* of 28 February 1903 announced that he was to drive a 50 h.p. Wolseley in the Paris–Madrid race and, if allowed, in the subsequent Gordon-Bennett race in France. (James Gordon-Bennett Jnr was a wealthy American newspaper owner whose interests were various and often profitably self-publicising – it was he who had sent Stanley to find Livingstone, raising no objection to Stanley's 'starting small wars in Africa in order to report them'.) Cumming's Wolseley was a racer which he had bought at the recent Crystal Palace show. Motor racing, then as now, was a rich man's sport; apart from the cost of buying their cars, drivers had to pay a £500 deposit to enter the Gordon-Bennett. Where did Cumming's money come from? At sixteen shillings a day, his 'active half pay', albeit six times what most private soldiers in the army were still paid, was nothing like enough to support a gentleman with a taste for speed and expensive new technology. Like most officers of the period, he probably had some family money but there is no indication that the Smiths, although very comfortably off, were anything like magnates; he would anyway have had to share any family money with his dozen siblings. Both his and May's wills indicate that there was a marriage settlement from which he benefited. It is possible that he also inherited money from Dora.

Early motor racing was no sport for chickens. About eight spectators and participants died during the Paris–Madrid race, in which Cumming's car was one of those that crashed. Driven by Sidney Girling, a Wolseley test driver, with Cumming beside him, it hit a wall. The *Autocar* of 6 June 1903 reported the incident:

> Up to the time of his collision with the wall in the Paris–Madrid race, Lieut. Cumming's Wolseley car was making splendid time. He tells us he left Versaille at 3.56 am, and arrived at Chartres at 4.57am. Out of this time has to be taken for the 15 minutes in control, so that the 74 kilometres were covered in 46 minutes. There was also a stop at Ablis through a misunderstanding of flag signals, therefore the average works out at about 100 kilometres an hour. Only one kilometre was timed and that came out at 110½. The collision with the wall was a regrettable affair in every respect as Lieutenant Cumming's car was in good form and had been thoroughly tested.

In fact, Cumming wrote his own report of his part in the race for the club journal, attributing the accident to an overheated crankshaft bearing which seized the clutch, though he doesn't mention the wall. He does mention a complaint common to other contemporary racers, about how the crowds that turned out to see them masked the turns, corners and other dangers: 'We drove for 100 miles into a solid mass of people at nearly 70 miles an hour.' He left the driving to Girling, he says, because 'I was very anxious for the success of the car, and knew that he would do far more justice to it than I could.' He goes on:

> The dust when passing other cars was awful. The mere physical pain of the stones hitting one in the face was considerable – my goggles were smashed by a stone thrown back by the first car we passed – and besides this, the dust was so thick that one could not see the road at all and could only steer by the shadowy forms of the people on each side. To race after another car, when one knew that a level crossing was not far ahead, with its double right-angled turn only broad enough for one, was exciting enough for anybody.

His car, he thought, 'almost human – far more so than many folks of my acquaintance – and I know of nothing more enjoyable than skimming along at a cracking pace, especially if you are picking up on the next car ahead!'

The first formal motor race in Britain had been staged only the year before, along the sea front at Bexhill, in Sussex. Early British development both of the industry and the sport was seriously inhibited by legal restrictions and passionate motorphobia in Parliament and among sections of the public and press, with calls for public-spirited citizens to empty their revolvers into offending motorists. There is no doubt that some motorists did indeed offend. 'My private opinion is that I should like to go as fast as I can and never be identified,' the later Lord Montague frankly confessed. It was a desire which Cumming probably shared.

Cumming did not in fact participate in the Gordon-Bennett

because he was deemed not to have applied in time, though the ruling provoked argument in the motoring journals and culminated in a letter from Cumming in the 6 June issue of *Autocar* in which he renounces any claim to participation while noting that the 'only rule which could not be broken or turned upside down' seemed to be the one that denied him a place. This note is echoed a number of times during the early years of his diary, usually in reference to the machinations of the War Office.

Cumming's automotive and nautical activities were also referred to in the memoirs of Montague Grahame White, *At the Wheel, Ashore and Afloat*. This genial and well-connected Lieutenant Commander RNVR seems to have measured his life in terms of developments of the internal combustion engine and to have been a founder member of practically every society connected with early motoring or motor boats, as well as designing some early Rolls bodies. He writes with artless complacency and matter-of-factness, an almost childlike assumption that one's own doings are of at least as much interest to the rest of the world as to oneself. After sufficient time, such memoirs are often more valuable than those of autobiographers of a more wily and reflective vanity. They can also be curiously effective. The description of his reconnaissance for the Automobile Club's One Thousand Mile Trial in 1900, for instance, is made all the more effective by the very limitations that come close to making it laughable. He recounts an heroic ninety-mile journey through snow storms over Shap Fell in an open, 5½ h.p. belt-driven Critchley – taking six and a quarter hours to cover the final ten miles to the summit – without any reference to frozen fingers, feet or faces, but almost entirely in terms of how many times they had to get off and fit new belt fasteners, or sections, or re-light burners, and how they found a way of reducing belt-slip on the move.

Grahame White was obviously familiar with Cumming, since when he first mentions him he gives him no introduction, though his account does tell us that Cumming chose to race Wolseleys after being strapped to the tailboard of one from Birmingham to London:

> The following day, accompanied by Lieutenant Mansfield Cumming R. N., I arrived at the Wolseley works, and after a series of trials we drove back to London [from Birmingham] with a mechanic deputed by Mr Austin to watch the efficient lubrication of the motor on the journey. The car having only two bucket seats, Cumming agreed to make the run strapped to the tail board, and he completed the distance in this most uncomfortable position, his enthusiasm for speed inducing him to order a car from the Wolseley Co. to compete in the Gordon-Bennett trials the following year, and nominating myself as the driver.

Grahame White's description of the geography and civilisation of India, whither he voyaged to see the Maharajah of Cooch Behar on motoring business, begins and virtually ends with: 'On arrival at Bombay, my first thought was to arrange the transport to Delhi of the Renault car on being landed: the Mors being towed behind a bullock's cart to the railway station and placed on an open truck before being coupled to the Calcutta Express.' Almost the only mention of the populace of India is when some of them drank the petrol intended for the cars. Years later, in London, Grahame White took an unwitting part in the suicide of Gertrude Atherton – 'one of the most beautiful women of her day' – but his account even of this event centres mainly on a taxi.

It is possible that they knew each other through sailing on Southampton Water. Grahame White, though eighteen years younger than Cumming, was born at Bursledon Towers (now a branch of Tesco's) and Cumming was probably prominent in the area by the time he was growing up. They nearly died together. In 1904 Grahame White found himself 'proceeding to Southampton to call on my friend Lt. Mansfield Cumming, R. N., stationed at the time in *HMS Argo*, lying off Netley.' Netley is very near Bursledon and the *Argo* was the elderly vessel in which Cumming had established his boom defence headquarters as well as – for some of the time, anyway – his marital home. Grahame White's project of the moment was the adaptation of two small steam yachts to motor power, a project sufficiently similar to the research Cumming was commissioned to do the following year on fishing vessels for there to be suspicion of a connection. Grahame White installed a French marine engine in his 52-foot yacht, *Mi-Ladye*, and invited Cumming to take it across the Channel with him so that they could compete in the forthcoming race down the Seine from Paris to the sea. Wisely, they decided to test the boat's sea-going qualities in moderately rough water and, taking a mechanic, set off for an evening trip into the Solent. Not far off Fort Monckton, near Gosport, they turned about in order to get back before dark, having no navigation lights:

> As the helm was put over the motor suddenly raced, and I instinctively pushed home the clutch lever, but the racing continued until I closed the throttle lever. The stern shaft had broken, and we found ourselves helpless in a strong east-going tide and approaching darkness ... We rolled from rail to rail beam on the sea for close on two hours, our mechanic lying in a huddled lump of sea-sick humanity on the floor of the engine room, whilst Cumming and I clung to the rails on deck looking around for any signs of assistance.

The only vessels in sight were a distant steamer and a square-rigged sailing vessel, both too far for any signals. The anchor-line was too short for the depth of water but Cumming eventually found a longer rope. While Grahame White was trying to fix it, an excessive roll pitched him overboard with the rope entwined around his sea-boots. 'Cumming quickly grabbed hold of me and after considerable difficulty assisted me over the rail, when I fell head first into the bottom of the aft cock-pit.'

The helpless, sick-making rolling continued, but eventually

Cumming spotted steamer lights bearing down on them. They quickly soaked engine-room mutton-cloths in oil and petrol, Cumming attached them by wire to a boat-hook and they lit and waved them. The steamer took *Mi-Ladye* in tow to Southampton.

Grahame White did not give up. *Mi-Ladye*'s shaft was renewed, her trim altered, a mast, jury-rig sail, long oars and crutches, engine spares, extra fathoms of cable and fire extinguishers were all added. Cumming, however, was unconvinced. He 'was not very keen on the idea of a hundred mile crossing in a single-screw motor-boat in those days, and from experiences I met with in later years I came to the conclusion that his decision was an extremely sensible one. Nevertheless I persuaded him to accompany me to Havre with an engineer and a deckhand.'

This time the problem was thick mid-Channel fog, in which during the early hours of the morning they were nearly run down by the Southampton–Le Havre mail. Surviving that, they cleared the fog and Grahame White had increased engine revs to a very satisfactory 750 rpm when the engine stopped. ' "What the devil is that?" said Cumming, as I went to enquire of the mechanic below. "Run out of petrol, sir, that's all," was his calm reply.'

Fortunately, they hadn't. The problem was the automatic feed from the main to the auxiliary supply tank, to which the mechanic had not attended because he had fallen asleep. They then discovered that he had been up for thirty-six hours, working all the previous night in the yard at Southampton. They told him to turn in, Grahame White taking his place in the engine room and Cumming at the wheel. They reached Le Havre without further incident early in the morning and set off up the Seine for Paris the next day.

The *Mi-Ladye* was not entered for the race – she was not a racer, anyway – but went back down the Seine with both racer and cruiser classes for the fun of it: 'my friend and I, in *Mi-Ladye*, proved considerably faster than any of them.' They ended up taking seven waterlogged or broken-down allegedly sea-going cruisers in tow, one behind the other, into Harfleur, Cumming, meanwhile, having 'expressed his pleasure in deciding to accompany me on the trip'.

Grahame White mentions Cumming's tour of foreign fishing fleets, adding that he was back in Southampton in time to organise reliability trials held by the Motor Yacht Club of which he was Rear Commodore. As one of the judges, he had to withdraw his entry, the *Commander*, a boat that he had, according to Grahame White, built in one of the yards at Bursledon, fitting it with a 20 h.p. Wolseley engine. It was in that boat, he says, that Cumming 'met with a similar experience to that he had shared with myself in the *Mi-Ladye*', this time through engine failure. Apparently Cumming and a gentleman named Maudsley Brooke in another boat suffered the same fate in the Solent on the same day, their boats pitching and rolling for nearly two hours before rescue. In each case the boats were half-filled with water, so things were presumably pretty dire.

Grahame White's final nautical references to Cumming occur in 1907 and 1908. By this time the *Enchantress*, one of the former Royal Yachts, had become the headquarters of the Motor Yacht Club in Southampton Water. Grahame White arrived with a number of visitors to find Cumming and others staying on board. An impromptu concert was arranged which included a violin solo by – of course – Grahame White, accompanied on the piano by a Miss Vera Stanley, while 'another member contributed some comic songs interspersed with some extremely clever card tricks'. We might have expected him to say if this was Cumming, though there is a family tradition that Cumming entertained children with conjuring tricks. A Captain Bayford, with his daughter, Sibyl, joined the party and 'added an extra turn to the programme'.

Following this during a violent snowstorm in April 1908, the 5,750-ton cruiser HMS *Gladiator* sank after colliding with a liner at the western end of the Solent. She lay on her side about three hundred yards offshore in about thirty-six feet of water. Early the next morning Grahame White, Captain Bayford and Cumming took a launch to the scene. The lengthy salvage operation was, of course, of consuming interest: 'no more interesting and instructive lesson has it ever been my fortune to acquire . . .'

There is one other nautical anecdote about Cumming probably dating from this period, or a little before. It is a family story originating with his nephew, Charles Molyneux Smith, who died in 1966, after a career in motor engineering, and who was very close to him both personally and professionally. The story is that Cumming was on a pinnace in the Solent in winter when a loose rope fell overboard and fouled the propeller. Cumming stripped off and dived into the cold water to free it, watched by those on board, one of whom was the then Mr Winston Churchill. Family tradition has it that Cumming subsequently came under Churchill's aegis. Molyneux Smith told sadly few stories about his uncle, being noted more for his discretion than his desire to entertain, but Cumming's diary does suggest, as we shall see, that he and Churchill knew each other. There is, however, no actual evidence of patronage.

Nor were Cumming's enthusiasms confined to road and water. In 1906, aged forty-seven, he became a founder member of the Royal Aero Club. This was three years after the Wright Brothers had made the first heavier-than-air flight in the United States and three years before Blériot made the first cross-Channel flight. It was a dangerous activity; in 1910, for example, some thirty-three aviators were killed, including C. S. Rolls, the collaborator of Royce, who perished on landing at Bournemouth after recently becoming the first to fly across the Channel and return without landing on French soil. This neither deterred Cumming nor, it seems, was it sufficient to persuade May to dissuade him from it, as Clementine Churchill did with her would-be aviator husband. He got his pilot's licence in 1913, an event recorded in the 22 November issue of *Flight* magazine:

47

Commander Mansfield Cumming, RN, a member of the Royal
Aero Club, has just returned from the Farman School at Etampes
in France, where he qualified for his aviator's certificate on a
Maurice Farman biplane on Monday November 10th, 1913.
Commander Cumming is probably the doyen of pilots, his age
being 54 years. He does not believe in extreme youth as a necessary or even desirable qualification for the making of a successful
pilot.

Cumming and May made Bursledon their home from 1906.
Originally a Saxon settlement on the wooded and sheltered
Hamble, a tributary of Southampton Water, the village had for
centuries provided ships for the Royal Navy (including HMS
Elephant, Nelson's flagship at the Battle of Copenhagen) but
was generally a quiet rather than a prosperous place from which
people journeyed to nearby Portsmouth and Southampton, more
by sea than by road. A toll bridge and railway were added in
the nineteenth century but it remained a secluded, if increasingly
sought-after, backwater. It still is, despite modern development,
two bridges and a waterfront that has become part of the largest
yachting marina in the country. Susannah Ritchie, local historian
of Bursledon and author of *The Hamble River* and *Solent Days
and Ways*, remembers Cumming's *Argo* and other boom defence
vessels arriving from Southampton Water in about 1906. Land
access for the crews was via a wooden pier built across the
marshes at the bottom of Salterns Lane, the seaward end marked
by a platform constructed around the mast of an old battleship,
the *Sultan*. This might well have been the *Sultan* on which Cumming served in 1883–84; it would certainly have appealed to
him to secure the mast of one of his old ships and there is
evidence throughout the rest of his career of useful dockyard
connections. When the mast was tilted into the soft Hamble mud
it sank half its length under its own weight, deep enough for
freshwater to be found inside. Most of it was removed during
the Second World War, along with most of the pier, but parts

of both survive, the stump of the mast projecting from the mud and water like an inverted mushroom.

In 1905 and 1906 Cumming bought part of the saltmarsh foreshore and later was to build a house on the higher ground just inland. There is a family tradition that he could read the writing on Ryde pier, on the Isle of Wight, through a telescope sited on the lawn of the house. He is also reputed to have had cross-trees and rigging on the lawn so that he could demonstrate resistance to age – and, later, to lack of limb, – by climbing it with the aggressive agility insisted upon by the navy of his youth. Although he was in his sixties and suffering from angina when the house was built, and although no one who visited it recalls cross-trees on the lawn, he was fond of tricks and stunts and might well have performed them earlier on the *Sultan*'s mast – up which, as a young seaman officer, he might have spent a good deal of time.

It is easy to sense the appeal of the spot. Despite the two road bridges and the railway, despite the yachts now crowded all along the Hamble and crammed into the basin around the river bend, the saltmarsh – Hackett's Marsh – remains haunting and evocative. It comprises only a few hundred yards of foreshore, easily reached from the footpath running down from Bursledon Lodge, Cumming's house. The footpath runs through a small boatyard, past a handful of houseboats and other craft, through meadows of grazing cattle, over a stile or two and along young elm hedgerows until the treacherous, heavily-creeked marsh begins. The marsh is studded with the vertebrae of ancient craft, broken rudders, abandoned pier-posts, mute pieces of driftwood and, occasionally, a perfectly coiled rope nestling in the mud. Although the road bridges are never silent, the most notable sound is the constant clinking of wires against the metal masts of moored yachts out in the Hamble.

Reaching the shore and the mast is not easy since every seemingly unbroken stretch leads to further stumbling, jumping, slithering, wading, boot-clinging diversions, so that the explorer is for ever having to go about to come at what he wants. On the shore the going is firmer but there are hidden estuaries and ditches that rapidly fill with gurgling water when the tide comes in. The inverted rusty mushroom never seems far, yet is never nearer, apparently within reach but not to be touched, like the past it symbolises. The way back means more slithering diversions with the tide chuckling behind until, suddenly, it is on the flanks, a remorseless, gathering presence rushing to fill the gap between the old mast and the stunted oaks on shore, above which the roof of Cumming's house still shows. Death could quickly seize the unwary, a small event unnoticed by the evening rush-hour traffic on the bridges, unheard amongst the tinkling of yachts' masts.

The houseboat which he and his family occupied for most of the rest of his life was actually a converted floating bridge which he named Bridgewater House. It was, according to Susannah Ritchie, built by Hodgekimon of Southampton and as early as 1856 used to convey the 'Red Rover' Bristol to Brighton stagecoach across the Itchin. It continued in this role until sold in 1896, and it is not known whether Cumming bought it then or later. As is evident from photographs, it was rather more house than boat. The central part, formerly a drive-through portion for the stagecoaches, was converted into three good rooms, the central one having top lighting from dormer windows. The side rooms, formerly passenger accommodation, were converted into bedrooms, bathrooms and so on. Kathleen Murray (see below) remembered 'a cook and maid, a living room and dining room, several bedrooms for guests and his office was lined with beautiful books.' The Cummings eventually sold it and its attendant launches to a Mr Hanbury of the New Forest, who took good care of it until the Second World War, when it was left on the marsh and eventually broke up.

Cumming liked to eat plaice, recalls Doreen Vetcher née Martin, who, as a local child, used to watch him gather them from salt pans on the marsh. Another local girl with memories of him – albeit, as with Doreen Vetcher and Susannah Ritchie, mainly from later in his life – was the late Kathleen Murray. Born in 1906, she was the daughter of a theatre manager who kept another houseboat, the *Brilliant*, at Bursledon. There were, she recalls, 'quite a few' there, some of which were evidently substantial. 'Ours would sleep 16 comfortable or 32 in a squeeze.' She later settled in America and left to her daughter, Miss Judith Buford, several pages of reflections of Cumming and some 23 letters, mostly written between 1920 and 1923, which we shall consider in due course.

Few of the houseboats, though, were as substantial as the one that Cumming and his family occupied for most of the rest of his life.

The Cummings could presumably have well afforded more comfortable and conventional quarters. The choice was most likely his, reflecting his quirkiness and fondness for small boats; to what extent May was a willing or merely an acquiescing partner in this can only be guessed at. Meanwhile, Alastair, Susannah Ritchie recalls, was educated a few miles away at Seafield College, Stubbington. Cumming must have been persuaded of the benefits of this form of accommodation since he later acquired another floating bridge, had it towed down from Barrow-in-Furness and named Ferry House, in which he installed his niece, June Hill, née Larkin, whose army officer husband was killed during the First World War. It is possible that he at one stage moved into this houseboat himself, since Kathleen Murray remembers him living in one that had been towed around the coast and in a letter to her dated 2 April 1920 he refers to his houseboat as Old Ferry House.

There is no single item of personal correspondence known to have survived from Cumming's pre-Bursledon years, while from the Bursledon years themselves there is only one postcard, dated 8 November 1907 and addressed by May to Miss V. Smith of Jameston, Woking: 'I hope you will stay on for a few days next week. Do try to do so. We look forward to seeing you all on

Friday. Shall the car meet you at S. & When?' That last sentence is eloquent of a time and manner of life, perhaps of a fairly social existence, and it is easy to imagine it in the soft Scottish accent that May is said to have had. Violet Smith was a cousin of Alastair's, to whom he was thought to have been unofficially engaged.

Accustomed as we are to biographical subjects whose correspondence has survived, this dearth with regard to Cumming may seem unusual, or even suspicious. But time's maw, indiscriminate and unassuagable, consumes virtually everything about everyone, so it is in fact unusual for any person to be written or spoken of, or even known about, a century after they lived. It is all too easy, when dealing with subjects whose families were historically conscious, or who were publicly prominent, to forget that oblivion is the norm. If history appears to be densely peopled, stacking up behind us, it is only because we know nothing of the overwhelming unmentioned majority.

Nevertheless, Cumming came from a large family that does seem to have been conscious of its history and he eventually achieved an official position in which many knew him and found his personality and career of interest. We might therefore expect more personal records and recollections, and indeed it is likely that they did exist but were destroyed. We have already mentioned his nephew, Charles Molyneux Smith (later Carrington) who not only worked with him but shared his interests, particularly his passion for motoring. In 1909, Molyneux Smith held the world records for fifty and three hundred miles and in 1911 he won a handicap at Brooklands with a fastest lap time of 94.15 miles per hour. He was one of Cumming's executors, is frequently mentioned in the diary, and, after Cumming's death, was apparently left or given various artefacts, such as Cumming's swordstick, portrait and silver. It is possible that he was also given papers and letters. However, when he died in 1966 after a career in motor engineering he left only two anecdotes about Cumming. The first, concerning Churchill, has already been noted; the second concerns Cumming objecting to a man in the train who took off his boots. The man refused to put them back on when asked to do so by Cumming, who then said, 'Only one place for these', opened the door and put them on the running board. There is no record of what happened next.

Molyneux Smith's wife, Barbara, apparently disliked the Smiths – she may have been the impetus behind her husband adopting the name Carrington – and on his death apparently made a bonfire of papers and books, some of which are believed to have been Cumming's. She also sold Cumming's silver for smelting, including a retirement plate autographed by his staff. May Cumming must also, of course, have had papers and memorabilia but when she died at Gordonstoun School in 1938 she left most of her possessions for sale or dispersal.

Apart from the ladies already mentioned, two living witnesses to Mansfield and May's later Bursledon years are his great-great-nieces, Alison Watkins and Pat Campbell. Pat Campbell recalls Cumming as a larger-than-life figure who gave seemingly wild parties on Bridgewater House and who, after 1919, had not only a telescope but a First World War tank in the garden of Bursledon Lodge. He used to take children for rides on the tank, though he declined to entrust it to the bridge over the Hamble. He was apparently adored by children, giving Christmas parties at Burnford House for those at Bramshaw as well as taking the Sunday school there. There is a family legend to the effect that he held baby Alastair in his teeth over the stairwell (at Burnford?) in order to demonstrate his grip. Aunt May, on the other hand, struck the children as being rather prim, though she gave the impression of being slightly less so when she took them to see *Charlie's Aunt*. Doreen Vetcher also recalls a biplane on the spacious – but surely by now rather cluttered – lawn of Bursledon Lodge, opposite the dew pond and not far from the tank. Cumming gave car rides to local children, instructing, 'Ladies inside, boys hang on by your eyebrows.' One day as he was driving round the garden with a carload of children, May came out saying, possibly angrily, 'Mansfield, what are you doing?' 'Having fun, my dear, having fun,' was his reply.

Susannah Ritchie recalls a sale in about 1920 of a field of seaplanes, at Lee-on-Solent, of which Cumming apparently bought a number, towing them to a field near Bursledon Lodge with a Lancia lorry and selling them off at five pounds each to be converted into boats. They were towed tail first, she recalls, throwing up much dust. (In fact his diary, which always very precisely records details of vehicles owned by the Secret Service, does show ownership of a Lancia lorry.)

The Cummings are not remembered to have had much to do with village life in Bursledon, though for at least the decade after 1909 they must have been very largely London-based. Mrs Vetcher recalls Cumming going swimming, unscrewing his artificial leg to do so, and also that he once jumped in and pulled her out of the water when she fell in. He taught her the doggy paddle and apparently sought permission to put a natural swimming pool on the marsh, but it was opposed by wild fowlers and never constructed. Physically, she recalls him as thick-set, short and gingery, and as sometimes attending Bible readings in her parents' crowded house. He was 'charming . . . a typical naval officer who would try anything'.

Susannah Ritchie recalls May as taller than Cumming, slender with brown hair that had probably once been fair, and very pro-Scottish. She gave Susannah a hymn book and used to send her books at Christmas. Her father worked for Cumming on the boom defence and after Cumming's death was given by May a clock that Cumming made. Susannah Ritchie has generously donated it to SIS and it now stands in the office of CSS (Chief of the Secret Service). It is an imposing seven feet, two inches high with a solid oak case, built in the early twentieth century style with a square top and open glass front. Since it does not strike, it is strictly speaking, a timepiece rather than a clock, though the movement (which is visible) is so well built of (dockyard?) phosphor bronze and chromium plated steel that it could arguably merit the term 'regulator'. The unusual deadbeat escapement is based on Lord Grimthorpe's 1840 gravity escapement which he invented for the Westminster Clock, better known as Big Ben. The face which has plain Roman numerals, forms the perimeter only, thus further exposing the handsome works. It is an engineer's clock, solidly constructed with everything accessible and nothing awkwardly small, the work of a patient, painstaking, conscientious, no-nonsense hand. It still keeps good time. The only other of Cumming's artefacts known to have survived is a half-model of one of his first boats, the *Commander*, now in the Royal Motor Yacht Club, on loan from Susannah Ritchie. He probably had a workshop aboard Bridgewater House, or at least on the shore nearby, and he certainly had one in Bursledon Lodge in which family tradition has it that he sometimes made coffins. No one knows for whom, but it would probably have appealed to him to make his own.

Kathleen Murray remembered the Burlesdon Lodge workshop as 'huge', occupying the whole of the basement. In it, she recalled him 'trying to perfect an artificial leg that would be light-weight – the legs at the time were heavy; he had one, so he knew the veterans of wars would like a better artificial leg'.

The impression of gregariousness and love of children is confirmed by the twenty letters Cumming sent to Kathleen, mostly while she was away at school during and after the post-war building of Burlesdon Lodge. The letters are playful, affectionate and tender, and it is clear that Kathleen was one of a number of local children whom the Cummings entertained. He sent her books to read at school – an arrangement apparently made while she was being rowed past Bridgewater House. She wanted boys' books; Cumming's selection included Conan Doyle's *The Memoirs of Sherlock Holmes* and *The Adventures of Brigadier Gerard*, along with Baroness Orczy's *The Scarlet Pimpernel*. He felt, he told her 'rather a responsibility in sending you books. It is so long since I was a little girl [sic] that I have forgotten what kind of books they like – & more important still, which books will not give them the wrong ideas about life . . .'

Later, when she was to leave school, he worried that she would 'become a grand young lady. I shall be very frightened of you for I have no society manners and don't know how to make myself agreeable to young ladies!' His letters and affection were obviously reciprocated – perhaps helped by the fact that he also sent chocolates – and Kathleen several times stayed with him and May during her holidays.

One of the letters confirms, in passing, his possession of a tank. 'We have got the tank down at last & the other day we went for a voyage in it down "Dirty Lane" [now Saltern's Lane] that runs from the house down to the river. Although this was choked up with brambles & other growth & was very hilly & rough, the tank managed to go up and down without any difficulty & I hope sooner or later to make a road down which a car can go.'

He had the Lodge built in 1919–21 on a site that stands proud of the marsh and still, despite tree growth and some recent building, commands a view down the Hamble and across the Solent to the Isle of Wight. It was divided into three in 1955 and is now something of a hotchpotch, with garden and grounds sold off for other development and no more tanks or aeroplanes to adorn it, but the original unity and substance of an Edwardian gentleman's residence is still discernible. The owners of the main part, Mr and Mrs Sneezum, reckon the very heavy roof timbers to be naval or dockyard surplus. When, in 1924, the house was sold after Cumming's death (for £8,500), it was described in the deeds as the 'messe or dwelling hse known as Bursledon Lodge the power house wood working shop garage and other bldgs erected or being thrown Togr also with the engine dynamos batteries switchboard and other generating plant in the power house'. He had a small mortgage on it, with the mortgagee given as Clarence Frank Leighton, a City solicitor who was one of his executors and who conducted discreet legal work on behalf of the Secret Service. About five acres of land were sold with the house but other land seems to have been retained by May until 1929. The buyer then was a very appropriate gentleman, an engineer called Noel van Raalte, who had been chosen by W. O. Bentley in 1921 to test his new 3-litre creation and who built and raced fast motor boats. After his death in 1940, Burlesdon Lodge's engineering tradition was continued by the Folland Aircraft Company, which took it over when dispersing to avoid bombing. Suzanna Ritchie recalls a sale of effects when May sold the house, including much of the library that was above the workshop. She recalls a red-leather-bound set of Marryat's seafaring novels, somewhat nibbled by mice after removal from Bridgewater House for wartime storage, and she herself had a Weber piano which had to be removed by crane.

The importance of Bursledon is not only that it was where Cumming and May chose to live, but that it shows what they aspired to, what they wanted; it was also the place where he left his mark. He was forty-seven when they moved there fulltime, though from the age of fifty – as his diary shows – he was nearly always in London. He hardly had time to live in the completed house before he died and May did not live there at all during her sixteen years of widowhood. Despite the fact that the now divided house, his grave in the churchyard, his long-case clock and (possibly) the remnant of the *Sultan*'s mast, are the only physical remnants of his presence, Bursledon remains the one place outside his other creation, the Secret Intelligence Service, in which you can, as it were, finger his footsteps, sense what he was and what he aspired to be. And it was very much his mark rather than May's, who, as we shall see, had life enough left to her to make her mark elsewhere.

Apart from the quoted postcard, there is one other piece of written evidence dating from the early Bursledon years. It is Cumming's and May's contribution to a booklet compiled by his doctor brother, Walter, and entitled 'Quotations Grave and Gay'. Friends and relatives were invited to contribute, the Cummings obliging as follows:

Commander MC, Bursledon
'. . . Get leave to work
In this world – 'tis the best you get at all,
for GOD, in cursing, gives us better gifts,
Than men in benediction.'
E. Barrett-Browning.

Mrs MC, Bursledon
'All things are literally better, lovelier, and more beloved, for the
imperfections which have been divinely appointed, that the law
of human life may be Effort and the law of human judgement
mercy.'
Ruskin.

Both were quoting well-known writers of their youth and
their choices suggest some serious reading. They also suggest
what was probably one of the guiding principles of their lives:
Cumming's diary, as we shall see, bears plentiful evidence of the
seriousness with which he regarded the duty to work and to
serve, an inclination that May, to judge by her contribution,
shared. Yet her contribution also strays into territory into which
it is hard not to suspect a more personal reference. Did she
simply approve the sentiment in general or was it a more pointed
reference to, say, her husband, whose imperfections might have
called for such a determinedly generous moral in his spouse?
There is a family tradition, endorsed by his late great-niece,
Diana Pares, who knew him well, that he had 'an eye for the
ladies' and that there were a number of peccadilloes which May
had to tolerate or endure. Susannah Ritchie, too, remarked on
his charm and, as we have already seen in the anecdote about
the exposed upside-down Irish lady, he could be gallant to good
effect.

The diary, too, contains evidence of his gallantry but the
hours it shows him as working appear to have made it all but
impossible for him to have done anything else. There is no evi-

dence either for or against the assertion by Richard Deacon, in his biography of Cumming's sixth successor, Maurice Oldfield, that Cumming was a 'notorious womaniser'. When sexual matters are mentioned in the diary, or when others mention them in reminiscences of him, the predominant theme is humour. At least one who knew him does not seem to have seen him as a regular debauchee, or sexual sophisticate. Edward Knoblock, the American-born playwright who worked for Cumming during the First World War – having been recruited on Cumming's behalf by Compton Mackenzie at a party – left a good description of him in his autobiography, *Around the Room*, which concludes:

> There was another side to him, the naughty side, which to anyone like myself who had long lived in Paris, was almost childish. With great mystery he would invite one to his office and take out of a secret drawer in his desk an illustrated portfolio of Le Nu au Salon, in which such reproductions as Bouguereau's 'Venus Rising from the Sea' struck him as particularly 'tempting'. It was considered a great privilege to be shown these pictures while the Old Man enlarged on the beauty of 'the female form divine' . . . But of course this was only in his spare moments, for the Skipper worked harder than any of us.

For all that spymasters are popularly assumed to have mistresses as a perk of the job, we simply do not know whether Cumming was a faithful or an erring husband, any more than we know whether his marriages were happy, unhappy or mixed, nor at what stage in life he began to sport the monocle that appears in one portrait, nor whether he smoked and if so what, nor what his favourite tipple was – though it seems safe to assume he had one. Nor do we know what happened to the pocket watch he probably wore, like most men of his day. Perhaps it, too, was smelted.

Also, despite knowing a good deal more about the middle-aged Cumming and his second marriage than about the young Lieutenant Smith so briefly married to the even younger Dora, we do not know enough to trace, in inward and emotional terms, a clear line of descent from Lieutenant Smith to Commander Cumming. Perhaps there was a sequential development into maturity or perhaps his inward life broke on the stalk after Dora's death, and a seemingly new plant grew up alongside. Whatever happened, seas were gathering beyond Bursledon that would bring, for Cumming and May as for millions of others, both death and a new life.

3

Why a Secret
Service?

Espionage is never an end in itself but always has a context;
people spy because other people want to know something.
The Secret Service Bureau was founded in 1909 as a response
to worries about German naval and military expansion and German espionage. It grew out of attitudes and actions that led up
to the First World War.

The problem with even the most cursory attempt to explain
the past is on the one hand beguilement by seeming inevitability,
and on the other awareness that at every point everything could
have been different. The act of tracing the history of something
– German expansionism, for example – imposes on selected
events a pattern that is the more persuasive the more coherent,
and that very coherence leads us to feel, even if we don't believe
it, that no other course was possible. At the same time, identifying moments or tendencies that could have led another way,
such as the record of Anglo-German colonial co-operation in
Africa or the fact that the Archduke Ferdinand's car in Sarajevo
might not have reversed unexpectedly, bringing it virtually to
the barrel of Gavrilo Princip's pistol, leads to an equal and
opposite persuasion of the arbitrariness of events.

Like all of us, Cumming and his contemporaries lived through
events and trends that they believed were shaping their times.
As a result of those beliefs, people acted in ways designed to
further or frustrate the shapes they saw emerging, thereby

sometimes giving those shapes greater reality. Yet all the time alternative perceptions were possible. For instance, Cumming and the circles he mixed in would have been aware of the degree of Great Power co-operation between Britain, France, Russia, the USA, Germany and Japan during the Boxer Rebellion in China in 1900. There were joint operations, including one in which a German naval officer supervised a British bombardment. In October of the same year, Britain and Germany signed an agreement establishing a policy of co-operation in the Far East, having already agreed to co-operate on a 400-mile railway into the interior of German South West Africa. The Kaiser ordered that English should replace French as the compulsory language in Prussian schools. Two years later the two powers agreed to act in concert in Venezuela and embarked on joint naval operations. When Queen Victoria died in 1901, her Kaiser grandson was at her bedside, cancelling his engagements for the Russian bicentenary. Before returning he proposed an alliance between Britain and Germany, 'the two Teutonic nations', and was disappointed and resentful when the governments concerned did not pursue it as he wished.

In parallel with this, German criticism of British conduct of the Boer War produced sharp exchanges, the British launched their first naval submarine in Barrow-in-Furness (a further fifty-five would follow during the next decade), a German naval bill set out the scale and pace of naval building right through to 1920, while the Kaiser had instructed his troops departing for China that 'No quarter will be given, no prisoners taken', and urged them to be like Attila's Huns.

As Germany, Austria-Hungary and Italy were apparently drawing closer together, so too were Britain and France as a result of mutual unease about Germany. The process that became the Entente Cordiale of 1904 began as an agreement on spheres of interest and as a procedure for resolving disputes by reference to the Court of Arbitration at The Hague. Prominent among these spheres were control of Egypt for Britain and Morocco for France. It was never a military alliance and neither country undertook to aid the other in the event of attack – as Britain and Japan did only a year later – but it symbolised a growing identity of interest and arguably assumed the psychology, if not the legality, of a military pact.

Both Britain and France were increasingly feeling the costs of empire. The Boer War had been Britain's most serious colonial war and there was trouble on India's North West Frontier, while France was compelled into significant military intervention in Morocco in order to save the Sultan. Germany, meanwhile, still sought her famous place in the sun and poured money and troops – 10,000 men by 1905 – into her African colonies. Although Germany was eager for empire, she calculated the cost: her 1904 colonial trade was worth £2,313,600, as against expenditure of £6,352,600. In March 1905 the Kaiser angered the French by visiting Tangier and criticising French policy. This was not a mere diplomatic spat confined to a few officials on each side, but was taken sufficiently seriously for the French prime minister to be forced to resign over his policy of not irritating Germany. The real possibility of war with Germany began to solidify in French official minds.

In 1906 Britain launched the first Dreadnought, a new class of battleship that represented a great leap in warship design and power. The armaments race was predominantly naval so far as the British were concerned. They had no continental ambitions and were reluctant to confront the possibility of significant engagement in a continental land war, but at sea they remained overwhelmingly dominant. However, the assumption that the emergence of the Dreadnoughts would enhance this position was wrong. It actually undermined it because the new class of battleship made all others obsolete, an obsolescence that applied as much to the Royal Navy's pre-Dreadnought ships as to those of rivals; except in terms of numbers, therefore, rivals had less catching up to do because they could start from the new techno-logical base.

Although there were many in the German Parliament who opposed it, Germany's colonial and military expansion was in tune with national sentiment. When in 1907 the French bombarded and occupied Casablanca, the Pan-German Congress condemned the action as 'in the highest degree damaging to Germanic prestige in the Islamic world', and there were suggestions that if France were to seize Morocco, Germany should demand equivalent territorial compensation. There was further Moroccan trouble the following year when Germany sought to aid German deserters from the French Foreign Legion. Both powers, along with Britain, meanwhile competed for the favour of the Turks. The British government probably thought it was doing rather well in getting Admiral Limpus appointed head of the Turkish navy with a particular brief to strengthen the defences at the entrance to the Dardanelles. How good a job he did became apparent some years later.

Relations between Britain and Russia, long soured by mutual suspicion and antagonism with regard to Persia and Afghanistan and influence in India, improved following the settlement of disputes over those regions. The Great Game – war, spying and intrigue in High Central Asia – was over at last. Tsar Nicholas II and Edward VII met at the Russian Baltic port of Reval and thereafter, with the French already in alliance with Russia, this triple alliance was perceived by Germany and Austria-Hungary as a force that could be – perhaps even was intended to be – turned against them. It was not actually a military pact but, like the Entente Cordiale, it was the burgeoning shape of things to come. In 1909 the Tsar arranged for four Russian Dreadnoughts to be built under British supervision.

Meanwhile, in 1908 a retired German civil servant, Rudolph Martin, called for a fleet of Zeppelins to be used in an invasion of Britain. The resulting outcry persuaded the British government to take more seriously the military potential of air power. Despite prophetic promptings by Churchill, however, it was not taken seriously enough: when the First World War broke out, Britain had only 113 effective fighting planes, France 120 and Germany 232. (By the end of the war, Britain's air force was the world's largest, with 22,000 fighting planes.)

Also in 1908, Field Marshal Earl Roberts, the respected Commander-in-Chief of British forces during the Boer War, made a widely publicised speech to the effect that a successful German invasion of Britain was feasible, and called for a greatly enlarged army. It was not a rabble-rousing speech but a considered, official, thoughtful appraisal. Germany had no such plans, at least in part because it lived in fear of the Royal Navy, but it was true that the British army was little more than a colonial bush-fire force, well trained and disciplined but too small to take on a major continental land opponent or to resist a determined invader for long.

In 1909 the newspapers, particularly Northcliffe's *Daily Mail*, ran a plethora of spy stories and invasion alarms – warning, for example, that the many German waiters and barbers in Britain were all spies. This reached such a pitch that the government was compelled to deny to Parliament that there were 66,000 German soldiers secretly established in England awaiting the call to arm themselves from an arsenal hidden within a quarter of a mile of Charing Cross. Alleged sightings of invaders and Zeppelins became common. 'Things which are being said and done in England these days strike us Germans as magnificent material for farce and comedy,' commented one German newspaper.

Such absurdities and exaggerations often conceal small, indigestible truths. The half of the Secret Service Bureau that was to become MI5 did indeed discover an important German spy who was also a barber; Zeppelins did bomb London; and Germany did, in 1909, commission three new Dreadnoughts and an armoured cruiser, ignoring a British proposal for a mutual limit on warship construction. Finally, there really was a German invasion plan, albeit not of Britain. The Schlieffen Plan was the crocodile that lurked beneath the waters of Edwardian peace.

Devised in 1905 by the Chief of the German General Staff,

Count von Schlieffen, it proposed an attack on Paris via Belgium, by-passing France's border fortresses, so that France could be rapidly defeated and the German army could then turn its attention eastwards, towards Russia. It was, with modifications, the plan used by the German army in 1914. It was known about much earlier and became the subject of staff talks between France and Britain as they drew closer, yet nothing significant seems to have been done to counter it. Perhaps the governments of both countries were unwilling to contemplate seriously such an unpleasant, expensive and as yet hypothetical eventuality. Britain, anyway, with her conviction that her contribution to any future war would be overwhelmingly nautical, trusted the French army to shoulder the burden on land, aided by a modest British expeditionary force.

In 1909 the retired von Schlieffen published an article predicting an attack on Germany and Austria-Hungary by an alliance of Britain, France, Russia and Italy. The Kaiser read it aloud to his senior generals. Just as the British spy scares were largely but not wholly without substance, so none of the four countries named by von Schlieffen planned to invade Germany; the British, though, conducted covert reconnaissances of landing sites on Germany's North Sea coast and all four countries were to unite in a war against Germany that all had sought to avoid. Perhaps because we live partly in an imaginary world, one that reflects our desires and apprehensions, the exaggeration of what turns out to be essentially true may be the price paid for the imaginative apprehension of that truth.

The spy stories of the early twentieth century were symptomatic of this apprehension. They were absurd and wrong in almost every particular, yet the danger they hysterically protested came to pass. The most colourful, fantastic, successful and – it is grim to consider – probably the most influential writer, was William Le Queux (pronounced Kew). As prolific as he was awful, in 1909 he produced no fewer than six novels, of which the most influential was *Spies of the Kaiser*. He claimed that all his fictions were based on disguised realities that the governments of the day wilfully and supinely ignored. His books persuaded his readers, as he seems to have persuaded himself, that there were thousands of trained German saboteurs lying low in Britain, waiting for the moment to strike. He armed himself with a revolver when searching at night for secret German signals in Surrey. Like others of his ilk, he was undaunted by failure to find what he said was there; the lack of signals simply meant that the Germans were even more cunning than had been thought.

Le Queux was no Childers. The awfulness of his books is as obvious as it was effective and popular. *Spies of the Kaiser* republished in 1996 is in fact still in print, with an informed introduction by Nicholas Hiley. Passages chosen at random give a sufficient taste of the whole:

'There is just a chance of us falling upon something interesting about here,' Ray was saying, as he pressed the tobacco into his pipe, and by the expression upon his clean-shaven face I saw that he had scented the presence of spies.

'I wish for that tracing,' I said, whipping out the revolver I always carried. 'Give it to me.'

'What next!' he laughed, in open defiance. 'Who are you, a mere servant, that you should dictate to me?'

'I am an Englishman!' I replied. 'And I will not allow you to take that secret to your employers in Berlin.'

The book ends with: 'What will happen? When will Germany strike? WHO KNOWS?'

No one knew, including the Germans, yet Le Queux convinced not only himself and thousands of his readers but also influential officials and politicians. As with *The Riddle of the Sands*, another novel born of passionate conviction, the umbilical cord from life to art looped back into life, in this case with a vengeance since Le Queux found ready support for his views in the War Office's Directorate of Military Operations. There, the section numbered MO5 was headed by Lieutenant Colonel James Edmonds who, greatly concerned by the threat of German espionage, had been cataloguing suspicious activities and sightings. These included sightings of foreign travellers with maps, especially in the eastern counties where invasion was most likely. What he was actually cataloguing, as Hiley points out, was an index of public nervousness. Le Queux and Edmonds co-operated and the resulting jumble of fact and fiction, which neither could or would distinguish, contributed significantly to the prevailing spy fever. Newspapers, too, fed the fever. The *Weekly News* ran a spy-spotting competition and appointed a Spy Editor.

Le Queux's and Edmonds's perceptions began to find wider favour in Parliament and parts of the bureaucracy, although fortunately there were always some more interested in evidence than excitement. An essential truth – that there was a German threat – was correctly apprehended, but its interpretation – that the prime threat was of invasion – was wide of the mark. There was German spying in Britain but it concentrated on dockyards and warships rather than invasion plans.

In March 1909 Prime Minister Asquith – not a man to be panicked by scare stories – was persuaded that a sub-committee of the Committee of Imperial Defence (CID) should 'consider such evidence as may be brought before them regarding the nature and extent of foreign espionage that is at present taking place in this country'. Much of the evidence was produced by Edmonds in unacknowledged association with Le Queux, and, though the sub-committee was rather more vigorous and detached in its assessment than most of Le Queux's readers, it nevertheless concluded in April 1909 that a working party should consider the formation of a secret department to deal with espionage and counter-espionage (referred to by most practitioners in those days as contre-espionage) at home and abroad. Three months later the working party proposed to the sub-committee that there should be a Secret Service Bureau.[1] An early result of the sub-committee's acceptance of the proposal was the letter dated 10 August 1909 sent to Commander Cumming at Bursledon. A later result was Le Queux's boast that information he had passed to Edmonds led to the founding of 'a certain nameless department, known only by a code-number'.

It would be pleasing to claim that the British intelligence services owed their existence to literature, however broadly defined, especially as their historical development has been paralleled by the development of the literary espionage genre; but it would be at most a half-truth (which, it might be thought, is quite enough). The other half – probably rather more than that – was that there was growing bureaucratic awareness of the genuine likelihood of war and of the form it might realistically take, along with awareness of the need for further information about the German armament programme and the need to protect details of our own. This awareness had been growing since the Boer War, in which the absence of intelligence sources and organisation had been keenly felt. Lord Roberts, after taking over as C-in-C, complained that 'he had to do for himself what an intelligence department ought to have done for him'.[2]

A Royal Commission inquired and the House of Commons debated, following which Balfour set up the Committee of Imperial Defence in 1902. Although it never had any executive authority and its wartime functions were dispersed among other bodies, this was to prove the principal advisory body on home and overseas defence issues until the outbreak of the Second World War. It occupied elegant offices in 2 Whitehall Gardens, later demolished to make way for what is now the Ministry of Defence monolith, and it commissioned influential reports on such issues as reorganisation of the army, the provision of an expeditionary force on the Continent, conscription and the defence of India. Crucially, it also considered the likelihood of invasion by Germany, concerning which there was a dispute between the Admiralty and the War Office. The former argued that there could be no successful invasion of Britain so long as the navy commanded the seas, though large raids could be mounted. The latter argued that the need to defend merchant shipping and the Empire could mean that the Fleet was lured away for long enough for an invasion fleet to reach these shores. The CID sub-committee, set up by Asquith, heavily favoured the Admiralty view, and this therefore prevailed.

The sub-committee that proposed setting up the SSB was a side-effect of this debate, reflecting the War Office's increasing concern both at the lack of intelligence on Germany and the lack of any effective way of dealing with German espionage in Britain. Lieutenant Colonel Edmonds was by no means a lone voice and the comical hysteria of Le Queux's writing should not be allowed to obscure the fact that there was genuine, reasoned concern. A minute written by Colonel Count Gleichen of MO2 in May 1907 gives the flavour to be found in numbers of papers at this time:

> As it at present stands, we have no Secret Service agents whatever in Europe, entirely owing to the fact that we have no money to pay them with and this, although £60,000 is annually allotted to the Government for Secret Service (last year it was £65,000). For anything outside our dole of £2,600 (for extra European affairs only) we are dependent on the charity of the Foreign Office . . . If relations with Germany (or any other country) become strained, we should have no organised means of finding out their preparations or their intentions . . . the breaking out of war would find us without means in the enemy's country of finding out what they were doing . . . the whole blame would fall on this Directorate.[3]

Gleichen goes on to ask for money to set up a 'Secret Service for Europe', concluding: 'The only consolation in the present state of affairs is that every foreign government implicitly believes that we already have a thoroughly organised and efficient European Secret Service!'

The secret service to which the government allotted £60,000 a year was not actually a service at all but a vote of money to the Foreign Office for the payment of – usually ad hoc – sources of intelligence, and of pensions. What was happening in the War Office was that those who would be expected to cope with an enemy had woken up to the fact that no one had thought of giving them the means to do so.

Nor was Le Queux Colonel Edmonds's only source of information. Over some years he had developed a liaison with a Major Dame, who worked in the equivalent of Edmonds's section in the German Defence Ministry, and from this he had learnt a good deal about German espionage, including the fact that the Germans had formed a new section specifically to deal with espionage in Britain. Edmonds produced a paper giving details of German and French Secret Services and comparing them with Britain's. Both the War Office and the Admiralty then petitioned the Cabinet, via the CID, for more organised counter-espionage measures in the UK and an increase in intelligence effort against the German military.[4]

The result of all this was Asquith's appointment of the Haldane Committee, named after the Secretary of State for War who chaired it in March 1909. Among the ministers and officials who sat on it were the three who were most important to the nascent Secret Service Bureau: the War Office Director of Military Operations (DMO), Major General J. S. Ewart; the Admiralty's DNI, Rear Admiral the Hon. A. E. Bethell; and the Foreign Office's Under Secretary (now more commonly styled Permanent Under Secretary or PUS), Sir Charles Hardinge. Of the four matters on which it was required to report,[5] the first three concerned counter-espionage, which was the committee's central preoccupation. The fourth – to consider 'whether any alteration is desirable in the system at present in force in the Admiralty and the War Office for obtaining information from abroad' – was what led eventually to Cumming's organisation and the Secret Intelligence Service of today. On this point, the committee noted the defects of current methods of getting information, particularly in Germany, and pointed out that the Admiralty and the War Office

> are in a difficult position when dealing with foreign spies who may have information to sell, since their dealings have to be direct and not through intermediaries. They are therefore compelled to exercise precautions in order to prevent the government from becoming involved, which would be unnecessary if an intermediary who is not a government official was employed in negotiations with foreigners.[6]

This paragraph, representing the enduring desire of most British governments to spy without admitting to it, was to shape SIS's role and operational strategy for decades to come.

The Haldane Committee's deliberations led to the proposal to form a Secret Service Bureau with three objectives: first, in conjunction with the Home Office, to take necessary counter-espionage measures, including the use of agents within Britain. Second, to act as a screen between the War Office and the Admiralty on the one hand and foreigners willing to sell information on the other; third, to deal on behalf of the War Office and the Admiralty with agents spying for Britain abroad. Detailed recommendations as to composition and function were set out on one typed paper which was held by the DMO, the committee having decided that 'the organising of the Bureau should be entrusted to the DMO in co-operation with the Admiralty and Commissioner of Police'.[7]

Thus, not only was the primary role of the Bureau conceived to be counter-espionage but the DMO was to be mainly responsible for its formation and running. The ambiguous role of the Admiralty and the Commissioner of Police led, particularly in the case of the former, to various subsequent interpretations. It is also clear, by omission, that political intelligence remained the business of the Foreign Office from whose budget the Bureau was ultimately funded. The military, therefore, were in charge, the Admiralty had a role of some sort and the Foreign Office paid. Given the direction in which Cumming eventually sailed his fledgling organisation, it is important to keep these original intentions in mind, as otherwise his most significant achievement will remain as unappreciated as it has been hitherto.

Cumming kept a carbon copy of a typed paper, from which it appears the sub-committee met again on 25 August 1909. He repeats the three aims and adds; 'By means of the Bureau, our N and M attachés and government officials would not only be freed from the necessity of dealing with spies, but it would also be impossible to obtain direct evidence that we had any dealings with them at all.' The Post Office and Customs were enjoined to assist.

Meanwhile, other parts of the bureaucracy were moving in a similar direction. In 1906 Lord Fisher, the formidable new First Sea Lord, had formed the Ballard Committee, a secret committee to draft naval war plans in the event of war with Germany. This committee considered the need to secure the home bases, the need to defend Britain against blockade, the need to enforce a blockade against Germany and the need to deploy forces over- seas in conjunction with seapower. Its secretary was a young Royal Marine who had already proved himself an outstanding naval intelligence officer, Maurice Hankey. Hankey was to become the first, and archetypal, Cabinet Secretary and would still be near the centre of defence policy-making two world wars later. In 1908 he was also appointed Assistant Secretary to the CID, whose concerns overlapped with those of the Ballard Com- mittee. For all the spy fever and invasion scares, government, in its innermost councils, correctly assessed the threat as real but not sensational, and it is in this context that the establishment of the Secret Service Bureau should be seen. It was a small part of a wider bureaucratic process.

There was also an historical context: the history of British intelligence organisations. It is possible to argue for earlier

beginnings than the latter half of the fifteenth century but defi-
nition becomes ever more attenuated. At that time Henry VII,
first of the Tudors and a man much plotted against, established
his own personal secret service. Personal instigation and control
were features of such early organisations, either in the hands of
the monarch himself or in those of a trusted courtier with a title
such as Keeper of the Secret Seal, or the King's Secretary.

However, it was not until after the fall of Cardinal Wolsey
in the next reign and century that control of the King's secret
agents became a regular function of an officer of state. Henry
VIII appointed Thomas Cromwell his Private Secretary, which
included this and – given Cromwell's protean abilities – many
other functions. During this period the King's enemies were
transmogrified into his country's enemies and Cromwell maintained agents in a number of European countries. They reported
to the King's ambassadors abroad and to his Private Secretary
at home.

It could be argued that the modern Secret Service should look
to Thomas Cromwell as its progenitor rather than to Sir Francis
Walsingham, Elizabeth I's Private Secretary, whom it affection-
ately regards as its first chief. More, of course, is known about
Walsingham's agents than about Cromwell's, and Walsingham
did, anyway, serve at a time when the threat to England was
more dramatic. He is known to have had about fifty agents
abroad, maintaining a permanent presence in thirteen French
towns, as well as having nine agents in Germany, five in Italy
and Spain, three in the Netherlands and three in Turkey.[8] It was
also in Walsingham's time that a regular postal system began to
emerge and Walsingham quickly developed great expertise in
secret interception. A near contemporary, William Camden,
described him as a 'man exceeding wise and industrious – a most
subtle searcher of hidden secrets – inasmuch in subtiltie and
officious services he surpassed the Queen's expectations'.

The intelligence service he built was admirably successful but
this – his successors might note – availed him little. When he

died in 1590 he was destitute and was 'buried by darke in Paul's Church at London without any funerall solemnity'. He was by no means the last chief of the Secret Service to fund spying operations from his own pocket.

The next significant figure, also featuring in the modern Secret Service's gallery of chiefs past, was John Thurloe, Oliver Cromwell's Secretary of State. Foreign espionage was in a bad way by the time he took it over, but he rapidly rebuilt it as well as developing agents in England itself. In 1655 he took control of the Offices of Post for Letters, divided into the Foreign Office and the Inland Office according to the mail handled, and established in a private room a cipher expert, Isaac Dorislaus, whose task was interception. It was a successful appointment.[9] During Thurloe's time an 'allowance for intelligence' is first recorded in the state archives as a payment to the Principal Secretary. It appears not to have been an annual payment but reappears thereafter in the form of warrants for varying, generally increasing, amounts.

The Restoration in 1660 saw the office of Principal Secretary rival in importance that of the Chancellor and Treasurer, but government interest in and expenditure on the Secret Service diminished. After an incident in which the French fleet, which was safely in the Mediterranean, was reported as aiding the Dutch in the Channel, money was again produced 'out of the Pole Tax, for intelligence and other private services relating to the Dutch War'. By 1689 it was agreed that set sums for the Secret Service should be paid to the two secretaries of the Northern (Home) and Southern (Foreign) Departments in instalments throughout the year.[10]

Early in the eighteenth century the Post Office became a department of state in its own right, though Secretaries were still empowered to 'inspect all letters at their discretion'. Fortunately, the times produced a Mr Secretary Williamson who largely (although not entirely) ended the custom whereby every Secretary regarded all official letters and memoranda written to and by himself as his own personal property. Thus the eighteenth-century archives of clandestine activity are, thanks to Williamson, fuller than they might have been.

Marlborough's continental campaigns between 1701 and 1714 produced an upsurge in espionage, with increasing use of cipher in agents' reports on, for example, enemy shipping and troop movements. Many of these agents were run from London but Marlborough had an extensive network of his own reporting to his headquarters in Europe.[11] One agent, a Rotterdam merchant named Richard Wolters, provided one of a number of examples, then and later, of entire families who spied for England or Britain. He ran his own network and had agents in Paris and every French naval base from Ostend to Toulon.[12] During this period spying within Britain also increased, with the Jacobites a prime intelligence target. As is well known, the writer Daniel Defoe was an agent.

A 1711 Act passed in the reign of Queen Anne permitted continued interception 'by an express warrant in writing under the hand of one of the Principal Secretaries of State', but there was still no monitoring of how Secret Service funds were used. Despite growing parliamentary disquiet, it was not until 1742 that a secret committee investigated the intercept operation and finances. The committee was surprised to discover that the intercept office had existed since Thurloe's time, that it had a staff of five, that its annual running cost was just over two thousand pounds and that the Chief Decipherer was the very respectable Dean of Lincoln, later Bishop of Bath and Wells, Dr Edward Willes. When considering financial arrangements, however, the committee had a more difficult time. The Treasury solicitor, Mr Paxton, was sent to Newgate Gaol for refusing to give the information required, while the Secretary, Mr Scrope, in a robust rebuttal of public accountability, told the committee 'he was fourscore years of age and did not care whether he spent the few months he had to live in the Tower or not, but the last thing he would do was to betray the King, and next to the King, the

Earl of Orford'. Scrope won, with the help of the House of Lords, and was 'dismissed without further molestation'.[13]

Parliament had good cause to be worried about the uses to which secret funds were put in the eighteenth century. Expenditure on intelligence or security was defensible, but using funds simply because it might embarrass the government if certain payments were public, or to supplement ministerial salaries, discharge debts, make charitable grants or bribe MPs, was not. With regard to political bribery, Lord Bute's secretary reportedly claimed that 'the peace of 1763 was carried through and approved by a pecuniary distribution ... With my own hands I secured about 120 votes on the vital questions to ministers. £80,000 were set aside for this purpose. Forty members of the House of Commons received from me £1,000 each: to eight others I paid £500 a piece.' These were very large sums, far greater than the £3,000 and £2,000 issued to the two Secretaries of State by the Treasury, or the £2,000 spent on interception.

The more flagrant of these practices were ended by Edmund Burke's Economic Reform Act of 1782, which established an annual and accountable £25,000 Secret Service charge on the Civil List with purposes similar to those set out in modern legislation governing the intelligence and security services. His Act also abolished the old Northern and Southern departments and created what became the Home, Foreign and Colonial offices.

At least until 1792, the annual budget of £25,000 covered payments to all agents in all countries including, for instance, the man who provided copies of dispatches sent by the French court to India, and reports on shipping in Rochefort, at a cost of sixty guineas a month, with a bonus of two hundred and fifty guineas at the end of his assignment. Many secret service activities were conducted by ambassadors abroad, but both the Admiralty and the army had their own agent networks and finance.

The French Revolution and subsequent Napoleonic Wars led to an explosion in spying. By 1805, for example, the vote for the secret service had increased from £25,000 per annum to

£172,830. There was success and failure on both sides, but over-all the secret service delivered what its government wanted: security at home and intelligence from overseas. A number of examples of the latter are known – many more remain unknown – but two in particular have achieved some fame. The first concerned the Treaty of Tilsit, agreed between Napoleon and the Tsar of Russia in the first week of July 1807. It is alleged that, for reasons of security, negotiations took place on a raft moored in the River Niemen and, according to some authorities, that a British spy hid beneath the table. Whether or no, it is known that the secret clauses to the treaty were being read in London by the 21st of the month and that this resulted in the seizure of the Danish fleet at Copenhagen on 8 September and the consequent sabotage of Napoleon's plan to extend his Continental System against Britain.[14]

The second episode concerned James Robertson, a Scottish Franciscan who travelled Denmark disguised as a cigar merchant. His activities resulted in a switch of allegiance on the part of Napoleon's 9,000-strong Spanish Corps who, instead of remaining in Denmark to help Napoleon, were returned by the Royal Navy to Spain where they significantly assisted Wellington in his Peninsular Campaign. Wellington, too, had a comprehensive espionage system of his own.

Apart from India, where intelligence operations were a necessary prop to British rule, the rest of the nineteenth century seems to have been predominantly a period of espionage decline in Europe, with budgets only partly spent. The Foreign Secret Service vote continued to be administered on behalf of the Secretary of State by the Under Secretary at the Foreign Office, dispersed to ambassadors as necessary. The navy and army continued to run agents on their own accounts, though the extent to which this happened naturally varied according to the campaigns in which they were involved. Increasingly the Foreign Secret Service vote was used for the payment of pensions to spies, or their families or descendants, dating from the Napoleonic era. The account books referring to these are in the Public Record Office and contain frustratingly brief reference to various exotica – Persian princesses, six Portuguese nuns, Dr Morrison, compiler of the first English–Chinese dictionary, and so on. As so often, however, we do not know what we do not know because many of the papers were destroyed; activity may have been greater than we think, since the habit of regarding secret service papers as personal was remarkably persistent. Even in the mid-nineteenth century Lord Hammond, Under Secretary from 1854 to 1872, considered all papers the personal property of the Secretary of State and regularly destroyed those of substance. Nor was the distinction between covert and overt activities as well defined as Burke's Act had envisaged.

The personal and proprietorial attitude often taken towards the Secret Service vote is best illustrated by the mechanics of handling the Foreign Office share. The money was held in the Secretary of State's name at Drummond's Bank and payments made as decided by him or his Under Secretary. Indeed, the legal position had a Secretary of State died in office was that his executors could, as pointed out by Disraeli when Chancellor of the Exchequer, have claimed the unspent balance. (Lord Clarendon did in fact die in office in 1870, but the secret vote survived.)

The best known Secret Service event of the period was the Mazzini affair, in which the interception of the correspondence of an Italian nationalist exile, Guiseppe Mazzini, became public knowledge. This caused a parliamentary inquiry into interception in 1844 and subsequently the abandonment of the practice. The affair is well documented,[15] and arose because the normal procedures for interception were, against the advice of the experts, abandoned in the case of Mazzini. One consequence of the parliamentary inquiry was an increase in pensions paid from the vote as the Bode and Willes families were pensioned off. The then Reverend Edward Willes began what became a family monopoly in 1716 and his descendants (also clergymen) were still at it when pensioned off 120 years later. The Bode family had a similar monopoly on the opening, transcribing and translation of foreign dispatches, having begun when the first Bode was imported by George I in 1736 from the Hanoverian Bureau Noir at Niemburg. When the office was closed in 1844 the Bode family, until then busily employed, not only joined the ranks of what one secretary termed the 'sturdy beggars' receiving pensions from the secret vote, but were able to ensure the same for their relicts and survivors. The last traced payment to a Bode was in 1893, 157 years after the first. The Secret Service has often been a family affair, but not usually to this extent.

While the parliamentary inquiry was in progress and receiving considerable publicity, the French government denied that it had a Bureau Noir of its own. Lord William Harvey, British Ambassador in Paris, commented with tart authority on the veracity of the French, since he regularly and secretly purchased French intercepts after they had completed their circulation within the French government.

In times of peace as well as war, the Willes and Bode families had done good work in return for their generous emoluments, and their priceless discretion. During the Greek War of Independence their work ensured that the British government was the best informed of all the parties concerned, including the Greek, and was informed also of all other governments' intelligence organisations. Between 1823 and 1842 William Bode received gratuities, usually of about £100, for breaking Brazilian, Spanish, Saxon, Sardinian, Columbian and Portuguese ciphers.

Whether the combination of high-mindedness and complacency that led to the abandonment of interception after 1844 had a beneficial, negligible or deleterious effect on how Britain conducted its international relations is happily outside the scope of this book. So many other factors come into play that it is probably impossible to do more than find reason for an existing prejudice, though there is no doubt that if a nation has a foreign policy that is any way forward or aggressive, or if it faces any kind of threat, then knowing what other nations wish to keep from you must surely be of some interest. It was not until the twentieth century that the world's greatest imperial power saw fit, once again, to snoop on other people's correspondence, and even then there were those who thought it unfair or ungentlemanly – the latter, of course, a consideration that would not have occurred to the gentlemen of a century or more before.

The only intelligence activity of note after this period resulted from the long spasm of mutual suspicion between Britain and Russia, made famous by Kipling in his novel *Kim*, and more recently by Peter Hopkirk in his excellent account, *The Great Game*. Despite the belief that vast imperial interests were at stake, there was no attempt to form a unitary intelligence service nor, more importantly, to establish a permanent relationship between intelligence and operations, or intelligence and policy. The Foreign Office, the army on the ground, the War Office in London, the Indian government, the India Office and various Empire political services all operated more or less independently – often, it must be admitted, with courage, verve and success, though there were incidents such as the one that Hopkirk records in which two officers were dispatched by different departments to Afghanistan, by different routes, to demolish the same bridge. This was discovered only when the second officer reached the demolished target.

In his memoir, *A Picture of Life 1872–1940*, the former Viscount Mersey, then Colonel The Hon. C. C. Bingham, recalled his own attachment to the War Office Intelligence Department in 1900. Its sixteen officers then occupied nos 18 and 20 Queen Anne's Gate and he spent most of his time compiling military handbooks for the generals and regions comprising Section E – Austria–Hungary, the Balkans, the Ottoman Empire and parts of North Africa. However, his first job on arrival was to travel to Paris to seek out the editors of two newspapers that were 'scurrilously abusing Her Majesty the Queen' and to bribe them 'with a few £5 notes'. The money was, of course, taken from the tightly-controlled secret service vote, in which it was put down to 'Remounts'. Press coverage of the Royal Family in more recent years suggests that this efficacious tactic may have fallen into abeyance.

Intelligence shortcomings were made more dramatically apparent by the Boer War, but still nothing permanent was done. It took the German threat to achieve that. Consequently, by the end of 1909, Britain at last had the formally established, permanent intelligent service it had long been assumed to have; but it would be some time yet before it actually spied on anyone.

4

FORMATION AND FRUSTRATION

Cumming's diary begins with typical forthrightness:

> On the 10th August, 1909, I received a letter from AB, (1) requesting me to come up and see him as he had something good to offer me. I called upon him on the 12th and had a conversation with him, in the course of which he told me that the appointment he had to offer was that of Chief of the SS Service for the Navy – a new Department about to be formed at the instance of the IDC.

This refers of course to the letter printed on the first page of this book: AB is Bethell, the IDC the Committee for Imperial Defence and from the first words it is apparent that Cumming was at this stage writing retrospectively. By late September he is writing more or less contemporaneously. The diaries for the period 17 August 1909 to 19 January 1914 are all typed in a single bound volume. Internal evidence suggests that the typescript was an improved version of earlier handwritten volumes now lost. The title page announces itself as Volume II, with no mention of a previous volume, but it is likely that it comprised filed copies of letters to which Cumming refers. The diaries from January 1914 onwards are in the form of their probable predecessors: handwritten annual volumes of Walker's Desk Diary, size number 9.

During this first briefing Bethell told Cumming that he would be responsible for obtaining all information required by the Admiralty and that he would 'have charge of all the Agents employed by him and by the WD (War Department)'. There would be a junior colleague 'associated with me in the work'. Cumming's pay was to be £500 a year and he would receive his pension free of deduction. Bethell would enquire as to whether he would be allowed to retain his boom defence command. This was a consideration that weighed heavily with Cumming, as is evident from a letter he wrote to Bethell on 17 August, following their meeting:

> I have been here for ten years and have stuck my roots down rather deep. I have been looking forward for a long time to being able to complete my new Boom Defence, which I intended to be, and believed would be, the most efficient in existence. With that end in view I have got together here the most perfect little establishment, which I hoped would some day lead to bigger things and might perhaps prove useful to the Service in other ways. I reckon roughly that I have spent in connection with the Boom Defence here – for the Land (leased to the Admiralty at one shilling a year), my Houseboat, Pier, Motor and other boats, Workshops and Plant generally, considerably over £5,000. All this would have to be abandoned and sold off – probably at a considerable loss. I only mention this fact to show that it really would be a wrench to give it all up. If only you could see the place you would understand this.

Nevertheless, he would accept the new job even if it meant giving up boom defence entirely, the offer being a 'wonderful opportunity of doing more work for the Service before I am finally shelved'. He argues, though, that he could retain control of the boom defence, with someone else doing the day-to-day running, and that such an arrangement would be useful cover for his new work. He reminds Bethell that Bethell had previously suggested that he should be promoted to a 'general supervision of Boom Defences', a position which would not be questioned by anyone who knew him but which would leave him free to do what he liked, and where.

With regard to money, he was 'amply satisfied' with his present pay and would take on the new job without any more, though he would like a rail pass for travelling between London and Bursledon. Since it was his custom to work late at night and early in the mornings, it would be an advantage to have a room attached to his London office where he could sleep and always be on hand. He asks only that when he retires he be given whatever is the appropriate retirement pay rather than that of a lieutenant (the rank at which he had left the active list), then adds:

> I can foresee that there are certain risks in connection with the work. The only one that seems serious is the possible loss of reputation owing to any supposed malversation of the funds supplied. I understand that there are means of safeguarding oneself against this. I hope that the time may come when it will be to the interest of certain persons to get rid of me, and this might offer a ready way.

Following this somewhat opaque passage, he rather touchingly urges that all his suggestions be disregarded if they are impractical or inadvisable: 'they are only offered as a means of keeping this place, of which I am extremely fond'.

Bethell replied three days later, apologising for his delay. The money had already been agreed and he was reluctant to reopen the issue; Cumming would therefore have to give up his boom defence pay. It would be hard to achieve the sort of office Cumming requested; Bethell was reluctant to involve more people in negotiations within the Admiralty since at that time only he, the

First Lord and the First Sea Lord, knew anything of the new appointment. He concluded: 'I had no idea your billet was such a good one or that you had so many interests in the place and I doubt its being worth your while to take this appointment – but you must decide this for yourself.'

Cumming replied two days later, withdrawing his 'suggestions' but then, with a combination of frankness, deference and persistence that was to become very familiar to his masters, asked that he should be allowed to 'retain a nominal connection with the job – just sufficient to enable me to come down occasionally' so that he could see that his work was not thrown away. He wanted no pay but would like to keep his quarters in the *Argo*, without any suggestion of his holding on to two appointments. He proposed to visit Bethell again unless he heard to the contrary, ending: 'You must forgive me if I show some natural regret at giving up the work into which I have put all my interests for a long time.'

The exchange of letters continued into early September, during the course of which Bethell moved from telling Cumming what could not be done, to lobbying for what Cumming was asking for. Sir Graham Greene, Secretary to the Admiralty (its senior civilian, also uncle of the novelist), and Lord Fisher were consulted and it was agreed that Cumming could maintain his watching brief by being put on to the Boom Defence Committee, while his pay would be the £500 a year stipulated for the new job, with nothing for boom defence.

Cumming visited Bethell at his home (Gardenhurst, Old Catton, Norwich) during the course of all this and it was agreed that the Bureau would open for business on 1 October 1909 in offices rented by a Mr Drew (referred to usually as 'D' or as Sketchley), a private enquiry agent who would receive £500 for the use of his name and services and would pay all charges. If he was deployed operationally he would receive a pound a day in England, one pound ten shillings abroad, plus expenses. Cumming would have no set agreement 'as my berth would be a permanent one so long as I did my work satisfactorily'. And so it remained for his successors for many years.

It seemed at first to Cumming that he had got the job on the terms he wanted, but after another visit to Bethell he was 'disappointed to find that I was not to be Chief of the whole Bureau' but was to share it with a War Office representative with whom he was to work on equal terms. This War Office man was retiring in order to take up the job and was to have a two-year agreement. Furthermore, 'no recognition of our work would be possible as we were to be disassociated from the authorities entirely, and not recognised except secretly.'

The confusions flowing from these two statements were to loom large in Cumming's career. The misunderstanding, which was probably Bethell's, over control of the Bureau and whether Cumming was to lead it or share it, led to friction between the War Office, the Admiralty and the Foreign Office. The War Office thought it controlled the Bureau, the Admiralty thought it controlled Cumming, while the Foreign Office, which paid for it, did not at this stage want too much to do with it. The desire of His Majesty's government to disassociate itself from the opprobrium of spying was reinforced by the wish for a mechanism that prevented unscrupulous information-peddlers from thinking that they were on to a good thing by being directly in touch with government.

The link between government and the Secret Service was thus intended to be untraceable, whereas in practice it could only ever be at best deniable (i.e. unprovable). Maintaining this fiction persisted among peacetime governments until the last decade of the century, but in the process the reasons adduced for it changed. It was always said that SIS remained unavowed so that governments could not be questioned about it in Parliament (wrongly, since even with a fully avowed intelligence community governments can still refuse to take questions on intelligence subjects). It was also thought that it usefully supported another cherished confusion, the notion of 'political embarrassment'.

This is what generations of British officials believed that British governments would feel if they were caught spying; how much that mattered, who would be embarrassed, what happened if a government decided to remain unembarrassed, and the thickness of political (as opposed to official) skins, were questions generally unasked. This leads also to a deeper point, which there is room only to mention: the link between British hypocrisy and British power. The ability to believe one thing of oneself while practising another – as in, say, Victorian sexual morality and Victorian sexual practice – may in international relations be a source of strength, in that the capacity to act pragmatically is unaccompanied by debilitating principle. In the case of intelligence, this officially-imposed hypocrisy contributed to the mystery surrounding the Secret Service, which became an important component of its mythology and power.

On 24 September, a week before the Bureau was to open for business, Cumming called on Colonels Edmonds and MacDonogh in the War Office Intelligence Department. Edmonds – friend of Le Queux – we have noted already, but George MacDonogh (later Lieutenant General Sir George) was an impressive, forceful, energetic, highly organised and organising man without whom the British army would have been even less prepared for a continental campaign in 1914 than it was. A Royal Engineer officer and former barrister, MacDonogh was a formative influence on the youthful Intelligence Corps and a major factor in Cumming's new professional life. It is easy to see the past as galleries of major heroes and horrors, and chastening to see how short is the shadow thrown by those whose public profile is lower, yet whose influence on events was sustained and sometimes decisive. Among those who were neither politicians nor front-line generals, yet whose influence was sometimes as great or greater, Maurice Hankey was outstanding, Admiral 'Blinker' Hall (whom we shall meet later) was arguably another candidate and George MacDonogh – often referred to by Cumming by his nickname, Blitz – has a good claim to be a third.

In the Army Intelligence Corps Museum in Bedfordshire is a memoir of MacDonogh left by another general, Sir Walter Kirke. Kirke virtually founded the Intelligence Corps and before the First World War worked under MacDonogh in the War Office's Intelligence Department. MacDonogh was head of MO5, the section created in 1907 for special duties, which included protective security, ciphers and the censorship of post and telegraphs, though MacDonogh's interests and responsibilities seem to have ranged ever farther. Kirke's view of the infant Secret Service Bureau is quintessentially that of the War Office, which clearly found it difficult to conceive of this fledgling organisation as anything other than an extension of itself. Kirke records that MO5 had 'a small CE [counter-espionage] branch under Major Vernon Kell, comprising only two or three officers. MacDonogh was also responsible for directing the activities of Captain Mansfield Cumming, RN, who controlled an organisation whose task it was to obtain secret information about any prospective enemy.'

Kell headed the other half of the Bureau, and was thus the founder of MI5. Kirke's phrasing suggests that Cumming was rightly viewed as more independent than Kell, despite coming under War Office direction (no mention of the Admiralty). Mac-Donogh's staff were 'not allowed to know anything about the Secret Service activities. These he kept entirely in his own hands, though we were on the best of terms with Kell and his officers, and with Captain Cumming, who brought a breath of fresh sea air into the somewhat musty atmosphere of the War Office.'

MacDonogh's censoring duties included the censorship of all British-controlled undersea cables on the outbreak of war, which Kirke described as 'like censoring the world', as well as the laying of new cables, the cutting or diverting of enemy cables and the chairing of an inter-departmental committee on the new technology, wireless. During the years before the war, Kirke says: 'Everything about which no soldier could be expected to know anything appeared to have been off-loaded onto Mac-Donogh.'

At one time MacDonogh took Kirke on a two-week walking tour of those parts of the French and Belgian frontiers rightly deemed vulnerable to German attack. This fashion for foot reconnaissance of areas into which the British army might be deployed had been started by the future Chief of the Imperial General Staff, Sir Henry Wilson, and MacDonogh apparently thought nothing of marching a regular twenty-five miles a day. Officers tried to pass themselves off as simple holiday-makers, not always very persuasively. MacDonogh apparently enjoyed the attentions of women who thought he and Kirke were German spies and was delighted to jump on and off a tram rapidly enough to fool his supposed surveillant into staying on it.

He had no interest in sport and it was said that his only hobby was work, for which he had a formidable memory. During the war he apparently carried the entire German orbat (order of battle) in his head and could recall what it had been months previously. He was reputedly taciturn, uncommunicative, unconcerned to establish friendly relations, secretive and reluctant to delegate, but Kirke found him a delightful walking companion and pleasantly warm, even lovable, interpreting his awkwardness as shyness.

In 1908 the War Office decided there should be a nucleus of intelligence-gatherers to be expanded on mobilisation in order to support, in conjunction with intelligence staff, the proposed British Expeditionary Force (BEF). Probably because of the deep-seated military reluctance to accept a significant continental commitment, nobody did anything about it except MacDonogh, who had his list of suitable men. In August 1914, therefore, a number of academics, journalists, writers, artists, businessmen and linguists were surprised to receive War Office joining instructions, and to cross the Channel with a few soldiers and seconded policemen on 12 August as the nucleus of the Intelligence Corps. On arrival at a rainswept camp near Le Havre they were issued with rifles and 100 rounds of ammunition. Cumming's son, Alastair, was among them. During that hectic period, MacDonogh and his MO5 officers remained in their offices day and night for a week.

By then MacDonogh was not unfamiliar with emergencies. The Agadir crisis in 1911 – provoked by a German gunboat's symbolic support for the Moroccans in their disagreement with the French – found the War Office entirely unprepared, and also the Admiralty which apparently had its own, contrary, ideas about the destination of any proposed BEF. After this, MacDonogh and his staff 'settled down to 14 hours a day completing our preparations for "the Day", which was obviously approaching'.

During the subsequent crisis over proposals for Irish Home Rule, the then DMO, Henry Wilson, an Ulster Protestant, persuaded almost the entire Directorate of Military Operations of the War Office to make it known that they were prepared to resign, except for MacDonogh. He had converted from Methodism to Roman Catholicism and he held out, maintaining that a soldier must do his duty, no matter how distasteful. Although there were significant casualties in the affair, including the Chief of the Imperial General Staff (CIGS), Sir John French, and the Adjutant General, and although the Prime Minister, Asquith, never forgave Wilson, MacDonogh's stance cost him no one's good opinion and he and Wilson never ceased to cooperate.

Once war was properly under way MacDonogh was appointed to the British General Headquarters (GHQ), in charge of the field army's intelligence effort. His major achievement was his early realisation – a personal deduction based on scraps of intelligence – that the Germans had gathered three fresh army corps with which to attack the British left flank. Sir John French, then in command of the BEF, was planning an offensive to turn the German right flank and push the enemy back to Antwerp, but was persuaded by MacDonogh's evidence to adopt a defensive position on the Lys and around Ypres against which, Kirke recalled, 'the new German corps with prodigious losses, hurled themselves in vain'. Thus it was that the

German invasion of their neighbours was halted, the future pattern of the war was set and, though it could hardly have been evident at the time, the seeds of eventual German defeat were sown.

Later in the war Asquith and Kitchener were taken in by German concealment of their movement of troops from the Western to the Eastern Front, and were fearful of an imminent German attack. MacDonogh, again through his assessment of myriad pieces of evidence, saw through the German concealment and persuaded Asquith and Kitchener that no such attack was likely. When, however, such an attack was in preparation – the German Spring Offensive of 1918 – MacDonogh was back in London as Director of Military Intelligence (DMI), his place taken at GHQ by John Charteris. Unfortunately, Charteris was a sick man when the Russian Front collapsed, failed to grasp what this meant for the Western Front and encouraged Haig with the prospect of early (1917) victory. MacDonogh, keenly aware of the error of this advice, contrived without rancour, bitterness or any hint of malice, to bring about the removal of his successor. So far as Kirke was concerned, 'no better DMI than MacDonogh has ever existed', a judgement that many of his contemporaries – including Lord Curzon to whom MacDonogh was apparently close – would doubtless have echoed. In fact, Churchill later described him as 'the best Intelligence officer in Europe'.

This, then, was the formidable and energetic staff officer upon whom Cumming called on 24 September 1909 to discuss his new post. He found, not for the last time, that what was uppermost in his mind was buried in his superiors' pending trays. Both MacDonogh and Edmonds, he recalled, 'were very busy with recent manoeuvres reports and appointed the 4th October for a meeting there'.

Although his office did not yet possess one, Cumming evidently had access to a typewriter from the earliest days. There are no diary entries for 1–3 October but there is a letter headed

'Suggestions' with '3rd October' and 'not presented' written in manuscript. In it he sets out what effectively becomes his agenda. The first paragraph reads: 'I wish to take over a small Flat, in which I can live, and which will be my headquarters. I will pay the whole cost of this myself, but I wish it to be understood that I am to be found there, and that I am doing my work from there. I shall live there under my own name, and I shall make arrangements for answering calls on the Telephone when I am away.'

He proposes he be given an allowance for the flat at the expiry of the term on the disliked Victoria Street office he was supposed to occupy, and assumes that it will cost the same. With regards to agents in Germany, he thinks he should have one in each of Wilhelmshaven, Hamburg and Kiel, plus another who could travel around discovering new sources. When there are enough people abroad for him to interview, he will travel himself but in the early days they would come to him. He also seeks 'some Official nominal post – such for instance as "work in the NI Dept. in connection with suspected persons in Dockyards"' – which would give him 'some pretext for trying to get help outside'. At present, he says, 'I have no pretext or cover whatever in approaching anyone.' He cites the sort of people who might help him as including 'Erskine Childers, Alan Burgoyne, Rothschild, and others'. It is useless, he thinks, to seek volunteer help abroad 'unless the volunteer knows that he is helping me personally and not some unknown entity'.

Two days later Bethell came to stay the night aboard the *Argo* and they had one of those long discussions that Cumming calls a 'yarn': 'he told me a great deal about the success in the past, and explained that E [Edmonds] had done all the work up to the present but that it was now to be handed over to MD [MacDonogh]'.

The meeting on 4 October comprised MacDonogh, Edmonds, Cumming and Captain Vernon Kell, the officer with whom Cumming was to share the Secret Service Bureau and who was to become the founder of the Security Service, MI5. The man they called the GOM (Grand Old Man) – General Ewart, DMO – dropped in and Cumming was introduced to him. Kell, as an Assistant Secretary of the CID and formerly deputy to Edmonds, presumably knew him already. This is the first recorded meeting between Cumming and Kell and they were, naturally, to see a great deal of each other during the years to come. At thirty-six, Kell was a good deal younger and his background was rather more that which most people would think of as appropriate for the head of a foreign espionage service. If the selection had been made on the basis of their CVs, Kell would surely have been the first Chief of MI6 and the fifty-year-old retired commander would have been thought more appropriate to the defensive role of MI5.

Kell's father was an army officer and his mother the daughter of a Polish count. He was educated privately and had a cosmopolitan, peripatetic upbringing during which he acquired fluent German and French. After Sandhurst he joined his father's regiment, the South Staffordshires, and in 1898 went to Moscow to learn Russian. Two years later he went to Shanghai to learn Chinese and in 1902 returned to the War Office to work on an analysis of German intelligence. His CID duties involved compiling the history of the Russo-Japanese war.

In character, too, the two men were quite different. While Kirke found Cumming 'the cheeriest fellow I have met, full of the most amusing yarns', Kell was quieter, more studied and tactful, perhaps more bureaucratically wily (though not, in the end, always more successful). In the words of a later colleague, he would 'scheme quietly and, with the use of exceptional charm, get his way'.

Kell was never formally senior to Cumming but there is little doubt that, in War Office eyes, his part of the SSB was the more important, and this is reflected in Cumming's diary. This was to some extent natural – ultimately, the ability to defend yourself has to take priority over the ability to attack (though the latter may well be part of the former) – and to some extent historical, since the threat of German espionage was thought to be more urgent than the lack of intelligence on Germany. The fact that Kell was already embedded in the War Office intelligence machinery doubtless made a difference; Cumming, despite coming under War Office direction, seems to have been seen as a sea-boot in the door on the part of the old rival (if not formally the enemy).

An ardent supporter of the new SSB, and someone who would probably have agreed that the threat of espionage was the more urgent priority, was the youthful President of the Board of Trade – shortly to become Home Secretary – Winston Churchill. He and Kell probably knew each other from Sandhurst and, on being briefed on the SSB within weeks of its formation, Churchill swiftly put the resources of the Board of Trade at its disposal. As Home Secretary, he subsequently did all he could, including pushing through the draconian 1911 Official Secrets Act and preparing alien registration legislation. It is illustrative of the frequent irony of politics that, nearly thirty years later, in 1940, it fell to Churchill to order the sacking of the head of MI5 – still Vernon Kell – because of his service's incompetent and indiscriminate pursuit of aliens.

The 4 October meeting, meanwhile, began with a brief account by Edmonds of what had been done in the past and then moved on to a briefing on the agents and their qualifications. This should not have taken long since there were few enough of them and it is not clear how many should properly have been termed agents. In later intelligence parlance, the word came to mean anyone, paid or unpaid, who consciously and secretly helped the service over a period (by providing either intelligence or other services), had a numbered file and was not a member of staff. The person with whom the agent was in contact was usually referred to as his or her case officer. Thus, agents were paid or unpaid helpers of the service, while case officers, intelligence officers and other officials were salaried staff working within it. In the early years, however, this distinction was not always drawn and there were various people who appear at different times in either, or even both, categories.

One such was the first 'agent' mentioned, referred to by Edmonds and MacDonogh as M: 'He and MD said they were going to keep M (the best man we have at present) in an office of his own, to which letters could be addressed.' In fact, M was a man called Melville, a former police inspector whose responsibilities included surveillance, checking up on people and liaising with the more conventional authorities. His office was in Temple Avenue and he was mostly of assistance to Kell, although Cumming had a fair amount to do with him at first. Another, who was slightly more like an agent, was referred to as L and was in fact a man called Dale Long, a German- and French-speaker who worked mainly for Kell and was to be sent to Brussels as 'chief agent'. (Brussels was then something of an intelligence marketplace, as Vienna reputedly became after the Second World War. It had the advantage that espionage was not illegal in Belgium.) Chief, or head agents as they came to be known, were employed for many years in a variety of theatres. The theory was that the case officer would recruit a head agent who would then recruit a number of sub-agents, each of whom would know nothing of the others and would report solely to the head agent, theoretically without knowing who the head agent's case officer was, or even that he had one. Intelligence would be passed from agent to head agent to the (usually visiting) case officer, with money and instructions travelling the other way. The theory was that if an agent was caught or turned (around, thus making him a double agent) he would not know the identities of others in the network nor of the case officer, so that damage could be contained. In practice, the head agent was both crucial and vulnerable in equal measure and there was little control over the agents, which meant that reports could be exaggerated or invented. Nor was it unknown for the agents themselves to be the invention of the head agent, as satirised in Graham Greene's

Our Man in Havana. (It is believed that Greene got his idea from a Second World War German spy ring in Portugal where the head agent took his German masters for a very long ride.) Nevertheless, there were many successful examples of the system and in Cumming's time no one seriously questioned it. There were also situations in which, perhaps, no other system was possible.

Two other agents were mentioned during the meeting: B, 'a good man who had done good work in R [Russia]' and K, 'of whom they did not know much as yet'. Cumming and Kell were to share a clerk whose allowance would be £150 a year, but Cumming said he had no use for one and Kell asked that someone he knew should be appointed.

There then followed a briefing on what came to be known as tradecraft:

> E [Edmonds] told us never to keep names and addresses
> on the same paper. Never to use paper with a watermark
> on it. Never to see any of these scallywags [sic] for the
> first time without M or someone present. Never to use
> the Office to meet anyone but to use the XXX address
> for this purpose and pay two shillings and sixpence a
> time. He told us he had ingeniously found out that there
> were no English in Oldenburg, by taking a Transfer war-
> rant to a lawyer there and telling him it must be wit-
> nessed by a British subject!! We were not to take notes.

There are two points about this. First, any exposition of trade-craft makes it difficult to take seriously. Indeed, its serious practice is frequently undermined by the natural contrariness of things in general, so that even when life and liberty depend on it absurdity and oddity keep abreast on a parallel tack, often uncomfortably close. Some sense of the absurd is a useful corrective of perspective in all fields, not only in tradecraft, but if it leads to sloppiness, to not giving any credence to all the boy-scoutery of chalk marks on walls, cigarette packets on window-sills, disguises and so on, it can also be fatal. One of the enduring attractions of espionage is this highlighting of strata that are closely conjoined throughout life but of whose proximity we are normally less vividly aware. The serious and humorous are only ever a hand's breadth apart and it is often impossible not to touch both.

The second point is Cumming's reference to agents as 'scally-wags'. This doubtless reflects the terms in which the agents were described to him, and that itself is a reflection of the times. Two world wars and nearly half a century of Cold War have meant that the mythology surrounding spies, particularly in fiction and films, has emphasised the ideological, the patriotic and the motiv-ationally complicated, with an admixture of the spy as victim. These elements were present in Cumming's time, as we shall see, but in the years before the First World War espionage in Europe was less a matter of causes than of cash. At a time when for many there seemed no particular reason beyond the personal to spy for one country rather than another, and with little or no employment or social security, there was a free market in espion-age in which some who had saleable information sought to pro-vide for themselves in this way. Just as Shakespeare's Richard III might send out for a pair of serviceable villains, so an intelligence organisation in 1909 might send someone to Brussels in search of scallywags with intelligence to peddle. The danger for the employer was that he might find himself buying anything that the scallywags thought they could get a price for.

Not that scallywags always sold rubbish or went out of vogue during later periods when the political importance and tragic potentiality of many spies were more widely recognised. The Second World War Cicero case, for example, involved what Cumming would probably have called a confounded scallywag. Elyesa Bazna was valet to the British Ambassador to Turkey, Sir Hughe Knatchbull-Hugessen. Sir Hughe persistently and flagrantly disobeyed instructions regarding the security of secret documents; Bazna photographed many of them, including some referring to the Moscow and Casablanca conferences and the invasion of Europe, and sold the results – along with the key to the British diplomatic code – to the Germans, who codenamed him Cicero. Unusually, we have Cicero's published account (*I was Cicero*, 1962) and that of his German case officer, L. C. Moyzisch (*Operation Cicero*, 1950). From this Bazna emerges as elementally greedy, vain, lustful, treacherous and resentful, a Shakespearean villain who proclaims his villainy openly, proudly and convincingly. Put together, the two books form a classic study of espionage and an example of how spying intensifies life. All the elements are there – the more creditable ones on Moyzisch's part – and, just as the novels would have it, Sir Hughe's seniority protected him from the disgrace he deserved. The case and Moyzisch reach a conclusion with an appropriate twist in the tale.

Following the tradecraft briefing, Cumming and Kell were instructed as to the use of their new office opposite the Army and Navy Stores in Victoria Street. They were never to see anyone there and if they wanted to meet a stranger they should hire a room. They were neither to send nor to receive letters and were to assume different names. Kell simply added a 'y' to his and Cumming turned his into Cunningham (though he permits his diary no knowledge of this, substituting for his adopted name a series of asterisks). It is not clear how they were supposed to function under these conditions and Cumming notes rather plaintively that he had understood from Bethell that they were simply paying Drew, the private enquiry agent in whose name the office was rented, for the use of his room and headed notepaper. Since Kell was not free to start for a fortnight, it was agreed that Cumming 'should commence work by copying out all the Records in MD's office – as soon as I had procured a safe in which to keep them'.

After the meeting he and Kell began what was to become one

of the better traditions of both services, by going off for a good lunch and 'a yarn over the future, and [we] agreed to work together for the success of the cause'.

Two days later Cumming bought two second-hand safes and had the keys altered. He was to be introduced to Melville at Edmonds's home that night – official premises presumably being deemed too risky – but 'was disappointed to find on my arrival that a note had been left for me saying that the authorities had decided that the meeting had better be postponed'.

Theoretically, the SSB opened for business on 10 October 1909, since it was from that date its two officers, its office, its part-time use of Mr Drew and its telephone begin to be paid for; £6,200 a year was allocated to the War Office from the Foreign Office Secret vote to cover all expenses. In fact, Cumming started work three days earlier, on 7 October. He 'went to the office and remained all day but saw no-one, nor was there anything to do there'. Given the conditions laid down, it is hard to see how there could ever be, but worse was to come. The next day he went to MacDonogh's office to pick up the records he was to copy and 'was disappointed to find on arrival that MacDonogh would not allow them to be taken out of the place and he said he must consider the matter and would write to me about it'.

Cumming might have been forgiven if he had returned to the sepulchral calm of his new office in order to try out drafts of his resignation letter, but he was keen and, despite what must have begun to feel a little too like humiliation, he was tenacious. He wrote to MacDonogh urging that he should have the papers and was told in reply that MacDonogh proposed to hand over all War Office work to Kell and to communicate with Kell alone on such matters, though Cumming was to stand in for Kell when the latter was on leave. There was no mention of the records. Cumming's response was somewhat Pooterish – 'This letter made me feel very uncomfortable as I could not help feeling that, under the circumstances, it was a distinct rebuff' – but he persisted.

On 13 October it was agreed that, although none of the papers was to leave MacDonogh's office (in fact, a reasonable precaution under the circumstances), Cumming could have access to them whenever he wished.

However, the day before he had written to Bethell, typing his letter at 119 Piccadilly West, the then address of the RAC where he was probably staying. He expressed himself with more feeling than he usually reveals in the diary, or than he might have shown to MacDonogh, protesting at the absurdity of the arrangements and adding:

> K tells me that Col. M said that he wished for one or other of us always to be in the office in case he should want to ring us up. On the other hand Col. E told me that he had informed the authorities that they must not look for any results for two to three years. Surely we cannot be expected to sit in the office month by month doing absolutely nothing. I hoped that I was to have the opportunity of working up a system that in a year or two's time would have agents and branches everywhere of importance, but I cannot possibly organise such a scheme by sitting in an office to which I cannot have anyone to see me.

He tells Bethell of the difficulty of getting access to records, adding:

> I don't wonder at his [MacDonogh] preferring to communicate with K. The latter has worked with him for sometime and of course he does not know me . . . I should feel that any exclusion of myself in favour of K would be fatal to my success, and as the latter is a much younger man, would raise up a jealousy between us that would hamper the work.

He urges the separation of the naval and War Office work, dislikes the idea of a shared clerk, complains that 'Half the secrecy that we are maintaining is of no practical good', concluding: 'I am quite willing to work along the lines dictated by my superiors and am not writing to make any fuss, but I cannot help feeling cramped, and having an uneasy suspicion that K will take charge of the Bureau, and I shall find myself of no use.'

It was an inauspicious start for a secret service. We may see in Cumming's complaints the seeds of strains and stresses which were to dog him for the next decade, indeed for the rest of his life. We may also see what was probably a powerful driving force within him: the desire to serve, to be of use. His concern over access to the War Office records was not mere fussiness or prickliness, but was soundly based. Any intelligence service is only as good as its records, since without them it does not know how it has got what, from whom, or who has access to what. This depends, of course, upon its making proper use of its records – knowing what it knows – and there have been examples of services seeking information they already hold or, more dramatically but thankfully more rarely, attempting to recruit people they have already recruited. Cumming needed the War Office records in order to establish what was known, and how, and where he should start, otherwise he might well have suffered the embarrassment of attempting to repeat recent history. To deny him was to deny him the wherewithal to begin his job. Whether the access MacDonogh reluctantly granted proved sufficient or whether, due to subsequent changes in Cumming's tasking, the records became less relevant, he does not say. For whatever reason, there is no further mention of the problem.

There are, however, more references to time spent fruitlessly in the office. Cumming's entry for 14 and 15 October reads: 'Office all day – no one appeared.' Since no one was supposed to know he was there, this was hardly surprising. He had nothing to do pending a 21 October War Office meeting and a 28 October Foreign Office meeting, at which arrangements were supposedly to be 'all squared up'. He spent his time reading up (the records?) and learning German.

He was also writing to Bethell, complaining that he and Kell should not use the same building and urged that he should have a private flat, meeting agents in rooms hired for the purpose elsewhere. One of his objections to the Victoria Street office was that its position opposite the Army and Navy Stores meant that he was constantly running into people he knew who wanted to know what he was doing there.

However frustrating and unsatisfactory this was from Cumming's perspective, we should not lose sight of what it might have looked like from MacDonogh's. MacDonogh was almost certainly overburdened anyway and the setting up and running of the Secret Service Bureau had been thrust upon him at short notice by the Haldane Committee at a time when what would now be called his core concerns all needed his urgent attention. He had to decide how the Bureau should work and who should do what, while being bombarded by complaints and demands from one who, so far as he was concerned, was the impatient junior partner of the Bureau. Nevertheless he had by 21 October produced a provisional directive and a reasonably clear-cut division of work.

Cumming summarised these in his diary. Kell should undertake all home work, both naval and military, 'espionage and contra espionage', while he would undertake all foreign work, naval and military. Kell was to have charge of Melville and Drew and their offices, and Cumming was to have nothing to do with them. What Cumming calls 'the foreign' were to be left as they were with an allocation of £2,700 to be confirmed at the Foreign Office meeting. He concluded by noting that MacDonogh 'conceded my request about the office, and we are not to stay in as "keepers"'.

Cumming transposed into his diary the detailed notes he took, entitled 'Duties of the SS Bureau', along with notes of his and Kell's subsequent questions and answers. Since the original aims given to the fledgling MI5 and MI6 are usually understood only in the most general terms, it is perhaps worth quoting Cumming's notes in full:

Duties of SS Bureau

1. To act as screens to Ad & WO.
2. Conduct investigations.
3. Correspond with all paid agents and persons desirous of selling secrets.
4. Act as representatives of Ad & WO.

Espionage – (C) Organise an efficient system by which German progress in Armaments and Naval construction can be watched, being careful in doing so that every thing which would point to concentration should be reported.

Both to keep WD thoroughly conversant with what we are doing. If K goes on leave MD will do his work.

Contre-espionage (*). To counteract all measures hostile to GB taken by foreign Governments.

Objects of SS Bureau

1. To obtain information of any movement indicating an attack upon this country.
2. To obtain information of interest to this country as to hostile action or preparations for any such.
3. Watch all suspected persons – such as foreigners residing in British territory and take all means within the existing state of law to prevent them from communicating with their Governments.
4. To counteract all movements hostile to British Government taken by Foreign Governments in this country – storage of arms – organisations of nationals for hostile action, and formation of demolition centres.
5. Organise a scheme of permanent correspondents both at home and abroad, who will furnish information within the enemies lines in time of war.

Means of obtaining information.

1. Retired officers – such as Schultz.
2. Disaffected persons – such as Poles.
3. Information as to technical matters.
4. Schemes of Instruction.
5. Can only watch.
6. Same as 3.
7. Special service must be organised in East and SE countries.

Replies to K's queries.
In reply to K's queries –

1. That all documents should be kept in the Office.
   Ans. No.
2. The unpaid agents to be still seen by WO and certain of them introduced to us under own names – other otherwise.
   Ans. No.
3. Information required (or received?) to be forwarded to WO and thence to us.
   Ans. Yes.
4. Our identity (assumed names) a secret except to MD, AB, M & L.
   Ans. Yes, as to last two, No as to M & L.
5. M to keep in touch with us, and be always called upon to be present at interviews with rascals.
   Ans. No.
6. As to the employment of a second Detve.
   Ans. No not at present.
7. To keep a Diary.
   Ans. Yes.
8. All information sent to WO to be forwarded direct to us.
   Ans. Reverse this.
9. Codes to be arranged between K, MD, & M.
   Ans. Yes.

10. Not to give out to anyone that we are open to receive information nor – suggested by me – to speak to any friends (such as J, Q & C) whom we think could help).

   Ans. No.

11. Each to be responsible for his own Dept., but to have access to the others information.

   Ans. No obligation as to this, but no restriction, leave to our own discretion.

12. C & K always to consult as to how specially paid men are to be employed.

   Ans. (Not given)

13. One Clerk between the two.

   Ans. This matter postponed for the present.

14. Direct dealings with CCs [Chief Constables] of counties.

   Ans. Not given. Intention, I think, Yes.

15. Not to remain in the Office of necessity as Office keepers.

   Ans. No.

16. If possible to avoid employing D.

   Ans. Yes.

17. Arrangements to remain as they are in foreign countries.

   Ans. Yes as far as Military matters are concerned.

18. Paid and unpaid workers to communicate with WO as before.

   Ans. Yes.

19. All translations to be done in the office by K.

   Ans. Yes.

20. To send in a Report in a year's time as to the system.

   Ans. Yes.

21. Written sanction to be obtained for the expenditure of all money.

   Ans. An imprest of £10 to be allowed to C & K.

In answer to my suggestions –

1. That I should be introduced to EH.

Ans. No.

2. That I should be allowed to approach friends like J, Q & C.

   Ans. Not at present.

3. That we should each be provided with the list of suspects, and any other documents that will help us with our work.

   Ans. Yes.

4. Hunt up a Retired Officer in Brussels as agent.

   Ans. Yes.

5. That we should be free to employ M & L.

   Ans. To be K's men in future.

6. Communicate with certain Swedish and Danish friends of mine.

   Ans. Not at present.

7. May commence a German course – hours 10 a.m. to 11 a.m.

   Ans. Yes.

8. Would a photo copying plant be any use?

   Ans. Yes.

Most of this is obvious but there are a few points to note. First, there is a contradiction between 'Duties of SS Bureau' points 1 and 4 – the Bureau could not in practice act both as a screen to the Admiralty and the War Office and as their representative. In any significant action or negotiation the Admiralty and the War Office would necessarily be involved. Second, Cumming's brief under espionage (C) specified only Germany, and only German armaments and naval construction with no requirement for political intelligence on German intentions, although it is interesting to see from this early reference to 'concentration' that the fear of sudden attack was already present. Point 5, under 'Objects' – communications in time of war from behind the enemy lines – is always a demanding and difficult objective and was to cause Cumming increasing cost and trouble as war approached. The problem is that important secret intelligence in peacetime is hard to come by because there often isn't much of it, although communications with agents who might get it are relatively easy. In wartime, however, the range of important secret intelligence is vastly greater, but communication with the agents who have it is at best horribly difficult, sometimes impossible. To put it in a Cold War context, if MI6 had run an agent in a Russian mobile missile regiment, the operation would have been fraught with difficulty and danger but would nevertheless have been possible and would have yielded much intelligence on weapons, command and control systems, deployment, staffing, tactics and so on. Although important and welcome, however, the agent and his intelligence would not have been of absolutely vital significance until the day when his regiment deployed, in the receipt of a particular coded signal, with live rather than practice warheads and real target data. But that would be the one day on which it would be most difficult, probably impossible, for the agent to make contact.

Among the questions and answers that Cumming notes, we see that scallywags have degenerated into rascals (5), that Kell was to have access to chief constables (14), that the unfortunate Drew was already on his way out (16), that Cumming was forbidden to enlist the help of friends (2 & 6) but may find an agent in Brussels (4). Finally, the objective numbered 4 under 'Objects' – discovering secret arsenals and 'demolition centres' in Britain – suggests that there was an extra chair at the meeting for Le Queux.

On 20 October Cumming wrote again to Bethell from the RAC, complaining that the War Office 'are not disposed to give me their confidence or to make use of me in the same way as my colleague – their representative'. After rehearsing his desire to make a success of the work, the story of the denial of records and of his non-introduction to Melville, noting that Kell has since met him, he continues:

There is no getting over the fact that up to the present I have been put on one side in favour of my colleague, and that if this attitude is maintained I shall have to take a very second place in the Department and shall become in all practical respects subordinate to him as regards my relations with my superior officers. This is quite contrary to what I understood when the appointment was mentioned to me and I do not think it would prove a good plan, nor tend to the success of the works. K is a man of brilliant attainments and is an interpreter in many languages, but he is a much younger man than I and is very junior to me in the Service, so that I do not think I can be asked to work as his subordinate either nominally or in practice.

He asks again that he should be allowed to work for the Admiralty only, or – although he is prepared to wait to see how things develop – to 'retire while I am able to do so without discredit'. It is possible that this letter was drafted but not sent; whether or not, it indicates the strength of his feelings.

In a subsequent letter to Bethell, Cumming thanks him for his comments on a pleasing annual report from C-in-C Portsmouth (presumably on boom defence) and describes in slightly more cheerful tones further discussions with MacDonogh which featured his apparently growing reputation for creating waves, nearly always unwelcome in Whitehall:

Thinking over what I heard as to my employers being frightened at my supposed over energy, I can not find fault within myself for anything I said to them. The whole thing was halted until K was ready to take on – though I could not know this – and since then they have dealt entirely with him and just left me out. They are not even going to let me do his work when he is on leave – as suggested. Col. M says he will do it all himself. To add to all the other difficulties, I can see only too plainly that I shall have a hard struggle to gain his confidence, and without it my work is bound to fail altogether.

He cites support for his working only for the Admiralty as having come from Capt. T, who was almost certainly a Captain Temple, a Royal Marine officer who was Bethell's staff officer in the Naval Intelligence Department (NID) and who appears frequently in the diaries as 'Tab'. He and Cumming seemed quickly to have established easy and mutually sympathetic terms. On the day of his letter to Bethell, he also wrote a note to Temple: 'I hope you will try and impress on the DNI the advantages of having his representative directly under his own orders and not under MO5' (MO5 was MacDonogh's designation). He adds:

> I can see very plainly – only too plainly – that Col. M gives all his confidence to K and does not really want me at all. K is an old friend, who has worked for him for years . . . 'A nod is as good as a wink to a blind horse' and I should have to be a very dense man if I did not see plainly that I am not included in Col. M's scheme, and I don't think I should be wise to start with such a handicap if by any possibility the arrangements can be altered.

He amplifies the arguments against the Victoria Street office in favour of a flat of his own at which he could promise 'being available at all times when required and my servant would be able to answer a call and say when I shall return if I were away – in the usual manner'. This is a timely reminder that most biographical subjects up to and a little beyond Cumming's period could assume a structure of domestic support that was generally unmentioned because it was taken for granted. As well as his own flat he wants to set up a 'Photographic Copying plant' for copying plans or documents, something that would be impossible in the Victoria Street office. Again, he thinks that 'half the precautions we are taking to preserve secrecy' are useless or worse, and that he should be able to approach people he knows and trusts. He points out, truthfully, how much more difficult it will be for him to find reliable agents abroad than for Kell at home where 'every third man one meets would be glad to help his country' and where there are many helpful organisations who provide information: 'The Army, Police, Retired Officers, Scouts, Commercial travellers and many others.'

As for his own operations abroad, he is expressly forbidden to approach the one organisation that might be able to give serious assistance, the Foreign Office's Consular Service. This was a serious operational handicap that was to continue, with exceptions, for many years. Not knowing that the Bureau in its early days was actually forbidden consular contact has led some historians to criticise it for attempting to find out information that was already known to consular officials. Similarly, the fact that Cumming was not at this stage allowed to seek political intelligence has led to his being criticised for a perceived failure to do so during the run-up to the First World War. Political intelligence was still very much the Foreign Office's concern and interlopers were not welcome.

Cumming continued turning up daily to his office, learning German and reading whatever papers were permitted him. On 28 October, the day of the Foreign Office meeting, he received his first month's pay – forty-one pounds, thirteen shillings and eight pence – through Kell, with a note from MacDonogh asking him to call for it on the 25th of each subsequent month.

It would be easy to get, and give, the impression that relations between Cumming and MacDonogh were stiffly bureaucratic and antipathetic. But to do so on the basis of what little we know might be to underestimate the camaraderie of the armed services, the often-mocked but more often valuable insistence on good-chappishness, no matter what the professional disagreements. Thus it was that in many army messes talk of 'shop' (work) was forbidden, along with other interesting but potentially divisive subjects such as women, religion and politics; though perhaps more often honoured in the breach than the observance, the existence of this convention was useful for men who often had to live, work and fight together for prolonged periods.

This is well illustrated by Ford Madox Ford who, as a middle-aged novelist, joined the army in the First World War, and, after early experience of the Somme, ended it in an administrative post in Redcar, from where he wrote to his mistress:

> I have been having the most frightful strafe all this morning and afternoon with the Quartermaster . . . as to where 'postings' are to go on arrival – and, as no one in HQ knows anything about it, we both invented ACIs [Army Council Instructions] and authorities as hard as we could go and roared at each other and grew purple in the face with rage – and then went off arm in arm to the Mess and had drinks. It is funny how you can get into the most violent rages over duty and yet be the best of friends in the Mess two seconds later, without a syllable of what went on over the road. I wonder if it wouldn't be possible to conduct married life on that sort of line: it would be a tremendous solution.

It should be no surprise therefore to find Cumming and Mac-Donogh having an amicable lunch on 27 October, the day before the Foreign Office conference, even though they couldn't talk much shop because of the nearness of strangers. They were probably in a club.

In all-too-common Whitehall practice, the Foreign Office meeting took place without those most directly involved in implementing its decisions, Cumming and Kell. Nor was Cumming, because of Bethell's unavailability, able to submit his thoughts in advance. He was given the general conclusions by Bethell immediately afterwards, and had them expanded over dinner the following week. They were, briefly, that he was to do all the 'foreign work' and Kell the 'home work' but that 'The Foreign Agents are to remain as at present', which seems to have meant that they would remain under War Office control and not be transferred to Cumming. There would be no more money and Cumming was to 'see what I can get done voluntarily'. He was not to call at the Admiralty 'except under special circumstances' and was to get a list of agents from Edmonds or Mac-Donogh (which suggests that he didn't yet have one).

The restriction on his calling at the Admiralty was presumably a reflection of the continuing desire that the Bureau should act as a screen. It is repeated a number of times over the next few years, a reflection of his daily disregard of it. It was in fact arbitrarily reversed by Bethell over dinner, who said that Cumming could say he was employed by the NID. Thus from early on the NID was for Cumming what later came to be known as a 'cover department', a practice used by nearly all intelligence services and often essential to their overseas operations.

He was, of course, disappointed by the conference's conclusions and wrote to MacDonogh saying so, asking for the list of agents. MacDonogh replied the same day without the list, suggesting another meeting at which, this time, Cumming and Kell would be present. On 1 November Cumming mournfully recorded: 'Office all day. Nothing doing.'

The following evening, however, there was something to do: he 'went to an address and interviewed C. J. with T'. But the mysterious CJ spoke German the whole time, and Cumming understood only a few words. He arranged to have lessons at the Berlitz School the following day.

He let off steam during a 'long yarn' over dinner with Bethell.

I told AB that I felt powerless to do anything – especially in the office – and that I was left no opening nor scope for doing any work for myself. That I had done literally nothing up to the present date except sit in the Office and I had only received one letter (containing my pay). That the arrangements settled at the conference appeared to me to prevent me from doing anything at all except receive the reports (from the War Office) of the existing Agents.

[Bethell tried to reassure him, saying]

> That I need not do anything to justify my appointment. I must wait patiently for work to come. That I need not sit idle in the Office but could go about and learn. That I should not be watched, and that he had every confidence, that as I had not made a 'loafing job' of the BD I might be trusted to work at this job whenever it came along.

The dinner was not wasted. Cumming received permission to 'take a Flat (at my own expense of course) and work there, but Records must be kept in the Office, so that K and I may have access to each other's papers, as it was for this object, primarily, that the Office was taken'. This was an important first step towards some sort of independence. Bethell told him that, if working from his own home proved successful, the Foreign Office would 'no doubt take it on, but he couldn't promise anything'. Bethell concluded by assuring Cumming that 'the War Office are to have nothing to say to my work, which is to be managed entirely by me, under him (the DNI)'. In this as in other matters, Bethell's goodwill seems to have outrun his accuracy.

There is no doubt that Cumming was in need of cheering up, since on the day of the dinner he had already typed a note which seems to have been intended only for himself and, as evidence of his state of mind, is worth quoting:

> Cannot do any work in office. Been here five weeks, not yet signed my name. Absolutely cut off from everyone while there, as cannot give my address or telephoned to under my own name. Have been consistently left out of it since I started. K has done more in one day than I have in the whole time.
>
> Introduction to 'M' – postponed.
> Copies of documents – put off.
> Introduction to EH postponed indefinitely.

List of Agents – postponed.

The system has been organised by the Military, who have just had control of my destinies long enough to take away all the work I could do, hand me over by far the most difficult part of the work (for which their own man is obviously better suited) and take away all the facilities for doing it.

I am firmly convinced that K will oust me altogether before long. He will have quantities of work to show, while I shall have nothing. It will transpire that I am not a linguist, and he will then be given the whole job with a subordinate, while I am retired – more or less discredited.

This was probably written at his lowest point before the dinner with Bethell, which doubtless did help.

By the time of the next War Office meeting on 9 November, Cumming had made some slight progress, in that he had achieved a promised list of German shipyards. This time he and Kell were present. It was settled that he would be allowed to meet someone referred to as 'B' but he could not be allowed to meet 'Q' because he had no official position. He 'begged for this, as K has one – or the equivalent of one – but although MD and E recommended it, AB [Bethell] was against it.'

Bethell seems to have backtracked on his offer of a notional position in the NID, and thus is history made. The fact that from the start MI5 was officially acknowledged in one form or another, and that its director general had an official existence, made it easier for it to secure co-operation from other British authorities. Officials like to deal with other officials whose provenance is explicable. MI6 would not have suffered if it had been avowed from the start; indeed, it might well have been able to operate to better effect. It might also have been less vulnerable to criticism, particularly during the 1950s and 60s in the wake of spy scandals, for being too much of an old-boy network. Yet its unavowed status meant that it was compelled to be this since it was not allowed, theoretically, to exist.

Nevertheless, something might have been lost with earlier avowal. The old-boy network actually functioned very well most of the time; SIS must have obtained enough intelligence that governments wanted and generally kept its doings quiet enough for it to have survived throughout decades when, because of the fragility of its existence, a single Cabinet Office minute would have sufficed to see it off. The cultivation of relationships and the ingenuity necessary for survival served it well, and the ethos it developed of mysterious, nothing-in-writing exclusivity probably contributed usefully to its mythology. It developed a culture of informality in which, being forbidden to ask for things openly, anything was quietly fixable provided it was defensible under British law and the government wanted it.

Another result of the earlier Foreign Office meeting was that Cumming and Edmonds got together for Edmonds to give 'useful advice and tips for dealing with foreign Agents etc'. Cumming was relieved to find that Edmonds 'evidently thinks as I do, that my first duty is to protect my agents from any breath of suspicion attaching to them through any act of mine'.

The protection of agents should be the cardinal principle of any intelligence service, and certainly became so in the one that Cumming founded. No service could function for long if its agents did not believe that they and their work would be kept secret. To compromise an agent through carelessness, or worse, is to sin against the Holy Ghost of espionage. No service can forgive it. As Cumming pointed out, though, he was very far then from being any sort of threat to the security of any agent – 'I have done literally nothing and have spoken to no one.'

Edmonds advised never to pay an informant in his own country, as he might then resort to blackmail, but to take him across the border and pay him not too much at first, with the promise of further payment by results. Names and addresses should never be written on the same paper and paper should never be watermarked. No agent should ever be referred to by his name – a practice continued in the later SIS – and no address should be used too often, nor should it ever be used for more than one agent.

They also discussed a series of people signified only by initials, with Edmonds approving Cumming's idea as to 'the K-L-ch-Y envelopes' but caring less for the plan to employ 'the Rs at the Kiel Regatta, or the Jorgensen plan, Burgoyne, Childers et hoc c o'. The early diary is full of such frustrations but the context makes it clear that he was still seeking approval to ask the help of such people as Childers, with the clear implication that they were all known to him. Indeed, the discussion moved right into *Riddle of the Sands* territory: '*Cynthia* was a convenient little steamer which ran from Delfzill (opposite Emden) from whose deck one could see a lot. He suggested my going as an American.'

This last sentence is the first indication that Cumming himself might undertake foreign reconnaissance and is typical of many of the spying missions mounted by the Admiralty and the War Office in which serving officers were dispatched to conduct visual reconnaissance, rather than simply trust to agents. Cameras were then less commonplace and less portable, and there was no aerial reconnaissance, still less any satellite snapshots. In war, discovering the whereabouts of the enemy was one of the major problems, while in peacetime, knowledge of, say, how many warships were being built, where and what sort, was as important to obtain as it was, sometimes, difficult.

A couple of days later Cumming was again in the Admiralty ferreting out a world chart he had chanced upon. He also chanced upon a discussion of 'the matter of SRT 1425, a foreign informant's offer, dealing with Forst etc.'. Finding that it was to be handed over to Kell, he told those concerned that he 'could not help making a mental note of the circumstance, as this was my department'. Again, the remark is Pooterish, but tone is something that can change with transcription, and it is hard sometimes to assess it. Cumming's statement might have sounded more an assertion of resolve, a thus-far-and-no-further warning, despite his having no official position, no rank and an ambiguous role. He spent the next two days sitting uselessly in his office.

The following day, 17 November, he astutely took Bethell to the motor show, after which congenial diversion Bethell said he might visit him at the Admiralty whenever he wished and should 'come right into his office if he was not engaged'. He undertook to 'think out some plans or give me a foothold in the Admiralty later on if practicable'. The advantage of a foothold, an official position, was not simply that it would be useful in terms of cover, but that Cumming could get the bureaucracy to work for him. As it was, having no official existence he was still having to beg and borrow even such basic items as maps. He next got Tab down to Bursledon for the weekend, where, during the predictable long yarn, they agreed that they should aim to get two agents in Germany under B, a head agent, as well as a third who could travel and 'once in three months, visit the big yards and send in reports'.

Three days later, after seeking out more maps in the Royal Geographical Society, he lunched a Captain Richardson in order to find out whether there were any retired British officers in Brussels whom he could recruit. There were a couple of likely-sounding individuals but he was inhibited from asking further details by not being allowed to give any reason for his interest. On 26 November, however, he had his first proper agent meeting. It was a day that marked a change in his fortunes and morale, the first flicker of light in his part of the Bureau, but it was nearly hijacked.

It had been agreed that Cumming should be introduced by Tab to B that night. But at noon Kell appeared and told him that it had been decided that Tab was not to attend the meeting. Kell showed Cumming written instructions that differed importantly from those that had been agreed with Bethell, adding that he had B's pay in his pocket 'which he was bound to hand over to him', and that Cumming was instructed to compile some coded messages with their corresponding 'blind sentences'. From Cumming's detailed record of the resulting to-ings and fro-ings, it appeared that B was clearly understood by him and the Admiralty to be a foreign-based agent who produced intelligence about German shipbuilding and was thus squarely in Cumming's area. However, B had previously been 'run' (that is, seen and tasked) by Edmonds on behalf of the War Office, which now belatedly woke up to the fact that it was losing control of the case. What is odd, and least defensible, is that the War Office should have attempted this hijack without trying to argue the case beforehand.

Cumming saw this as a moment of decision: would his part of the Bureau function under him as an equal and independent arm or was it to be wholly under War Office direction, and treated as a sub-department? He told Kell he would not agree to the change without Bethell's authority and proposed that they go at once to see him. Kell insisted that they should also see MacDonogh, adding that it was impossible because he was tied up all afternoon. Eventually, they took a cab to Bethell. Quite what went on in the cab will never be known but when it reached Whitehall Kell got out of the far side and went over to the War Office, while a surprised Cumming proceeded alone to the Admiralty. There he found strong support from Bethell, who sent Tab with a message to General Ewart, the DMO, saying that he considered Cumming to be in sole charge of all the foreign work and arrangements, and that the division of the Bureau's work as agreed at War Office and Foreign Office meetings was to be maintained. If, as Kell had relayed, it was thought by the War Office inadvisable that more than two people should be present with B, then it should be Kell who stayed away.

When MacDonogh heard about this he went to see Ewart, but Ewart agreed with the Admiralty. MacDonogh 'begged' that Cumming would not change the addresses to which messages should be sent as they were long established and it was a bad time to change them. He suggested that Edmonds rather than Kell (who was not allowed to attend) should pay B because 'the man who was the employer should be the paymaster'. This showed that the War Office still did not fully accept Cumming's assertion of independence, qualified though it was. Cumming stuck to his last: 'I said that this was precisely the reason I wished to pay the money myself and it was eventually handed to me to pay over to B.'

It is not difficult to imagine the bureaucratic feather-ruffling that all this provoked and no doubt it took some time for the roosts to quieten. Nor is it ideal to have such fraught preliminaries to a significant agent meeting; he spent the hour that remained working in his office on the message-sentences. He thought the results not good enough for a permanent code but got them done just in time to meet Tab and head for the 'JS address', where they found Edmonds. When B arrived Edmonds introduced him to his new case officer and left. The conversation was in German which Cumming could just follow, 'but not enough to understand his ideas and opinions'. Tab translated. B 'seemed to think he should have no difficulty in getting us the information we wanted, as he said that all the TRs were open to bribes and could not resist the sight of a gold piece.'

'TRs' means the Germans and this is the first use of the abbreviation in the diary. It is a shortened form of Tiaria, which Cumming first uses within a week of this date to mean Germany. The origin is nowhere stated; it could be Secret Service parlance but it is more likely to be of naval origin, such as the name given to a fictitious enemy, which everyone knew to be Germany, in exercises. Or it may have had some altogether non-official origin.

They arranged with B that he would recruit a sub-agent in Wilhelmshaven as well as one who could travel around the big shipyards every three months. Cumming asked whether his men might be able to get lists with English people in the towns they visited 'but he deprecated this very much and evidently does not mean to do it'. Cumming then suggested that he might get details of four Dreadnoughts supposedly about to be built at Pola and elsewhere in the Austrian Empire, 'but he jibbed at this immediately and said he was an Austrian and could do nothing that could hurt his native country'. This showed, thought Cumming, 'that he will be of little use should Austria join Germany in a war against us'. B volunteered his name, writing it because he said it was hard to spell correctly and also giving his telegraphic address in Berlin, but Cumming did not ask his home address, 'as I thought he would wonder at my not knowing it'. At the last moment Cumming asked if he spoke French 'and was surprised and pleased to find that he speaks French as well as or better than he does German'. With fuller intercourse now possible, they arranged to meet again the next day. Cumming's verdict on B was: 'He is definitely an intelligent and bold man and I think will probably prove my best aide, but the difficulty about his patriotic feeling for Austria will have to be considered.'

For a first meeting, this seems to have gone well. It was essential to agree communications – the life-blood of any secret agent relationship – and tasking, and Cumming would have tried to leave B feeling confident that he knew what was needed and also confident enough to say what he could not do. Certainly, it seems to have buoyed up Cumming, who perhaps thought that he was getting down to the job at last. A couple of days later when he notes calls on Bethell and MacDonogh he uses their nicknames – Luz and Blitz – for the first time, possibly an indication of his own more relaxed and confident state.

When discussing these communication arrangements with MacDonogh the next day, Cumming discovered that the War Office Resident Clerk would receive messages out of working hours up to 11 p.m., but that after that they would remain in the Post Office until the following day. 'This must of course be altered,' he commented, noting that he would have to wait until introduced to the senior GPO official (Mr de Wardt) who was responsible for confidential matters. He also reminded MacDonogh that he had now taken a flat of his own and was having a private telephone wire laid in. This flat, in Ashley Gardens, Vauxhall Bridge Road, was thus the first actual headquarters of what became the Secret Intelligence Service, since that in Victoria Street had never functioned as such.

The next few days were spent arranging further communications, acquiring foreign currency – financial control being tight, receipts for each amount had to be taken personally to Tab – and visiting the Admiralty and the War Office whenever he had an excuse to poke his nose in. He acquired from MacDonogh a 'roll map of Tiaria' and a copy of a letter from someone offering information from Germany. He shared the case with Kell because it 'touches both of us, K, because the man mentions two persons whom it is his business to know about, and me because he offered information'. Thus began the first of many cases run jointly by the two services.

The following day he and MacDonogh had lunch and a yarn at the Naval and Military Club, following which a number of administrative issues were satisfactorily agreed, including authority for Cumming to acquire a 'typewriting machine' instead of the services of a clerk. They also tried unsuccessfully to devise better agent telegraphic arrangements, with Cumming concluding that the present arrangement 'will never do, and I must get some better scheme as soon as possible'. The image of MI6 affairs being arranged behind the polished doors of London clubs, beloved of spy books and films, was, from the earliest days, always at least partly true.

The bureaucratic struggle went on, with MacDonogh producing a list of written instructions which he required Cumming to sign in his presence. These might have been in response to Cumming's letter of 29 October and some, at least, appeared to Cumming to re-open questions he thought settled. One clause, he pointed out, 'apparently limited my field of action to one country and thus did not conform to the terms of the arrangements made at the Meeting'. But in other ways it gave him at least some of what he was asking for. It began, 'I now propose to hand over to you the whole of the TR intelligence system, subject to the following restrictions conditions' [sic]. Among these were that B should be paid and retained whether used or not as 'he was found useful in Russia and might be required to work there again. FO has approved this.' Cumming was not to exceed his budget on any account, was to produce receipts for all expenditure and was to submit his financial requirements on the 20th of every month for payment on the 25th. Military subjects were to have their full share of his attention and he was to seek military intelligence to the best of his ability, a stipulation which suggests that the War Office was worried that it might, because of his provenance, play second fiddle to the Admiralty's requirements. MacDonogh at last provided the names and addresses of five agents, requesting that any new recruits were to be reported to him and that he was to be kept fully informed of whatever Cumming was doing. Subject to all this, Cumming was free to recruit, to discharge, to communicate with and to instruct his agents as he chose but must 'Arrange such a system for the transmission of intelligence both in war and peace that will ensure it reaches the N & M authorities with the minimum of delay'.

After this meeting Cumming dropped in on the Naval and Military Club in the justified hope of finding Bethell. Bethell thought the instructions symptomatic of divided control and War Office intransigence, a guarantee of bureaucratic frustration and rancour. He was more right than he knew. In the 1950s, when those concerned were long dead, the War Office once again tried, albeit half-heartedly, to wrest back the control it had lost long before and was already losing in December 1909. Not that it seemed like that at the time. Cumming commented ruefully: 'It is difficult to know to whom I am to be responsible and to whom I should apply for instructions, orders and help.'

There were more agent meetings during the next few days, one at the lodgings of another of the DNI staff, Captain Roy Regnart of the Royal Marines. He was to play a significant and not always helpful part in Cumming's life over the next few years. The agent he met at Regnart's lodgings was referred to as WK, about whom he commented: 'seems intelligent and probably straightforward, but I am not quite certain that he ever saw those guns!!'

On 13 December he met the man involved in the case he was sharing with Kell, variously referred to as 'Von de T' or 'ST 635'. He and Kell were obviously not co-ordinating closely since Kell had arranged to see someone else at the same time and place and had already 'been down to ST's place disguised as a philanthropist [sic] but had not succeeded in finding out anything about him'. (The place is referred to as a 'TR Lab home', which may have meant a hostel for German workers or labourers.) Kell was put out that Cumming was to see the man, and Cumming put out that Kell had seen him without his knowledge. Cumming protested that he was 'in no way to blame for the muddle as I had carried out my orders to the letter, and if I was misled as to what K was doing, that was not my fault.' Kell hurried off to see MacDonogh – he seems to have had a penchant for hurrying off during confrontations – while Cumming kept his appointment 'at the Trysting place but ST never turned up, something having frightened him away. It could not have been my letter, but it might very likely have been the timely visit of the philanthropist . . .'

The following day, he and Kell met again at ten o'clock and 'had a yarn. We settled that I should do more about ST (and I hope we shall work better together in future).' However, Kell also said that MacDonogh wished that messages between himself and Cumming should pass via Kell in future. Whether this was because MacDonogh felt unduly pestered by Cumming or was trying to assert War Office predominance, or simply thought it might be more efficient, is not known. Cumming was too wary to agree: 'K promised to get this in writing.'

Notwithstanding MacDonogh's request, two days later Cumming was in his office again, confirming his order for a typewriter and asking to be allowed a set of press cuttings. Even this humble request was, it seems, too much. Press cuttings 'could not be allowed – in fact they were not obtainable – as the papers were sent in their whole condition to him and he extracts the matter that interests him himself.' On 20 September he visited MacDonogh again, handed in his requisition for pay for B, and found that the question of control of B was not settled after all. MacDonogh said that if Cumming 'had no objection he would prefer K to pay B's wages himself, for the present, and to hand me the money to forward to him, the receipt being returned to Blitz . . . a farce.' Cumming was not to write to B but 'I may ask when he is likely to be going to Krakow and where he will be staying when there'.

No case officer could accept such conditions and the lack of any apparent protest from Cumming suggested that he had given up seeing himself as such, at least as far as B was concerned. His only comment was that the stereotyped letter sent to B (presumably to do with pay or meeting arrangements) 'was very compromising' and not as good as his own.

On the other hand, MacDonogh conceded that there did not need to be two people at each agent meeting and that Cumming could conduct them by himself. Nor did he object to Cumming having a German teacher for private German lessons – 'if my niece joins the class and it is not held in the office'. They also discussed the 'Ess man [Essen?]', with regard to whom MacDonogh 'had no authority to sanction the payment of any fee, and that if I do have this (up to twenty pounds) I may requisition on him afterwards, but must not have a grievance if it is refused. On the other hand he will not think I am trying to force his hand if I do pay it.'

For all that these entries tell us little about the agents concerned or the intelligence produced, they do reveal the tenor of Cumming's discussions with his masters and the almost crippling degree of financial control. MacDonogh approved the purchase of a 'cheaper Typewriter'.

During the run-up to Christmas there are dealings with Tab, arrangements and postponements of meetings, arrangements for communications and daily visits by Cumming to check PO boxes or other addresses issued to agents. In the early days of the Bureau he did everything himself and such clandestine communications, in almost any form, are time-consuming.

On 22 December he was told by Bethell to 'ask FRS to go to F (Fiume) for me and also to Arctic P and to find out what progress has been made in laying down ships for Ds [destroyers?]'. FRS was probably a naval or army officer, or someone reasonably well known to the bureaucracy, rather than a secret agent in the normal sense. He was to start as soon as convenient and was to have his expenses paid, first class. Bethell did not wish to see him and Cumming could tell MacDonogh 'at my discretion'. They also later discussed the payment of B's men in such a way as to suggest that Cumming was still dealing with him. What most likely happened was that B remained a War Office case, with Cumming tasking and debriefing him on Admiralty requirements.

The following day Tab 'came to lunch here' – it is not clear where, but probably Cumming's Vauxhall Bridge Road flat – and gave Cumming 'the blue book on the ship building and capabilities of the principal Naval Powers'. Such a seemingly mundane matter is important for any intelligence service since a portion of what governments think they want to know is often known to them already. It has happened that intelligence services have risked gathering in secret what a little effort on their part, or on the part of their taskers, would have discovered overtly.

When picking up his pay from MacDonogh, Cumming had arranged to be introduced to 'D' at the RAC on 21 December. While there, he ran into Kell and agreed to put him up as a member of the Portsmouth Club; and a few days later he wrote to the secretary of the Royal Naval Club seeking honorary membership for Kell. MacDonogh, meanwhile, said that the DMO had asked him to 'give DR a job to test his capabilities' and asked Cumming to fix it. It is worth noting just a few of these daily arrangements because they were the context against which, or within which, the larger bureaucratic issues took place. However great the disagreements, other aspects of working life had to go on and, since bureaucrats are natural compartmentalisers, serious disagreement in one area did not nullify friendly, or at least civil, relations in others.

On Christmas Eve Cumming called on FRS and obtained his agreement to the trip Bethell had proposed, for expenses only. 'We had a discussion as to plans and arrangements, it being understood that I was a mere go-between and had no interest in the affair, other than obliging my Chief by mentioning a suitable man.' This is a good example of why confusion has often arisen as to on whose behalf espionage operations were mounted. Many serving officers, let alone agents, were not always clear as to whether they were working for Cumming, for the DNI, or for the War Office, or for all three. Who, for example, did FRS think he was working for? Whatever unlikely disclaimer Cumming may on instructions have made, it was he who did the asking and tasking, and presumably he to whom FRS reported; but it was a DNI operation.

Christmas Day and Boxing Day pass without mention in the diary. Cumming seems not to have taken time off between Christmas and the New Year since, apart from other business, he notes for the 28, 'Working in office all day.' He wasn't alone. MacDonogh was also at work and arranged that Cumming should be introduced to another War Office agent, known as 'U'. He also said that Cumming should make any suggestions for the next year's work before 10 January, and at the same time telling him not to hurry since 'the Paymaster [Sir Graham Greene, Secretary to the Admiralty, also referred to by his nickname, Tin] would not consider I had sufficient experience to justify their adoption'. Cumming obligingly replied that he did not consider he had 'sufficient experience to suggest anything'.

On 30 December he took 'DP' (who could be identical with FRS) to Portsmouth Dockyard in order to show him what he should look for in foreign dockyards. On New Year's Eve he briefed the agent 'D' at the RAC following confusion on D's part as to Pall Mall numbers. He recorded the main points of the meeting for his diary, from which it is apparent that D's main role was that of providing warning of war – 'I promised him £500 if he could send me accurate news of the imminence

127

of war before any other agent, and at least 24 hours before any declaration' – though Cumming clearly did not have great confidence in him, finding him 'timid and accepts as a foregone conclusion that at the outbreak of war he will fly (and bring his message with him)'. D was apparently one of three such 'passive' agents whose sole purpose was to warn of sudden attack by Germany. Such worries were not confined to the British and the fact that it didn't happen, and that there was no such intention, does not mean that worry about it was necessarily otiose. It is one of the responsibilities of military establishments to take precautions against what could – but probably won't – happen, since unless they do that they have very little chance indeed of anticipating whatever does come to pass.

Cumming's downbeat assessment of D is reassuring. An enthusiastic case officer's desire for results can lead him to persuade the agent, himself and his colleagues that the case is better than it is. This in turn can lead to treating poor intelligence as good and, at worst, partial truths as whole, or false as true. Cumming seems not to have suffered this weakness – or not yet – and, as we shall see, in one major area of his First World War operations he took the most sensible measure available to any intelligence service to counter it: the separation of intelligence assessment from intelligence-gathering, so that the assessors of reports have no interest in furthering the cases that produce them.

The year 1909 ended with the diary as silent about New Year as it was about Christmas. In its four months of life the Secret Service Bureau had achieved little or nothing so far as Cumming was concerned. There was more going on on Kell's side, which is unsurprising, but the very fact that the Bureau was already effectively if not formally divided in two was a significant step. Yet the problems of command and control were unresolved and Cumming was often in a position that many would have regarded as intolerable. The agents and operations he inherited were few, tentative and amateurish, largely because they were conducted by amateurs who were themselves few and uncertain, and the intelligence machinery was neither properly co-ordinated nor tasked. When Cumming proposed setting up his own operations, as he was supposed to do, he was met with suspicion and restrictions. The fact that he stuck with the job was probably due to the traditions of obedience and loyalty in which he was reared, to his patriotism, to his strong desire to serve and to the probability that at the age of fifty he was pleased and surprised to be offered another job. The challenge of setting up the British Secret Service was too good to relinquish easily, no matter how unsatisfactory the early realities.

5

THE FIRST FULL YEAR

The year 1910 was to prove fuller, more productive and more troubled, with larger events played out against the background of almost daily to-ing and fro-ing with Tab in the Admiralty and with the helpful de Wardt at the GPO over agent communications and post boxes.

It began quietly, however, with Cumming translating accounts from *Le Petit Temps* of the trial at Rheims of a German spy caught in France. As with MacDonogh having to do his own press cuttings, the structure of support later taken for granted in government departments did not then exist. Kell forgot a lunch they had arranged at the Naval and Military Club and U was too ill to attend a meeting.

Cumming then turned his attention to writing a report: he had been asked by MacDonogh to make suggestions for next year's work on what he thought of the present situation of the Bureau, and to make suggestions for the future. He worked on it until the early hours and presented it around 10 January, after Bethell had approved. It is headed 'Suggestions for general working of SS' and is the first known paper on which the famous 'C' signature appears, albeit not yet in green ink. He calls for attention to four points, the first three concerning agent communications in time of peace, approach to war and war. From these it emerges that he has inherited five principal agents, three of whom have the sole task of warning of impending war and are quite untried, though their success 'would be worth more than all other information obtained at any other time'. He thinks

131

they should be offered a substantial fixed sum to be awarded to the first to communicate accurate news of imminent war. He then analyses the problems of wartime communications, especially that of motivating from a distance agents for whom discovery means death, and asks for suggestions.

His fourth point – a call for 'The establishment of a system in foreign countries (other than Germany) which could be readily developed should occasion require' – is a call for what later came to be described as third country operations: 'It may often be possible to get information about Germany through another country, and secrets that may be carefully guarded from us may be more readily accessible elsewhere.' He names France, Italy, Austria, Belgium, Holland, Sweden and Denmark as countries in which he would like to have agents or 'correspondents' who could get at German intelligence.

The interest of this document is not only that it shows how Cumming's mind was working in the early years but in his generally accurate analysis of the problems and priorities and its – for the time – radical third country proposal. This often later proved effective against 'hard targets' and the fact that it seemed innovative in 1910 indicated the previous lack, in Britain at least, of serious thought about how to learn the secret intentions of a likely enemy. Perhaps we should not be surprised at this. Only a European enemy could have posed a threat to Britain itself – the 19th-century Russian threat was towards the British in India – and there had been no such threat since Napoleon. There had thus been no need to spy seriously on European powers, albeit that they – particularly France, Russia and Germany – found it necessary to spy on each other, and so had more developed intelligence services.

After this Cumming received a paper from Bethell entitled 'General Instructions' which is so uncompromising in its insistence that Cumming is answerable to the DNI above all others that it is impossible not to suspect collusion over Cumming's problems with the War Office, e.g. 'You are to hold yourself directly responsible to me for all matters connected with your duties.' It is also striking in its continued insistence on the importance of feigning independence of government and on the importance of Cumming being given access to all agents reporting from overseas and full autonomy in handling them. He is told that it is undesirable that he should keep a written record of all his operations and arrangements, though he must keep notes sufficient to enable him to report. His principal duty is to

> obtain early and reliable information of all important movements of Naval and Military forces, or official views indicating any unusual activity among Naval or Military forces, and to make such arrangements as will make it certain that timely warning of impending hostilities against this country on the part of any foreign state within the range of your information, will be received, and you must take every precaution to eliminate all risks of failure in this regard and must concentrate your attention upon the organisation and improvement of such a system as shall reduce this risk to an absolute minimum.

In other words, he is to be a trip-wire.

Interestingly, he is 'not to neglect the possibility of changes involving a similar interest in other countries [than Germany], and you must carefully consider what arrangements you would be prepared to make should information be required from elsewhere'. He must do this, however, 'without the expenditure of money, and for the present at all events, you are to devote your attention to the country where your Agents are placed'.

MacDonogh's reaction to this assertion of Admiralty control was surprisingly positive, but there were no immediate changes. Cumming's days were spent mostly in laborious communications with existing agents and in hanging around hotel lounges waiting to interview potential agents. Although these included a number of semi-professional spies willing to sell information to the highest bidder, a better kind of agent, the British businessman, begins to feature more frequently. Cumming was to use many of these, and they generally served him well.

He must also have applied himself rigorously to his German lessons because, by the early months of 1910, he was spending most evenings, and some nights, translating German reports. His most constant concern, however, remained the setting up of a credible early-warning system and for this he continued to think in terms of a travelling representative, or head agent, based in Brussels under civilian cover and building up a network of agents operating into Germany.

On 10 January 1910 he settled with de Wardt at the GPO arrangements of cover and telegraphic addresses, involving the establishment of the rather attractive-sounding Rasen Falcon & Co., Shippers and Exporters, as a cover company with a box number address. It was the Secret Service's first public appearance, suitably disguised with a name-plate on a door to secure listing in the Post Office London directory. He also arranged two telegraphic addresses which were not in any directory. One was 'Sunbonnet London' used for the general run of communications, with telegrams delivered by the usual messenger service. The other was 'Autumn London' for emergency communications with immediate delivery by special messenger and a duplicate sent by special messenger to the Admiralty. He tested each system.

On 13 January he had a long talk with Edmonds about sending officers on reconnaissance missions around north German ports. In view of events later in the year, this was perhaps an historically significant conversation:

He had recommended – and the Paymaster had cordially approved – a scheme for sending several Officers every now and then round the German coast, landing in Denmark and going round to Korsor, Kiel, Sønderborg, Burnshuttel, Cuxhaven, Bremerhaven and Emden. His own trip last time – extended over a fortnight – cost about twenty eight pounds. He says he believes that Blitz drew money for this scheme this year, having asked for a large sum for travelling expenses with this scheme in view.

It is clear that these trawling expeditions could be either War Office or Admiralty inspired, but it is unclear how frequent they were and how far the two departments co-ordinated them. They seem to have been fairly common practice and could also later have originated from Cumming himself.

They also discussed Edmonds's conversation with the Japanese military attaché, who reported that during a recent visit to the Krupp works in Germany his movements were restricted for the first time. 'Not only this,' Cumming wrote, 'but when a Japanese Prince recently visited the works he was not allowed to see anything until permission had been obtained from the German Admiralty, and even then it was found that many of the slips were unaccountably deserted that day.' Krupp, the major German armaments manufacturer, was of course a prime intelligence target.

On the same day Cumming called on 'Queer' at his hotel. 'Queer' was one of his businessmen, possibly a Mr Strange, who proved to be very helpful. He had not been to the Krupp works himself but knew about them from a Mr Capron, of Davy Brothers, Sheffield. 'His men were only allowed in the slip in which their work was going on, and they were carefully screened in with canvas while at work, so that they could see nothing.' Queer gave details of new shells and guns and later introduced one of his co-directors, a Mr Fairholme, who was half-Bavarian, fluent in German and knowledgeable about ordinance technicalities. Cumming thought he might be of 'immense use' and tasked both men accordingly.

This illustrated not only how business contacts can work and how naturally and easily one leads to another, but also the degree of access to foreign information that industrialists often have in their own fields. The result was the Secret Service's first known intelligence report, which Cumming produced on 18 January. It is numbered 77, which probably refers to its position in his file of letters and memos, mostly now lost:

The following information has been received from a reliable source. It is reported that Krupp are making a very large Howitzer, 29.3 cm. firing a projectile weighing 300 kilos, with a MV [muzzle velocity] of 450 metre seconds, which pierces a Nickel steel 'deck armour' plate of 10 cm. at an angle of 55 degrees. The projectile penetrated the plate at a velocity of 253 metre seconds and was unbroken. The projectile was filled with Tri-Nitrol-Tuluol. It is stated that the new 30.5 gun is to throw a projectile weighing over 500 kilos, with a MV of 2800 ft, and which will penetrate a 12 in Krupp plate at 1600 ft secs.

[In reply to some questions asked] What steel, nickel or nickel-chrome is Krupp using for guns? It is stated that Krupp is using Nickel-Tungsten steel for all small guns. A great deal of the segregation trouble is got over by its use, and a longer life is claimed for the gun on account of the lesser erosion.

Do they push bore or draw bore? They push bore from both ends simultaneously for the rough cuts and then draw bore for the fine and finishing cuts.

Whether any wire construction used &c? It is not thought that Krupps are building any wire guns at all. It was stated that a number of skilled men left Woolwich at the time of the reduction of the Arsenal staff, and went over to Germany. It is believed that some of these have not returned and definite information could be obtained as to this if required. More information will be available from this source later on.

Shortly after this there is in the diary a copy of an agent report – that is, a report written by an agent, not by Cumming – from someone referred to as WK. WK obviously had good access to

German naval matters and gives details of harbour construction, ship performance and, especially, the submarine-building programme. In order to circulate the report to his Whitehall customers, Cumming would have edited and partly rewritten it, but as an example of raw intelligence of the time it is worth quoting in full, as he received it:

Copy of WK's Report for December 1909

Heligoland.

The last year commenced building operations for a new Harbour for small Cruisers and Torpedo boats, has this year been greatly furthered. It will however still take several years to complete this gigantic work which will cost several million Marks. It will be situated on the Southern point of the island, and a Mole built of stone devised to defy any storm however furious has been carried several hundred meters into the sea. The work progresses slowly as all the necessary material, such as Cement, Stone and Wood have to be carried by ship to the island. Heligoland will then be of greater strategical importance, and in consequence the strength of the Fort which now comprises 150 men, is to be doubled as soon as the required Barracks have been erected.

Imperial Yard Wilhelmshaven.

Several hundred men have been paid off through want of work, and it is probable that further reduction in the staff will be made in the coming summer, as the new building programme has as yet only provided one small Cruiser for this yard. The Searchlight work and Flashlight Telegraph business will in future be carried out by men who will have the same as their sole occupation, and not as before by members of the Engineering Department. A new Deck-Officers & Engineering Training school will be built at Kiel at a cost of two million Marks and a plot of land has been secured at Wik consisting of 18,000 sq meters. The Lineships 'Schlesien' & 'Zahringen' are undergoing repairs at Wilhelmshaven.

Speed of latest additions

The new 18,000 ton Lineship 'Nassau' has with full armament attained 20 knots. The record before stood at 19.26 made by the 'Schleswig-Holstein'. Just as satisfactory has been the Armoured Cruiser 'Blucher' which with a warranted speed of 24 knots, reached 25.3. The Armoured Cruisers 'Gneisnau' and 'Scharnhorst' reached 23.6 and 23.7 respectively, but their trials have not yet been completed and it is possible that this speed may be increased. The 'Ziethen' arrived at Wilhelmshaven on the 11th inst, the 'Stuttgart' & 'Hay' left Heligoland on the 10th inst and proceeded to Sønderborg where they arrived on the 11th inst after having finished High-Sea shooting practices.

The Mineship 'Pelican' left Cuxhaven on the 8th inst and proceeded in the direction of Kiel, having on board the members of the Mine-finding Commission.

The new Torpedo boat V.164 arrived from the Baltic at Cuxhaven on the 14th inst, having made a speed of 34.46 knots. She will continue practising between Cuxhaven & Heligoland, and for that purpose will remain for some time stationed at the former place. The G.171. attained a speed of 34.62. This remarkable speed has only been possible through the use of Turbines and experiments are about to be made, using four Turbines.

Submarines.

To the first German submarine 'U.1' from the Germania yard in 1908, and the 'U.2' from the Imperial Yard, Danzig, have this year been added 'U.3' and 'U.4' also built at Danzig. In 1910 the strength will be doubled by the completion of 'U.5' to 'U.8' now building in the Germania Yard. It has therefore been found necessary to appoint a special commission to deal with the training of the men engaged in this branch of the Navy, so that it may become a standard of perfection and render valuable service in time of war. We learn on good authority that a formal Committee was appointed on the 1st Oct, to carry this into effect. The 'U.3' and

'U.4' recently completed the 540 sea-mile route from Cuxhaven – Skagen–Kiel in 40 hours.

The Training ship 'Wurttemburg' stranded on the afternoon of the 9th inst in the bay between Hollnitz & Glucksburg in thick fog as she was returning from practice.

It is also reported that the Battleship 'Wurttemburg' likewise stranded in the same bay, and that in her efforts to get clear two 'screw wings' were broken. The bottom here is however fine sand, and no heavy damage is feared. Some time ago she was in a similar precarious condition.

The Training school Torpedoboats of the North Sea Division who had just finished their first practices and trial trips this winter, returned with one exception to Wilhelmshaven on the 9th inst. The missing boat was the 'G.89' which stranded near Husum, in the terrific storm on the night of the 3rd inst as the four Torpedoboats attached to this Division sought refuge there. The Boat stranded on the highest point, the propeller bored into the sand, though she was free both after and forward. The Northern Salvage Association, who have carried out successfully many difficult salvage operations for the Navy, despatched their Tug 'Reiher' to render assistance. The Torpedoboat arrived at Wilhelmshaven on the 20th inst, and after repairs have been completed will again join its Division.

On the 11th inst the second series of practices was commenced by this Division and these will last until the 8th Jan. Meanwhile the damaged Torpedo (? boat) on which I promised to report further has been replaced by one of older type. Referring to the new Torpedo on which I promised to report further as to the result of experiments, it may be said that a hundred dummy soldiers had been drawn up in two lines with a space of 4 metres between each, and every one was knocked down by one shot.

Submitted Jan 12th 1910.

A good report could be written from this, detailed, specific, with plenty of follow-up questions.

On 19 April Bethell inspected Cumming's premises in Vaux-hall Bridge Road. Cumming seems to have regarded himself as, if not quite permanently on duty, at least never really off it. He was always there, always available, as aboard ship: 'On my asking his permission to go down to Sheerness to stay with the Nevilles, he told me he did not wish me to ask for leave for such visits. I was to use my own discretion.'

A couple of days later he learned that the DMO had approved his ideas on the direction of his work but had stressed that he 'did not want any espionage work done in France just now, as our present excellent relations might be disturbed thereby'. This cry – albeit probably based on a misunderstanding, since Cumming wanted a man in France to spy on Germany, not France – is almost as old as espionage itself. It has superficial plausibility but contrary to what is usually thought, there have been very few, if any, examples of friendly relations between states being seriously damaged by espionage. Politicians are too routinely cynical and relations between states, more a matter of interest than emotion, usually too complex to be disrupted by a spy case.

On 23 January FRS, the official who had been travelling on Cumming's behalf, returned after surviving a train that was overturned by floods and a ship that had to be abandoned at night. He presented an 'interesting' report on shipbuilding along with heavy expenses, the latter, he maintained, un-avoidable. He reported that the people of Austria, though cordial to Englishmen, 'freely discussed the possibility of their having to join Germany in fighting against us'. It was not only in Britain that war was anticipated four years in advance.

Another feature of Cumming's daily official life was his fre-quent calls on Bethell and MacDonogh, with the latter predomin-ating. As an example of what much of the diary comprises, in the early years, the following is given in full – not because of any particular interest but because it is typical:

Called upon Blitz by appointment. He told me to ask 'B' why Reichart should require so much money considering that he is not asked to buy anything, but has only to go round these different places and keep his eyes open. I may arrange a Liebers Code series of sentences with him.

He gave me authority to arrange with 'B' to correspond in future direct with me, using the addresses I have arranged. He (Blitz) himself, is returning here on the 21st prox, and I am to have 'B' over after that date. I may change the large Safe in the V. office for a smaller one, and bring it here.

He authorises me to spend a sum not exceeding £40, on Frs' expense at K, this year. He gave me the names of two men who have offered their services. (".&P.). He lent me the 'scheme', made out some four years ago, and alluded to on p 10.

He showed me a short Paragraph in today's 'Morning Post' which I must look in to. I presented a copy of Queers report (No 77). He gave me authority to buy a Liebers Code @ £2.2.

I handed to K the cutting from 'Answers' about the Libury Hall establishment [a farm in Hertfordshire which had German connections], and told him the yarn about the Monastery, on the Aldershot–Portsmouth road.

I called on Tab, who says that a DNO man questions the weight of the projectile thrown by the 30.5 cm gun, as it is so high. He does not think they could get the MV stated.

Called on Luz, but he was on Committee.

Went down to Sheerness by the 4.20 train, to Admiralty House. Blitz says that the GOM is in favour of having a man in FJLd but that everything will depend upon getting hold of the right man. I gather that I may look around and let him know if I heard of a suitable one.

Cumming was in Sheerness to see Admiral Neville and had a discussion at the Eastchurch Flying Ground with C. S. Rolls, Royce's collaborator. Zeppelins were an intelligence priority and Rolls referred Cumming to a Colonel Cupper of the Balloon Factory, Farnborough. MacDonogh subsequently turned up some sort of source on Zeppelins and Cumming stayed up until 3 a.m. to write his report.

FRS's shipbuilding report had meanwhile attracted high-level attention. Bethell 'told me that he wished to introduce me to the Ruler [Fisher, the First Sea Lord] and that I must stand by all day, to be rung up, as the best time to see him was generally in the evening about seven. He said that the Ruler had been across to see xxx xxxxxx xxxx as he considered the news so important.' Leaving aside Cumming's exasperating habit of concealing the names or positions of people who were almost certainly important public officials and whose public business it was to know about these things, this must have been very gratifying recognition that his efforts were at last beginning to yield something of what people wanted to know. Although they would have known each other, the First Sea Lord was probably God as far as Cumming was concerned and the fact that the report reached him so quickly, and engaged him so immediately, indicates not only the importance of the material but the existence of a system for passing intelligence up the chain of command, and something of Cumming's place within it.

When summoned he

Went over and found Luz in the Ruler's room. Both had copies of the FJL [i.e. FRS's] report which the latter had evidently read through and thoroughly grasped. He said that the report was an extremely interesting one, and that the importance and gravity of the news depended not only on the fact that the ships were being built, but that they were being built in a clandestine manner, as ** had informed them quite recently that nothing of the sort was going on. He questioned me as to the character of the reporter, and I told him that I thought his facts were probably quite trustworthy, but that he might of course have been mistaken as to the size of the vessels that were on the slips. The Ruler pointed out however that this was probable as – in the case of the S. T. yard for instance – they were building the ship on the largest of the slips, although others lay vacant close at hand. This they would never do with any ship smaller than a battle-ship, knowing as they did that it was only a question of time before the orders would be given. Luz suggested that there had been rumours that the £4,000,000 which remained in Austria after the settlement of the Servian affair, was to be expended upon ships and perhaps this was the solution of that idea.

The Ruler talked to me about Krupps works and the number of men employed by him. I gave these as 65,000, but he corrected this to 68,000. He said they had already thought of the plan of getting a tally of the guns as they crossed the road, and thought this a good scheme if it could be arranged. Luz said that he had been informed that Krupp had 30 12 inch guns completed and ready to turn out (Naval guns his informant called them).

This early report was something of a coup and, again, the speed and level of reception suggests a virtually ideal reporting system.

An agent recruited in 1910 who provided just this sort of information was Hector Bywater, a British journalist and naval expert then resident in Germany. In his little-known book, *Strange Intelligence* (Constable, 1931), he gives convincing descriptions of his penetration of German dockyards during 42 months of spying (although not claiming in that book the experiences as his own, there is strong evidence that they were – see W. H. Honan's biography, *Bywater*, Macdonald 1990, ISBN 0-356-19125-4). He also describes Cumming in very recognisable terms. There are diary references on 2 March 1910 and 28 June 1910 to the recruitment and debriefing of 'HC' (Bywater's initials) and references in 1913 to an agent codenamed H20 who was very likely the same man (Cumming, like the later KGB, enjoyed giving code-names suggestive of the person: see Appendix for details of the correlation between Hywater, 'HC' and 'H20'). In his book, Bywater refers to a small core of expert nautical agents like himself, none of whom was every caught, contrasting them with 'amateur' agents such as military officers on leave. He also describes the comprehensive intelligence coverage of the Germany Navy achieved by 1914, resulting in detailed photographs and silhouettes of every German warship afloat, often along with design details and specifications of armour and armament. He berates the Admiralty for its tendency to record rather than act upon the information.

Meanwhile, there had been talk of a 'Regatta expedition', probably a reference to the Kiel regatta, and a proposal to spy on the German navy via selected participants or spectators. It is probably such expeditions that are referred to elliptically in the following paragraph:

I then called on McJohn, and told him of my meeting with the young officer in the waiting room and I asked him what course he usually followed in such cases. He said that he always sent for these young men and enjoined them to confine their search for knowledge exclusively to their own business, as they were always

> closely watched and apt to act without much tact or dip-
> lomacy if they attempted any research work. If they
> really came across anything of interest they were to com-
> municate personally with the NA [naval attaché] who
> would take the proper steps to follow the matter up.

This illustrates why it is sometimes difficult to reach satisfactory conclusions about intelligence-gathering missions by serving
officers, since whether they were sent, or simply volunteering
while on holiday, and the extent to which they were selected,
targeted and briefed, is often unclear. This has resonance for
developments later in 1910.

Towards the end of January there was a series of unsatisfactory agent meetings, probably typical of most conducted by
Cumming at the time. They were more productive of opinion
than hard intelligence: the Germans intended to attack Britain
but would not be ready for three years, they would begin by
surprise submarine attacks on British ships in harbour, they
would seize Holland and perhaps Denmark, the Triple Alliance
was shaky and would take little to dissolve, and so on. Informed
prophecy, insightful predictions and general analysis were probably what many agents thought was required of them. But if
intelligence were to form a basis for action, it was information
that was needed, not opinion: how many 'U' boats the Germans
planned to build, for example, their tactical doctrine of deployment, policy decisions with regard to Austria, whether Germany
had actually drawn up plans for the invasion of Holland and
Denmark. Opinion could be a basis for action if the source were
particularly well-informed and authoritative – the view of a head
of state or his deputy or private secretary, for instance, as to
how the country might react to international negotiations – but
in most cases it was not. Commenting on one of these cases,
Cumming seems to have recognised the lack of precise requirements: 'He is very willing to help us and will get any information
he can if I will let him know exactly what we want.'

The agent referred to as U is another example. He may have been a British businessman, introduced to Cumming by a relation of Sir Charles Hardinge, the Under Secretary at the Foreign Office. Cumming was disappointed to find that he did not live permanently at Kiel, could not name any of the ships recently launched even when prompted and never questioned any of his allegedly forthcoming German officer friends for fear of arousing suspicion. However, he offered to hurry across the Dutch frontier and send a telegram should he 'smell war in the air'. He believed that the Germans were dissatisfied with their previous big-gun practice and that they had more torpedo boats and submarines than we knew of. He had also lost the Victoria Street address Cumming had given him. 'I should be very sorry to depend much upon him,' Cumming notes, but he had little choice at the time.

An example of the lack of co-ordination in the intelligence community occurred when Cumming interviewed another potential traveller in February and briefed him on the Zeppelin requirement before discovering, just as they were parting, 'that the man was going on a trip with a man named Sue!!' 'Sue' was Sueter of the DNI.

On 8 February he and Kell lunched Colonel Cupper, the man from the Balloon Factory whom C. F. Rolls had recommended. They discussed Zeppelins and Cumming produced a fairly basic report, whose satisfactory reception indicated that the British government had no co-ordinated mechanism for acquiring and assessing information – open or secret – which it believed it needed. The material in Cumming's report need not have been secret but because the information came only from him (though it was available openly), it was.

More letters and reports, some needing translation, began to come in. Meanwhile, Cumming visited the harbour master at Southampton to discuss interviewing ships' pilots in order to get reports on German shipping and dockyards. Kell called confessing that he too now wanted to leave the Victoria Street office and had actually tried to take a flat in the same building as

Cumming, but 'the authorities' had refused and told him to go on with Victoria Street for a while. He had engaged a clerk to work there. Cumming was not pleased: 'I think he should have consulted me before going so far, as I do not think it would be at all a good plan to have him in the same building.' For good measure, Kell added that he wasn't sure whether the War Office was satisfied with the home/foreign division of work between him and Cumming, and then backtracked by saying that he wasn't certain about this. Finally, he said that he was introducing someone to 'Q', prompting Cumming to reflect: 'This is the man whose name I suggested as likely to be useful, but was not allowed to see.'

Four days later he learned from Roy Regnart, of the DNI, that two of his customer departments in the Admiralty 'often treated our information slightingly and often stated that the facts given were already known to them, but they would rarely hand on any information they had to our department, and would never divulge the source by which they had obtained it'. This was a further symptom of the lack of any co-ordinated requirements and assessment machinery. Large firms such as Vickers were well able to get information relating to their fields and were 'only too willing to give it to those who can give them orders running into millions of money ... great rewards have been paid to their reps for these services'.

Shortly after preparing a report for Kell on Libury Hall, Cumming set out on his first recorded trip overseas on behalf of the Bureau. Had he known it, the frustrations of the journey were useful preparation for many trips to come. He planned to take the Le Havre boat at midnight after a rendezvous with Roy Regnart in Southampton, then the train to Paris and another to Antwerp. However, 'it came on to blow so hard in the afternoon that I decided to abandon this plan and go up to town and cross by Dover'. He telegraphed Roy at two addresses but missed him at both. So Roy took the train from London to Southampton as Cumming took one in the opposite direction. They eventually met in London just in time to get the midnight boat for Dover, reaching Paris after a 'fresh' crossing on the morning of Sunday 20 February.

They travelled on to Antwerp and put up at the Queens Hotel where they were to meet 'our man' (referred to as 'KK'), who did not turn up. Eventually they wrote to him and continued their wait. Two days later, on the Tuesday morning, they received a letter appointing a meeting at 8 a.m. on Thursday. Cumming had a meeting in London with 'B' on Wednesday so crossed the Channel again on Tuesday night, arriving in London at 5 a.m. on Wednesday. After a bath and breakfast, then collecting letters from his various PO boxes, he met B at a hotel room at 10 a.m., along with an interpreter. The meeting lasted two and a half hours but produced little apart from some fairly basic information about a new class of battleship. B wanted more money for one of his sub-agents who allegedly had the entrée to a great many shipyards and knew a number of people employed in them.

After another meeting with Bethell, Cumming re-crossed the Channel, reaching Antwerp at 7 a.m. the following morning. There was a hasty breakfast, then he and Regnart returned to the station to watch every train between 8 a.m. and 11 a.m. before going back to their hotel 'rather dispirited'. They telephoned a friend of KK's, asking if KK had left, but the reply was unintelligible. They hung around the rest of the day before returning to London the following morning. The day following their return, Saturday, 'Roy came down to the ship with me [the *Argos*, presumably] and we worked hard at a code we were drawing up for general use.'

One of the main themes of these very early years was Cumming's continuing, but generally unavailing, attempts to get existing agents to introduce him to a reliable and worthwhile source, while conducting a series of encounters with people offering their services. Although among the latter were businessmen who picked up information during trips, most offers of service came either from well-meaning people with little to offer, or from hyperbolic charlatans. It is easy to be amused at these early attempts – as Cumming was himself, among his frustrations – but less easy to see how else he could have gone about it, given the restrictions and resources with which he had to work. Even in more favourable conditions and after years of practice, he, like other intelligence chiefs, would still find it difficult to recruit good agents against serious, watchful targets. The most desirable agents were usually the secretly disaffected but they were precisely those whose disaffection was always most difficult to uncover, for either side. Nor, perhaps, was ideological disaffection as clearly defined a state in 1910 as it was to become during the subsequent struggle between capitalist democracies and the totalitarians of the left and the right.

On 12 February, for example, Cumming called on a Mr Brass of the Portsmouth Dockyard who had recently visited Pola in order to demonstrate an invention for detecting petrol and other gases by electrical means. Mr Brass had been allowed everywhere in the restricted dockyard but 'felt himself bound not to reveal anything to our Naval authorities'. Many saw spying less as an extension of the conflict between states and ideologies than as a business of rogues, fraudsters and, in Cumming's term, scallywags. Cumming did not argue with Mr Brass but secured a promise of lunch in town and resolved to 'see what I can do with him later on'.

Intelligence services were commonly seen by the needy and the venal as a potential source of money, though what was offered in return was not always straightforward intelligence. On 1 March, for instance, Kell tried to interest Cumming in a 'scheme connected with a Baron de Roenne, who wishes to start an "Aerial Defence League" with a passenger service between large towns and a government subsidy to follow! He has invented some patent metal sheath for his dirigibles, which renders them nine tenths invisible. He wants ten thousand pounds each for them.' It is not clear what Kell's role was but Cumming thought it sounded 'too much like other schemes of which I have heard before'. A few days later, however, he had to stand in for Kell at a meeting with the Baron, who spoke little English. Over tea 'with Knox and the rest' (it is not clear who Knox was, but one, and perhaps peripherally two, of the four gifted Knox brothers were subsequently involved in intelligence), the Baron described his scheme, with a lot of technical detail about materials and a metal that was supposedly 'almost invisible in sunlight especially when corrugated'. They talked of lifting strengths and gases and of 'pneumatic injectors with which he could fire shells with great accuracy'.

More mundanely, Cumming recruited a Captain Dixon of the Royal Engineers to spy for him at the forthcoming Kiel regatta. A gentleman from the Royal Geographic Society offered his services (initially to Kell who passed him on) and the editor of the *Motor Boat* magazine undertook to put Cumming in touch with one of his pseudonymous contributors. On 8 March he had to stand in for Edmonds at a meeting with a lady agent, 'A', a case controlled by MacDonogh. Disappointingly, he found that she had 'a very slight grasp of what is required, and very little power of obtaining any news of importance'. He seems to have been more focused on results than some of his War Office colleagues, who were perhaps continuing cases because they were cases, rather than because they were useful.

While being warned that he 'had better not be seen loafing about the passages outside Luz's door' in the Admiralty, Cumming was summoned by Bethell and asked to call upon a Sir L. Lock, a British Consul in Germany at present at home in London. Lock helpfully suggested where agents might be located to monitor shipping and rail movements, identified a couple of potential sources and told Cumming a blackmail story involving a man called Robertson, which Cumming knew already. He commented: 'This is the same man who wrote to us for £100 and then bolted (market garden and all).' Lock thought the Germans would not listen for a moment to any suggestion of limiting the arms build-up, which is what Churchill repeatedly sought, because there was a 'deep jealousy in the heart of the commercial part of the population, and we should come to an issue eventually over some question of trade'.

This is further indication of how widespread was the conviction that there would be war with Germany. The imagined circumstances and reasons were variously inaccurate but what is striking is that the popular sentiment, in the teeth of all sensible reasoning about there being no need for war, was right about the big thing. It was rare for Cumming to be allowed access to anyone from the consular service and he and Lock arranged to keep in touch; but he was later warned off, so he had to call on Lock again and advise him that his contact should continue to be the DNI, as it apparently had been in the past. Nevertheless, Lock kept Cumming's address because 'there might be information to be sent which could not be put into an official document'.

There were problems over the pay of one of B's sub-agents, Wilhelm. Although B and his team do not seem to have been very effective, and although payments seem if anything to have been over-generous, the system itself was also at fault. Giving head agents the money for their sub-agents and leaving it to them to deduct what they thought due to themselves, while paying the same whether they were producing or not, was not likely to encourage industry or honesty. Cumming was not alone in complaining of the expense and lack of productivity of the 'permanent' agents, but the system was well entrenched and it was some time before he was free to do anything about it. He drafted an uncompromising reply to B, which MacDonogh persuaded him to tone down. In explaining why he thought it should be toned down, MacDonogh laid bare another continuing problem for Cumming. His two masters had different requirements, one chiefly wanting information about shipbuilding and armaments, the other chiefly wanting early warning of war. Visiting agents, such as businessmen, could cover the first requirement reasonably well, but only resident agents could properly cover the latter and it would have to be accepted that they would be unproductive for most, if not all, of the time.

It was the end of March before Cumming had properly rid himself of the unloved Victoria Street office, transferring a large safe from there to Ashley Gardens and bequeathing a small safe and his desk keys to Kell, who was still seeking a second office and still had his eye on Ashley Gardens. 'He asked me if I should object to his coming next door, but I told him that I thought it would interfere with my privacy in my own Flat and I begged he would not go forward with any such scheme. I would rather he were not in the immediate neighbourhood at all.'

Kell's desire to camp on Cumming's doorstep was not the only source of irritation. Kell announced that the CID were considering appointing someone to visit and debrief consuls overseas and use them to get in touch with merchant shipping. This was Cumming's patch. 'I told him this was already in train,' he noted tartly. 'I think he had himself in mind as a possible man.' A few days later Kell said that he had recently interviewed a Miss Yonger, who had written in with an offer of information. Cumming already knew of the offer and had at first received permission to follow it up, only to be later refused any details of her, including her name. This was again refused even after he had discovered it and pointed out that she had written to the press. He commented:

It now appears that though they kept the name from me they communicated it to K and he has seen the lady, although her information is entirely in my department. Secondly, K told me that he had made the acquaintance of the editor of the Standard and through him, that of a man named 'Half Term' who had supplied him with some information, and for whom he had got a retainer of £50 per year. I was expressly forbidden to approach the Editors of any paper.

Kell went on to say that he had secured the permanent services of L (the engineer, Henry Dale Long), prompting Cumming to comment:

> His staff must now be four times as big as mine and far more expensive. He has not been allowed to engage the rooms in the Temple, however, but is to have them next year. He says he always puts in for any taxis he takes when on duty and when away in his Car he is allowed sixpence a mile for it if he considers that its use helps him more than the train. If not, then he gets the train fare and cab fares that he would have had.

This sounds heartfelt, perhaps unsurprising in one who was paying for his own office at the time, but Cumming's disadvantageous position was probably due more to negligence than design and reflected Kell's long association with the War Office intelligence community. It is difficult to form a judgement as to how largely such issues loomed in Cumming's concerns; selecting for and confiding in diaries – indeed the very act of writing them – lends to concerns an intensity which they do not always have in the small change of everyday life. Discontent may be expressed in a diary not because it is overwhelming but because there is no other outlet. Context is also important, and that is what is generally missing from diaries.

Despite these dissatisfactions, Cumming and Kell agreed that payment of agents by results would be preferable to paying regular salaries, and the following day Kell told him of forthcoming visits by two men of interest to him. One was a former Krupp employee who had quarrelled with the firm, and the other, 'a Swedish Col, who might take the place of the late Col. Schultz'. Cumming couldn't resist noting that both men should have been handed over to him from the first, but also notes that when he and Kell next met, Kell 'professed his wish to keep our two departments separate and was very cordial'. Along with Cumming's removal of himself from their joint office, this is further indication that the two services would eventually go their separate ways and that the desire was always mutual.

Cumming produced a report which included photographs and sketches of German ships in dock, on which an official called Darnaway commented that it was 'very valuable to him as the construction of our own vessel was being delayed, owing to experimental work with girders not turning out satisfactorily. He proposed to take the sketch at once to Barrow and have a test girder built. He said that the plan was worth its weight in gold.' Given the expensive action taken on the report, it must have been another coup. Kell's Krupp man, meanwhile, claimed to be the inventor of a system of rolling rifle barrels 'and other things', while the Swedish colonel had apparently served in the German army and made a study of German mobilisation which he wished to communicate. This was presumably very important since, in the approach to 1914, German mobilisation plans were probably among Cumming's top three requirements (the others were almost certainly naval construction and the degree to which the Schlieffen Plan was to be implemented). There were other offers of service, none of which led to much.

Meanwhile, Cumming was taken up with producing a report on the first six months of the Bureau. Kell did the same for his side. His report is now in the PRO while Cumming's, dated 10 April, is not. Although the relevant file has long since been destroyed, we are fortunate that a copy has survived in his diary. It provides as clear and detailed a snapshot as it is possible to have of his side of the Bureau at this time. Like other examples of his official writing, its frankness and forthrightness make it almost as much a personal statement as an official document, despite the formality. It was almost certainly addressed to Bethell and is given here in full:

Report on the Workings of Secret Service Bureau, April 1910

I have the honour to submit a report on the work of the SS Bureau, during the first six months of its existence.

At a meeting which was held on the 9th November last, it was decided that the duties and responsibilities of the Bureau should be divided into two parts:-

1. All matters of espionage and contra-espionage in the United Kingdom.
2. All similar matters abroad.

I was given charge of the latter, with certain restrictions and limitations as to expenditure etc.

For the first two months I have no work of any kind, as the arrangements made were such as did not admit of any initiative on my part, and the nature of the work prevented me from attempting to seek or create it without risk of disclosing my identity, and I was therefore compelled to wait for the work to come to me.

Since the 1st December however it has increased rapidly until at the present time I have as much as I can tackle, and there is every prospect that it will continue to grow as the circle of my correspondents widens. I found that the Office provided for the Bureau had certain disadvantages, of which the most important were that the very precautions taken to secure secrecy, resulted in making it very difficult to prevent my friends – and especially my brother officers who are working with me on Defence matters – from being suspicious, owing to my not being able to give them my office address or allow them either to write or meet me there. Moreover the fact that no letters arrived at the office would sooner or later have caused suspicion, and it appeared to me that this would be extremely undesirable under the circumstances. With your permission therefore I took up my quarters in a Residential Flat and established an Office there, and up to this point I have found this arrangement to work very satisfactorily. I have had a private telephone line laid on to my room, and I can interview anyone in the room without any risk of my conversation being overheard. Arrangements have been made with the authorities at the Gen. Post Office which will ensure – as far as it is humanly possible – that the most important messages will reach me at any hour of the day or night, and that these as well as ordinary communications will be received and forwarded to me with all trace of their destination cut off in their passage through the GPO.

These arrangements have been carefully tested from abroad. With regard to my staff of Agents these are of two kinds:

1. Those who are not required to collect definite information or send in periodical reports, but who are expected to keep a good look out for any unusual or significant movements or changes – either Naval or Military – and report them. From these agents 'no news is good news' and in the absence of any evidence to the contrary, it is to be believed that they are doing their duty and are earning the pay they receive. It has been pointed out that this negative news is of great value and that although we may wait for years for any report, it may be invaluable when it comes. On the other hand this class of agent should be very carefully chosen and should be of proved character, as very much will depend upon them, and the temptation will be strong when the critical moment arrives, to avoid risk by doing nothing.

2. The other kind – those who in addition to giving warning of extra-ordinary activity on the part of those they are deputed to watch, are expected to collect information of all kinds and forward it to me at stated intervals – I can not as yet speak with any authority, as sufficient time has not elapsed since their appointment to enable me to form an opinion.

The principal Agent – whom I will call 'B' – is employed on peculiar terms. He has three men working under him for whom he is allowed £360, £500 and £642 respectively. He is not paid anything at all for himself, but is supposed to retain some part of his men's salaries. There is no check whatever on the proportion he deducts and I think that this in itself is a mistake, as it invites him to employ the cheapest men he can get. I have no control whatever over these men. I have never seen them or heard their names, and I am not by any means certain that they exist at all. The reports sent in are very meagre and do not up to the present justify the large salaries paid – more than is paid to all the other Agents put together.

'B' himself is intelligent and he has I understand rendered good service in the past. I believe that he has the ability to do good work, but I do not think his present system of payment will ever get the best work out of him. He has no incentive to send in good reports, as he is paid the same whether they are good or bad. Valuable information can not be obtained without hard work and some risk, and he naturally will not exert himself or take more risks than he can help, without incentive. I should like to pay him a fairly large retaining fee for himself, and offer payment on a liberal scale for all information supplied and approved, with a definite fixed sum of large amount for early news of impending hostilities. I think he is allowed too free a hand. To put the case strongly I should say that I believe I could do a great deal if I were allowed £1,500 a year and not asked to account for it but I should not have the smallest chance of having this granted, yet this is what is given to 'B' who is a foreigner, a potential enemy (for he is an Austrian) and a professional spy. I don't by any means wish to get rid of him, but I should like, after the present system has been given a year's trial, to review its work and compare it with those of others, and if necessary alter the terms of his employment and pay in such a manner as to get more out of him.

The next in importance – from the point of salary – are the three 'Ks'. Of these only one is actively employed, the other two following their trade abroad and presumably keeping a look out at the same time. Their reports are nearly all taken from the newspapers and are not of much value, and I should propose that as their period of trial is now coming to an end, that their joint salary of £600 should be discontinued, and that the youngest of them '2K' should be taken on at a salary of £200, to rise to £240, if he gives satisfaction. I think he could be very useful after a little practice, though he is inclined to be lazy if not kept up to the mark.

The three passive agents 'A', 'B' and 'U' are difficult to appraise as to their value, as they send in no reports, and their whole worth depends upon the amount of reliance we can place in their sending early information of war. The last two are so timid that I doubt their finding sufficient courage when the times comes, but as the last of the group has just been dismissed from his employment for shady conduct, perhaps he may improve as an Agent, and the effect upon him up to the present time is certainly hopeful.

The most valuable information that I have been able to supply, was produced by a man who was sent abroad to ascertain definite facts [probably FRS]. Although his task was a difficult one, involving some risk and calling for resource and nerve, he accomplished it successfully, and although some of his information has been questioned, I believe that his report was correct in all essential particulars.

A good deal of information has been procured from persons who have written to the authorities offering their services. The information offered by these persons must perforce be received with caution, and it is feared that a large percentage of it is likely to prove of little use when submitted to expert investigation, but it is hoped that experience will enable the SS officer to sift the good from the worthless, as time goes on.

A valuable source and one which it is hoped will be greatly extended, is that of the voluntary help given by those whose business or profession gives them special facilities for finding out what is going on abroad. I have received intelligence in this way from several whom it is not necessary to specify by name, and have sent in reports of their information from time to time. I am afraid that it will always be difficult to get voluntary help from people living abroad – even those of British birth. The risk they run is so great, and the consequence of detection so serious, that it is only in rare cases that they are likely to be of any use. I have however found one man – a Scotchman who occupies a position which will give him exceptional opportunities of knowing if anything in the nature of war is impending, who has promised that in such a case he will come over himself, or if that is impossible, will send a messenger in whom he has absolute confidence, to give warning. I feel bound to say that I place more reliance upon this man – who is of sturdy and independent character – than upon any of the others who have undertaken this important duty. [Written in the margin of this paragraph, in green ink – the first observed use of it by Cumming – is 'Rollo'.]

But little Military intelligence has been obtained in comparison with Naval work, but I think the reason for this is that the information required by the Military authorities is more of the negative kind than is the case with the Naval. The only questions for which I have been asked to procure replies, have been very difficult ones, and quite beyond the powers of any ordinary agent.

1. Should like to know how much I can count upon for travelling expenses for myself and for Agents and those who offer information.
2. Should like to have power to spend £10 at home or £40 if abroad, upon Agents, travelling expenses, payments for information, plans etc. that I have to buy outright. The case of 'CJ' whose friend the WO of 'Nassau' we lost, owing to the delay of two days in asking for permission to send him £6.
3. Should prefer to keep my plans, assistants, methods and meetings entirely to myself, as secrets shared with anyone else, cease to be secrets. [If we were to ask what most typifies Cumming's attitude towards secret service, this would perhaps be it.]

As far as my experience goes up to the present, the two offices – the Home and Foreign – have little or nothing in common with each other, their connection being a purely theoretical one. I know practically nothing of what my colleague is doing and we appear to work in totally different fields. If we should be more closely connected, there is considerable risk that one or other of us would be 'marked down' and our usefulness would be very much impaired. I think it is a pity that the SS Agent [by which he means himself] should be obliged to tell even his Chiefs what he is doing – certainly he should not tell more than *one* person – and I think it would be far better if he could keep his work, his methods and all knowledge of his assistants entirely to himself.

Of course this implies great confidence in the man, but if he cannot be trusted to work conscientiously, I think he should be got rid of, and another appointed in whom confidence can be placed.

There follow two pages of notes of payments to agents and frustratingly elliptical assessments of some, along with Cumming's own operational expenses. B's three supposed sub-agents are referred to by their first names and there is a further undated page headed, 'Advantages of my present Office', which lists six reasons why he should have the flat to himself in Vauxhall Bridge Road.

It was true that he was becoming busier and April was to prove more so, with many late nights, more travel and a number of missed meetings. In this latter respect the clandestine experience resembles that of the military, in that the natural contrariness of things in general is found in a heightened form in both activities. It is not hard to see why this should be in the military, since moving large bodies of men and equipment is always more difficult in practice than in theory, being subject to weather, breakdowns and misunderstandings, not to mention enemy action. Superficially, the clandestine ought to be no more difficult than the rest of life, yet it appears it is. If in normal life an arrangement is made to meet in a pub a red-haired stranger carrying a copy of Gibbon's *Decline and Fall*, then this unusual encounter would generally take place without hindrance. If, however, an intelligence officer arranges to meet the same man, as his agent, then the chances of the pub burning down, or of there being a police raid, or of the agent's ex-wife and mother-in-law turning up, or of there being a convocation of red-haired Gibbonians that evening, are surprisingly high.

When, therefore, on All Fool's Day (his birthday, though he never mentions it), Cumming was summoned to meet a 'certain Swedish gentleman' he should, perhaps, have been prepared to wait vainly in the hotel foyer for an hour, then for a further one and a half hours at home, then to find that the man had been in the hotel all the time: 'I think he was very nervous and had hidden himself.' Cumming refers to him as TG and it is possible, though no more than that, that he was the Swedish colonel referred to earlier. In the more relaxed surroundings of the RAC the Swede agreed with Cumming and Regnart to 'join a regiment in Kiel and send us periodical reports for fifty pounds'. After dinner they apparently retired to Cumming's rooms – 'precautions being taken that he should not be able to locate them' – where TG talked more freely, in German all the time. Cumming did not think he was a trap but doubted 'his capacity to make an agent of first class calibre . . . he has no driving incentive . . . I cannot make out why he has volunteered to do this work, as the pay is small and the risk very great. He has not the most elementary idea of protecting himself, and occasionally asks us to write to him under his own name.'

He was right to be uneasy because sustained spying requires determined motivation. If TG was to infiltrate the German army and become that risky, valuable asset, an agent in place, then it would clearly be preferable for him and everybody else to be clear as to why.

Authority to take on and pay TG had to be sought from

MacDonogh, Bethell and the DMO who, according to MacDonogh, was 'very nervous about all this SS work', as well as from Sir Grahame Greene. This was all achieved the following day and TG set off with money and communications, which involved picture postcards as signals for meetings. He was to figure frequently in the diary.

Among all the missed and unproductive meetings was an encouraging one with 'U', who appeared more willing than at his previous meeting. He reported on an excursion with German naval officers to some high ground near Kiel where he saw that

'an old vessel was anchored out from the shore and that they were firing at her from the fort. At each discharge the shell burst on board and there was a copious discharge of greenish yellow smoke which issued from the ports etc. of the ship. A number of dogs, sheep etc. were tied up on board and between each shot the ship was visited by a party of Officers, including some Doctors who remained on board about twenty minutes.' He was told they were experimenting 'with some shell that emitted suffocating fumes'.

There is no record of reaction to this early report of German preparation for chemical warfare but it showed that U had the potential to achieve reasonable, if occasional access. He also gave details of two possible recruits.

Cumming sought permission from Bethell to 'hand over the Leg of Front matter to Roy as they knew me there and I should find it very difficult to preserve my incognito and moreover they were always in such a state of thirst for recognition in any form that I felt sure they would give the affair away in their Journal'. The Legion of Frontiersmen was indeed to be avoided. It was born in 1904 in the mind of Roger Pocock, an eccentric of Le Queux's persuasion who wanted 'an army of observation, a unit of field intelligence in peace and war . . . in case of any menace to the British Peace'. It secured favourable recognition from one or two leading figures, such as Lord Roberts, Baden Powell and Prince Louis of Battenburg (then DNI), but by 1909 Pocock's behaviour was so odd that he became a victim of the mania he had sought to create, and was ousted because of suspicions that he himself was a German spy. There is no record of how well Cumming knew those involved or of what Bethell had asked him to do, but his desire to distance himself was emphatic.

As for other matters, further conversation with Bethell enlisted the belated acknowledgement that 'the authorities had laid too much stress upon the secrecy of the two managers of the Bureau ... the managers, instead of acting as a buffer between their employers and employees, had found their employers acting as a buffer for them'. He got MacDonogh's permission to buy a few cameras, Brownies at five shillings each, to lend to agents. (Permission for any expense had to be secured in advance; it was one of Cumming's frequent complaints at this time that neither he nor Kell was allowed to spend anything on his own authority.) He quotes a War Office official who 'always maintained that we wanted some smart and good-looking young officers to approach ladies and get help from and through them'. This appealing idea, which in the mythology of espionage is what spies do all the time, seems not at that stage to have been acted upon by the War Office since 'we had no-one who could undertake this department'. He did succeed, however, in getting an agent transferred from Kell to him and in getting his 'long wished for' pass – to the War Office presumably.

Cumming and Regnart now embarked upon a period of intense activity during which the former was often working (writing and translating) until two or three in the morning, on at least one occasion summoning Regnart from his club to help. As we shall see, Regnart (who at this time was still Bethell's man rather than Cumming's) was not popular with the intelligence community but Cumming supported him loyally, albeit perhaps misguidedly, despite the evidence he himself produces of Regnart's obstinacy, arrogance and resentment. We hear less of his virtues, which probably included conscientiousness, frank-ness and dedication, so in Regnart's favour it is only fair to quote what Cumming says of a late-night discussion they had in April about the people they had spying for them in Europe: 'He said that – as I had supposed – these people are queer, and their motives more than doubtful. They are striving for recognition and must be handled very carefully.'

This shows some perceptiveness on Regnart's part. The desire for recognition was doubtless a significant element in some of their cases. A few people who felt unrecognised or unrewarded in their professional lives compensated by earning praise from the sympathetic case officer of an appreciative foreign intelli-gence service, especially when they could justify their secret work because it coincided – or could be made to coincide – with their political beliefs. It was not so much that this kind of spy was more in need of recognition than most people, as that spies were some of those 'most people' who had found an unusual way of achieving it.

Cumming and Regnart planned another overseas trip in order to examine a new German firearm which an agent, JR, had secretly arranged to borrow from the manufacturer for a few days. It seems to have been a personal weapon that could be concealed in luggage, was the new model of an existing type and was manufactured by Mauser. Cumming paid some of JR's expenses from his own pocket and records that the DMO for-bade them to bring the firearm into Britain, saying that he could find out all about it from Mauser himself during the latter's forthcoming visit. Cumming, supported by MacDonogh, argued against this on the grounds that 'it was extremely unlikely that M would give anything away that was not already adopted by his Govt, and that he probably had *two* f.a. patterns, of which he would be willing to sell us one that was not adopted by the Gs'. Cumming won the day, as also on the issue of whether they should meet JR in Amsterdam, which was being urged upon him because it was cheaper, or Paris, which he preferred 'because everyone goes there and no excuse whatever is required'.

He had to agree that a technical expert should join them in Paris to examine the firearm, and insisted they met beforehand so that they would know each other in a strange place. He was therefore 'introduced to a Mr Reavell, who is not an educated man and seems to me scarcely the right man for the job. However I made all the arrangements possible.'

In the event, a Mr Orgie was substituted for Mr Reavell, while the meeting with JR took place in Belgium following another with B in Paris. Cumming and Regnart travelled overnight arriving, sleepless, on the morning of 19 April. When B joined them in their hotel room later that day, he was 'offhand, unwilling . . . very unsatisfactory'. He asked for three more men, was refused, then for more money. He also proposed a system of communication in wartime which he had evidently been urged to devise and which Cumming pronounced 'insufficient'. After the meeting Cumming commented: 'I could not feel absolutely sure that he had three men in his employment at all, though perhaps this is only the suspicion that grows upon one after the first few months of the work.'

The following day they journeyed to Brussels and put up in a quiet hotel patronised by commercial travellers. This was a mistake: 'This was not a good policy as I found afterwards as these commercials are a very close clique, and they look rather askance at any stranger, and make enquiries about him from the Hotel Servants.' Large, modern, anonymous – and therefore expensive – hotels were probably better.

At 5 a.m. on 21 April they met the substitute technical expert, Mr Orgie, at the station and put him to bed in the nearby Palace Hotel. Cumming comments that he couldn't take him to his own hotel because he was staying there under the alias he used with JR which Mr Orgie, to whom he had been introduced in Mac-Donogh's office, presumably either should not know or could not be trusted to use. They were to meet JR later in a café in 'Li' [Lille? Liège?], so they arranged to meet Orgie on the steps of his hotel a quarter of an hour before the train. Cumming didn't want to hang around long because 'Br is full of spies and the station especially seems to have a lot of people loafing about who look very suspicious'. At the appointed hour, however, Orgie was nowhere to be found and Cumming had to go on alone, leaving Regnart to continue the search.

At the café he successfully met JR who had travelled from Berlin, and they waited for the others. It was then that Cumming learned that the 'thing' was not with him but was in Tindal, a suburb. They left written directions for Regnart with the '*caisse*' who promised faithfully to pass them on to the two gentlemen who would later appear and ask for JR. It was an hour's carriage ride to Tindal and light was failing by the time they reached JR's place, where he had the 'thing' and (by pre-arrangement) a photographer. Cumming also had a camera but before he could see the 'thing', JR said that he had been warned by 'Peter' (evidently known to both and seemingly the Berlin end of the operation) not to let anyone see it without prior payment in case, as had happened with some plans he had shown in London, 'they said after examination that they weren't interested, and paid him nothing'. Cumming 'was obliged to agree, and paid him the twenty five agreed upon and also a further ten for the answers to the questions set out by the airship people'.

He and the photographer then set to work in very bad light, made worse by the lace curtains which JR would not permit to be drawn. The photographer exposed three plates, Cumming two. He twice rang the café but there was no news of Regnart and Orgie. They had no tools to take the 'thing' apart and JR was reluctant for it to be handled, fearing damage. As soon as the photographer had finished his developing, JR said he had to go because he had to return the 'thing' to Berlin early the next morning and 'had to walk a long distance to get it across the frontier'. He also mentioned that an Englishman, whose name began with R, was reported killed at the Brussels station that morning. 'This was lively!' wrote Cumming, fearing it might be Regnant. Nevertheless, in the few minutes remaining he was able to handle, measure and sketch the weapon – 'but was surprised afterwards to find out how much I have managed to leave out'. He was untutored in the sort of detailed examination that Orgie was to perform and 'could not find out from any evidence offered by the "thing" itself that it was a.f. at all. It looked exactly like the ordinary military affair, except in the matter of the fore end of the barrel, which was apparently double and cased.'

JR, fidgeting, was nervous about the windows, door and time. He would not let Cumming borrow scales to weigh the weapon but promised to send the weight later. The mechanism was 'evidently very simple' but entirely enclosed. The sights were 'marked for one hundred to seven hundred metres and from eight hundred to nineteen hundred metres on the raised part, but he said he was told that it was only effective to fifteen hundred. It fired five shots.'

Cumming hurried off and just got his train, after bumping into – with the unwelcome coincidence that often accompanies anything clandestine – Pourtrait, another agent who was himself en route to Berlin on other business. JR suggested that Orgie be sent to Berlin to examine the weapon in Peter's house where it could be hidden for a couple of days before return to the stores, but Cumming thought it wrong to 'ask a man like Orgie to run such a risk'.

It became apparent at this point that JR was also in touch with the French Secret Service, whom he disarmingly said would 'give him a good character for reliability, accuracy and moderation'. In fact, a number of Cumming's early agents were working both for the British and the French – not always as candidly as JR – and this was one reason for his subsequent close liaison with his French equivalents. They were always fishing the same pond.

He did not meet Regnart until four in the morning back at the Brussels hotel, and they spent the rest of the night talking. Regnart and Orgie had reached the café not long after Cumming and JR had left and had waited there the rest of the afternoon because the '*caisse*' had forgotten about the letter. When eventually they got it they started immediately for Tindal, reaching it again just after Cumming and JR had left. They returned to the café and waited until Regnart was able to telephone Cumming later in the evening and be summoned back to Brussels.

The next day, having seen Orgie off early for London, they themselves left by a later train. This, Cumming confessed, was a mistake. Orgie was lost until late the following night when he eventually returned, having missed various trains and boats after a journey that began by his 'being taken down in the lift of his Hotel to a lower floor than he had gone up from, and as he could not understand a word of French, he could only shout "station" in various tones of distress, but without any result . . . Although no doubt a very good man at his particular job he was quite unfitted to travel alone.' Like most Britons of the time, he had probably never been abroad before, nor ever met a foreigner.

On his return, Cumming went straight out and had his negatives developed: 'One was hopelessly under exposed, and one showed a shutter defect (not surprising, as I had not used the Camera for ten years) but the third was capital – the best of all the photos taken.'

The 'thing' turned out not to be the weapon it was thought to be. Cumming was disappointed and offered to repay the £25 he had paid for his brief sight of it. MacDonogh approved such action but wanted to take advice before agreeing:

He said that it was not fair to make me responsible for all the failures – a certain proportion of which must occur – and that not many officers could afford to make good such losses. I told him that no officer who had not private means could take up my work at all, as up to the present (including Office etc.) I reckoned that it had cost me the whole of my pay to keep it going.

It was probably not an untypical trip.

In a separate conversation, perhaps with money on both their minds, MacDonogh gave him a letter from someone referred to as Alexander 'to whom he said the Govt. had paid twenty two thousand pounds during the [Boer?] war to set up an agency in France, but from whom they had received nothing in return'.

Cumming's flat was still apparently a contentious issue because he gratefully records Kell's promise to back him up on the question at a forthcoming meeting and to 'ask for one for himself of a similar nature to mine – viz. a set of private chambers, where he can sleep if necessary and receive visitors and letters. He agreed that our work was totally different and that our connection was only one of name, and that it would be better for both that we should work separately.'

Although the separation of the two halves of the SSB into what became MI5 and MI6 seems to have been uncontentious, this conversation on 28 April 1910 may perhaps be described as decisive. Thereafter, it was 'when' rather than 'if'. The conversation took place, as it would have in most spy novels, while they were walking from Cumming's flat to Kell's office and discussing how Cumming would set up a man of whom Kell wished to get a discreet view. That was achieved later in the day, after which their conversation apparently resumed because Kell said 'that the Tr o s [precise signification unclear but meaning German spies] who are coming over will be liable to penal servitude for life, for aiding and abetting in a felony. This is pleasant to hear, as no doubt I should share the same risk if I go over, and I must be careful when sending anyone to warn them of this.'

April ended with queries and reassessments about some of Cumming's ship reporting (reports from FRS and WK appeared to conflict) but with an overall favourable verdict from the First Sea Lord, a considerable accolade. Bethell told him to try to get plans of two new cruisers of the improved 'Mainz' class and briefed him on the recent theft of the plans of *Indomitable* and another ship, concerning which Cumming put him in touch with Kell. Then, presumably, he left for Bursledon because his last entry for April is to record another call on the harbour master at Southampton: 'no satisfactory result as regards the Pilots'.

6

Gains and Losses

May 1910 was important for two reasons. The first was that on the 9th and the 11th there were attempts to address the problems of the Bureau as adumbrated in Cumming's first six-monthly report, which occasioned a good deal of bureaucratic musketry.

Kell's six-monthly report is of an entirely different nature and format, partly accounted for by the fact that he had an official position which enabled him to work through and use other official organisations such as the police and Customs, whereas Cumming had to seek informal help while pretending he didn't exist. Thus Kell, unlike Cumming, stated confidently in his report: 'I have no hesitation in saying, from my year's experience of the work, that this section of the Bureau has justified its institution.' He calls for better official secrets legislation (granted the following year) and for more money to pay more staff.

For Cumming, however, the shortage of funds was crippling, since he had no official agencies to do his legwork for him and virtually all the information he acquired had to be paid for one way or another. On 2 May he was forbidden by MacDonogh to spend any more until after the forthcoming meeting and to get all 'authorities' given him by MacDonogh in writing because, as Cumming disarmingly confessed, 'What I said to him when he is bothered by other matters went in at one ear and out at the other and he forgot all about it.' MacDonogh's forgetfulness included the promise to pay £40 to FRS for his ship reporting although, as Cumming says: 'I told him [Blitz] that we had built a boat on the strength of the promise.'

MacDonogh himself was in an awkward position. The £6,200 he was given to finance both sections of the Bureau was quite inadequate and left him with about £830 to meet all the Bureau's travelling and operational expenses for the rest of the financial year, although April alone had consumed some £230. The standing costs he had to meet and was unable to reduce (though he would have liked to get rid of the expensive permanent agents) were: salaries for Kell and Cumming, £1,000; office rent, £500; salaries for M and L, £980; for Kell's clerk, £150; for B and his three sub-agents, £1,485; for the K family of agents, £600; for agents A, D and U, £525; for TG, £50; and for M's office, £80, a total of £5,310. MacDonogh did not see the Bureau in empire-building terms; he had more than enough on his plate and it was one more headache to add to others; he would have been happy to share financial responsibility and headache with Bethell, if permitted. That night, Cumming records: 'Roy called in the evening and showed me a new "case". I am afraid that we shall have to drop it, as I have no money to pay the man's travelling expenses.'

The following day MacDonogh wrote to Cumming setting out the new financial regime, which included such unworkable instructions as, 'Money will only be issued by me on written demand, which should reach me at least four days before it is required', and such unwise ones as, 'In order to save travelling expenses it will be desirable to reduce the number of meetings with agents as much as is possible and trust largely to the post'. The tone and content of this letter reawakened Cumming's fears that the War Office was trying to get rid of him, in which persuasion he was encouraged by Regnart who 'thinks the letter is intended for a censure, and that they mean me to resign'. He had no intention of doing so, 'so long as I have the confidence of my real chief – Luz'. He did: 'Luz says that I am too sensitive in supposing that the Arkis [the War Office or Army, just as the Admiralty or Navy was sometimes called Sipahi a Hindi word meaning, oddly, 'soldier'] want to reduce my berth to a mere nothing.' He was also reassured by someone he refers to as XX 'that my disburser was a slow cautious man with a legal mind but no go, and that I must ask for more than I wanted and use the funds as my discretion dictated'.

Cumming drafted his own reply to what he saw as the attempt by the War Office to stifle him, but sent instead one drafted by Bethell which reminded the War Office that authority for Cumming's activities stemmed from the Admiralty, not from the War Office, and that Cumming must be permitted reasonable freedom in the matter of expenses. Bethell also drafted, but probably did not send, another more trenchantly expressed letter: 'Nothing can be done without money, and if difficulties are put in the way of attaining it the whole shop might as well be shut up.' On 6 May Cumming wrote an account of how he was obliged by the new regime to postpone, and probably lose for good, meeting a potential agent 'of the highest possible value' whom TG had with difficulty been persuaded to introduce.

MacDonogh tried to reassure then both that he did not intend to put Cumming in a position any more impossible than that which he was in himself, with a rate of expenditure far exceeding supply and a time-consuming, inflexible system of financial control. 'I argued', writes Cumming, 'that it was not right that an officer holding a public position should be told that his expenditure was liable to be disallowed but he said this was the case with himself, and his sanction of my expenditure might be repudiated.'

The 9 May meeting was held in Bethell's office in order, in his words, to revise the 'methods and procedure of the SS Bureau'. MacDonogh gave a detailed and fair summary of arrangements, making the point that work could not seriously be said to have begun until 1 January. A large part of Kell's work involved talking to chief constables (many of whom were retired army officers referred to by Cumming – and perhaps by others – as 'Hear Hears'), and he made the point that Cumming's work was more difficult. The permanent agents – some of whom, Bethell said, he would 'cheerfully throw overboard' – were agreed to be too expensive. MacDonogh defended B, saying he had done valuable work when relations were strained with Russia, having 'supplied us with the actual way bills of the trains, showing what troops were being moved, and he had undertaken to let us know when any troops were moved to the Afghan frontier'. Cumming also spoke up for him, while suggesting that his payment should be more on a results basis, and it was eventually agreed that MacDonogh and Cumming should make recommendations as to which agents should be retained and on what salaries. Cumming's request for authority to promise large sums for early warning of war was not agreed but it was agreed to put in a request that the SSB budget should be divided into two with the respective heads allowed reasonable expenses and payments without prior reference. Towards the end of the meeting, Mac-Donogh again mentioned the Boer War, this time claiming that £28,000 had been paid 'to a certain person without any return'.

At a meeting in the Foreign Office a few days later, chaired by the Under Secretary, Sir Charles Hardinge (whom Cumming often refers to as the Paymaster), the request for a divided SSB budget was turned down (because Hardinge did not wish to go through two separate accounts) but Bethell was given authority to allow Cumming to act, travel and spend without further reference to the Foreign Office or Sir Grahame Greene. MacDonogh explained his difficulties, chief among which was that the £70 a so a month left for operational and travelling expenses was currently being consumed at three times that amount. Hardinge's response was heartening and forthright: 'The Paymaster said that if the work required it, the amount must be increased. There was no intention to stint the money or cripple the work in any way, and that whenever application was made to him for money, there would be no difficulty in the way of getting it supplied.'

The permanent agents were then examined individually and in detail, with the DMO protecting Hans, one of B's sub-agents, 'who has sent nothing but a bare statement that all was quiet, and this was valuable from their point of view'. That the Under Secretary of the Foreign Office should make time to go through the list of Cumming's agents, discussing the merits, values and costs of each, must surely have been unusual. Also, perhaps less unusually than those outside the bureaucracy might think, decisions were taken immediately and rulings made, such as that M and L were approved as indispensable, B was to give notice to his sub-agents and do more himself to justify his salary, A's salary was to be reduced to £100, D was to be dispensed with, U put on three months' notice unless he improved, the two elder Ks to be discharged and the younger WK put on a year's trial, JR was to have a retainer of £50, and TG to have his salary increased to £100. The private inquiry agent, Sketchley, was to be given notice in December and the Victoria Street office got rid of with Cumming and Kell having separate (officially funded) offices. Cumming was to be allowed 'to expend what was necessary and [in Cumming's capitals] NO RESTRICTION WAS TO BE PUT UPON USEFUL SERVICE. There was no wish to restrict the work in any way and if money already granted was not sufficient, more would have to be found from elsewhere. All he [Hardinge] wanted was to make sure it was spent wisely.'

This was a ringing endorsement of the SSB and Cumming goes on to record, possibly more euphorically than accurately, that in addition his request to offer £1,000 for warning of impending hostilities was 'cordially authorised'. There was, however, no sign of extra money, apart from that released by the proposed discharge of agents, until a year later when the new Under Secretary, Sir Arthur Nicholson, convened a meeting which decided to raise the budget from £6,200 to £8,050. This was a nugatory sum given the devastating costs of the war that this money was supposed to help predict, and even this small increase required the agreement of the Foreign Secretary, Sir Edward Grey.

Normality for Cumming had become a procession of problems connected with agents, or with communications with agents – generally, secret communications failing to remain secret, and the open failing entirely. Fortunately, the comedy and variety of bureaucratic life also continued. Cumming was summoned by Bethell to be told of one, Hugo Thomas, who had 'victimised the German Naval Attaché by writing to him to the effect that two ladies had picked up a Pocketbook belonging to a distinguished Admiral, in which were certain papers giving information about German naval matters, plans of Wilhelmshaven, Minefields etc.' The attaché must have had a guilty conscience because the German embassy handed over £40 in gold and £60 in notes in return for Mr Thomas's promise to retrieve the pocketbook from his lady friends. He shook off the men they sent to follow him and no more was heard until he wrote again, threatening to expose the attaché if more money was not sent. At this point the German embassy sought help from the Foreign Office, which advised recourse to the law. Bethell had summoned Cumming hurriedly in case he 'was connected with the matter in some way'.

No work was done in public offices on 17 May, the day of King Edward VII's funeral, except by Cumming, Bethell and Regnart. On 23 May Cumming appeared at last to have relinquished his boom defence responsibilities: 'Went round to Portsmouth and called upon C-in-C re Boom Defence. Turning over to him and his Secretary.' He did not, however, relinquish his interest, because on 30 May he was back in Bursledon to witness trials of a new boom system. He also again failed to find the right Southampton pilots but had useful conversations with businessmen about German munitions, mines and armour. The next day he 'had a conversation with Lionel Rothschild this afternoon, and he told me that whenever his firm received information from the correspondents abroad, they sent it directly to the Prime Minister or to the Foreign Secretary.' He spoke also to a man who was 'lately manager of the Mercedes Co in Berlin and he told me that he often dropped across information . . .'

Meanwhile, Regnart had asked a fellow Royal Marines captain, Bernard Trench, whether he wanted to undertake a discreet tour of the German North Sea coastal defences, particularly the northern and eastern Friesian Islands (*Riddle of the Sands* country). This was the sort of fishing expedition that the Directorate of Naval Intelligence, like the War Office, regarded as one of its mainstream activities. Royal Marines officers were frequently used in this and other intelligence roles, largely because the corps offered a very limited career to commissioned ranks. Its proper role was thought to be service at sea, where few officers were required, and there was no permanent ground force trained for operations ashore. Many officers therefore opted for seconded duties in the colonies or at home in specialist areas such as ordnance, signals, intelligence and, later, flying.

Captain Trench accepted the offer. An interpreter of German and French, by then learning Danish, it wasn't his first spying trip: in 1908 he and a friend, Lieutenant Vivien Brandon of the Royal Navy, had undertaken a similar expedition to observe German naval facilities at Kiel, for which Trench received official commendation in his service record (it refers to his 'useful report on the coastal defences at Kiel'). Trench asked if his friend Brandon could accompany him again, and the request was agreed.

Trench and Brandon were doubtless aware that they were part of a very much larger programme, extending well beyond their personal involvement and considerably pre-dating it. In an interesting privately-published account of the 1910 operation, ('*Royal Marines Spies of the World War One Era*', Royal Marines Historical Society, 1993)[1], Professor Donald Bittner drew on papers then withheld by the PRO but available in America to show that from at least 1901 the British were taking a keen interest in the small fishing village of Emden, thirty miles from the North Sea, and the island of Borkum. Both were tactically significant to Germany's reinforcement of her North Sea fleet and to any possible landings in Germany. A series of British

177

Admiralty reports and assessments in the US National Archives (passsed to the Americans by the British) feature an agent called 'Z' who reported in detail on the potential of the area should the Germans choose to use it. The ground covered and the tactical assumptions are so similar to those of Childers in *The Riddle of the Sands*, published two years after Z's account, that it is very tempting to imagine that Childers was Z, or was with him; tempting, but none the less speculative.

In 1906 the NID produced a consolidated report on the area, listing information still required and concluding that a landing could be opposed at once or within a few hours at most. By 1910 the NID was still monitoring recent German reinforcements of defences, booms, garrisons, canals and roads, since seizure of Borkhum still seems to have formed part of Fisher's war plans and it was to Borkum that Trench and Brandon were primarily directed for their three-week 'walking tour'. They were, it turned out, to be away for rather longer than that.

Cumming makes no direct reference in his diary to the decision to mount the operation and it seems unlikely, both from his many later references and from Trench's account, that he originated it. He was none the less involved, albeit not always as he wished, and the operation is perhaps a good example of what probably happened more often than we realise: the Admiralty and War Office made use of Cumming's facilities for operations of their own, while he made use of their facilities for operations of his. The result is that it is often hard to tell which was whose and assumptions based on clear evidence may be wrong because the evidence, though clear, is incomplete.

When Trench and Brandon set out on 6 August as officers ostensibly on leave, they planned to go first to the Netherlands and deposit there any incriminating papers. However, they went instead directly to Borkum, having heard that military exercises were about to take place, and stayed near the restricted zones around new forts. One night Trench penetrated the barbed wire surrounding a restricted zone and conducted a reconnaissance;

the next night Brandon did the same. Unfortunately, Brandon was equipped – perhaps had equipped himself – with a camera and flash attachment, which he unwisely used. The flash was seen by a German sentry, Brandon was illuminated by searchlight and caught.

He was taken by train from Emden and seemed at that stage to have been regarded more as an errant tourist or enthusiast who had broken the rules than a spy. Trench joined the train and was allowed to speak to him. Throughout the trip the two men had photographed, sketched, taken bearings on guns and searchlight positions and generally gathered as much tactical information as they could. Trench realised that closer examination of Brandon would lead to the material they had gathered and so he returned to their hotel in Emden and hid incriminating documents in, unfortunately, all the obvious places. He then sought to escape to the Netherlands but before he could get away he, too, was arrested.

Brandon was interrogated in French by a Lieutenant Luck-amm who, on seeing Brandon's photographs, identified those of the fortifications on the island of Wangerooge. Brandon claimed he had confused two islands, then said that these were the only ones of interest for the newspaper for which he claimed to write. His annotated guide to Heligoland he tried to pass off as being only 'a few distances which I had estimated roughly with the eye because Heligoland was of interest to me as a point of defence in view of the many newspaper articles on the subject'. Sketches of harbour works and notes of distances he considered himself 'authorised to do as all this can be freely seen'. Not surprisingly, it didn't wash.

Accounts of the arrests appeared in the German press and then in the British between 22 and 24 August. On 5 September the Foreign Office denied to the German government any official British involvement in what the arrested men had done: 'HM Government has no knowledge of the officers in question, nor of their movements, which were entirely unauthorised.' Efforts were made to back up Brandon's cover story by preparing evidence that he worked for *The Sphere*, a journal that carried stories about ports and forts, but he himself undermined it by authorising the examining magistrate to examine letters which he knew had been sent to him at Defzl in Holland. One at least of these letters gave clear evidence of intelligence connections.

Meanwhile, consideration was given in London to a round-up of suspected German spies who could be held in exchange for leniency, but nothing was done. Quite by coincidence, however – and it was coincidence, as Kell's diary makes clear – a German officer, Lieutenant Siegfried Helm, was arrested on 7 September after making sketches of Fort Wilde, Portsmouth. He was doing exactly what Trench and Brandon were doing, and was found to have made sketches and measurements of other forts, but the War Office decided his material was 'of no great military value'. Convicted under existing secrecy legislation, he was treated leniently, fined and allowed to return to his unit in Germany.

The Helm case had little or no effect on what happened to Trench and Brandon, perhaps because of the greater sensitivity over what they were doing and the amount of evidence. After Trench was arrested in August the papers he had hidden in his hotel were not at first found, but on 23 December the hotel proprietor found notes and sketches under the bolster of his bed and during the subsequent police search other papers were discovered between the mattresses and elsewhere in his room. What the Germans now had was an espionage haul: notes on Kiel, Wilhelmshaven, Borkum and the Kaiser Wilhelm Canal giving depths, gun positions, arcs of fire and ranges, along with details of possible landing places and more undeveloped photographs. Trench later said he had not destroyed all these when he returned to his hotel because he thought 'the danger had passed'.

The trial, held in Leipzig before Christmas, was agreed by British officials and press to be impartial and fair. It was also lenient. The prosecution accepted that no information had actually been passed to the Admiralty by Trench and Brandon; that they were servants of their government, not traitors betraying the Fatherland; that they had not attempted to bribe Germans into betraying their country; that their activities, barring those at Borkum, had been confined to public roads and places; and that they had co-operated with the investigating authorities. They, in turn, acknowledged connections with intelligence, mentioning 'Reggie' (Regnart) as an officer 'connected with the Intelligence Bureau of the Admiralty' but refusing to say any more about him. Both were asked whether they had read *The Riddle of the Sands* and when Brandon admitted to having read it three times, there was laughter. They were sentenced to four years' detention in fortresses, Trench at Glatz in Silesia and Brandon at Königstein in Saxony. *The Times* commented on the amicable atmosphere of the trial, describing how afterwards the defendants remained for some minutes 'chatting with counsel and others and shaking hands with acquaintances such as the Juge d'Instruction who conducted the preliminary hearing ... They were very gay and perfectly satisfied with the result of the trial.'

Although they hadn't escaped as lightly as Lieutenant Helm, both charges and sentences could have been a great deal worse. Not only were there mitigating features but what they had done was not viewed by the Germans as ungentlemanly or unofficerlike. Rather the opposite, in fact: it was the duty of a patriotic officer to gather information about a potential enemy's dispositions. The prosecutor called not for public deprecation but for wide publicity so that the British public, whipped – as he saw it – into spy mania by the British press, should see that their own people were practising what they accused the Germans of practising upon them. The two officers had ignored or broken just about every sensible security precaution available to them, but this seems to have escaped comment.

The story of Cumming's involvement is probably best told in the order in which he records it in his diary. It has a context which not only partly explains what happened but is also indicative of the emotional underpinnings of what went on in the Naval Intelligence Department at that time. The context was Cumming's relations with Roy Regnart and the best snapshot of those at this period arises from a trip they made together to meet TG in Brussels.

They travelled overnight via Ostend and reached their hotel at 6 a.m. on 4 June, retiring for a couple of hours before greeting TG. If the forthcoming agent meeting, or meetings, was at all representative of most that Cumming had to endure during this period – and it probably was – then his forbearance and persistence were truly impressive.

TG was staying at another hotel in his own name, despite receiving mail there in the alias of Gluck. However, he failed to notice a letter awaiting him in his alias until Cumming and Regnart pointed it out: it turned out to be from his friend, Knight, whom he was to introduce to them. They arranged to meet for lunch at a café.

At mid-day they ran into TG in the street. He at first either missed or ignored them and when they addressed him he contradicted what he had earlier said about the letter from Knight, claiming that Knight was in Paris and therefore unavailable. They adjourned to a café for two and a half hours. TG was 'very slippery', alleging that Knight was too nervous to meet them both and would meet only Cumming (because, Cumming thought, Regnart's superior German would make it more difficult for Knight and TG to talk in asides or to bamboozle him). TG complained that he had no guarantee that they were not German spies, 'and that we had not a man with a camera taking the group as we sat'. They were 'too sly to be merely officers' and before he risked exposing his friend to them 'there must be proper arrangements', such as £100 down. After lengthy debate they agreed that Knight should be paid £10 after the interview, with a further £10 advance on salary if his information turned out to be good, with more to follow for more information. As they were leaving, TG tried vainly for another £10 down to help him 'persuade' his friend, who had long ago become available again.

When they met outside Cumming's hotel, however, TG was still alone, saying that Knight had not returned but would come shortly. Unfortunately for TG, Knight arrived while he was saying this, apparently relaxed and happy. TG immediately took him off and returned a short while later to say that Knight agreed to meet only if allowed to sit in the corner with his face to the wall, and so long as his statement of what he knew was not interrupted or questioned. TG was to select the room.

Later, the four spies in search of a meeting all met again and set off for a room that TG claimed to have taken. This time Knight was rendered nervous and frightened by meeting two policemen on a street corner. It then turned out that TG had not actually taken a room, so they had to find one, reluctantly giving their names and addresses. When eventually they settled down, Knight spoke frankly and freely (Cumming doesn't say which way he faced), giving information about the forts around Wilhelmshaven, suggesting an engineer whom he could introduce and – most valuable in any agent – 'when he came to a point he did not understand or know about, he said so frankly'. The interview lasted some hours, ending only when the landlord turned them out. It was then past midnight, and, as Cumming and Regnart had not been to bed for some forty-eight hours, they arranged to meet again at lunch the following day. It was, Cumming concluded, 'very hard work talking to these men in a foreign language and having to consider every word, both of theirs and your own'. It was also, it would not have occurred to him to add, a considerable achievement to learn anything of a new language in your fifties.

The next day, Sunday, they found TG 'loafing about' an hour before the appointed time, and repaired to another café. 'He was extremely jealous of Knight and warned that he might "fade away".' He had tried throughout to conceal Knight's real name but now he betrayed it, claiming that all that Knight had said was false and insisting that he himself should be made head agent. His qualifications, he thought, were his exceeding caution and the impossibility of his making mistakes. He felt that Knight's appearance had unfairly damaged his own position, as indeed it had. It had also demonstrated that TG had been withholding information.

Cumming's response was blunt: he was not at all satisfied with TG's work and he could either produce better and double his salary or do as little as hitherto and get nothing. It was up to him.

Regnart then took TG into yet another café while Cumming waited outside for Knight. When Knight arrived Cumming told him that he was nervous about TG and his carelessness 'and if he found at some later date that he would prefer to correspond with me direct, he could do so by writing to the address I gave him'. Cutting out TG was obviously desirable and Knight seems to have taken immediately to the idea, since there are frequent further references to him and his information in the diary although, frustratingly, his position is never given.

Later they all met up for lunch in Brussels, an event that lasted from one o'clock to five-fifteen. Cumming arranged to be introduced to Knight's engineer friend in London early the following week, but otherwise the lunch was dominated by dealing with TG who 'showed the greatest impatience at our talking to Knight in English, and kept up a constant flow of interruption. I had to turn aside to talk to him and keep him quiet several times. He ended by getting rather drunk, when he became very objectionable to the waiters and showed us a new side of his character that he had better have kept concealed.' He also showed them photographs of himself in various uniforms, prompting Cumming to comment that 'there is no doubt that he is what he says he is'. Next he described himself as the 'slyest man in Europe except for his brother, who is an attaché in Cairo'. He asked for various impossible guarantees and for medals and, once again, for money. Cumming relented slightly on the latter and finally, in an excess of self-esteem, TG 'told us that Count Mankovitch [probable] had invited him many times to join his service, but he had declined as he hated Russians – the natural enemies of his country . . . ever since he had been a Cadet, he had set this business [spying] as a goal before him'.

Agent meetings may be the stuff of spying but they feature little in spy fiction, particularly meetings such as this. Cumming no doubt found it part of the fascination of espionage that a bombastic, greedy, insecure, dishonest scallywag such as TG can, very occasionally and often without realising it, do something worthwhile, such as introduce a better agent or produce a nugget of real intelligence. The trick, as Cumming surely also found, is in knowing when to believe, when to say no, when to encourage and how to disengage.

Apart from giving us a glimpse of what it was like trying to spy in 1910, the episode also tells us something about Cumming's relationship with Regnart. They spent a lot of time together (on this trip sharing a room) in rather busy, sometimes fraught, circumstances. We must hope that the comedy of what they were doing did not escape them entirely, though Regnart's sense of humour remains an undiscovered realm. His hard work and conscientiousness are, however, well established and he seems never to have regarded himself as off duty, any more than did Cumming. On otherwise lonely trips abroad it could have been reassuring to have an experienced and probably courageous companion, though his judgement might have given pause for thought and the agreeability of his company remains, like his humour, a matter for surmise. Whatever the diary shows later, they could not have got on badly most of the time.

Not that on trips such as this they would have had leisure to cultivate their relationship; as Service officers they would have regarded that as a secondary matter anyway. Apart from travel, catching up on sleep and their meetings with TG, they also on this trip met JR, receiving him in their room at nine in the morning of the day of the five-hour lunch. He was still sulking over the affair of the 'thing', but had answers to a questionnaire on airships, for which he wanted a pound an answer, and gave them a French questionnaire that he had been sent by his French case officer, whom he identified.

When Cumming and Regnart left by train that night, they had a conversation which Cumming noted:

Private matter on this page

A conversation took place in the train which left a queer impression with me. I commenced it by telling my companion about a trivial incident with Swede [an officer in London] when he had hesitated to allot to me what I thought belonged to me by right. My friend said that he did not agree at all with my attitude on the question. He said that Swede as an Officer 'in an official position' had every right to give or withhold any cases that came up. That I must remember (as XX had pointed out) that I was not on the active list and had no recognised position, (what was my title?), that the folks opposite [the War Office] had behaved very well all through and it rested entirely with them whether to give me any work at all. That if I should ever complain to the GOM, he would have to back up his representative (Blitz) and I should have to retire. That I ought not to assume the position of a Chief of a Bureau, but should go to them as a 'client' and ask for work. I told him that I could not agree with this view. That I was as much in an official position as another. That I had been properly appointed by recognised authority, and that although I was not on the active list I was certainly an Officer. The division of the work had been made by the folks opposite – not at my suggestion or request and that it was certainly understood that all the work appertained to my part would be given to me. I did not consider it right to beg for work that I had been appointed to do. I reminded him that I had not come begging for the appointment, but had been taken from an important command to undertake this special work. He said that did not affect the question. He ended by saying that he supposed that it would be alright so long as Luz remained at the head of affairs, but after that I must look out. The awkward part of the matter was his evident implied reference to his own power to withhold any cases that might come to him, and either give them to me or work them himself as he thought fit. Coming after his proposal to join me as an assistant when his time is up, and his remarks about taking another man's work on that occasion, this was very significant, but he gives too much away on these occasions to be really dangerous.

This reads as if Regnart was a cauldron of bile and resentment. The exchange was evidently unusual enough for Cumming to record it in detail, though he does not express surprise, and his reference to Regnart giving 'too much away on these occasions to be really dangerous' suggests that there was a history. It also suggests a capacity for shrewd calculation and assessment underlying Cumming's normal bluff straightforwardness. This is the first reference to Regnart's possibly leaving the Marines and the NID in order to work for Cumming. Its relevance to the matter of Trench and Brandon, and possibly to other cases, is in the sentence, 'The awkward part of the matter was his evident implied reference to his own power to withhold any cases that might come to him, and either give them to me or work them himself as he thought fit.' What seems to have happened with Trench and Brandon is that Regnart did both, and neither properly.

The next page in Cumming's diary is apparently from his lost letter book from which we learn that Trench and Brandon were to have been contacted care of the Cook's Agency in Hamburg, that they were to visit fourteen north German towns, ports and islands and that both had code names – Brandon's was 'Bonfire', Trench's 'Counterscarp'.

On 7 June Bethell had agreed to Cumming's paying £30 to Trench (also £10 to someone unknown called 'Orange') and had approved Trench's trip. The next day Cumming 'went round to Roy's office and saw Counterscarp there. Arranged with him for his trip and gave him sundry cautions. Roy is providing the list of requirements.' There is no further mention of the two officers until 27 June when Cumming received a letter and telegram sent to Copenhagen and collected by Trench, who was studying Danish in Copenhagen at the time and probably helped out by picking up mail for agents and sending it back via the military or naval attaché. On 19 July Cumming notes that he agreed to find an extra '£10 to enable Counterscarp to have a companion on 6th of next month. We had authority for thirty pounds. They think they can do it for forty pounds the two.'

On 4 August, two days before the operation, he went to Regnart's office for a 'short talk with Bonfire, who is to meet Counterscarp in Porktown [sic – presumably Hamburg]. He gave me a short sketch of his proposed route.' The following day came the first sign of impending trouble. Cumming and Regnart were busy organising another agent's journey, when

Just as I was starting, Bonfire appeared in Roy's office where he had been waiting for us, so I remained a few minutes talking to him. It dropped out that he was to write to some private address given him by Roy. This is quite contrary to my wishes in the matter, as I feel very strongly that it is utterly wrong and mistaken policy, and has no single advantage to support it, but on speaking to

Roy about the matter he says that Bonfire was to write
to him only on a particular matter, that of a man who
had been recommended to him by a ship's captain. I did
not see why this should be separated from the rest, but
let it pass.

Thus, an operation which seems not to have originated from
Cumming was nevertheless funded by him and he arranged its
communications, but others also intervened; he evidently did not
have sole control. The degree to which his relations with Regnart
and the disputed question of control were factors in the affair
is made starkly clear by his diary entry for 13 August, some
days before the news of the arrests reached England:

I had another of those awkward discussions with Roy,
that leave behind such an unpleasant feeling that he is
playing some game of his own. In the first place, he told
me that he preferred to send his report into Luz privately
[Regnart had, by arrangement by Cumming, just concluded a reconnaissance of the shipyard in Trieste, checking agent information]. If this is a draw, it did not come
off, as I took no notice, the ground being too weak for
any discussion on that head. The next point was raised
by his asking if I had reported his going to Blitz. He
demurred strongly to this, but I told him that I had written orders to keep Blitz informed of what went on, and
was not going to disobey my orders for anyone. We then
got onto the subject of the two who had just gone out
(Counterscarp and Bonfire). I asked him if he did not consider them as my men, and he said certainly not. I asked
who sent them out and he replied, 'The representative of
the DNI' i.e. himself. This is of course absurd, as they
are paid with the money for which I had to show the

results. He said they were not connected with the CC [Secret Service] at all. In fact whenever there is anything likely to turn out well, he is to have the credit for it, and my bureau can content itself with the wretched scally-wags (not one of whom he has yet handed on to me).

Regnart then said he wanted to extend a trip by someone called Wren in order to photograph the shipyards at Pola, which, because of close guarding, Cumming considered so dangerous as to be 'little short of sending Wren to prison'. Regnart's reaction – that it wouldn't matter if Wren were caught as he was of no use and it would never be known – shocked Cumming: 'I entirely and totally disagree with this policy and I feel that it would be impossible for me to work with Roy, and knowing that he holds such views. It puts an ugly light on CJ's arrest.' He gave 'positive orders' that Wren should be brought home.

It is not known who the unfortunate CJ was, but the same ugly light is shed upon the forthcoming arrests. Was this callous, self-defeating nonchalance really Regnart's attitude or was he simply carried along by the current of contradiction? Cumming's response is very much in keeping with what came to be SIS ethos, in which the arrest of an agent was the most keenly-felt of disasters.

On 16 August Regnart sought MacDonogh's authority to send Trench and Brandon to watch the Danzig manoeuvres. MacDonogh discussed it with Cumming and agreed to provide a further £30 for this aspect of the trip. Afterwards, he talked about Regnart's position and

said that he was thoroughly uncomfortable about it. I told him that I was also, though for a different reason. He told me to send in a report on the subject, but I begged him to let me off that, as it would be a very awkward thing to do, and might lose us the services of a good man. To this he agreed, but he said that I must promise not to take Roy into any more of my schemes and must stop the private addresses altogether.

This the first of many occasions on which Cumming defended Regnart while acknowledging his faults. Whatever virtues are subsumed under being a 'good man', Cumming alone seems to have been aware of them, or at least to have thought that they counter-balanced Regnart's vices. Both then and later, when the Bureau expanded hugely, he was always short of people he could rely on because the Admiralty and War Office – always his main and for one period his only suppliers – could never be trusted not to snatch seconded officers back at a moment's notice. Regnart seems to have desired no other sort of work nor to have sought advancement in the normal way. In Cumming's eyes he probably offered experience, dedication and dependability. Nevertheless, Cumming's view of him over the next few years remains one that it is easier to sympathise with than to share.

On 27 August he recorded the safe return of Wren – 'although the work would have been valuable, we could not allow one of our workers to run risks.' He wrote a letter to Regnart but before delivering it saw in the evening paper the report of an Englishman arrested at Borkum, hesitated over sending this letter but decided to go ahead 'as case or no, it applies equally well – though if there has been a mishap, it would be the wrong time to rub this matter in'.

It was probably a letter setting out their respective positions with regards to his control of the Bureau, since it provoked a defensive barrage from Regnart: Cumming wished to run the whole department, Regnart included, and took too much on himself; he was working in the dark without consulting anyone; in Bethell's absence Regnart was to be regarded as the DNI's representative; the tone of Cumming's letter was objectionable and he would not send any such letter to anyone else; the

Bureau's funds were not Cumming's to dispose of but the NID's – and more in that vein. Cumming rebutted these assertions point by point, asserting his independence with regard both to the NID and the War Office (referred to, as usual, as the 'other side', a phrase rarely used of the German enemy) and reminding Regnart that 'he was very much my junior'. Once again, this time from Regnart's pen, there was clear indication of the intimate relationship between Regnart's concerns about his position and the operation that led Trench and Brandon to their fortress incarcerations: 'He said that if he were not allowed to completely control those he sent out, I should get no more, as these particular men were personal friends of his own, and he should not bring them forward for my benefit.'

Although strong words were spoken on both sides, they put the matter aside in order to discuss the news of the morning. Regnart was pretty sure the arrested man was Brandon and they considered sending someone over to collect the letters in Holland but Cumming argued that the Germans would surely have already discovered the address and would have collected them (in fact, as we have seen, they did not know about them until Brandon volunteered the information to the examining magistrate). Regnart decided to telegraph Trench saying 'Regatta postponed. Wire news.'

Over in the War Office Cumming found people 'in rather a panic'. He said that 'if the man was ours, I would certainly accept responsibility for him, but we could scarcely believe all the papers said. I told them "officially" that we knew nothing about the matter.' He spent the afternoon on boom defence committee work but in the evening Regnart brought him 'very serious news that he had just seen in the papers'. Bethell was at Cowes but they felt he should be briefed and caught the last train, arriving at the Royal Hotel at two in the morning. When briefed after breakfast the following day, Bethell decided that Fisher, the First Sea Lord, should be informed and travelled back to London with them, discussing 'various schemes for helping our rash friends'.

Bethell instructed that the official line that should be taken within the War Office (presumably with the departments other than those that knew about the case) was that 'we had ascertained that the two unfortunately were not military men at all, nor connected in any way with any CC work. We knew nothing at all about them.' There may be good reasons for official denials and disclaimers – such as that an admission makes a trial unavoidable, conviction certain or a sentence longer – but it is surely not good policy to try and fool your own officials, which is how this reads. It was possible, though, that this was intended as an unofficial line for public consumption. Bethell saw Fisher, who decided 'that nothing was to be done at all for the present, and that we know nothing about these men at all'. Regnart suggested that he should visit friends of the two accused 'in an assumed character' but, perhaps fortunately, there is no record of this being attempted. Regnart subsequently claimed not to know that Trench and Brandon had taken a camera with them and was sure they had not taken a questionnaire. Relations with Cumming meanwhile seemed to have been calmed by greater events; Cumming 'gave him back the letter to me unopened, according to our arrangement of yesterday'.

There was an Admiralty meeting about the case on 30 August. Kell recorded in his diary that 'I was asked if I could get up a "counter-blast" to the Borkum affair. I said I feared not.' Cumming, as usual, goes into more detail, although his first comment – 'Not much decided' – is a fair summary. British press interest in the affair remained fairly low key, thanks partly to the efforts of Trench's and Brandon's solicitor, Sir William Bull, Conservative MP for Hammersmith, who was also involved in discussions with the Foreign Office. He had already suggested a round-up of German agents in Britain and Cumming raised something similar at the meeting, but it was rejected on the grounds that 'even supposing we had a definite case, we should scarcely tell them who it was'.

When Cumming discussed the matter again with MacDonogh the next day, he found him

cordial and kind although evidently troubled about this
affair and chagrined that such a hindrance to our work
should have occurred . . . I told Blitz that I had understood from the first that Counterscarp was going for one
of the towns suggested by XX, whom I had specially consulted on the matter. This was in July last. The other
man had been suggested as an afterthought, and I had
consented to give £10 (as the limit I was allowed) for his
extra expenses. I saw both men just before starting, but
my object in doing so was principally to know them
again by sight in case I had to meet them abroad.

After that 31 August entry there is a gap in the diary until
22 November 1910, when it resumes without acknowledgement
of the gap. Kell's diary mentions Cumming or Cumming-related
matters nine times during the period, giving glimpses of the
progress of Cumming's affairs and of the Trench/Brandon case
but no more than that since it is naturally more concerned with
Kell's affairs – in which the arrest in Portsmouth of Lieutenant
Helm featured largely – and is anyway less detailed.

On 5 September Kell recalls: 'I went to see "C" for a few
minutes. He is in bed with high fever and will probably not be
up and about for some days – so I have put off my trip to the
SW of England until next week.' (This suggests that the rule
still obtained whereby they could not both be away at the same
time.) On the same day Kell was summoned to a meeting with
Bethell where he heard that Sir William Bull claimed to know
of two German spies in Britain (presumably with the implication
that they should be arrested). Kell then went to the Foreign
Office with 'Colonel MacDonogh' (he never uses the nicknames
that add colour and mystery to Cumming's diary) to discuss the
Helm case. There they found that Sir Francis Campbell was
'thoroughly apathetic and would give us no lead'.

On 12 September Kell met Sir William Bull in 3 Stone Buildings and discovered that the two German spies had now become three, but Sir William remained reticent about putting Kell on their track – 'he wanted to keep them up his sleeve until the Borkum case was finished'. He eventually agreed to give Kell all the information he had, provided Kell took no action without informing him.

Kell often had information about supposed spies pressed upon him and was usually energetic and even credulous about following such offerings, as, for instance, 'M. also told me that he had run across a German down at Ilfracombe who went under the name of Herr Leon and who was most likely a Spy.' Or, 'he warned us against the head waiter at the principal Hotel at Malta. He felt sure he was an agent.' Sir William's offerings, like these, appear not to have made a mark on espionage history, although later in the month Kell did discuss one, a Herr v. Grundherr, with the Chief Constable of Wiltshire who 'knew of the man and had long ago suspected him. He had left the County now . . . he owes some money in the neighbourhood.'

Cumming's illness lasted longer than anticipated. On 26 September Kell noted: 'Saw "C". He is better. I offered to lend him "L" to do his correspondence, etc., until he was able to get about again. "C" very glad to have him.' (This seems not to have been the agent, L.) On 11 October Kell dined with Admiral Limpus who suspected that 'Schneider, the German barber on the Hard at Portsmouth, was a spy'. Schneider had shown familiarity with all the details of the 'Borkum spies' and said that Trench had told him, before leaving, that 'he was going to Borkum and the other islands, to see what he could discover – or words to that effect'.

Kell next records seeing Cumming on 24 October, finding him better and working again at his correspondence, with L's help. To be found to be 'much better' after seven weeks suggests more than a heavy cold or touch of flu; possibly, given the reference to fever, some recurring illness that Cumming had picked up in the tropics in his naval youth. By 27 October, however, he was properly back in action, introducing Kell to a Mr and Mrs Redwood whom Kell wanted to use to investigate a Mrs Fleming at Little Chart, Kent. The following day Kell interviewed the 'very smart' Mrs Redwood in Cumming's office.

In mid-November, as already noted, the SSB's budget was increased to £8,050 in order to pay for an assistant each for Cumming and Kell plus a further 'Marine assistant' for Kell on the east coast and an agent for Cumming in Copenhagen. The Foreign Secretary's agreement had to be obtained. The attraction of an agent in Copenhagen was the city's easy access to German shipyards, though the War Office preferred Brussels because it wanted a stay-behind organisation on the Belgian–German frontier. It would be some time before either materialised.

On 23 December 1910, the day following the trial of Trench and Brandon, Cumming summarised the affair for himself in a way that emphasises once again the problems of divided command and control within the intelligence community:

It seems as if the result of the trial has been to exonerate me from any personal share in the scheme. This however is merely a fortunate accident, and up to the very end of the case I quite expected to find myself saddled with a certain amount of the responsibility although it has transpired that I had no control whatever of the parties concerned. I should like to have the position defined so as to prevent anything of the kind happening again. It is obvious from the evidence that –

1. The officers travelled on a different route to the one I believed them to be following.
2. That though I expected them to write to me and gave them addresses for the purpose, they had other instructions from Roy and did actually correspond with him.

3. That they sent home information to him of which I knew nothing, and for which my Bureau received no credit.
4. That arrangements were apparently made by which Roy was to go out to Defzl to meet them. Such a plan would not have been permitted if referred to authority.

This work is extremely difficult to carry on under any circumstances. Under those indicated above, it would be impossible. I could not accept responsibility for work done contrary to my directions, nor agree to a plan directly contrary to my own instructions. Roy proposed to take 70% of my month's funds, and to employ them independently of my Bureau. If repeated often this would have reduced my Bureau to nothing.

It must have been a discouraging end to the first full year of Cumming's side of the SSB. Some intelligence had been produced but fundamental bureaucratic and operational problems remained unresolved. It would be a mistake, though, to assume the Trench–Brandon affair dominated the latter half of the year. Other things also happened, other themes ran strongly throughout and there were some colourful encounters.

There was, for instance, the case of Mme Rachell. Cumming first heard of her early in July when MacDonogh, on return from his month's walking reconnaissance, told him how she and another woman had previously been run as War Office agents but had 'gone off very huffy' because they had been paid only £8 for some intelligence. Cumming, under pressure from Bethell to get details of the armaments supposedly carried by German merchant ships, wondered whether Mme Rachell might be able to oblige and got MacDonogh's permission to reopen negotiations.

He arrived in Paris at 5 a.m. on 16 July and was briefed by a man called Holmes who was probably on the staff of the military attaché at the British embassy. Before meeting Mme

Rachell, however, he had to see another potential agent, a Mlle Marguerite Depiesse. She was to call at his hotel where he was staying under an assumed name. In case of a trap he 'took precautions not to be recognised or identified for future action, by taking up a position in a small salon where I could see anyone entering the grand Salon' He was also, he adds with disappointing brevity, 'slightly disguised (toupee and moustache) and had on a rather peculiar costume'. Naturally, these precautions having been taken, he waited six hours – no doubt feeling he must look conspicuously under-employed – and no one turned up.

Afterwards, he set off for Enghien, where Mme Rachell lived:

On arriving at the house, which was quite a respectable one, I asked for the lady – who was evidently at home – and the servant took in my name. A message was brought out to say that she regretted she could not receive me. I sent back a message begging her to give me an interview as I had come all the way from Paris to see her, but again the message came back that she regretted that she could not see me. This time I sent a message begging for 5 minutes only, and raising my voice [presumably all in French] so that the lady in the inner room could hear me, I said to the servant, 'Say that I have come all the way from London to see her, and if that will not persuade her, say that I have come all the way from China to see her, and am not going back until I succeed.' This brought the lady out!

They got on. Cumming described her as 'of a certain age ... of medium height, on rather massive lines, good complexion, blue eyes, brown hair, coiffed in modern fashion but not in any extreme mode, plainly dressed, but in good and rather expensive style, quiet in voice and manner'. His own manner with what he doubtless would have called 'the ladies' seems from this and other evidence to have been formal and polite, with an undercurrent of playful gallantry. Before meeting her he had, he confessed, formed the impression that she 'belonged to the prostitute class' but saw at once that he was wrong and that she was 'a good type of respectable married French lady of the middle class'.

It transpired that Mme Rachell's information came from her sister-in-law – 'whom I am informed by Holmes is a Jewess of inferior class' – who had been deserted by her husband and who kept herself and her child by 'working in this way'. Her source was an officer in the German army engineers in charge of a balloon section, who gave her information 'for love'. Both women were very indignant with the British for having paid them so little last time that they were out of pocket, and her sister-in-law had 'strictly enjoined her not to correspond any more with us'. Cumming was sympathetic: 'I took the line of condemning them [her War Office contacts] also and said that these people were the *Military*, the *Marine* side being of totally different calibre and well able to appreciate valuable services.'

He pressed £20 upon her to reopen relations, settled communications and a system for agreeing the price of information in advance and then gave her some test questions. He thought she was 'inclined to be honest and . . . very intelligent', albeit 'a little careless about the papers, but as she was in her own house, this may not really have been the case'. For all his own charm, however – and his sensitivity to charm – he remained clear-eyed: 'My impression is that these two ladies deal with the French Government, and find it a good paying business . . . they only consent to deal with us because they sell to us the same information that they offer to the French . . . the French pay far better than we do, although I believe that for really valuable stuff we should always be able to get the money.'

When he returned to his hotel he found a letter from Mlle Depiesse saying that she had changed her mind about coming to Paris because she 'feared losing the money for her travelling expenses' and proposing, illogically, to meet instead in London. Two days later, Cumming sent to Mme Rachell a letter from London by messenger. The messenger called early in the morning and she received him 'in a wrapper', taking him into a small saloon which 'was rather untidy and with luggage littered about as she was just starting on a journey (to London)'. She read slowly because she was very short-sighted. They were interrupted once by the servant 'on a very poor pretext' and twice by 'Monsieur', whom the messenger reckoned to be about fifty, reckoning Madame at about thirty. She agreed to meet Cumming in London the following Tuesday. The messenger thought her 'straightforward, honest and very intelligent', and was convinced that Monsieur was 'in the know'.

They duly met in London over tea at the Trocadero, where she told him that her sister-in-law's lover required £100 for expenses and £100 for 'the report' (despite, presumably, doing it all 'for love'), which would include answers to any questions put. She had already sent her brother to Berlin to arrange for reporting on the Metz manoeuvres, a requirement that Cumming had mentioned earlier. (Mme Rachell's making of her espionage a family affair was not as uncommon as might be thought.)

Cumming got authority for these payments and then briefed her in the Piccadilly Hotel, having failed to find a private room elsewhere. They arranged to meet again in a month. The following day, after seeing her off on the boat train, he set about finding private rooms in which to meet agents and 'Found a likely set at 12 Park Place, St James's, where they promised to let me have a room at six shillings a time if disengaged'.

The case continued for the next few years. Unfortunately, as with nearly all the Bureau's cases, the product has been destroyed so we have no idea of its utility. It must have declined by the end of 1913 because on 13 December of that year, when Cumming was again in Paris, he called on Mme Rachell, her sister and sister-in-law. 'I told the latter that we could not do any more business unless she could produce better stuff. She asked if we wanted details of the new Tr Howitzer and I said that we did – if the information was genuine.' After that we hear no more of Mme Rachell.

We do, however, hear more of Mlle Depiesse. They arranged to meet in London on 21 July 1910. Cumming and Regnart went to the station at the appointed time, saw two trains come in, left a note at the appointed hotel, returned to the station, went home, received a telegram, returned to the station, waited four hours and finally met the would-be agent. 'The person,' wrote Cumming, whose expectations probably inclined to towards the trim and feminine, 'turns out to be a man of exceptional height and girth.'

He was a Belgian who claimed to have been a detective in the USA and was, in Regnart's words, 'a very big man and much of the farmer type'. He had remembered a 1907 Belgian press story about someone who had answered an advertisement offering a situation to a retired soldier, only to find that it was German intelligence. The man refused to spy and, since the police were not interested (espionage not being illegal in Belgium), he went to the press. Subsequently, Uncle Depiesse had recognised a similar advertisement and entered into correspondence with the Germans. When, in the spring of 1910, he wrote directly to the Germans offering French information, their response was desultory. He then wrote as Mlle Depiesse, offering 'English information', and the response was immediate. He concluded that the Germans already had a source in the French 2me Bureau and offered himself as a double agent to be run against them in order to discover more about this. He showed various letters as evidence.

They nicknamed him 'Delagardiere'. Regnart was keen to employ him in the role he suggested but Cumming, Bethell and MacDonogh were against. Not, it seems, because they didn't trust him but because they saw spying on other spies as a distraction from the main task of getting secret information about German naval and military matters. Cumming was interested in hostile intelligence services but apparently only as what came to be called targets of opportunity; resources had to be husbanded for the main tasks. There seems to have been no thought of turning such cases over to Kell, unless there was a specifically British angle, and no consideration of working them up into serious counter-espionage cases, as was later the practice (particularly with the KGB).

Despite the fact that a great deal of spy fiction and media comment assumes that spies spend most of their time spying on spies, the focus on other information insisted upon by Cumming, MacDonogh and Bethell was a more accurate reflection of what most agents actually did. An agent in a hostile country's treasury, defence ministry or ministerial private office may know more about political and military intentions than an agent in a hostile intelligence service – unless, as was often the case with communist governments, the intelligence service was itself more central to power than other departments.

Disagreements involving Regnart continued. He had previously been the NID's point of contact with the world of secret agents, having been responsible for liaison with the War Office, which did more in that area, and he probably resented what he saw as a superannuated, inexperienced interloper fishing in the same pool independently of him and placed neither over him nor under him. What was worse, the interloper had a charter that effectively took Regnart's work away. Bethell, who was in charge of both, seems not to have issued clear instructions to Regnart concerning Cumming's licence to operate. This may not have been entirely Bethell's fault since Cumming goes to some lengths to protect Regnart, stressing his usefulness and experience. MacDonogh, on the other hand, made no bones about what he would do if Regnart were under his charge: get rid of him. When he complained that Regnart's continued involvement with secret agents was contrary to Foreign Office wishes and intentions, Cumming continued to defend him, then and later: 'I asked him not to do anything about the matter officially . . .

this would weaken me very much as Roy was an enormous help . . . I promised to wean him if possible from the work, so far as "seeing the cases" etc.'

He did not, however, want Regnart appointed his assistant: 'I told him [MacDonogh] that I was half afraid of Roy, who is so strong a character that he would always be riding rough shod over my methods and indeed already does so.' This unabashed confession makes it all the more curious that Cumming defends and employs Regnart later. It might be thought to indicate weakness, though admitting he was 'half afraid' is more a sign of strength of character and, later, he showed no fear in disciplining Regnart. Yet it is hard not to feel that he was wrong to persist with him as long as he did.

A small example of the sort of dissatisfaction that Regnart spread around him in 1910 occured when he was away on a trip to Brussels with M, the retired policeman (Melville), and Cumming discovered yet more examples of his having given to agents addresses of his own for communications that should have been sent to Cumming. The trip, meanwhile, was disappointingly inconclusive but in one respect surprising: Regnart formed a high opinion of Melville and his methods, the tactical subtlety and penetration of which may be gauged by the following: 'He [Regnart] says M is much bolder than he when dealing with strangers. He goes right up to them and peers in their faces.'

Regnart also looms large in protracted discussions during the middle part of the year as to whether Cumming should have a 'Branch Centre' in a European capital. Cumming now favoured Brussels over Copenhagen because of its centrality in the event of war, its ease of access and 'its Club, its English society, and its modern and cheap mode of living'. MacDonogh, on the other hand, now favoured Copenhagen or Amsterdam as being 'less infected with spies'. There was much debate as to whether the man sent should be a serving officer on the active list or someone who had notionally or actually retired and whether he should be answerable directly to MacDonogh or to Cumming.

Cumming was against the use of active list officers both on security and control grounds, and he was against opening in several cities at once, preferring Brussels but being prepared to compromise on Copenhagen or Amsterdam. Meanwhile, 'We must wait until we find the ideal man – one who can settle down in one or other of these places with some real definite object and occupation, and who can and will live there for months doing nothing, until suspicions are lulled.'

It is hard now to appreciate what an advance this was on traditional British military intelligence thinking and practice. For the military, intelligence operations were generally carried out by officers using their wits to avoid capture; the idea of long-term deep cover operations carried out by people who changed identities and occupations and became, say, shopkeepers for years on end was much more the thinking of a dedicated intelligence service.

Cumming's cause was not helped by the fact that Regnart was his suggested candidate, though there were some persuasive arguments in his favour. When agreeing in November 1910 that Cumming could open a station in Copenhagen, the Foreign Office wanted more information about the man selected. Cumming told Lord Errington, private secretary to Sir Arthur Nicholson:

> Roy was possessed of special qualifications . . . spoke several languages, had considerable experience in Departmental work which was very necessary for a successful Agent who had to instruct his men as to what to look for, was independent as to means, did not care for Society, was prepared to sink his identity altogether . . . taking a shop under a trade name and working it as a bona fide business.

On this latter point he stressed Regnart's 'exceptional advantages' and access to expertise, which is probably a reference to his father's chairmanship of Heals, the furniture store. Regnart, of independent means and probably unmarried, perhaps had no pleasure or purpose in life beyond the satisfaction he found in secret, patriotic work. If so, this might account for his emotional reaction to anyone whose appointment appeared to threaten his. It is possible that Cumming divined this and, not wishing to deprive Regnart of his life's commitment or himself of his help, saw an overseas station as the perfect way of getting him out of the kitchen while retaining his services.

Cumming also discussed with Lord Errington the difficulty of finding a suitable office assistant, which was worsened by the need – as perceived by the Foreign Office – for him not to attract attention by being seen too often in the War Office or Admiralty. Cumming's reply shows that he was learning the language of bureaucracy: 'I replied that the way was made easy for me in both cases, but that I would endeavour to limit my private visits as much as possible.'

By the year's end, though, the appointment had still not been made and Cumming filled a couple of diary pages in setting out for his own benefit why he wanted Regnart and why recent references to 'Reggie' in the Trench/Brandon trial should not disqualify him. He concludes:

> I consider Roy a very difficult man to work with, as he plays an independent game and would not submit to control – I shall find him a constant thorn in my side. At the same time I believe he is the best man for the post . . . I would rather risk a certain amount of personal discomfort and worry than have a second rate man as my chief branch agent. The experience [of Trench and Brandon] will have taught us both a good deal.

It might not have pleased him to know that, despite the November 1910 agreement, no overseas Secret Service station would in fact be established until the autumn of 1913.

Nor was the question of an assistant for him in London an idle matter. It seems to have been generally accepted that he needed help and, following an August conversation in which MacDonogh had said he was going on leave for a week or two, Cumming noted rather plaintively: 'I said I did not see my way to get away at all, and he remarked that the work must be rather a tie. I wonder if any of them suspect how many hours a day I have to work? I reckon it 9.30am to 11.30pm, with two hours off, say twelve hours, but I get a very short Saturday afternoon and no Sunday.' No mention of home life, either, but he attempts to console himself: 'It is bound to continue for a year or two, but after that should settle down.'

The reason for Cumming's long hours was that he had to do everything: correspond (often in a foreign language) with existing agents, compose and circulate the reports of the productive ones, negotiate daily with the bureaucracies that controlled him, travel to see agents, receive visiting agents, and devise and mount new operations while running along to interview every scallywag, mountebank, genuine case and volunteer that he or anyone else heard of.

Typical of the sort of unscheduled event that could take over the better part of his day was an encounter on 21 December 1910. He was summoned by MacDonogh who met him outside his office to say that a lady offering information was inside being interviewed by one of his own men. The old Whitehall bogey of wishing to distance the organs of government from spies was in the ascendant that day. 'He wished me,' says Cumming, 'to meet this lady and get into friendly relations with her, but wished me to do this outside the office.'

Cumming, reasonably enough, assumed that anyone coming into the street after such a delicate interview would be 'displeased and alarmed at being accosted by a stranger' but nevertheless summoned a cab and told the man to wait for him.

When the lady appeared she naturally went straight for the waiting cab, at which point Cumming stepped forward, bowed and asked to be allowed to speak. She paled and said, 'I know you, you are "polish".' He assured her he was not a policeman and, as evidence that he was a member of the 'firm' (an early use of an informal term for SIS that survived among older members until late into the century), showed her the pass she had just used.

This wasn't enough. The man who had interviewed her had assured her that she wouldn't be troubled by anyone and she invited Cumming to return to him with her. Cumming had to refuse and so they parted, she to return to her interviewer and Cumming to MacDonogh. He got MacDonogh to send a hurried message to the interviewer to tell her that Cumming was 'a suitable and fit person to associate with her, though from some misunderstanding this was not the sense of the message she received'.

He regained the street just as she did. She insisted she did not want any more business with anyone. He persisted, 'walked along a good way with her and finally persuaded her to come with me to a good Restaurant, and have lunch with me'. He took a private room and they spent the ensuing two hours lunching together.

The comedy of this encounter may obscure the achievement. What came to be known as 'cold approaches' in public places are naturally chancy and demanding of nerve, as well as of the power to instil immediate confidence. Cumming must have been very persuasive and charming. The encounter also perfectly encapsulates the continuing ambiguity of his and the Bureau's position. It made no sense that, the lady having offered her services in official premises, the person whose job was to receive, assess and use those services should be forbidden any appearance of official connection, while at the same time enjoined to prove his official connection in order to have conversation with her.

However, it made for an interesting lunch. The unnamed lady, of Russian, Dutch and English parentage, divorced from her German officer husband, had been – as she saw it – grossly insulted by a royal prince while trying to get her two children into a German army home. This, she said, had engendered in her a desire for revenge and she proposed to pass information learned from her German naval admirer who 'would tell her or give her anything while allowing her to preserve her honour intact, for her children's sake'. She exercised a fascination over her admirer. 'When relating her grievances,' Cumming noted, 'she wept a good deal and I had to beg her to leave me to imagine what she had not already told (there was not much left).'

He found her rather difficult to bring to the point, partly because of her insistence that, although she would not work for money, she must have money for her expenses. While he mentioned plans of ships, secret books and so on, she mentioned 'several luxuries that she thought should appertain to her new dignity'. They discussed her alleged acquaintance with the owner of Krupps and with the Kaiser, as well as the ease with which she could get information on the German '35.5cm gun'. She longed to be invited to the British embassy in Berlin but Cumming told her that 'a person as valuable as she was going to be, must not risk suspicion by appearing to be intimate with a foreign Ambassador'. He promised to introduce her into good society when she eventually settled in Britain 'after satisfying her revenge against Tiaria'. They went over the information she had already given to MacDonogh's officer, and agreed money and communications.

Cumming's conclusion was, as usual, unsentimental: 'I do not think she will be able to get very much information of importance, as I think she relies entirely on her charms for the obtaining of this and these are considerably on the wane.' He was wary that she might be deceiving him and was suspicious of her claiming to have spotted two detectives, one of whom she said had followed her before: 'she would not explain where or when this occurred, and suddenly failed to understand my French, and to forget her own English.' He was also suspicious of her offer to carry a message to Captain Trench 'on account of his approaching execution!' On the other hand, when he made it easy for her to invite him to meet her in Germany she did not rise to the bait and she did not touch his notecase when he was out of the room. 'If she is a trap,' he concluded, 'she is an uncommonly good actress.' She made notes of his requirements in Old Norse.

'I regret to say,' he wrote finally, 'that she was rather insistent upon the "guarantie" which all spies ask for. They explain that it is a guarantee of good faith which is due to them in exchange for the compromising gift of their names and addresses, but my experience teaches me that it means an advance of payment followed by an unbroken silence.' There is no further record of what became of the lady.

Encounters with recruited agents, though generally more productive, could also be time-consuming and problematic. There were a couple of frantic days in London with the resentful and demanding TG, who spent what time he could spare from arguing for more money in trying, vainly, to discover Cumming's real name. The lady agent, A, had incautiously revealed her association with intelligence and had to be chided, while FRS, U, Fred Knight and a new source of German handbooks – Josef, who was seen in Paris – all had the happy knack of crowding on stage together. On 1 July Cumming received a letter from someone called Otto and arranged to send 'one of Sketchley's men' to pick up Otto's material, but Sketchley's man changed his mind after the briefing and argumentatively declined to go. This incident took place in a restaurant which Cumming had chosen so that 'he did not know who I was'. In Cumming's cryptic description we get a glimpse of how short and decisive he could be: 'He began to lecture me and eventually got rather abusive and I had to clear him out.'

On 5 July he learned something of the origins of the long-standing Austrian agent, B. He was told by an official called Foulnest (the status of this name is unclear) that it was he who had first introduced B on the recommendation of the 'Austrian

DMI, a Colonel Hordoiczke, who said that he had done capital work for them.' B had, said Foulnest, 'the faculty of going into a fort and being able to come away and make a sketch of it – put in all the details – with great accuracy.' They agreed, however, that he was lazy and needed keeping up to the mark.

Contacts with Kell are more fully recorded by Cumming than by Kell and seem to have become more relaxed and straightforwardly co-operative than hitherto, though there is one rueful note when Cumming is asked by Kell to question A about a man she recommended earlier: 'I think it is rather curious that he should be reading up the back correspondence of my agents – especially as I was never allowed to have it.' In early August, when Trench and Brandon were setting off, Kell introduced Cumming to Baron Tsarn von Roenne, describing him as a 'First rate engineer, draughtsman, and Tr scholar' who would 'willingly serve us'. The Baron had been employed by 'Zeppelin, Parseval, Krupp and one other Airship constructor', and over lunch at the RAC he agreed to help, subsequently going to Germany on Cumming's behalf. Intelligence on airships was in greater demand than intelligence on aeroplanes and over the next few years Cumming was productive in this area. (Presumably this was a re-introduction to the man Cumming had met in March; whether or not, this latter meeting seems to have been more useful.)

On 15 August K introduced him to another engineer, Henry Dale Long, the agent known as 'L'. It has been said that L was one of Cumming's agents, and it is possible that he worked for both, but he was certainly Kell's man initially and perhaps always mainly. Cumming briefed him on a forthcoming trip to Hamburg, Kiel, Bremen and Danzig. He liked him: 'I found him a smart looking fellow, very likely, alert and I think careful.' He briefed him for nearly two hours and, though he regretted L's ignorance of shipping and naval matters, thought this need not hinder him 'as his duty will be to get men, not facts'. L was to send Cumming a postcard on leaving each place, Cumming to write to him at an address in Brussels. If L found a potential recruit whom he thought Cumming should meet, he was to bring him across the frontier and telegraph. Cumming thought L would do well, partly because he spoke French and German and partly for the somewhat less predictable reason that he was 'something of the same make and shape as myself'.

This represented a considerable advance so far as Cumming was concerned. What he most needed was good agents, though what he was under pressure to get was the sort of information about German shipbuilding and military preparations that was normally provided by officers on trips such as that of Trench's and Brandon's. The Admiralty and the War Office felt they needed this information because German press and security restrictions were much tighter than those in Britain, where many details of warship construction were regularly reported. It would have been far better for Cumming and the Bureau had he been allowed to concentrate during his first few years on building up an agent network, rather than at the same time having to provide intelligence that others were simultaneously producing.

There was a change of DMO, with Major General Ewart handing over to Major General Wilson (the cockney-speaking future CIGS). Cumming's comment on his introduction – 'a smart o [officer] and will no doubt shake us all up' – reveals that he never spoke to the late GOM (Grand Old Man – the DMO) 'except on the three occasions when we met on Committee'. He hopes the new man will 'allow me to approach him occasionally' and takes heart from the fact that Wilson 'listened patiently to my long yarns about the work'. He concluded, with a dangerous lack of bureaucratic self-importance, that 'it does not make much difference so long as matters are generally and accurately reported but it is always easier to deal at first hand when possible'.

Meanwhile, on the 17th day of a very busy August, he 'returned home and went down South for BD [Boom Defence] trials'. How much he was seeing of May and Alastair, we do not know. Were they in Bursledon all the time, or with him in London, or both? Wherever they were, there is no doubt that work and service took priority.

7

Learning Lessons

The year 1911 was very likely busier than 1910 – particularly as it featured the Agadir crisis, easily the most important international event since the Bureau's foundation – but we know little about it because Cumming's diary is blank for all but 6 to 19 January. Kell's diary and other evidence shows that he continued to function and there is no reference when the diary resumes in January 1912 to any reason for the gap. Nor is there any reason to suspect a conspiracy to suppress; the original 1909 to 1914 typescript volume has no pages missing and, anyway, if Cumming regarded anything as too sensitive for his diary, he tended not to put it in rather than tear it out later. A possible explanation is that whoever typed the presumed handwritten volumes that underlie this typescript, started in January 1911 and then inadvertently missed the rest, continuing with January 1912. Or it could simply be that Cumming was too busy to keep his diary and resumed again the following year without feeling any need to explain himself to himself.

The period 6 to 19 January 1911 does, however, contain one or two colourful encounters, and one of significance. There was an offer of services from a Mr Canelly, who also used the name Joye. A former gunner in the Royal Horse Artillery who had been invalided out after the Boer War, he was 'a short man of about 27 years of age, clean shaved, fair hair, stoutish, of decent appearance, but rather shifty looking about the mouth and eyes'.

With disarming candour, he advised Cumming not to take up his regimental references, as 'his antecedents would not bear looking into very closely ... he had done nothing disgraceful but his character was not very good'.

Immediately after this, Cumming hurried off to be made up for his next encounter, a hotel meeting with a Major H.L.B. The major had brown eyes and hair, a large nose, a shifty look and was 'rather showily dressed, with an enormous pearl pin'. He later claimed to have a tie-pin camera with which he had photographed Bethell during a recent interview. His nationality was difficult to place and, despite having been brought up at the Vickers works in Erith, Kent, he claimed to speak many languages and always to travel on the continent as a Spaniard. Among his other claims were organising colonial regiments in Nigeria, being chief of police and artillery in Bolivia, receiving various papal and Italian war medals, blackmailing a German officer into showing him over Erhardts (a prime target of Cumming's) and having a Peruvian Indian ring containing a poison that would kill in three seconds. He also named a number of men whom he claimed were 'the smartest Agents in the German [Secret] Service' in Britain – one of whom could be handily identified by his four rows of teeth – and said that for the last three years he had worked for the French service until they 'broke their contract by asking him to work against England'.

Cumming concluded: 'He has probably been kicked out of the French service for some lapse, and now wishes to get another job. He is no doubt a blackguard, but is probably a clever one, and I should like to get something out of him. All my staff are blackguards – but they are incapable ones, and a man with a little ingenuity and brains would be a change, even if not an agreeable one.' He took him on for a trial trip to Essen to get details of a 14-inch gun with expenses in advance and payment by results. 'We could', Cumming suggested to him, 'share the profits.'

This was not illicit private enterprise. Because of the restrictions under which he had to operate, Cumming had presented himself to the major as an 'aspirant' for the NID who was forced to 'recommend myself by procuring valuable information'. He had to assure him that 'our authorities never had anything to do with SS work at all, and that there were strict orders that no offers of any such services were ever accepted'. However, the juniors were obliged to get information and so disobeyed orders, being prepared to pay generously for it since the younger men (Cumming had presumably disguised himself to look younger, a common professional vice) were mostly very well off.

Thus, both parties to this encounter were mouthing equal implausibilities, the one because he claimed to have something to sell and almost certainly didn't, the other because he claimed not to have authority to buy and certainly did. Such encounters doubtless contributed to the romantic but misleading portrayal of espionage as a world of mirrors, uncertainties, shifting sands, which itself is made a metaphor for the human condition. The problem was only partly the fact that the SSB was obliged to act as if it were nothing to do with the government that had established it, a ruse that fooled no one. The other part of the problem was that Cumming was obliged to interview and some-times use virtually every mountebank who offered because he was not allowed to operate more directly, and in particular still forbidden the one group who could most easily have pointed him towards potential agents with real access and real motivation, the Foreign Office overseas consular officers.

He disguised himself again on 12 January, going to Clarksons to be made up in a manner that was 'far more satisfactory – the disguise being perfect, and its existence not being noticeable even in a good light'. He had himself photographed so that the dis-guise could be repeated, then went off to meet the first of his encounters that day, a man called Ironmould. This man had already tried in vain to identify Cumming, whom he apparently already knew as Captain Currey (Cumming often used his own initials for aliases and seems to have yielded to the temptation to promote himself when under alias). Ironmould identified alleged

Austrian and Russian Secret Service personnel as well as a couple of British criminals he said were involved in espionage, Braywich Power (sometimes known as Wyndham) and William Guy Delaforce – 'The first is a Jew money-lender, and the latter is an ex-Scotland Yard Detective who was discharged for blackmailing women.' He volunteered to get plans of harbours and fortifications, with Cumming saying he would have to advance any money out of his own pocket and share the profits, then noting for his diary: 'I really don't think he could appreciate any arrangement that had not some suspicion of fraud about it.'

Following this, Cumming removed his disguise and went swiftly to meet a Professor Gerothwohl at one of the St James's rooms he had taken. Like most of Cumming's descriptions, that of the professor is brief and direct, with enough of the physical to convey appearance and enough observation of manner to suggest something of character: 'He is a thick set strongly built man of 30 years of age (looks older). About five foot nine, dark, brown eyes, dark hair, fresh complexion, rather puffy cheeks, a fidgety manner and an excess of self confidence. His arms are very hairy and look muscular – he says he is a good wrestler.' He was fluent in French and German, had friends in Brussels who might introduce him to people of influence, disliked his present employment and was prepared to drop a hundred a year to work for Cumming, for £500. The problem was, he had nothing to offer. Cumming thought his 'education and gentlemanly instincts' made him more valuable than most and that his occupation as 'a writer of some repute' would act as useful cover, but for what? 'When our new schemes are complete we may find a berth for him.'

The following day Kell's diary reads: '"C" gave me the names of five supposed SS agents who are said by "a Colonel" Burnstein to be over here. "C" was only able to give me the addresses of one of them. I have told "M" to investigate this one.'

Meanwhile, Cumming was embarked on yet another encounter, this time appearing as Mr Morris Carter opposite a quarry he named Mr Hiccough. Despite this, the encounter was to prove of rather greater significance than the others.

On 14 December 1911, page 8, column 4 of *The Times* carried two reports, the shorter headed 'A Bishop Bitten by His Dog' and the longer, 'The Espionage Trial in Leipzig'. This latter recalls the imprisonment of five people who spied for the variously named English Espionage Bureau or English Intelligence Service. First to be arrested was a ship dealer called Max Schultz, who was picked up in Hamburg in March. *The Times* reports that the evidence against the others was based largely on incriminating statements made by Schultz, who, on being told during his arrest that he was unlucky, was alleged to have said, 'Oh no, it was lucky, because if I had not been arrested I should have done a great deal more, and I should not have got out of Germany in less than 20 years.' He was sentenced to seven.

The others comprised a man called von Maack (three years), a man called Wulff (two years), a woman called Frau Eckermann (three years) and Engineer Hipsich (twelve years). Von Maack and Wulff were both recruited by Schultz in 1910, the latter being invited to correspond with 'English friends interested in naval matters'. He had worked in the Bremen shipyard for six years, installing and testing submarine bells for submarines and warships. When he visited England in December 1910 he passed on information on warship engines and both he and von Maack recommended Engineer Hipsich for recruitment. In March 1911 he was tasked to report on the battleship *Ernst Odin*, then building at Kiel. Frau Eckermann was Wulff's and Hipsich's landlady and 'had perfect knowledge of what Schultz was doing'. She had in fact helped procure them for him.

Hipsich was the most severely punished because he was deemed to have been motivated solely by gain. An Austrian by birth, he had worked for twelve years at the Weser yard and had been naturalised in 1909 after the German Admiralty had forbidden the employment of foreigners. He had supplied plans of battleships and other materials to 'the surprise and unconcealed pleasure' of the Englishmen who had paid an advance of £20 and a retainer of £2 a week (his main payment was presumably by result).

The Times report was far from sensational and the reporter's comment that 'the connection between the prisoners and any official quarters in England seems to have been established only by insinuation' may have reflected a degree of official briefing. Shultz, however, had a longer espionage history than was apparent in the report of the trial.[1] In fact, for the short time it lasted, this affair seems to have been a success.

Schultz was a Southampton shipbroker who dealt in yachts and had extensive contacts in private dockyards in Germany. He had sent information to the Admiralty in 1909 and by 1910 was regularly employed as a spy. By whom is, as usual, not entirely clear. He might have been reporting to both the NID and Cumming, or first one then the other. He was not in January 1911 a regularly paid agent of Cumming's, though they certainly knew each other and when Cumming refers to him on 12 January he does so familiarly. The context was 'Captain Currey's' interview with Ironmould, when the latter said that he had found out from 'Max S' everything about Cumming that Schultz knew. This evidently did not include Captain Currey's real name, but it did include a silly piece of invention: 'S was mad enough to tell I [Ironmould] that Captain C carried about a warrant for his arrest!'

Schultz reappears more substantially the following day, 13 January, arranging for Cumming's encounter with the mysterious Mr Hiccough who, it appears, was Engineer Hipsich. Cumming begins: 'An elaborate scheme has been arranged in order to attract a certain Mr Hiccough, whose acquaintance had been made by Max S when abroad.' Hipsich was apparently 'super-interested' in aeroplanes and had designed one that he thought would be revolutionary. Schultz had told him of a Mr GW who might be interested in developing the design, if recommended by his friend, Mr Maurice Carter, in which case Hipsich would be handsomely rewarded. However, when Mr GW was introduced he considered the design too impracticable; Hipsich was disappointed and in order to cheer him he was taken to the Aero Club where 'Claud's manager' arranged for some of the machines at Hendon to be flown especially for him. Such was his delight that – in the words of Cumming's third-person account in the diary – 'he threw his arms around Max's neck and kissed him loudly on both cheeks – he was quite prepared to do the same to Mr Maurice, but he eluded his approaches.' In the taxi on the way home he asked Max what he could do to repay such hospitality and was told that a good return would be to give Mr Maurice some information. Before he and Mr Maurice parted that night they had settled on a salary of £2 a week plus 'considerably larger sums' for any original plans or documents.

The following morning Hipsich answered questions in number 12 Park Place, St James's. It was immediately apparent to Cumming that 'his stock of useful knowledge was very much greater than we had anticipated'. Regnart was sent for and came with plans and data that enabled them to ask more detailed questions. The debrief lasted four hours and Hipsich passed 'a very considerable amount of information that I believe to be extremely valuable ... more than we have collected during the previous year from all the other agents put together ... we have ... for the first time ... more than value for money'. Cumming proposed to pay him three months' salary in advance and to ask for a permanent salary for Max, 'who has well earned it'.

Hipsich occupied a good position in his profession and was well paid; Cumming accounted for his willingness to spy by his having 'got into the hands of some unscrupulous woman, who no doubt is drawing him for money'. No doubt the woman was Frau Eckermann whom, to everyone's surprise, Hipsich had brought with him, which meant that the two of them had to be looked after and catered for the whole time, along with Schultz. Cumming ended the day by observing that he had not had time to attend to correspondence and would have to 'abandon going down to my ships tomorrow'.

The next day he took Hipsich, and presumably Frau Eckermann, to the flying ground at Hendon again, driving there in
Mr GW's car and inspecting the London-to-Manchester Farman
biplane and a Gordon-Bennett 100 h.p. Bleriot. Hipsich declined
the driver's offer of a trip in the biplane but Cumming, typically,
'availed myself of it'. Hipsich spent so much time enthusiastically
examining the machine that their host, GW, missed several
appointments before driving the party home.

This ingenious exploit was the type of many agent recruit-
ments made by intelligence services during decades to come.
Schultz was what would be termed an access agent, someone
whose primary use was not what he knew but whom. The access
agent 'talent spots' an individual who has the right information
and the possible motivation to spy. Seemingly innocent introduc-
tions are arranged, friends of friends introduced, the potential
agent is given a taste of whatever it is he seeks and is led to feel
under some obligation. If all goes well, when the recruitment
'pitch' is made there is hardly any need for it; as in this case, he
virtually recruits himself.

Cumming's concluding comment on the affair was shrewd
and perceptively foreboding. For once, he was confident that he
was not dealing with a rogue and time-waster and his doubts
were not about the agent himself. But doubts he had, from which
it is clear that his many hours spent with tie-pin camera mer-
chants and wrestling professors were not in vain:

The difficulty with Mr H will be the transmission of his
documents and keeping his work secret. I shall have to
get an agent of some kind abroad, and make arrangements to call for his stuff, or receive it if posted to some
Belgian or Dutch town. As for keeping him clear of the
woman, his friends Wulff and Maack, and Max S, this
will be almost impossible and their knowledge will
eventually wreck the scheme. I can control Max S, to a

certain extent, but no one can control the woman or her
partner Wulff. At first her demands will stimulate H, but
as she becomes more greedy, he will find himself hard
put to keep pace with them and will either quarrel with
her or get caught trying to do too much.

There must have been more going on beneath Frau Eckermann's
roof than is evident from the trial report.

The diary's final entry for 1911 concerns the 'termination' of
TG (i.e. ceasing relations with, not killing). Terminating agents
can be almost as difficult as finding them. There was a series
of arguments, misunderstandings and missed meetings over the
period 17–19 January, with Cumming referring exasperatedly to
TG as 'this man'. TG claimed that his life had been 'spoiliated',
continued trying to identify Cumming and demanded £2,500.
Cumming offered him '£15 for the letters', £5 for travelling
expenses and £5 for the 'work' that TG was to undertake. Bizar-
rely, TG threatened to complain to his embassy and sue for
damages, but Cumming was unyielding.

The following day, TG complained to 'Cumming's
employers', which he had promised not to do. After further
negotiations and missed meetings, they agreed £30 for the
'papers' – presumably letters either from Cumming, the War
Office or the NID – and then it turned out that TG had
deposited them in his country's consulate. This must have been
the last place most spies would consider depositing their incriminating documents; and in that respect, therefore, the best. He
and Cumming were to pick them up together but Cumming
arrived to find that TG had just left. As a result, Cumming

had a rather awkward quart d'heure there as the Consul
General requested me to remain and explain my
position . . . I had taken off my hat as a mark of respect,
but his attitude was not very pleasant, and upon one of

his clerks shutting the door in a somewhat significant
way, I replaced my hat and made as though to go out.
This they evidently did not mean to allow, and I
remained to discuss the matter without appearing to
notice that I was in any way detained.

It could indeed have been extremely awkward; the consulate was
theoretically foreign territory, Cumming a British official there
under false pretences in an espionage relationship with a national
of that country. However, he talked his way out of it amicably
enough and later, after a 'final and soul stirring struggle' with
TG, secured the incriminating letters for £22 and returned to
TG his own. He gave the letters to MacDonogh, which suggests
that TG was originally a War Office source, and TG walked out
of history with the threat that he had photographs of everyone. 'I
think', commented Cumming, 'this is his usual bluff.'

Although this marks the end of the diary for 1911, it was not,
unfortunately, the end of the spasm of arrests. Bertrand Stewart,
an officer of the Territorial Army's West Kent Yeomanry, was
arrested in Bremen on 2 August and charged with espionage. As
usual, it is not clear how Stewart, a wealthy Old Etonian lawyer
and member of seven clubs, came to be involved, nor exactly what
Cumming's role was, but the consensus among such writers as
Christopher Andrew and Nicholas Hiley is that his involvement
began at the time of the Agadir crisis in July 1911. It is hard, at
this distance, to appreciate fully the drama of this diplomatic con-
vulsion and its role in hardening attitudes. During the height of the
crisis, *The Times* reported on 21 July that the German High Seas
Fleet had left port and was somewhere in the North Sea. No one
knew where and the Foreign Secretary, according to Hiley, was
alarmed that the British fleet 'might be attacked at any moment'.
On 26 July MacDonogh was asked to help find it and went to see
the DMO, Major General Wilson, who noted in his diary: 'Mac-
Donogh came to see me this evening and told me that our Admir-

alty had lost the German Fleet and have asked us to find them. MacDonogh sent Stewart off to Brussels to see L. And send him round the German Ports. The whole thing is like a Pantomime.'

This makes the dispatch of Stewart sound like one of a pattern of regular deployments rather than a one-off, but another version, a 1947 memoir by Kell's assistant, Captain Drake (in the Sigismund Payne Best papers at the Imperial War Museum) has it that Stewart was an intelligence enthusiast who volunteered his services to the War Office with the idea that he should be deployed as a double agent to discover German objectives. Drake recalls that 'poor old C found that willy-nilly he had Stewart thrust upon him with orders to "let him have a run" . . . No objection on C's part had any effect and after being warned by C that he was running his head into a noose Stewart departed jubilantly for Holland.' Drake says he was told this by Cumming himself and gives details of Stewart's arrest in a public lavatory with a code-book planted upon him by a real double agent. The double agent concerned was a man called Rué, who had been recruited by Edmonds in 1907 and who, allegedly because he was poorly paid, worked for the Germans as well. (According to Hector Bywater, Frederick Rue was a Belgian born in 1861 who had a record for fraud, bankruptcy and robbery with violence; more than most he seems to have merited Cumming's 'rascal' verdict.) The German fleet, meanwhile, had actually been located on 23 July.

Kirsteen Tait, a descendant of Stewart's who is researching a book on intelligence operations of the period, says that Stewart knew Le Queux (whose ideas his own resembled all too closely) and believes that if Wilson's account is right, he must have exceeded his brief and stayed on after the German fleet was found. It is also, she points out, odd that he was never charged with the more serious offence of obtaining the (albeit planted) code-book, but only with the lesser offence of asking questions.

A little extra light is thrown on the case by a typed letter from Bethell to Cumming dated 21 August 1911. 'S' refers to Stewart, 'K' to Kell and 'Max' to Schultz, while 'U' appears to refer to Rué. 'U' was, of course, one of the unsatisfactory agents whom Cumming had inherited in 1909 and who seemed to have dropped out of the picture. His reported loss of job due to 'shady dealings' would, it was hoped, lead to an improvement in his agent performance – as it did, for the Germans.

Clostessey House
Nr Norwich

21.8.11

My Dear Cumming,
Thanks for your letter. I am afraid S has made an awful ass of himself and it is very questionable whether U has not been a decoy all through. Anyway our organisation must be pretty well through over there by now and your connection with it as well. However I do not think they can get anything against Brandon and Trench as you never had any dealings with them. It is annoying but we must expect drawbacks such as these in this kind of business. The account of the arrest of S does not agree with what Tyrell told me – he said that the FO had heard it from the Consul, that S was arrested in bed at 1am. I hope he will get off as you say is considered possible. Personally I don't think they will let him go very easily – it is not difficult to rake up evidence over there! S has a lot to explain away in being under an assumed name and connected with U.

Max is past praying for I should say he has helped very materially to get himself a long sentence – he must be mad I think.

I see K has moved at last at Plymouth. I believe we have a clear case and I hope it will not fall through for sentimental and false motives like the last case did. K has backed it up very well and I hope for his sake the man will be convicted.

Come down here whenever you like. I can put you up and we can talk better after dinner than in a hurried manner between trains. I should be in town for a meeting of CID on Wednesday but I don't expect I shall have time to see you but you might look in to the Admiralty about 2 pm and if I can we will lunch together.

Yours sincerely,
BETHELL

The Times reported Stewart's trial on 1, 2, 5 and 7 February 1912, after which he was sent to serve his sentence in the same fortress as Trench.

The alarms set off by the Agadir crisis continued into the autumn of 1911 as German manoeuvres and other measures, as well as various coincidences, fuelled suspicions of imminent invasion. In September, MacDonogh told the Foreign Office that all German sailors were being recalled from leave, and Kell reported that the Germans were buying and storing all the wheat they could get. British consuls in Germany reported the call-up of naval reserves and the gathering and conversion of steamers to transports, while German manoeuvres along the Belgian and French frontiers further heightened tension. By the end of September, a surprise attack across the Belgian frontier seemed more than ever likely.

The fact that it did not happen does not mean that the reporting, as much overt as covert, was wrong. Nicholas Hiley is persuasive when he argues that the intelligence networks were so geared to reporting preparations for attack that this combined with the inherent Germanophobia of the agents to produce a false impression of imminence, so that the Secret Service did not so much report accurate intelligence as reinforce prejudice. But this is only half the story. We do not actually know what the great majority of Admiralty, War Office and SSB reports said, because we do not have them. Even if they did reinforce prejudice, the prejudice was, in essence, accurate – Germany did have hostile intentions and did later invade Belgium. The Secret Service was prevented from finding out what the government most needed to know – the intentions of the German leadership – by the fact that political reporting remained the preserve of the

Foreign Office. All that agents and overt observers could do was to report on what the Germans were actually doing – calling up reserves, moving troops and so on – while German intentions had to remain a matter of inference. No doubt many of those involved in intelligence believed wrongly that an act of war was in preparation; the fact that it did not happen, however, does not mean that their reporting was wrong, but their assessment; also, the fact that neither the British nor the French governments over-reacted to the German autumn manoeuvres suggests that at some level there was accurate assessment.

The blank in the 1911 diary means we know little of the extent to which Cumming was involved. The evidence from Kell's diary is that, for Cumming, it was very much business as usual for the rest of the year. Kell was much taken up during the first few months of the year with the possible future of 'L' in Brussels (which indicates that L was not there already, except as a visitor, and confirms that he was Kell's man, not Cumming's), and on 24 February he passed Cumming information about battleships and torpedoes reported by Baron von Roenne. Later in the spring Kell received regular reporting from his new officer assistant, Ohlson, who began systematically debriefing the skippers of merchant ships plying between Britain and the Continent, passing relevant information to Cumming. In May, Kell asked Cumming to let him know the regulations for the employment of foreigners and naturalised subjects in Germany and at the end of June Ohlson reported Cumming's complaint thus his (Ohlson's) activities were encroaching upon Cumming's territory. The matter was settled amicably with MacDonogh agreeing 'Ohlson should report through Cumming to the Admiralty, with reference being made to the source'. In his round-up of the year, Kell records the arrest and conviction of Heinrich Grosse, a German spy in Portsmouth. It could not have been much consolation to Cumming, who had lost his best source, but it was doubtless gratifying to his masters, and may have made the political climate for overseas operations easier.

8

FRENCH LIAISON

The diary for 1912 is almost as short as that for 1911, though there is slightly more meat to it.

It begins in January with a long rigmarole by a man who claimed to have been approached by the Germans to spy on the British. His story sounded unlikely and Cumming had his doubts, but nevertheless treated it with a certain cautious credulity which was unfortunately enhanced by an accidental encounter with the First Sea Lord who decreed that it should be followed up. Luckily perhaps, we hear no more of the case.

The tall stories swallowed by intelligence services, often by the very people deemed most sceptical, deserve a volume of their own. When the occasional intelligence fraudster succeeds it is usually because the intelligence service is under pressure to produce on something it knows little about and the new source is assessed by people who are not expert on the subject he offers. Typically, the larger and vaguer the claim the harder it is to verify, but most fraudsters fall down on questions about specific details. Thus, the claim that 'a Russian submariner told me in a café in Minsk that the High Command is considering sending them to sea with dummy nuclear missile war heads on grounds of cost' may be virtually impossible to verify, but details of the circumstances of the conversation – date and time, the colour of the tables, what was drunk, how much it cost, who served them, who else was there, how many were at the bus stop, physical and biographical details of the submariner – are more likely to reveal contradictions, vagueness and checkable facts. There have been determined hoaxers on nuclear missile technology who got the physics right but the colours of buses on the nuclear base wrong.

Another reason for credulity may be in the psychology of professions such as intelligence or journalism that live by purveying information. Both are occasionally vulnerable to stories they have long wished were true. There is something, too, in the psychology of certain individuals that leads them to devote a great deal of time and ingenuity to seeking involvement with an intelligence service, as if their lives were thereby lent a greater and more vivid reality. It is not always a question of money.

The diary resumes on 8 March 1912, with Cumming going to Paris to begin a significant new relationship: liaison with the French intelligence service. There are indications that this was his long-cherished ambition and, like most routes through bureaucracies that stray outside the 'usual channels', it was probably achieved only after a great deal of persuasion. In Paris he met a Captain Linard and a Captain Zopff and received the regrets of their chief, Colonel Dupont, who promised to meet him the following day. Linard's duties were 'confined to information procured in peacetime', while Zopff's task was 'organising the SS in time of war and the preliminary period of "tension politique"'.

Linard asked Cumming and his companion, referred to as 'F', if they had any letter to prove their identities. Naturally, they did not; they were not supposed to exist. In Whitehall's legalistic eyes, a letter might have compromised Cumming's deniability more conclusively than his physical presence could ever have done. Cumming explained that as the visit had been arranged via the French military attaché he assumed that Linard had been advised of their arrival. He might, but did not, have added that Linard's presence might also have suggested this was the case. Instead, he 'told him enough of our business to show that we were the persons indicated' and then, observing that Zopff evidently thought Linard over-cautious, tactfully 'took his [Linard's] side and commended his attitude, and promised to try to get some form of identifying introduction before I presented myself to his Chief next day'.

Thus, on this rather comical and uncertain note, began SIS's first and most enduring foreign liaison relationship, one that was to prove a genuinely close, mutually beneficial and understanding link. It was, for Cumming, a very important step forward.

They discussed the structure and organisation of the French service, keeping this first meeting to 'subjects that were not of the first importance as regards secrecy'. However, they did frankly discuss 'several persons who had served us both as agents' and the French retailed some of their painful experiences with swindlers, as a result of which their rule was not to buy goods unseen. With regard to means of communication during the period of *tension politique*', Cumming thought them 'much impressed with our idea of a mobile wireless station, but doubted if the Belgians would allow anything of the kind in their country, as savouring of partisanship'.

They professed ignorance of a plan, which Cumming knew they had, to pass scouts through the advancing enemy lines to report from the rear, but did say that their favourite means of communication was carrier pigeon 'which they have used to a large extent'. Cumming thought it would be difficult for the British to do the same because British 'fanciers' would either have to settle abroad, where they would be spotted, or the pigeons would have to fly home to England, which would be impractical. (In fact, he was wrong: the British made extensive and successful use of pigeons during the war.)

Cumming told them that he 'could not undertake to plant agents in Tiaria, and was not inclined to trust the Trs'. The French advised him to do what they did and use people from third countries – Norwegians, Swiss and so on – but 'they did not rise to the suggestion that they should find these men for us, as they evidently have plenty of employment for all they can get'. The meeting resulted in an agreed note which Cumming summarised as: '(1) We must each know officially what the British force would be expected to do – where it would land and in what district it would act – and (2) They would like their Chief and ours to meet us, and tell us when all together, in what way and in which district we can work "ensemble" and what amount of confidence each side may repose in the other.'

It is interesting to note here that the certainty of BEF deployment in a war which was taken for granted is equalled by ignorance as to what it would do. The notion that they might work 'ensemble' is not as unlikely as it might seem. Although in intelligence co-operation during the war the two nations tended to division of labour rather than sharing (though they shared product), the necessary groundwork of trust and the habit of co-operation were begun at this meeting.

With regards to agents they ran in common, Cumming was shown 'dossiers of HCJ, Bernstein, and Rué'. The first had reported to the French on his meeting with Cumming 'and had evidently told them the truth all through, and his having stated that I had allowed him to give them his reports to me, had evidently had a good effect'. He was slightly worried, however, to find that HCJ's reporting on armed German merchantmen was accepted by the French 'principally because he had told them that I had done so – which I pointed out was somewhat simple on their part'.

Bernstein, who was possibly also in touch with the Germans, was as much a mystery to the French as to Cumming but much more was known about Rué, the betrayer of Bertrand Stewart. The French, too, had employed him for a long time and reckoned his best report (its accuracy confirmed from other sources) was that on Borkum, which he had made originally for Cumming. They also had a copy of another report on the German schooner *Helena* (a vessel which features in Kell's diary as being sought during the summer of 1911), as a result of which they had 'very nearly caught her engaged in espionage work on the French coast, but had missed her owing to the clumsiness of their contra-espionage department (which he described to me as being very inefficient)'. What they did not know about Rué, until Cumming told them, was that he was also a German agent.

Conversation appears to have been in French throughout but the only problem Cumming mentions was keeping to the subject when everyone talked at once. One subject that wouldn't go away, though, was the question of evidence of his identity:

> Before leaving the two Captains I promised to get some evidence of identity, and they suggested that I should go to the Embassy (which was of course not possible). They cannot understand our secrecy as to personality. They themselves are well known to all their comrades and they are officially recognised. It would only have accentuated their doubts if I told them that I could not be recognised by our Embassy.

French bafflement was understandable. Cumming eventually rang London and asked for a letter to be sent.

There were two further meetings the next day, for the first of which they were joined by Colonel Dupont and a wireless expert. The Colonel received them cordially, saying he had heard from the French military attaché as to Cumming's and F's identity (F was almost certainly an official of the military attaché's department called Fairy). Although the atmosphere remained cordial, it became clear that the closer they got to the practicalities of co-operation, the more difficulties there were:

> we were not sufficiently equipped with the necessary knowledge to be able to confer with him to any useful purpose. I could not admit my ignorance of our plans, so I told him that I had not received authority to talk about

things . . . he thought it would be much better for both parties if the two Generals – ours and his – could meet together and tell us how far we could confide in each other, and particularly what districts we should regard as mutual ground.

The French were frank and friendly but 'a little nervous about telling to strangers of another nation the matters they had kept secret for so long. He [Colonel Dupont] was however very strong indeed as to the vital necessity of our meeting each other and deciding now at once upon a plan of concerted action to take when the crisis comes.' Contrary to what Cumming had thought, the French had been favourably disposed to a 'personal rapprochement' for some time.

What came to be known as the need-to-know principle is both a necessary and admirable practice and a problem. It was right to keep knowledge of BEF deployment plans to as few as possible, and those few did not include Cumming; but if at the same time he was authorised to prepare wartime co-operation with his French equivalent, then it was clearly necessary for him to be as well informed of British thinking as they apparently were of French. That he was not was a consequence of his anomalous position within the British bureaucracy.

Nevertheless, he seems to have kept his end up, at least when it came to exchanging views on the likely thrust of the expected German invasion:

they shared our view that the TRs would keep to the South of the Meuse, in their march across the Belgian frontier, yet they were by no means sure that this would be the case, and they wished us to extend our (supposed) organisation farther to the northward than we had it at present. He suggested the district between Liège, Aachen, Koln up to Gladbach, and hoped that we would not with-

draw any of our men from the Belgian frontier but
would extend our system as suggested.

The French reservations were, of course, to be bloodily vindicated by the events of 1914.

When Cumming again regretted that he could not 'place
agents in Tiaria', adding that the difficulty was in finding men
who could pass as German or settle in the country without
suspicion, Colonel Dupont charitably 'quite understood this and
said that they had the same difficulty but had forty years of
experience to help them'. The French had, of course, been anxiously spying on the Germans ever since the Franco–Russian war.

Cumming had a wireless car under development and spoke
about it again. When the French expert queried whether it really
could have the 250-mile range Cumming claimed, he 'assured
him that we had tried it with complete success and promised to
get the power, height of aerial etc. for him'. Dupont doubted
that the Belgians would permit its deployment but one of the
captains thought it might be managed if car and equipment were
purchased through a Belgian government official who was an
agent of theirs. Cumming doubted the 'soundness' of this idea,
but kept his reservations to himself. Dupont had suggested Méz-
ières as a 'centre for information', preferring it to Cumming's
suggestion of Givet, and proposed that Cumming should post a
liaison officer to him and another in Brussels (not the military
attaché) who would 'receive and forward all information from
the scouts' and keep in close touch with the French representative.

When they met again in the afternoon, Dupont had changed
from his uniform into civilian clothes and they were joined by
a Captain de Fregete Somborn who looked after naval matters.
He and Linard spoke some English, Dupont and Zopff none.
Somborn thought they should be 'introduced and commended
to each other by our respective Chiefs before we could frankly

compare notes', and credited Cumming's organisation with having produced very good naval information and having 'given the TRs an infinite amount of trouble during the last two years'. (This was no doubt a welcome compliment from a quarter Cummings had every reason to respect, and it suggests that some sort of intelligence exchange was already in existence.) The Germans, meanwhile, had caught 'a very large number of Frenchmen, but none that were of any importance'. One had been caught bringing information out of Krupps, on which the French were largely ignorant. They discussed French naval requirements and the French admitted 'slight and unimportant' dealings with three men – Glauss, Jakob and Reich – whom Cumming seems also to have been in touch with. They asked him to check on a man called Beckett, who had given his address as 54 Shaftesbury Avenue (which turned out on checking to be a Kelly's Library) and had offered them alleged plans of Bremerhaven.

It appears from this that the French experienced the same problems as Cumming with unreliable agents and German restrictive security. The differences were the scale and duration of their operation and their own more settled and sensible place within the French bureaucracy. What was evident at the start of the relationship, and thereafter came to characterise it, was what might be called mature goodwill. This enabled it to survive changes and vicissitudes without seriously undermining the acknowledged identity of interest. Infidelities were mutual, neither side was genuinely shockable and the importance of remaining on terms was always overriding.

Following this Paris visit, there is a gap in Cumming's diary until 9 December 1912, when he records a meeting with Kell, Regnart and Ohlson to discuss Kell's intrusive scheme for the latter. This, as we have seen, was to get the captains of merchantmen to collect information from foreign ports, send it to Ohlson, who would send it to Cumming, who would send it on stating that it came from Ohlson. Kell wanted a code so that urgent information could be wired and Cumming promised to 'get out a code for him by next April'. Although he never gives details, codes were evidently something that he took very seriously (devising them probably appealed to him) and there are frequent references to his working on them. Appropriate to this case, he thought, would be a 'similar style of code to my own but with alterable numbers, so that the loss of it by one agent will not necessarily compromise the whole edition'. No examples survive.

His main concern, however, was what it had been from the first: that this scheme trespassed on his territory. Kell admitted this but 'assured me that he had no intention either now or in the future of attempting to usurp my duties'. Cumming agreed to help Ohlson with his organisation, which he saw as supplementary to 'my own scheme of warrant officer travellers', and admitted to himself that until he had permanent agents in all the ports of interest, Ohlson's men were likely to be more valuable than the occasional and casual reports that he currently received. Nevertheless, he continued to find it 'a little disquieting that K should insert the thin end of the wedge in my dept., as with his large staff and the assistance he gets from our mutual superiors, he would be a formidable rival'. There was nothing paranoiac about Cumming's fear of absorption, firstly by Kell, then for a period by the Admiralty and later, much more seriously, by the War Office. It hung over his service throughout his career and probably played a greater part in his thinking and bureaucratic actions than we can now imagine.

The following day, 10 December, he interviewed a Mr O. Ruff, a 'short commonplace looking man of German birth' of whom he expected little but agreed to give him a trial by sending him off to Germany with some fairly basic tasking. He also referred to a reporting scheme he had organised, apparently unofficially, among Foreign Office consuls. The game had been inadvertently given away by one of them, called Erskine, and Cumming had been ordered to stop it. He did, but continued to see Erskine and get oral advice on such matters as the locations of Baltic wireless stations. For all his deference to his superiors and respect for orders, Cumming was badger-ish in his persistence.

9

PREPARATION FOR WAR

The year 1913 saw developments in the cases of the three imprisoned officers, Trench, Brandon and Stewart. In May, Kaiser Wilhelm II's daughter, Victoria Louise, married Prince Ernest Augustus, Duke of Cumberland. King George V and Queen Mary attended the Berlin wedding, a visit that was not, according to the Royal Archives, a state occasion but merely 'a private family affair' during which the King was unaccompanied by government ministers. Thus it was that the British government – perhaps also the German – was taken by surprise by the Kaiser's sudden release of the three officers.

Trench and Stewart were released from Glatz, a fortress prison housing Germans convicted of duelling, and Brandon from Konigstein. The first two returned to London by train, Stewart being met at the station by his family and his brother officers from the West Kent Yeomanry who gave him a tumultuous reception and conveyed him away in a car, while Trench slipped off unnoticed. Brandon returned in more leisurely fashion, via Paris.

According to Trench's account, there then began an uneasy period of negotiation with the Admiralty concerning responsibility for their trip, their arrests and everybody's costs, from which Captain Jackson, who had replaced Bethell as DNI, does not emerge well. Cumming does not feature in Trench's account and there is only one reference to the affair in his diary at this period.

On 27 June he was summoned to a meeting in Sir Grahame Greene's room with Jackson, Bethell and Regnart:

> Only a few questions were put to me by GG and they were such as I could answer without hesitation and tended to show that I had very little to do with the matter. GG asked me in reference to my telling him that Col. E [Edmonds presumably] had said that a certain route was a good one and cost about £28 for each traveller, 'Then I suppose it was that which caused you to suggest to Roy that you should send these two persons?' I saw through this little trap (which was very clumsily put) and replied that I could not admit that I suggested any such thing to Roy or anyone else. The proceedings lasted only a short time and I heard nothing of what had gone before me.

Disputes apart, the two men resumed their marine and naval careers, and flourished. During the First World War Trench served partly at sea and partly as an interrogator, while Brandon commanded three ships and ended the war as assistant to the DNI. He retired as a captain in 1927, his last job being naval assistant to the Hydrographer of the Navy, dying in 1944. Trench undertook a number of intelligence assignments after the war before retiring as a lieutenant colonel in 1927. He was recalled, however, during the Second World War and was apparently a most effective interrogator, dying in 1967. They also remained friends, Trench being best man at Brandon's wedding in 1915.

Stewart's was a less happy tale. He seems to have been convinced that his arrest was none of his responsibility and that he was owed compensation. Before the releases, on 1 April, Cumming told Jackson that Stewart had smuggled out letters, remarking that 'they do not contain one single fact or piece of information of any value whatever. He has never done anything for us which merits even the barest thanks.' On 23 May, following Stewart's release, Cumming's defensiveness becomes more specific (Blitz, is, of course MacDonogh, while BS refers to Stewart):

This afternoon Blitz rang me up and said that BS was at the War Office and was then closeted with the chief. I asked if I might come over, and I waited in Blitz's office until BS looked in. He seemed surprised to see me, but on our being left alone shortly afterwards, he talked away freely about his experiences and his trial. He inveighed against this in strident terms and said that he had not been given a fair hearing and that his evidence had been purposely confused. The authorities had wished to secure a conviction for political purposes and to help their Navy Bill. When Blitz returned, BS turned to me and said 'One of your mistakes was in not sending me some secret ink into the prison as I could have sent you quantities of information.' I told him that his friends had particularly asked that we should not attempt to communicate with him as this would prejudice their chances of getting a pardon. I said, 'You emphasise "One of your mistakes" – what were the others?' He replied that he could not go into that question now but would see me next week. After he had gone I repeated to Blitz my hope that he would not be allowed to go round to my employers and tell them a one-sided yarn in which he would try and shift the blame of his own carelessness on to my shoulders. Blitz begged me not to justify myself at BS' expense or 'rub in' any points that told in my favour.

Three days later Stewart called on Jackson but was rebuffed and then tried to call on the First Sea Lord. Jackson assured Cumming that no complaint made by Stewart would be heeded but Cumming was not satisfied: 'I urged in vain that this man might do me a great deal of harm if allowed to go round to my superiors and tell a one-sided story, and that I should like to be allowed to meet him and answer any charges he had to make.'

When Stewart tried to involve MacDonogh, Cumming

pointed out that it was scarcely fair to me that this man should be going about – both the War Office and the Admiralty – and making a charge against me which I was not allowed to hear or to answer, but he [MacDonogh] only repeated that he did not wish to go into that now. I asked him if he thought the charge a justifiable one, and he said decidedly not. I suggested the introduction to Rué [the agent who had betrayed Stewart], and said that BS had accepted an appointment which would cause him to deal with dozens of such men, and Blitz said that this was a complete answer to the charge. I can't see why this secrecy and mystery should prevail in a matter that concerns me so directly, but I am quite ready to meet any charge that BS can bring forward and only wish I could be confronted with him.

The wish seems never to have been fulfilled but for some time the affair rumbled to and fro between the corridors of Whitehall and the offices of lawyers. On 16 December 1913, for instance, MacDonogh showed Cumming a letter from Sir William Bull, Stewart's lawyer:

In it he claimed for Bertrand (1) That he had been contrary to his agreement sent into Tiaria and exposed to risks. (2) That we ought to have known that Verrue [Rué] was a rascal. (3) That we had injured his cause by writing to Verrue after his arrest. He claimed £10,000 and declined our offer of £1200 [actually typed as £12.00]. He also said that he wanted a letter sent by the Chief to the King, Sec. for War and 1st. Lord, to say that he had done well. I spent the whole afternoon in M's office while he composed a report on the whole case for submission to the S. for War. In it he repeatedly alluded to me as the Chief Agent – the term employed by Bertrand. I protested mildly but he said it meant nothing and was only used to make matters easier for the S of S.

Cumming was thus able to state his case, albeit not directly. That was not quite the end, however. In the account by Captain Drake, already mentioned, Stewart was said to have rejoined his TA unit 'and went to France with it and was killed. His widow, much against C's advice and wish, was granted £10,000 which I am nearly certain C had to pay out of his SS funds.' The bureaucratic ripples provoked by Stewart outlasted their originator.

And so Bertrand Stewart, too, walks out of history, vanishing in the conflagration which was to consume so many. Regardless of where real responsibility lay, his brief entry probably had all the ingredients of comic spookery, which even the serious consequence of imprisonment seems not to have lessened significantly. Nobody came well out of it, except perhaps his widow and Verrue who both seem to have done rather too well.

Recriminations, rights and responsibilities were, thankfully, only a small part of Cumming's concerns during that final pre-war year. He was far more taken up with efforts to establish a network of agents who could report on German ground movements both in the approach to hostilities and after they had started. As war approached, this subject predominated over the prime requirement of the earlier years for reporting on the German naval build-up. The chief difficulty of the task was no longer the acquisition of agents – though good ones were always hard to find – but the establishment of reliable means of communication, particularly means that would endure once war had started. Another major difficulty, becoming more acute, was continuing responsibility for organising Secret Service reporting for the BEF when it took the field, while not being allowed to organise in its intended operational area because he was not supposed to know it.

Two head agents who were very likely serving or retired officers, referred to as DB and AC, feature largely. On 3 January 1913, AC suggested a scheme for the posting of agents and scouts to Belgium in time of war, which Cumming wanted to take farther but MacDonogh was away and he had to spend the rest of the day dealing with someone called Church, who devised codes.

He still spent a great deal of his time running around London trying to see people who were out, or engaged, or in the wrong place. When AC called again the following week he wanted to discuss not his scouts scheme but his claim to be paid subsistence allowance when on leave, on the basis that he was still on call (though he had not been called). Cumming reluctantly agreed to leave this to MacDonogh's judgement and MacDonogh invited them over, but was engaged by the time they reached him.

He was still not free by the time Cumming had to go off and see DB who, despite waiting in 'a very comfortable place', was apparently 'very queer tempered' when they met, complaining about the rottenness of 'the system' and offering his resignation. Cumming promptly accepted it and began calculating the pay due to him then and there, which had the effect of making DB 'glad enough to pass on to other subjects'. He was still liverish and wanting to be made much of when they parted, saying that nothing would go right with the Bureau until the Bureau had a central office with him in it. Cumming's response was brisk: 'I told him that it was I who wanted the assistant to get through the immense pile of correspondence that he sent in to me.'

It is not clear precisely what the respective roles of AC and DB were, but it does appear that one was to take on some of the other's responsibilities in the field in the event of war, and that they were to work closely together. However, they didn't know each other and Cumming argued that they should, since they would have to depend on each other in the event of war. He proposed that agents near the frontier should convey information to 'the place chosen in France as a centre' and suggested that he could have a man in Maubeuge who would communicate with AC and forward everything from him. MacDonogh disagreed: 'He said that he was unable to divulge the place of landing of our Army, and that therefore he could not indicate in what district they were to operate. I must therefore confine my organisation to Belgium, leaving it to him to provide the link to carry the information received over to our headquarters in France.'

Cumming protested that this made his task impossible but MacDonogh was adamant: DB 'must not even suspect that our Army may be landing at any particular place. At present he thinks we are to land in Antwerp, and he must be led so as to retain that idea.' They both called on DB in his office and presumably proceeded to mislead him, noting his request for a pigeon service 'in addition to the cycle riding scouts'.

These latter were in fact first mentioned by Cumming in a November 1912 meeting, when he proposed that they should cycle in pairs posing as tourists in advance of war. He also proposed buying two motor cycles and keeping them in Belgium. After the usual months of negotiation, one motor cycle was reluctantly authorised, purchased and sent over to AC for safe keeping. There is no record of it, or the cyclists, ever being deployed.

After persistent argument from Cumming, MacDonogh did

eventually concede that on the eve of war AC could 'come to Brussels to meet his five officers and DB, and shall then return to his own Headquarters. Suitable addresses must be found for these people to go to, and a place of meeting arranged at once – by L – to be approved by us, next time we send.' L was of course Dale Long, Kell's agent who was deployed to Brussels.

Two years after it was agreed he should have one, Cumming still had no representative of his own abroad, and thus no over-seas station. It was not for lack of trying but part of the problem, at least, was his dogged desire not to accept the man offered but to send Roy Regnart, of whose suitability he had yet to persuade anyone else. Jackson, the new DNI, was strongly opposed if it meant that Regnart had to retire for the purpose, as he was 'in difficulties with another man who had been induced to retire and who now – though quite unfit for his post – he was unable to get rid of, owing to his claim on account of his retirement'. Cumming argued that Regnart intended to retire anyway and that he was 'a first rate man for the work' – essentially, the job was to be a Brussels-based organiser of communications – though he had to concede that he was 'undoubtedly very difficult to work with and had a queer temper – especially when opposed'.

Regnart was probably pestering Cumming daily about the job during the first two months of the year and on 16 February Cumming records him as suggesting that he should take over AC's job: 'He suggested to me that he should offer AC either £500 down or £100 a year for ten years, to clear out and make way for him.' This novel way of getting the posting you want was, Cumming said tactfully, 'worth considering but not practi-cable', confiding darkly to his diary: 'Roy must think he would soon clear me out, or he would not offer such a sum.'

About a week later DB returned from Belgium to report that he had recruited men in nine out of the ten places he had been directed to find someone. He was confident that there would be war immediately, with Russia and France starting it on their own account. When Cumming accused him of being alarmist, he insisted that nothing else was talked about up and down the whole Belgian frontier, adding, 'without my asking or suggesting anything, that we intended to land our expeditionary force at all the ports each side of Calais – and as far south as Rouen – and join the French force at Lille'. This was, of course, precisely what MacDonogh insisted that no one, Cumming included, was to know. Loyally, Cumming suggested that Antwerp was more likely but DB 'scoffed at this and said that we should have liked to land there but the Belgian Government would not allow it as they believe they can hold Antwerp themselves'. He added that when he had said this to MacDonogh in September 1911, Mac-Donogh had 'made a face'. Cumming reported this exchange to MacDonogh, saying further deception was pointless and that he 'disliked the principle of this immensely'. However, MacDonogh 'would not admit that DB's view was correct and said that this "rumour" had appeared in the papers!!'

When Jackson was asked to report to the CID on what resources existed for getting information from abroad in the run-up to, and during, hostilities, he asked Cumming to go through the papers on the subject with him. Cumming was surprised to find a number that had been presented some time before, evidently without any reference to him. They 'made it appear that there was at that time a most perfect organisation for the supply and transmission of warnings and other information of all kinds and at the shortest notice. Of course this must have been "super-optimistic" as there can have been no organisation of which I should not have known, and I know that there is nothing of the kind.' They reviewed what arrangements actually existed which, in Cumming's words, 'made out a fair case but by no means a sufficient one or one that will allow us to rest'.

They arranged to meet again and prepare a report but when Cumming called on 7 March Jackson was busy and he saw Regnart instead. Regnart, never shy of raising the subject that was uppermost in his mind, said he had decided to retire and asked what were his chances of being taken on. Cumming, who was of course supposed to discourage him from retiring in order to take the job, 'could not give him any definite assurance as of course most of those who have influence in the matter are against his being employed'. He promised to do his best, though, reasoning that it would be most advantageous 'to get McJ [Jackson's nickname] to agree to this when he is making out his case for the CID, as he will then have the weakness of our present arrangements brought home more fully to him'.

Meanwhile, AC had reported intelligence on which Cumming was complimented. This made Cumming uneasy because he did 'not know what he [AC] would do should war be declared, as he has no instruction from Blitz. I understood that he was to concentrate his agents on Marche, but he said that the latest plan was to collect all his information at Charleroi and pass it on to Mons. He has no instructions for sending anything over here.' This was hardly encouraging preparation for war and for Cumming it must have been particularly dispiriting because he was in the uncomfortable (but by no means uncommon) position of having responsibility without power.

On 1 April 1913 – his fifty-fourth birthday – Cumming heard Jackson's account of his appearance before the CID:

McJ gave me an account of the meeting he had with a Committee he called the 'Invasion Committee'. He stated that he could not undertake to say that the TRs would find it impossible to embark 20,000 men without our knowing about it. In spite of what Sir J. F. [presumably Sir John French] had stated on a former occasion, we had no organisation that could promise to give timely warning of such a movement. He said that we had abandoned the system of fixed and permanent agents and now increased our numbers but did not pay them salaries but promised them a very large reward for information received as to an imminent embarkation. The First Lord said that every DID [Director of Intelligence Department – DNI] had certain funds for this purpose and was not supposed to state how they were employed.

Although there is no evidence in the diary of the results of this meeting, it seems reasonable to assume that efforts to establish an early warning system were increased. At the same time, Cumming learned from MacDonogh that his financial estimates for the year were to be cut by the Foreign Office, though no one yet knew by how much. We do know that his figures for the quarter ending that day were reduced from £3,925 to £2,103, though he comments that this was partly a matter of spreading money over different periods. He then says: 'the surplus he [Mac-Donogh] offered me on Friday, he now tells me has been completely expended elsewhere – I presume K has got it.' With Cumming's money being reduced at the very time further demands were being placed upon him, it is perhaps not surprising that he drew more frequent contrasts with Kell at this period, though there is no reference to any awkwardness.

In fact, Kell was trying to get Cumming to 'find a berth' for his Royal Naval seconded officer, Ohlson, whose work was to be taken over by the Admiralty. Cumming was disposed to help so long as it did not prejudice his chances of getting Regnart to Brussels. After months of manoeuvring, the matter was taken out of their hands by a meeting comprising General Williamson (by then DMO), Jackson, MacDonogh and Sir Grahame Greene, which decided that Ohlson should return to his ship. Kell and Cumming were kept outside the door at first but allowed in later for Cumming again to make his case for employing Regnart as 'someone capable of organising a system of communicating information at time of war'. There was the usual debate but General Williamson supported Cumming and it was agreed to put the question to Sir Arthur Nicholson, Under Secretary at the Foreign Office, the following week.

At this meeting, on 7 May, Cumming again made his case but was opposed by Jackson who argued that Regnart would do no good if allowed to go about his work in his own way, while if any attempt was made to control him he would kick over the traces. Cumming proposed that he be appointed for only a year at a time and eventually a compromise was reached whereby Regnart could be appointed provided he retired first of his own accord, without being told he was going to get the job. Jackson warned the meeting that they would all regret it.

Sir Arthur Nicholson asked Cumming if he was satisfied with the information the Bureau was getting. Cumming was not – 'I did not consider that the stuff obtained should be taken as a criterion of the value of the Bureau, but my organisation was increasing and I hoped would prove useful when called upon.' They still, he said, lacked means of communication during time of crisis or war, but he hoped the appointment of Regnart would improve this.

He also recalls that before the meeting he had looked in on Jackson and found him engaged with two captains. Jackson was 'very rude and said that he was not in the habit of being late and shut the door in my face'. Relations did not improve as they walked along Whitehall. Cumming had heard that the fraudster, Delaforce, whom he had interviewed and rejected, had wormed his way into Churchill's good opinion via someone called Glyn and that Churchill was proposing to buy 'Delaforce's shell etc. for £800'. Cumming warned Jackson that the whole thing was bogus and that Churchill should be told, but Jackson 'did not take this in good part and said that the money spent by WC was of no concern to me as it would not come out of my funds. I replied that I considered it my duty to warn him that the man was a thorough blackguard and his information faked.' Then they reverted to the relatively uncontentious subject of the difficulty of getting reliable information on Borkum.

By the autumn Cumming had got his way, with Regnart resigned from the Marines and installed in Brussels. It is possible that what Cumming had in mind – the organisation of communications – might have coincided with Regnart's presumed strengths, in that he might have been better at dealing with method and organisation than with people; but there is almost nothing in espionage that does not involve people and it soon became clear that all the warnings were wise. They met on 12 December in Paris, when Cumming was reviewing wartime arrangements with his French counterparts. They had exchanged reports and he had earned plaudits for those the French had given him. The omens for this visit, however, were not propitious.

Cumming had devised a scheme for wartime communication called the A scheme which had been approved by his immediate superiors but 'the authorities' apparently did not like it. He still did not know why when he had to leave for France on 11 December, though he did learn from MacDonogh that General Williamson had decided that nothing should be said about the scheme until he had himself been to Paris and seen General Belin [probable], and no one knew when this would be.

This [wrote Cumming] is extremely disappointing and upsets all my hopes of progress or success. I cannot understand upon what principle these affairs should be discussed and decided without my presence . . . and I am told that the authorities disapprove of the plan – but of what plan? They have never heard mine . . . these schemes ought to be put forward by me and not submitted to the authorities at third or second hand. I don't suppose for a moment that the French General will sympathise with my wish to have a means of communication under my own control. I feel the difficulty – the impossibility of my position but can do nothing.

Regnart reported from Brussels, soon after his arrival: 'Roy complained loudly that he was not given £300 or £400 to spend as he wished . . . he had to advance money out of his own pocket . . . laid great stress on the interest value of his furniture . . . we had a long and rather peevish talk, and I left him to dine alone.'

It seems that Regnart had set up some sort of furniture-related cover business and had been finding agents. After his solitary dinner, he was more compliant, admitting that his father had been getting at him over money. Cumming reminded him that he had always said he was rich enough to work the business 'upon a liberal scale' and Regnart conceded that he had not been misled as to the extent of official funding. He none the less tried to persuade Cumming to make over to him part of his official funds. It was late when they parted.

The following day they went off together to meet a man variously referred to as Jacot, Jacottet and Jacques, a French agent whom the Deuxième Bureau had made available probably because they thought the British better able to assess his naval reporting. Cumming had already had unsatisfactory dealings with him in London but this meeting must have been memorable. Regnart assumed a disguise, 'which though very efficient is rather terrifying', and they set off to find rooms away from their hotel. It was not easy: 'We tried a well known brothel or "house of call" but they would not let us have a room and evidently badly mistook our intentions,' Cumming noted laconically. Eventually he went off alone and found a *'cabinet particulier'* in 'one of the lesser known restaurants', where he installed Regnart and to which he brought Jacot from the agreed rendezvous.

Jacot gave them a report on German naval trials which he had already given to the French and which Cumming, unknown to him, had already seen. They pointed out that on a date mentioned the ships he referred to were not in the North Sea but in the Baltic. He dismissed this as a trivial mistake. He offered further documents, describing them as copies of official reports for which he wanted £400. Cumming pointed out that the date had been altered and that it was wrong, anyway. Jacot had no explanation. They questioned him about the subjects on which he was reporting, and found him blankly ignorant. 'He left without any demur or fuss.'

Jacot's departure prompted a renewal of Regnart's pleas for money which Cumming continued to refuse, but he did agree to refer to MacDonogh Regnart's request for further funds to recruit men in Maastricht, Venlo, Nynmegen, Groningen, Hanover, Munster and Wesel. They parted at four o'clock, after which Cumming made his somewhat sad call on Mme Rachell, her sister and sister-in-law, which we have noted already.

He recalls that he then 'spent all my spare hours at the Aero Exhibition and saw a lot of new things that I hope may prove useful later on'. Since his first flight in 1911, he had not only gone on to get his own pilot's licence but had campaigned for the use of aircraft to gather intelligence. What became aerial reconnaissance seems now so obviously useful that we take it for granted but, some years before it became a reality, Cumming fought a lonely and unsuccessful battle to get it accepted. By 1913 he had drawn up plans and figures for purchasing, maintaining and flying a Secret Service Bureau aircraft and was discussing them with General Henderson, Chief of the Flying Department at the War Office. The War Office showed little enthusiasm for this novel way of finding out where the enemy was, objecting on grounds of cost and the unreliability of aircraft. Cumming insisted that both would be reasonable and controllable, deploying the original argument that his aircraft would fly only in good weather and only 'over easy country and will never fly over any route that the pilot has not previously gone carefully over on his bike'. He got some way with this and it looked for a time as if he was going to win, but he never deployed his aircraft; on this, as on much else, the War Office was eventually moved only by grim necessity.

On his return to London he renewed his battle to co-ordinate the roles of Regnart, AC and DB during wartime. The results were no more satisfactory than before. MacDonogh decided that AC was to 'have all DB's men and to arrange to collect and refer all their reports to HQ, but to have nothing to do with SS. After the TRs have passed over their line they will become SS men and Roy will undertake to handle them.' When Cumming protested that in that case Regnart and DB should get to know each other now, MacDonogh decreed that they would meet for the first time in Brussels on the declaration of war. Cumming's continued objections that this was unworkable again got him nowhere; nor did his argument that it was 'distinctly my job and I must have it done in the way that I can see daylight through, which I cannot do through this plan'. They broke off without reaching agreement. On 17 December Cumming spent what was probably an enjoyable, engrossing and therapeutic day at his favourite activity, the boom defence trials.

In fact, he got his way, more or less, though not until the early months of 1914. Then it was agreed that 'DB is to introduce Roy to six of his best men – by means of a letter to each. Roy will take charge of these and use them as a nucleus for his war staff, but they are not to be employed in collecting news now.' AC, who had his motor bike, was to take a PO box at Lille through which Cumming and the 'B. section' (presumably the War Office's Belgian section) would communicate with him. He was to 'work from now on the Western frontier, S. of Courtrai, to N. of Erquilinnes', examining the railway between Valkenburg and Heerlen and looking out for possible bridge sites over the Meuse between Liège and Visé. DB was to go to Dinant – 'on the left bank of the river and should concentrate his carrying force there'. He was not to know of AC and his role until the time came, so was introduced to him in London as Captain Francis, 'an officer working in England, with whom he would work in time of war'.

It is possible that the subject of all this discussion was a plan for the acquisition of intelligence behind enemy lines by one group of agents and for its transmission through the lines by another group. The arrangements begin to have the whiff of plausibility about them, at least on paper, and it was only the fact that the war did not proceed according to French and British plans that prevented their being tested.

Before 1913 ended there was one affair which seems to have involved Cumming as much personally as professionally. This concerned an officer who worked for him referred to as TP, and who was almost certainly Lieutenant Commander Talbot Ponsonby. He apparently did good work and Cumming liked him but he became increasingly dogged by illness throughout 1913. After he developed a very bad throat on 18 December Cumming advised him to press his doctor for a straight answer as to whether anything was seriously wrong and, if so, to 'clear out of this country for the winter and go to the Cape or wherever his man advised him'. On 23 December TP told him that he had a tubercular swelling of the vocal cords and that he had taken Cumming's advice and booked tickets for South Africa.

Cumming's reaction is both revealing and tantalising:

> I did not say much to him at the time as I was too
> shocked and had not time to discuss the thing carefully.
> He will be a great loss to the office for not only have we
> wasted a large sum of money on his training abroad, but
> he is a most excellent ambassador to high class clients
> and gets on with them capitally – as no other officer
> could do. I suggested that we should stop his pay but
> keep him on, indefinitely, and he cordially agreed to this
> plan. I shall be only too glad to have him back, but
> believe that he will never return.

This mixture of personal and professional reactions illustrates the extent to which Cumming already lived his work, and was to go on doing so. It was probably his wholehearted giving of himself to what he did that earned him the affection and esteem with which his agents and staff (when he got some) came to regard him. The affair also illustrates his kindness and compassion, and his bleak realism. His reference to TP's role is tantalising – who were the 'high class clients', why did Cumming think that no one else could deal with them, what was his expensive training abroad? Did TP have access to European royal families whom he could influence, or, without their realising it, debrief? He seems to have spent some time attached to what Cumming calls 'the French HQ's', possibly for training purposes and in May 1913 he had successfully solicited the help of some Danes who were able to pass on international cable traffic. There is also a reference to his having reported on German plans to use a naval coal store in Iceland.

On New Year's Day 1914, Cumming took TP and his wife for a farewell lunch in the RAC, removing from TP his key and pass. TP 'promised he would come back at any time if I were in a difficulty or an emergency, and certainly in the case of war'. Two days later he travelled down to Southampton to see them off in the *Edinburgh Castle*. 'By way of comforting him, I told him that if he felt well enough to come home but not to live in England, I might be able to find work for him in Italy – or elsewhere. He is a great loss to me, for I have no one to take his place or do the excellent work he did in travelling abroad and interviewing people of all ranks and classes for me.' He adds that he returned home that afternoon and worked late in the office, which further suggests that 'home' was no longer Bursledon.

Someone who obstinately did not go away was Bertrand Stewart. Cumming seems to have had no more to do with him directly but twice in January 1914 he refers to conversations with MacDonogh about 'evidence in the BS case'. On the first occasion it involved letters and an amended statement from Dale Long and on the second it involved correspondence with Regnart about Long's evidence. On the first of these occasions, incidentally, Cumming records that MacDonogh told him he was not to do any work in Sweden 'for fear of playing into the hands of our rivals'.

There was also a fair amount of reporting from someone called H_2O, who could just possibly have been a Mr Archer, a former naval officer who with his son was paid £1,200 to hire a yacht and spend a year ship-watching and fulfilling other naval requirements around southern Norway and Denmark. The intelligence results were apparently fair but, to MacDonogh's annoyance, the £1,200 budget was considerably exceeded.

Money remained an issue throughout the year, albeit of varying severity. It ranged from the abrupt imposition of cuts, to Cumming's tentatively wondering whether he might broach with MacDonogh the question of a side-car to go on A C's £60 4 h.p. motor bike, to a rather surprising offer from General Williamson on 6 March of a round million:

A very busy day. A large packet of valuable stuff came in from our friends [probably the French liaison], and I took this over and showed it to Wmson, who thought it extremely valuable and is to show it to Sir J. F. at once. He talked to me about the state of affairs and said that it was an extremely good move to get hold of these people, and hoped that we were doing something for them. I told him what a slow and heartbreaking job this billet was and he agreed that it was quite impossible to hurry matters and asked if unlimited money would help – a round million for example. I told him that I thought the supply of such a sum would probably lead us into great mistakes, and that it required experience and time to form a decent organisation, and unlimited patience upon both my part and my superiors – with which he cordially agreed.

This is interesting not only because of its indication of the quality of the intelligence exchange with the French but because of Williamson's rather surprising offer. Did he have a sudden insight into the potential of intelligence in the war to come? In view of what 1914 was to bring, Cumming might have done better to have accepted.

Cumming's entry for Christmas Day and Boxing Day 1913 (he worked all day on Christmas Eve) memorably begins: 'In the office but nothing to record.' This naturally again raises questions about his marriage and family life, although it is at least possible that May and Alastair were in the Ashley Gardens flat with him and that he merely went next door to escape Christmas for a while, as many would like to do. Whether or not this was the case, family Christmases – especially extended family Christmases – would not feature greatly over the next few years.

10

WAR

Nineteen fourteen brought recognition, albeit mentioned by Cumming in only two words on 29 June, long after he had knowledge of it: 'Invest.re today'.

He had been awarded the CB, an honour which, though not uncommon among senior naval and military officers, was considerably less common at his rank and pre-dated those of Kell and even MacDonogh. He would not have been so recognised if his work had not been well regarded. It was a sign that, despite all the debilitating bureaucratic struggles – and despite all that were to come – the Chief of the Secret Service was making his mark in the heirarchy before the First World War had started. The only way he could have done that was by the intelligence he produced and the best available account of that is in Hector Bywater's *Strange Intelligence* (see page 143). Bywater's pre-war espionage was conducted on Cumming's behalf, whereas his wartime activities were on behalf of the Director of Naval Intelligence, Admiral Hall (see below). Apart from comprehensive specifications of German warships, he also claims penetration of the Berlin Navy Office, counter-measures ensuring that only one of Germany's secret armed liners and merchantmen was able to leave port during the early months of war, a detailed 1913 description of the secret armed liners and merchantmen was able to leave port during the early months of war, a detailed 1913 description of the secret fort-reducing howitzer known as 'Fat Bertha', the acquisition of naval war plans and world-wide coaling and intelligence facilities and the transmission of Whitehall desks of the important German Fleet Law Amendment Act before it was tabled in the Reichstag (proofs were apparently obtained from the printers).

Cumming was very unlikely to have been cynical about honours; like almost all in his day, and most in this, he probably was pleased and flattered. The fact that he does not use the diary for any sort of reflection or comment suggests that he continued to regard it as an official record, the bureaucratic version of a ship's log, rather than as a personal confessional. He was not alone in this respect. 'Old 'ard 'art' Wilson's (see p. 18) diary comment on returning home after the action that won him the VC was 'Docked Ship, received VC'.

The typed portion of the diary ends on 19 January 1914, after which all is in manuscript. However, for the first nineteen days of 1914 we have both versions and are thus able to see that the typescript is indeed an expanded version of an earlier original. For instance, the already quoted typescript for 3 January – in which Cumming sees TP and his wife off at Southampton – is in manuscript rather briefer: 'Travelled down with TP and his wife and saw him off in the *Edinburgh Castle*. Suggested to him a possible berth in Italy. Retd home and worked late.'

There is no indication why the typescript ends when it does but it is possible that it was either dictated later, when he was ill or convalescing, or that with the approach of war he simply became too busy to transcribe it.

The new year brought more agents and more urgent requirements, though some old familiars persisted. On 26 January Cumming learned that Bertrand Stewart was claiming 'an immense sum' and alleging that Cumming had sent him on purpose in order to get him arrested. Later, General Williamson wrote to Sir William Bull to try to stop the Stewart correspondence, and on 21 May Cumming learned of 'Bertram's bombshell', a Petition of Right 'fired in by BS' which apparently accused Williamson, MacDonogh and himself and claimed £12,500 from the government. MacDonogh took down Cumming's replies to extracts read to him and the following day he repeated them to Sir Graham Greene, 'who will inform WC' (Churchill, presumably). On 29 June, the day of investiture, he learned from MacDonogh of 'the Prime Minister's decision re BS'.

When the Archduke Franz Ferdinand was assassinated in Sarajevo, General Williamson was talking to Cumming of more apparently significant matters, such as governmental unease over Egypt and India if troubles in Ulster worsened. The Germans, meanwhile, completed the extension of the Berlin–Baghdad railway to Basra, thus gaining access to the Indian Ocean, while MacDonogh worried as to whether Sir William Bull would agree to arbitration over the Stewart case. There is another possible reference to Stewart on 9 August, though it is not clear that it is the same man. Cumming was discussing codes with Sir Alfred Ewing and MacDonogh, and afterwards 'Met BS and went into question of extra men for him . . . Stewart brought Major [indecipherable] . . . who promised help'.

The affair of Trench and Brandon spluttered on into 1914, albeit more benignly than that of the unhappy Stewart. On 2 February Cumming wrote:

Bonfire and Counterscarp called on me and stayed two hours. They discussed their case in all its bearings but were quite friendly. They want to see Roy and I told them I would write to him . . . B & T absolutely exonerated me from any share in giving them instructions: they said the whole trouble arose from Roy springing the Danzig business on them at the last moment, which made them hurry up everything and take risks. He had arranged with them to meet them in Holland (unknown to me) and in giving the TRs authority to collect their correspondence at D, they thought he would certainly have cleared the PO first as it was a week after their arrest.

This latter point, unless it is merely post-hoc justification, is some mitigation to at least one of their actions.

Regnart, however, clearly was Cumming's responsibility. His temperamental demands continued into 1914 until he rejoined the Royal Marines and was swallowed up by the war. He was angry not only about money but about Cumming's refusal to let him communicate with German agents. There seems to have been one in particular – 'the Tr agent' – who was possibly of some consequence. Regnart threatened to discover his identity and communicate with him independently, which resulted in Cumming issuing formal orders to the contrary and Regnart finally quietening down. (The following day, Good Friday, was quieter anyway; all offices were closed except, of course, Cumming's.) On 1 May he agreed with MacDonogh to terminate Regnart's appointment if he did not keep within financial limits, but three weeks later he included in his annual report a further twelve-month appointment. This was agreed, but soon rendered irrelevant by events.

And so, troubled, troublesome and temperamental, Roy Regnart disappears from the diary and – unless anyone chooses to follow the rest of his life – from history. His departure could be seen to mark the end of the first phase in the life of the fledgling Secret Service, the phase of essentially nineteenth-century assumptions and practices. Some of these Cumming struggled against, others – exemplified perhaps by Regnart – he accepted, even at the price of making life more difficult for himself. From August 1914 he had to find ways of operating in the midst of war, particularly getting intelligence across borders that were mined, wired and machine-gunned in time for it to be of military value. This involved agent motivation differing from anything that Regnart would have been used to and agent-running techniques unlike anything he practised. By 1914 Cumming had outgrown his earlier dependence on Regnart and it was perhaps as well that the speed and extent of the German advance removed Regnart from the Secret Service.

Nor was Regnart the only problem that dissolved under pres-

Crowther Smith's copy of an earlier portrait of Mansfield Cumming, with awards and decorations added. They are the Neck Badge of a Knight Commander of The Most Distinguished Order of St Michael and St George; the Neck Badge of a Companion of the Most Honourable Order of the Bath (Civil Division); Breast Star of a Knight Commander of the Most Distinguished Order of St Michael and St George; Breast Star of the Order of St Stanislas, second class (Russia); India General Service Medal (1854-95) with 'Perak' clasp; Egypt Medal (1882-89); British War Medal (1914-20); Badge of an Officer of the Legion of Honour (France); Khedive's Star (1882-91); Order of St Stanislas, second class (Russia); Order of St Vladimir, second class (Russia); Officer of the Order of St Leopold (Belgium).

Cumming as
Sub-Lieutenant
Smith, RN.

Cumming on the deck of the *Enchantress*, by kind permission of Susannah Ritchie.

A post-card produced of Cumming qualifying for his pilot's licence. By kind permission of Susannah Ritchie.

The clock made by Cumming and given to Susannah Ritchie's father.

Cumming featured as one of the pioneers of 'motorism'.

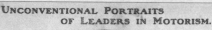

UNCONVENTIONAL PORTRAITS OF LEADERS IN MOTORISM.

XLIII.—COMMANDER MANSFIELD CUMMING, R.N.
"Motor Yacht Club."

Cumming's Wolseley racer, 25th April 1903. The caption reads 'A front view of Lieutenant Mansfield Cumming's 50 h.p. Wolseley racing car. Last week we published a side view of this vehicle and this, in conjunction with the front view will enable those who have not inspected the vehicle to realise that it is one of the best looking high-speed cars that has ever been turned out. The position of the motor enables the weight to be kept down and further back than usual, and arrangements have been made so that the engine can be got at from the footboard very easily by a capable mechanic when the machine is travelling.'

Cumming at the wheel, 2nd May 1903. The caption reads 'Lieut. Mansfield Cumming on the Wolseley Racer just after he arrived at Clipstone.' The conditions did not permit of Lieut. Cumming testing his car over the course.

Cumming before the race. 9th May 1903. The caption reads 'Lieut. Mansfield Smith-Cumming's 50-h.p. Wolseley Racer, the owner driving and Mr H. Austin seated beside him. We gave a view showing the other side of this vehicle last week, Mr Girling, one of the Wolseley Company's skilled drivers, being temporarily in charge of the car at the time when our photograph was taken. This car is now in Paris preparatory to taking part in the Paris-Madrid Race.'

'Waiting for the Off', 30th May 1903. 'Paris-Madrid.- At the start. Taken by flashlight. Lieut. Smith-Cumming's 50-h.p. Wolseley Racer waiting its turn to start. Mr Sydney Girling is at the wheel, the owner standing at the side.'

Cumming's Boom Defence headquarters and home, HMS *Argo*, with (right) the mast of the Sultan in position. By kind permission of the family.

Cumming's houseboat at Bursledon. By kind permission of the family.

The wreckage of what is believed to have been the car in which Cumming and Alastair crashed. By kind permission of the family.

Alastair's grave in the military cemetery near Meaux. By kind permission of the family.

Cumming's successful and controversial head of Rotterdam Station, Richard Tinsley (1875–1944). Crowther Smith mounted him on a plinth, perhaps to indicate both his shortness and his view of himself.

10. II. 09.

Private

1.

My dear Mansfield Cumming. Boom defence must be getting a bit stale with you & the recent experiments with Bærel 2 Mbr discounts yours at Southampton you may therefore perhaps like a new billet. If so I have something good I can offer you & if you like to come & see me on Thursday about noon I will tell you what it is.

Yours sincerely

The letter to Cumming from the Director of Naval Intelligence, inviting him to start the Secret Service.

Burnford House, Hampshire, which Cumming rented.

The modern view from approximately the site of Cumming's wartime office in Whitehall Court.

Part of what may have been Cumming's workshop in Whitehall Court.

Photograph taken by TR/16 of the Deutsche Werft yard at Kiel, June 1916.

Photograph taken by TR/16 in June 1937 of a destroyer fitting out in the Germania Werft yard at Kiel.

Self-portrait by Crowther Smith, the cartoonist who worked for Cumming. He was a fanatical croquet-player

Cumming's grave, whe partially uncovere

The remains of HMS *Sultan's* mast in the Hamble mud.
By kind permission of Susannah Ritchie.

sure of approaching war. Since the inception of the Bureau in 1909 Cumming had sought permission to use a press-cutting service. This very reasonable request had been regularly put and as regularly refused, with the consequence that he was in constant danger of discovering that, say, details of a ship's armament that an agent had risked imprisonment to acquire had, in fact, just been announced. Intelligence is often in danger of having its legs cut from under it in this way and Cumming did not, unlike some, appear to see duplicated reporting as helpful corroboration. On 21 January 1914 he tried again with MacDonogh but was discouraged. On 16 July, however, he had better luck: 'Called on M: explained to him that we were behindhand even with published news and got his consent to order Press cuttings to be sent daily to a call address. This after trying for five years! + will be a great boon.'

He also persisted with his attempts to be allowed to conduct aerial reconnaissance, this time involving the French who, General Williamson told him on 23 February, approved the idea. The arrangement was that the French would house the machine and that Cumming would cross to Boulogne by rail and fly it from there. The sum of £1,300 had been authorised, with Cumming to pay a further small sum to French Customs which the French service would refund. He could go ahead, Williamson told him. Excited, Cumming went to Hendon and inspected a 100 h.p. Sopwith biplane, taking 'two exhibition flights . . . mounting to about 2,000 feet'. After a dinner in aid of a putative 'London Aerodrome', he arranged to buy a 70 h.p. Renault, keeping it at Etampes and purchasing as if through a Belgian agency. He also arranged the loan of a shed at Hendon.

Once again, the German invasion of Belgium interfered with well-laid plans, though there is one final, hopeful reference to the 'aero' on 20 August: 'Called on Maj. Fisher who will take our aero if delivered here.' He may even have got it, therefore; but almost certainly he never used it. On the day of this arrangement he was asked to deliver £6,000 to the British headquarters in France, which he had recently visited and was shortly to visit again. It is probable that the money was for intelligence purposes, since the British GHQ ran its own networks, but the only comment Cumming makes is that it was 'too late now'.

If we were to summon Cumming from the dead and ask what were his main preoccupations during the first seven months of 1914, he would probably say that his principal concern was still to establish a reliable system of tactical military reporting before and during hostilities. There are not many references to it in the diary for 1914 but where they occur they read as a continuing concern, not in need of introduction or explanation. We get, as it were, still shots taken from a major feature film which we shall never see.

We also know that there were at least two other films running concurrently: naval reporting, to which there are many fewer references than in earlier years, and the recruitment and performance of new agents. Fewer references to the former may reflect an established flow of intelligence rather than any lack of requirement on the part of the Admiralty, or efforts on Cumming's part to seek it, though there was an Admiralty request in March 1914 for more intelligence on the secret building of German submarines. There is evidence that naval coverage varied from very good to unsatisfactory at different times (probably a reflection of changing requirements) during the war to come. A 1939 Admiralty letter to Cumming's successor but one, Stewart Menzies, compares early Second World War reporting on the German navy unfavourably with the good coverage – especially of Baltic ship movements – apparently achieved in the First World War. Clearly, there were achievements, quite early on, that were more than embryonic.

It is generally accepted by historians that, almost to the last minute, the French government and the senior French military had no knowledge of exactly how and where the British would deploy the six divisions of the BEF. Yet on 19 January 1914 Cumming records working on his continental scheme which involved DB and his agents, A C, Regnart and French liaison. General Williamson had been to France and seen General Belin who 'approved of the scheme and blessed it but wished to mention it to General Joffre and I must therefore wait a bit longer'. This and other references suggest a detailed working-level arrangement with the French regarding the deployment of British and French tactical reporting networks, and the B E F. It is possible that there were different degrees of co-operation at different levels and that on both sides tactical preparations and intentions were not always fully co-ordinated. For all that reality made most plans irrelevant, Cumming's arrangements as to who would operate where – for instance, that D B should deploy on the left bank of the Meuse and 'concentrate his despatching force there' – were so specific that it is not possible to doubt that he and his French liaison shared common assumptions about areas of military deployment.

Towards the end of January, when he was debriefing one of three agents[1] who reported on shipbuilding (by driving him around London in a taxi because there were so many Germans at the meeting place), he was preoccupied by an operation going on in Berlin which he refers to as 'the Berlin mission' and which involved L and Regnart. We do not know what it was, but he was greatly relieved at L's return at 5 a.m. on Saturday 24th. A good deal of time was also taken up by a pair of agents called Sage and Sagette, apparently a father and son who were taking a yacht around the Baltic (probably not identical with the mysterious H_2O mentioned earlier). There were arguments about money, with Sage at one point refusing to give Cumming the names of his sub-agents and Cumming commenting: 'He is very unreasonable – very greedy – and quite unscrupulous and is a bad man of business into the bargain but I think he is clever and has probably done his work very well.'

Ironically, in the midst of his taking Sage to task for running up bills without warning, he was summoned by MacDonogh and asked 'to consider any possible work which I could do and which would require a sum of money as he had a surplus'. This was a fairly common predicament for government service budget holders who were prevented by the Treasury from carrying savings over and were therefore compelled to 'use it or lose it' at the end of each financial year. Cumming suggested that he buy a car for use in Belgium but MacDonogh preferred that he undertook another overseas mission, which Cumming argued could not be organised by the end of the financial year. His own budget figures at the time show a requirement of £800 to get him from early March to the end of the financial year and 'a supposed surplus of £1,280'.

Sage and Sagette were paid off and discharged during a meeting with Cumming at the Union Club on 23 May, apparently in reasonably amicable fashion. Their sub-agents would be paid off and Sagette kept on a six-month salary until 1 September while he collected and forwarded reports; Cumming would also pay for the fitting out of 'the yacht', a total of £288. The frequent references to sub-agents suggests that Sage and Sagette might have used their cruise to recruit people who could report sightings of German shipping – there are later references to Danish and Norwegian lighthouse keepers and so on – and these might well have been the basis of the Bureau's good intelligence coverage of the Baltic. This might also tie in with the discussion of Norway and Sweden he had on 23 June with a man called Homes, who apparently had valuable connections and had been 'in the habit of working the wireless on the steamers going over'. He assured Homes that he 'did not want any Norwegian information, but only Tr stuff that may be got from there'.

As on Good Friday, Easter Monday found Cumming in the office – 'Attended to correspondence, but the office was closed for the day' – but on 4, 5, 26 and 28 May he actually took leave, the first two days of which he spent in Le Havre and Paris, whither he had travelled on business.

Throughout early 1914 there are increasing references to pigeons and pigeon ciphers, with Cumming supplying the latter both to the Admiralty and the War Office. Communication by pigeon is often unthinkingly regarded as primitive, even as a joke. Primitive it may be, but in both world wars and in other theatres this century it proved a useful resource, sufficiently so in the First World War for the Germans to threaten with execution any civilians found in the occupied territories with the eight-page questionnaires attached to pigeons by the British. (Captain Landau, who, as we shall see, worked very effectively for Cumming in Holland, recalls the June 1915 sabotage of a Zeppelin in Brussels whose presence was allegedly reported by pigeon.) The Germans also granted fourteen days' leave for any front-line soldier who shot down a pigeon.

The subject deserves more study than it can be given here but, briefly, the sport of pigeon racing was founded by a cockney solicitor's clerk named Alfred Osman who was born in 1864 and who was in charge of the Army and Navy Pigeon Service during the First World War, when virtually all pigeons for military and espionage use were supplied by British working-class pigeon-fanciers. Reuters News Agency was founded on carrier pigeons and, before wireless, Royal Naval ships carried them. They were used not only for longer-range agent communications but for tactical reporting in the front lines.

Meanwhile, in those last months of peace, agents and agent reporting remained the stuff of daily life. Some of H_2O's reports were queried and needed revision and on 14 July Cumming discussed with Regnart the fate of the three Bangs, Mr and Mrs Bang senior and the younger brother, Bang Junior, whom Regnart supposed to have been arrested, though Cumming doubted it. The Bangs make a number of appearances with no indication of what they were doing; there is a final puzzling assertion by Regnart, in the context of their possible arrests, to the effect that 'neither of the Bangs were working for us'.

Some agents are referred to with even less detail, such as the interestingly named Back and Sense. On 2 June TP made a temporary return but was disappointed by what his doctor had to say and proposed to return again in September. Cumming spent Whit Monday decoding telegrams – evidence of agent productivity, perhaps – and on 18 June handed to the Admiralty a 'report of *Eden Hall* leaving Antwerp with Arms'. This may have been in connection with growing troubles in Ireland.

At about this time Cumming's handwriting goes through one of its periodic changes. Normally, it is even and concentrated, with small regular letters and brief elaboration of some capitals. It suggests energy and purpose with some artistic flourish. Occasionally, though, the letters become smaller, the elisions more common and the whole hastier, scrappier and less legible. Sometimes the context makes it reasonable to surmise an indulgent lunch, lack of sleep or illness but in this part of 1914 there are no such indications and it seems most likely to have been pressure of work and time. During very busy periods diaries tend to be at their least revealing.

It is thus tempting to look for signs that Cumming was working ever harder as war approached, but for the awkward fact that no one knew it was going to happen when it did. For all that war was felt to be approaching, no one knew that Gavrilo Princip's pistol shot on 28 June was its starting gun, as indeed it need not have been. At once unnecessary yet inevitable, the war seems to have been sensed by millions, reluctantly believed in by some, yearned for by others, and feared but not quite believed in by most policy-makers, especially British. It was one of those issues over which the better educated were more likely to be wrong; intelligent, informed and well-meaning people such as the British Foreign Secretary, Sir Edward Grey, could see no reason, right up to the last minute, why Princip's act had to commit millions to slaughter. They were right. Brought up to believe that rational people behave reasonably and avoid doing irrational, harmful things if they are aware of them, men such as Grey could see the unnecessity of this war more clearly than its inevitability. And it was unnecessary. As the military historian John Keegan pointed out in *The First World War*, even in the last hours of peace some use by statesmen of the new and unfamiliar instrument, the telephone, might have saved things.

Even so, it would surely have done no more than delay them; the war had become inevitable. We can postulate as contributing factors an inchoate yearning for conflict among European peoples, a demonstrable resentment and envy on the part of the German trading and commercial classes, the vanity and ambition of the Kaiser, the enthusiasm of the German General Staff and fear on the part of the French and British which paradoxically created that which they most sought to avoid, but there was one reason why it had to happen once German mobilisation had started. This was that the Schlieffen Plan operated to a rigid timetable of movement along railways and roads from the moment of mobilisation through the forty days of the German army's planned sweep through Belgium and France. Schlieffen, an obsessive who never saw action, was for fourteen years Chief of the General Staff, and apparently had no interests outside military planning; his only relaxation from work was to read military history aloud to his daughters. He died in 1912 before seeing the fruits of his life's work.

Cumming's handwriting returns to something like normal after his investiture on 29 June, though it still looks a little more hurried and less deliberate than before. Early in July, Regnart 'Admitted his man arrested but had no incriminating documents of any kind'. The following day, when giving the Admiralty drawings of German gun control and conning towers, Cumming 'reported W's arrest'. (It is possible that W was one of the elusive Bangs.) He interviewed a multi-lingual Russian-speaker called Argyll whom he was considering sending to Russia, though it is not clear whether as an agent to spy in co-operation with the Russians (which is more likely), or against them.

Throughout most of July life as represented in the diary seems to have continued normally with no sign of increasing tension. Potential agents were interviewed, reports gathered, payments recorded. There are several blank pages. On 21 July Cumming authorised DB to undertake a trip to Belgium to compile lists for the War Office pocketbook, adding: 'This trip is really to oblige him and it is to be employed by him to a great extent on work for his Hist. of Belgium.' Given, too, that the trip was to start on 1 August, it is reasonable to infer that, like almost everyone in Britain, Cumming did not expect immediate hostilities.

Things may have changed, however, on Thursday 23 July. In the single line entry for that day Cumming records handing to MacDonogh a report which he describes in one barely decipherable word, probably the German, *Mobilsmachung*. According to Hector Bywater, this was the prearranged secret signal for emergency war measures to be flashed from Kiel to Wilhelmshaven. It was intercepted by one of Cumming's agents. Intelligence that it had been sent was obviously of great importance especially as the Germans had not yet mobilised and indeed, on that same day Lloyd George described relations between Germany and Britain as being better than for many years.

There is no further entry until Wednesday 29 July when Cumming resumes again in his worst handwriting, with brief hurried entries. Extending from Wednesday to Friday 31 July these mainly concern the despatch of DB to Dinant and co-ordinating his activities with those of AC and others. A woman with an indecipherable French or Belgian name was sent to Austria.

On Saturday 1 August Cumming begins with the phrase, 'All emergency vessels despatched' in clear and deliberate script, as in the relative calm following a decision. The British Cabinet was in session throughout the weekend, trying to decide whether Britain was committed to war. They were under understandable pressure from the French to say on what issue and when they would declare support for France. There was no treaty obligation to do so but there was a widespread assumption shared, as we have seen, by MacDonogh, Cumming and many others, that Britain would support France; yet the British government had still not formally committed itself, although the sending of the fleet to war stations had been accompanied by a secret undertaking to France to protect its Channel coast.

In Germany on 1 August, however, there were no such doubts.

An impecunious young artist was part of a crowd gathered in Munich to hear the proclamation of mobilisation. He was, he wrote, 'not ashamed to acknowledge that I was carried away by the enthusiasm of the moment . . . sank down on my knees and thanked Heaven out of the fullness of my heart for the favour of having been permitted to live in such times.'[2]

While the British Cabinet debated whether to take the decision towards which the tide of events effortlessly bore them, those responsible for enacting the decision were more certain. Cumming drove MacDonogh to Southampton, where they appear to have had business with shipping offices. It must have been an early start because they travelled back to London on the 2.40 train, MacDonogh briefing Cumming (at last, it seems) on what precisely was required of DB and AC and their men. Cumming saw Williamson and later drew £108 in Belgian currency. MacDonogh spent the night at Cumming's flat. The following day, Sunday 2 August, Cumming saw the banker Alfred Rothschild at 1 Seymour Place, in London's Curzon Street, and Rothschild agreed to 'arrange for a large sum of £ in Brussels, which GG can call for'. This may not have been solely for financing Cumming's own Belgian operations but may also have been intended for use by GHQ. He also borrowed a car from Rothschild and dispatched a codist and a couple of others in it to Brussels, as well as interviewing a Mrs Rex Dan (probable) and promising her £100 if she would spend a month in Berlin.

A week later, on 7 August, he arranged with Rothschild for '5,000' in German currency to be available the following the day and recorded the numbers of promissory notes to Rothschild, each of which was for £500. This swift and easy arrangement with Alfred Rothschild, while not the first time that British intelligence and London merchant banks had co-operated – the Rothschilds were justifiably proud of their record of assistance to the British state – is none the less typical of the informal and effective co-operation that continued for much of the century; the stuff, for once, both of myth and reality. The next day, like many in August that followed, Cumming dispatched agents to the continent, recording who was issued with which code, with how much money and sometimes their destinations, but not, sadly, their tasks.

On the fateful Tuesday, 4 August, Cumming recorded – again in scrappy, less legible writing – a call made by what looks like Lord Montagu, whom he would have known from his motor racing days, with the surprising offer of 1,000 motor lorries. Cumming referred him to the army. He referred to Kell a lady who offered to spy for him but had no passport, and then interviewed a Major Charteris whom he proposed to send to Paris to take over his French liaison from an officer called Spiers, (possibly the then Lieutenant Speers [sic] the future general who liaised with de Gaulle in the Second World War) who was recalled – as were many of Cumming's serving officers – by the War Office for service elsewhere. In bolder, more deliberate handwriting, farther down the page, he wrote: 'War declared against Germany – midnt.'

The next day he was asked by Williamson for 'arrangements on Dutch coast', following which he called on the manager of Muller and Co., Leadenhall Street, who 'called to his firm in the Hague' to put agents at six points on the Dutch coast to report on German ship movements. MacDonogh authorised £580 for purchase of a 50 h.p. Mercedes, and Regnart called for the inevitable 'long yarn'. Cumming met and took on more people (the engagement calendar at the front of the diary shows twelve taken on during August, but that is probably not the total). There was a payment of £1,500 to Rothschilds and a handing over of the longed-for aero to a Mr Wethered, arranged by General Henderson and necessitating a payment from Cumming of £620, for which he notes that he is to be repaid. On Sunday 9 August he met Sir Alfred Ewing and took him over to the War Office 're codes'. This was an important meeting whose significance we shall look at later. There were no entries for the next two days.

The diary resumes on Wednesday 12 August with the by now

routine round of interviews and departures. Cumming was urgently seeking linguists to send to Switzerland. One line, however, separate from the rest, stands out: 'Alastair left for the front.'

This is the first of two mentions of Alastair in the diary. To a more informal, less disciplined age, accustomed to diaries that are indiscreet, chatty and personal, this may seem odd, an indication perhaps of coldness and emotional repression. But we should be wary of such judgements; we know enough of the impressions Cumming made on people to make this one unlikely and it would, anyway, be based on unjustified assumptions about for what and for whom he was writing the diary. No one writes for himself alone; the very act of writing implies a reader and even though you intend that no one else should read what you have written, in choosing what you say you are putting yourself in the position of a hypothetical reader. Cumming, as we saw, sought permission to keep his diary as a record of what he had done for a putative successor should anything happen to him. It was also a record for himself, necessary because he was not joining an organisation, but starting one, and because he was working alone for much of the time with no other means of keeping track of what was going on. Although it becomes increasingly less complete as the one-man service becomes an organisation, it remains essentially a personal reminder of professional matters, and sometimes a sounding board against which he works out his thoughts and reactions. It is not a personal history.

Yet it does become something else as well. On occasions when he is exercised, such as over the arrests in Germany, or by Roy Regnart, or by his planned deployment in time of war, or by perceived injustice, it becomes his dialogue with himself. He rehearses the arguments and events that concern him; hence his detailed accounts of meeting untrustworthy agents overseas, or his repeated setting out for himself the reasons for his obviously uneasy decision that he should continue to employ Regnart. This goes well beyond the mere keeping of a record, an example of which – started at the same time – is Kell's much briefer diary. Kell, too, has nothing of the personal, but also substantially less of his own reactions and virtually nothing of any sort of debate with himself.

In this context, therefore, it is arguable that Cumming's brief first reference to Alastair is an indication of strength of feeling rather than its lack, a rare intrusion of the personal into official matters. Alastair's going to the front may have been significant for Cumming in a way that, for instance, the award of the CB probably was – both had great personal significance but merited only brief mentions because they *were* personal.

Little is known of Alastair's life to this point. As we have seen, he was educated not far from Bursledon and some time after that he became friendly with Kurt Hahn, the German educationalist best known in this country as the founder of Gordonstoun School. It is commonly said that the two got to know each other at Oxford, but there is no record of Alastair having matriculated. It is possible that he was at a crammer's. We do know that he later joined the army and was commissioned into the Seaforth Highlanders, with whose first (regular) battalion he served in India. According to a Morayshire local paper he was at home on leave when war broke out and 'was offered an appointment on the Headquarters Staff of the Expeditionary Force by a General on whose staff he had served in India'.

There was, in those early days of war – as in all wars – a scramble by many on leave to get transferred to any post that would take them towards the war rather than thousands of miles from it. The assumption that anyone who didn't get in at the start would miss it was not as unreasonable as later events make it seem. The Schlieffen Plan was predicated on success within forty days, and the preceding wars in Europe, the 1870 Franco-Prussian War and the earlier six-week war between Prussia and Austria that led to the foundation of the modern Germany, had indeed proved short. Nor was it only serving soldiers who were keen. As we know, civilians flocked to the flag in their millions in all the combatant countries.

Of course, it is possible to see his father's hand in Alastair's successful transfer. He had the contacts to fix it. Also, Mrs Doreen Vetcher, then a Bursledon child, heard later from her parents that May had been against Alastair's going to France but that Cumming had encouraged it because he felt that she had been too protective of him and that military experience would make him more 'manly'. This is plausible, but in any event Alastair was doing no more than what thousands of others in his position did, or sought to do.

The element of the BEF that he joined was the newly formed Intelligence Corps. Prior to this, the corps did not exist as a full-time permanent body. Various headquarters and campaigns, such as those of the Indian army and the Boer War, or the 1906 Zulu rising, had brought into being their own army intelligence organisations, but these bodies were either temporary or restricted to particular commands and were disbanded, along with their experience, when the need faded. As we know, the War Office maintained its own intelligence staff and had prepared, largely through MacDonogh's efforts, a nucleus to be recruited and expanded on the outbreak of war. Among the War Office staff was Walter Kirke, who was made responsible for secret intelligence in the BEF and was later able to claim grandly at an Intelligence Corps dinner in 1938 that, in the first week of the Great War, 'I commenced to raise the Intelligence Corps.'[3] If Cumming did use his influence to get Alastair his post, then it would almost certainly have been via MacDonogh and Kirke, with both of whom he was in daily contact.

In his *History of the Intelligence Corps* Anthony Clayton lists fifty-five founder members, describing them as the 'original contingent who sailed with the BEF from Southampton 12th August 1914'. Alastair was one of them. Both the commandant and the adjutant were, like him, on leave from India. He commanded the motor cycle section, which was equipped with Douglas, Premier, Rudge and Triumph machines, a command that no doubt would have intrigued his father. The original fifty-five were accompanied by twenty-four volunteers from the Metropolitan Police.

Alastair left no diary but Clayton quotes from one kept by Major Baird, later Viscount Stonehaven. In summary, later, military operations generally read as if they proceeded smoothly without any of the vexatious muddle that almost inevitably accompanies them, perhaps particularly in the early stages of war. Baird arrived in Southampton from London on 11 August to find much grumbling in camp because there were no messing arrangements and because men who had joined as officers discovered they had to look after their own horses. Most had been embodied for a week and had already bought their kit, but a dozen were dismissed for failing a French examination. On 12 August they learned that another element of the BEF HQ staff who had travelled the day before had found themselves not expected at Le Havre, with no reception arrangements and great delay in disembarking.

It may be that Alastair spent the night before embarkation at Bursledon; Cumming has no diary entry for that day or the one before. They might have been together.

Baird recalls a cheerful crossing with singing of the National Anthem and patriotic songs, the route patrolled by three lines of warships, ten miles apart. They were off Le Havre at 9 a.m. and alongside at 11 a.m., but didn't start for their camp (guided by a boy scout) for a further five hours, arriving at 6 p.m. Baird spent 14 August trying to get orders, meeting MacDonogh, then running out of petrol with the commandant in a midnight downpour and sheltering for the night in a small house. The following day they set off at 7 a.m. with three cars and four cyclists 'to try and locate the Germans N and NW of St Omer'. They also had a Rolls-Royce manned by three Marines under a Lieutenant Smyth.

The first weeks of the war were fast-moving and fluid, with both sides seeking flanking movements to the west. Finding the enemy was everyone's problem, not only that of the infant Intelligence Corps, but the corps had other duties too: gathering civilian reports, co-operation with the French police, military ciphers, pass and permit control, questioning of prisoners, motor cycle despatch work, organising civilian working parties, searching for lost units, clearing roads of refugees, pre-positioning stores for retreating units, accompanying cavalry reconnaissance patrols and bridge demolition teams, investigating sniper reports (usually false), examining tunnels and mines that the Germans might use and spreading false information during the advance from the Aisne. Given their small number, fulfilment of these tasks must have been largely theoretical.

In London, meanwhile, it was a life of meetings. Cumming's discussions with 'CMS' became ever more frequent and almost certainly referred to his nephew, Charles Molyneux Smith, the engineer and racing driver who was now also a lieutenant in the Intelligence Corps. He seems to have been seconded to Cumming and it was likely to have been through him that he got his commission. They doubtless featured more in each other's lives than we appreciate, having only the dry and formal evidence of wills and odd periods in the diary, but this period at least indicates virtually daily contact.

On Saturday 15 August Cumming made the first of his wartime trips, crossing via Ostend to Brussels where he put up at the Palace Hotel and saw L 'who had made a fool of himself over a "suspect" cyclist'. (There is a later report to the effect that the outbreak of war found L taking an authorised holiday in Italy.) The plans involving AC and DB were evidently still extant since Cumming briefed the British legation and minister on them before driving out of Brussels. Outside the city he found Belgians hurriedly throwing up entrenchments, with guns, wagons and reserves being moved into position, stories of German Uhlans in a nearby wood and some French soldiers who mistook him and his party for German spies. He eventually met DB, returning to Brussels the following day to find roads barricaded and patrolled every quarter of a mile. There he met AC before driving to Ostend, where he had difficulty getting the car hoisted on to the boat, later dining at Folkestone and setting off for London in pitch dark. Somewhere in Kent his 'lamps' failed and he had to camp in the car until dawn. With his usual punctilious attention to all things mechanical, he noted taking the car to the Wolseley garage and that the problem was the dynamo. He was not put off night drives, though perhaps he should have been. On Sunday 23 August he drove down to Southampton and the *Argo*, setting off on the return journey at 10 p.m. in a thick mist and suffering a 'slight collision', following which both lamps and fuel gave out. He reached London at 6 a.m.

After further bits and pieces – interviewing two ladies at the *Daily Mail* about what they had seen at Heligoland, deciphering telegrams (he still had to do everything himself), being told by MacDonogh not to call at the Foreign Office any more and by the Admiralty not to do anything in Italy ('it scuppers all my plans there') – he set off again for the Continent. He travelled with a King's Messenger, on MacDonogh's advice, and recorded the trip in some detail.

They drove to Southampton in convoy, Cumming unwisely following the King's Messenger's Rolls-Royce and frequently having to stop and recover from smotherings in dust. After some difficulty he obtained a berth for himself and car, having the latter hoisted aboard before supping at Orwell (a frequent stop for him when in Southampton). Returning to the ship after supper he found that its destination had been changed, so he had the car hoisted out again and into another, settling it at 4 a.m., sailing at 5 a.m. Channel crossings at that time were as busy as they were confused and – it was thought – hazardous, with ships and berths in great demand. Somewhere on the way he picked up Bailey, his driver, and put him in a naval uniform which he supplied himself. The voyage to Le Havre was unexpectedly comfortable – 'Very luxurious ship. Lovely cabin with sitting and bathroom. Very good meals and every comfort' – and the car was hoisted out without mishap. After calling on generals and admirals at GHQ, he drove on to an hotel at Yvetot, unchallenged by patrols 'owing to uniform' and noting, 'Very well and kindly received everywhere by the French'.

They left for Paris at 6 a.m. the following day, and at Rouen were run into by a boy on a bike who emerged suddenly from the crowd. The boy was uninjured and Cumming gave him 50 francs for his bike. They were delayed by French troops crossing southwards and suffered two punctures due to bad roads. With the first of these they were helped by a peasant, with the second the local guard turned out and 'a lady stopped her car and made her driver assist (he refused my tip)'. Local people presented him with two French flags. In Paris he had discussions with British and French officials, including Major Wallner who was to run the army GHQ intelligence service.

On the return journey he arrived at Le Havre at 11 a.m. but found the British Transport Office packing up and cheerfully telling everyone there was no chance of a passage for four days. He would have to make his own arrangements. He did, getting himself and car aboard a crowded ship at 2 p.m. and having to wait five hours to get below decks. It was a smooth passage, which was just as well since the ship was packed with refugees and there was 'much discomfort, but everyone kind and considerate of the women and children'. Cumming slept in his car, allowing two refugees to join him. At Southampton it took three and a half hours to get hoisted ashore. After calling at Orwell, he drove to London – still with the unnamed refugees – had a bath and called as usual on the War Office and Admiralty. He turned in early that night, remarking for once that he was tired.

During the next fortnight or so a new and apparently important series of reports came on stream, which he refers to as the Bordeaux reports. The fact that they never came singly but always in numbers, and their geographical provenance, suggests they might have been wireless interception reports, but there is no evidence. What there is evidence of is an increasingly close liaison with the Russians, of whom General Yemoloff of the Russian legation was Cumming's principal contact.

Arrangements were made to meet the Russian 'SS' in The Hague but there is no indication as to whether Cumming himself went. A Russian proposal that he should visit Petrograd to meet 'Chief to Chief' was seriously considered by the Foreign Office, with talk of Cumming's temporary attachment to the British missions in Russia or Sweden, but it came to nothing. An early concern of the liaison, which lasted for as long as the Tsarist government lasted, was the sharing of information about German troop movements between the eastern and western fronts. Later in the war each side let the other read its reports and Yemoloff and his colleagues were frequent visitors to Cumming's office, while his own people in Petrograd actually had an office in the war ministry. He was, as we shall see, of considerable help to the Russians, and was later given two Russian honours.

He was still trying to get access to the consular system for Secret Service purposes, with a proposal that consuls should forward 'anonymous' reports handed in to them. Even in wartime, however, the Foreign Office was anxious to maintain what it saw as the political virginity of the Consular Service. Ronald Campbell, the Under Secretary's Private Secretary with whom Cumming normally dealt, told him that to do otherwise would 'upset the whole principle of keeping them clear of SS'. Roland, then his main Admiralty contact, argued the contrary: 'he was not out to uphold the principles but to beat the TRs'.

This disagreement was typical of the distinction whose fault-lines could be traced throughout the British establishment, a distinction characterised by Andrew Gordon in his book on Jutland as that between gamekeepers – necessary for maintaining the peace – and rat-catchers, needed for waging war. It is perhaps in the nature of all diplomatic services that gamekeepers should be a built-in majority but they flourished in the fighting services, too, as Gordon effectively demonstrates of the Royal Navy. The irony of this particular instance, of course, was that however sincerely the Foreign Office insisted on the virginity of its Consular Service, it was a virginity believed in only by those who proclaimed it, and scarcely credited by the foreigners it was supposed to reassure.

Cumming was also much occupied by his scheme for 'anti-German press propaganda' in neutral countries, such as Holland, Italy (at that stage), Switzerland, Norway, Sweden and Denmark. Although not recording how far any of this was put into effect, he does complain that with regard to Holland 'they [from the context, the War Office, possibly sometimes the Admiralty] are taking my men and suggestions and working them themselves!'

On 8 September he records that Kell called on him quite late, 're Shaw etc'. It would be more teasing than responsible to speculate that this was anything to do with George Bernard Shaw. The following day Cumming drove down to Brixton prison 'and saw Max B-L and had a long talk with him' – the origin, perhaps, of that part of Secret Service mythology that has patriotic cockney safe-crackers plucked from gaol in times of national emergency. A few days later he returned to Brixton, released Max B-L and took him to Hammersmith. There is no record of why. On the same day, 9 September, there was no Bordeaux report; the fact that he thinks this is worth recording indicates, presumably, that Bordeaux reports were coming daily.

Cumming had at last acquired an assistant, a former warrant officer, T. F. Laycock, whom he put up for a commission and whose gazetting gave him obvious pleasure. He also records a War Office request that he himself be transferred from the Reserve to the Active List, only to learn a few days later that he was already on it, but that nobody had thought to tell him. DB, meanwhile, was paid off on 11 September and two days later, a Sunday, Cumming was in Southampton on 'port duty'. On 16 September, during his daily Admiralty visit, he 'met Winston'.

AC, however, remained in employ and arrangements were made for him to be housed under cover in Brussels. By the end of September it had been decreed – apparently by the Admiralty, not the Foreign Office – that Cumming should not after all visit Petrograd but that he should open a station there. With Sir Arthur Nicholson's agreement, he chose three officers and saw them off from King's Cross with an accompanying Russian officer on 26 September. Among them was a Lieutenant Alley, who was to feature prominently during the next year or two.

Cumming was by now running two offices, the one in Ashley Gardens and another. He was also going to Southampton on 'port duty' and was on call every night. On 24 September, for instance, he notes of the previous night: 'Heavy night: six calls.' These were probably communications from agents. The following day he secured a revolver for someone and two days after that noted with satisfaction that he had secured the rank of commander, Royal Naval Reserve, for a businessman, Richard Tinsley, whom he had sent to Rotterdam to open up a station. Tinsley, a controversial figure, was to make a significant contribution to Cumming's war effort.

At the end of the month, on either 30 September or 1 October, he travelled to the Continent again, calling at GHQ en route for Paris. It was a fateful trip. The front line had still not stabilised; Antwerp was still (just) in Belgian hands, fighting between the Germans and French on the Aisne had more or less finished and the main action was now concentrating on what became known as 'the Race for the Sea'. It wasn't exactly that, so much as a race to exploit the gap between the Aisne and the sea. The French Tenth Army deployed along the River Somme just in time to check and defeat the German advance, while the BEF, moving north into Flanders, was soon to complete the blocking move by pouring into the crucible it would endure for four years, the Ypres salient. The Schlieffen Plan had failed and the war of attrition, which neither side had planned, was about to begin.

The day before he left for the Continent, 29 September, Cumming's single-line diary entry records, in his usual writing, a visit to Euston. There are a few scrappy, spidery lines for 30 September, suggestive of tiredness, illness or perhaps of having been written while travelling, and comprising reminders to himself of people, money and room numbers. There is no entry for 1 October and only three lines for the 2nd. The first two – 'Slept

Rouen. Left early 5am' – are at the top of the page. The third, in a rounder, looser hand, characteristic of the next few entries, reads 'Accident 9pm – near Trilport [probable]'.

There are four lines for 3 October: 'Picked up/6am Carried to Meaux Hospital / Poor old Ally died / 1st Operation – Dr Regnier of Paris.'

Cumming had picked up Alastair at GHQ and set off with him, probably for Paris via Rouen. If they left at 5 a.m. on 2 October and since the accident did not occur until 9 p.m. they had had a long day of it, perhaps having gone elsewhere, or having undertaken some reconnaissance of their own, or having been delayed by troop movements, punctures or a long lunch. They are believed to have been driving a Rolls-Royce (a well thought-of car then, but not yet the icon it later became). It overturned and struck a tree, trapping Cumming and killing Alastair. Early press reports had it that they were 'traversing the woods of Meaux' when a puncture caused the car, driven by Cumming, to collide with the tree. Alastair died soon after and Cumming later had his right leg amputated below the knee.

The version of events that subsequently entered both SIS and family lore is substantially that given by Compton Mackenzie in his autobiographical volume, *Greek Memories*. Mackenzie, who later worked for Cumming and was close to him, had it that it was Alastair who was driving:

In the autumn of 1914 his son, a subaltern in the Seaforths, had been driving him in a fast car on some urgent Intelligence mission in the area of operations. The car, going at full speed, had crashed into a tree and overturned, pinning C by the leg and flinging his son out on his head. The boy was fatally injured, and his father, hearing him moan something about the cold, tried to extricate himself from the wreck of the car to put a coat over him; but, struggle as he might, he could not free his smashed leg. Thereupon he had taken out a penknife and hacked away at his smashed leg until he had cut it off, after which he had crawled over to the

son and spread a coat over him, being found later lying uncon-
scious by the dead body.

'That's the sort of chap old C is,' said Sells [Mackenzie's
informant, who had already described Cumming as 'Obstinate
as a mule, with a chin like the cut-water of a battle-ship'.]

Unsurprisingly, it is Cumming's self-amputation that has
attracted most attention. Although it has not proved possible to
confirm that it happened, doctors with wartime and accident
experience have confirmed that in some circumstances the remnant of a crushed limb may actually inhibit, rather than encourage, dangerous bleeding. Also, he may not have severed the leg
entirely, but dragged the mangled stump with him. If the timings
Cumming gives are correct, his survival in this condition for nine
hours on an October night at the age of fifty-five is remarkable.

Another account by someone who knew him well and who
may have had it directly from him within a year of the accident
is that of Frank Stagg, who was seconded to him from the Admiralty in 1915. By then, Cumming's principal office was a flat in
the eaves of 2 Whitehall Court where he generally used the alias
Captain Spencer:

My first sight of 'Captain Spencer' [Stagg recalled later] was on
the stairway from the 6ᵗʰ to the 5ᵗʰ floor of Whitehall Court, on
a day the lift had broken down. He had not yet got his artificial
leg, and the old man was working his way *by himself* down six
flights to get to the car: two sticks, and backside edging its way
down one step at a time. I was very impressed!!! As is well known,
his only son was driving him 'somewhere in France' when the
car capsized and pinned them both down. 'C' said they talked
together and his son's voice got weaker and fainter – and then
he knew when it stopped that he was dead. How 'C' got clear of
his car I do not believe he himself ever knew. The legend that he
cut the last strips of skin off with a pocket knife *may* be true –
it would be like him.

It was also 'like him' to have had a pocket knife handy.

There are a few further diary entries for October. On the 4th he wrote: 'At Meaux. Sent in from Amer. Amb [American Ambulance] but was not at first allowed to leave.' On the 5th: 'Carried to American Ambulance Neuilly. Operated on by Dr Debouchet.' On the 10th he noted: 'CMS returned'; and on the 12th referred to a car that was either going to, or transporting him to, GHQ. On the 22nd he noted the names of six others, probably all French officers, who were 'In the ward number 63 with me'; and on the 24th the names and addresses of the nurses and others who cared for him. On the 26th there is a longer list of some fifteen names, along with the address of a shop – presumably in Paris – noted for its chocolates (La Coupe D'Or, Bde Haussman).

Among the few relics possessed by Cumming's family is an old photograph of a car spectacularly crashed against a damaged, fire-blackened tree, its chassis bent and twisted, steering wheel broken, wheels tyreless, body panels missing. It looks as if it had rolled violently and may well have hit other objects before the tree. There is no inscription on the photograph and the family has no evidence that it was Cumming's car beyond their otherwise puzzling possession of it. Opinions differ as to whether the chassis is that of a Rolls-Royce Silver Ghost of the period. Some experts believe it is not, others that it could be but with the rear springs untypically elliptical.

As with the death of Dora many years before, we can only imagine the effect of Alastair's death, though the fact that the two references to him in the diary are virtually the only personal references does give us something to go on. We should not be misled by the phrasing of the second – 'Poor old Ally died' – into thinking it off-hand or casual; it was an expression of the times, the seemingly cheery nonchalance which we often over-simplify as being a stiff-upper-lip repression of feeling when actually it may have been a more subtle code than we give it credit for, signifying that deep feeling existed but was subordinate to the determination to carry on, to endure. The writer

Ford Madox Ford, middle-aged like Cumming and also of upper-middle-class provenance (albeit unmilitary), encapsulated Cumming's mode of expression in his description of a wounded, half-crippled young soldier returning from the Boer War to be met by his father at the station: 'Their greeting was, "Hello, Bob!" and "Hello, Governor!"', and Ford comments, 'that a race should have trained itself to such spartan repression is none the less worthy of wonder.'

Ford's comment is seductive but – if it is not an impertinence – it is surprising that he, a man too aware for his own good of the layers and subtleties of feeling, should not have acknowledged the feeling and fortitude that may be behind the unspoken, along with the determination, born perhaps of generations of adversity and struggle, that what counts is keeping at it.

Although he died in an accident, the twenty-four-year-old Alastair is listed among the first four casualties of the Intelligence Corps (one list has his death wrongly attributed to a mortar rather than a motor accident). He was buried in a military cemetery near Meaux (cemetery 1347, grave 424), his grave initially marked by one of the plain wooden crosses that were soon to flower in their hundreds and thousands throughout Northern France and Belgium.

A Scottish obituary describes him as the only son of Commander and Mrs Smith-Cumming of Logie, Morayshire, with no mention of Bursledon or London. In his memorial service address the local preacher said that he knew Alastair from his visits to Logie, and made it clear that there were others locally who knew him better. He refers to the 'skilful and interesting entertainment' he gave at the local school, to Alastair's service in 'the intelligence department' and to his Christian moral qualities which apparently led his fellow officers in India to ask him 'to speak to the men and to advise them to resist the temptation which beset them and to lead pure, clean lives'.

It appears from this that real home, at least as far as May was concerned, remained in Morayshire. Cumming never once mentions it. The Imperial War Graves Commission entry on Alastair gives him as the son of Sir Mansfield and Lady Cumming of 22 Fitzjames Avenue, West Kensington, but that was a later address. As for what their loss did to their marriage, we have already noted Mrs Vetcher's opinion that Cumming might have pushed him against his mother's will into military adventures, and Mrs Vetcher believes that May never forgave him for their son's death. This sounds plausible but, as with so many areas of Cumming's life, we have no firm evidence. Their suffering, like the life and death that occasioned it, can be imagined, but not described or demonstrated.

The next substantial diary entry is on Sunday 1 November when, for no apparent reason, Cumming wrote nearly a page of notes headed, 'Carrying a letter across the frontier (peacetime).' The procedures involved are fairly straightforward ways of concealing a letter's destination from cursory inspection. There is then another gap until 11 November when he announces, 'Arrived home about three and commenced work at once.' Six weeks was not long to recover, especially given his age and the double shock to his system, but it sounds as if he couldn't wait to be back.

He never makes any reference to his injuries and we know only from Frank Stagg's description that he was on crutches or sticks for some time before his artificial leg was fitted. His naval record describes his injury in the following terms: 'Awarded a pension of £300 in compensation for injuries (loss of right foot and impaired use of left leg – nearly equiv. to loss of a limb) sustained 2nd October 14 while on duty in France. Pension to commence from date of injury.' It is from this period that date the stories of his buying an American scooter to traverse the corridors of Whitehall and, when exasperated, of sticking compass dividers in his artificial leg in order to startle unwary visitors or colleagues. The story about the scooter is later confirmed by the diary, while the second is confirmed by Frank Stagg.

Once thankfully back at work, Cumming had a long session

with his assistant, the recently-promoted Captain Laycock, which included a 'sketch account of all progress and work in the office during my absence'. An early subject discussed with Colonel Cockerill of the War Office was events in Petrograd, arising from personality squabbles. Cockerill, Cumming records, 'thinks Camp. should return'.

'Camp.' was Major Archibald Campbell whom Cumming had sent to Russia along with Lieutenant Alley on 26 September. Unlike Alley, who was a tactful man and had been born and bred in Russia, Campbell was a tactless Scot who swiftly made enemies among the British official community. Given the confusion and profusion of British representatives posted to Petrograd at that time, this may have been difficult to avoid. For instance, apart from the diplomatic officials, there was a military attaché who not unnaturally thought it his job to conduct military liaison with the Russian allies; there was also a wartime military mission who thought they were there for the same purpose; and there was Campbell and his staff whose role was not to spy on the Russians but to assist them and to pass back the fruits of Russian military intelligence. He and Alley were attached to the Russian General Staff and given offices in the Russian headquarters, overlooking the Winter Palace. Matters were further complicated by a multiplicity of Russian organisations. Not only the General Staff but every army group headquarters had its own secret service, along with the Ministry of Marine, the Court and the Holy Synod. There was also, of course, the famous or infamous Okhrana, the Tsarist secret police. Each, observed Sir Samuel Hoare, one of Cumming's later chiefs of station, 'would almost rather catch each other out than catch a German spy'. A commendably clear summary of the muddle may be found in chapter 6 of Christopher Andrews's *Secret Service*.

The Campbell issue flickers throughout the diary for the rest of 1914 until he, but not Alley, was withdrawn. Meanwhile, the then DNI, Admiral Oliver, had been replaced by a new man and his post renamed DID – Director of Intelligence Department. The new man was Captain Reginald 'Blinker' Hall (nicknamed for the obvious reason) and he called on Cumming on 12 November to discuss the Petrograd problems. He thought 'the English coterie are very suspicious of Camp and his mission and he thinks Camp should come home'. The following day they discussed it again and Cumming telegraphed Campbell suggesting he come home and leave Alley behind. When Campbell returned on 7 December they talked until midnight.

Russian liaison continued unabated, however, and was to be expanded considerably during the next two years. In early December Cumming was visited by a Mr Alexander Organchieff [?], who said that 'the Russians had only four million men mobilised as yet' and had plenty more but no equipment. He had with him an order for, among other items 'two million shrapnel with fuzes'. On 8 December there was the first reference to the 'Technicians', a scheme to send British wireless operators to the eastern front in order to improve Russian signals intelligence. It seems to have been proposed originally by the British military mission but by 8 December Cumming records that 'the matter of the "Technicians" is put into our hands to work'. Meanwhile, the military mission was warning presciently that the Russians 'wish only for closer touch and communication'. There follow numerous references to collecting and interviewing what becomes known as a 'corps of technicians'. Their tasks, Cumming notes, included the investigation of 'suspicious daily messages as to situation, acquired from wireless stations', the passing of German messages to cipher experts, communications back to London and the influencing of Russian plans so as 'to conform to our desires'. At one point he adds, prophetically: 'Russia will be the most important country for us in future and we should sow seed and strike roots now.'

While Cumming was convalescing his staff had expanded and by 6 December, when he makes a note of his establishment for the War Office, it comprised four officers (himself, Campbell,

Laycock and a man called Kenny), four clerks, two typists (Miss Woodyear, Miss Moore), one messenger and two 'outside men', Rivers and Bailey.

This, then, was the headquarters of Britain's principal espionage arm after four months of war. It directed and processed the work of individuals and networks overseas, whose extent we cannot be exact about but we have some indication because Cumming noted his estimate of monthly expenditure as at 23 November 1914. The total, £4,310, included headquarters and travel expenses as well as what he refers to as Dutch, Belgian, Danish, Norwegian, Swiss and German organisations. This was not a complete picture of his deployment, since he does not mention Russia or France, but it probably indicates some countries in which, or against which, he had permanent staff working. Easily the greatest portion, £1,250, was spent on the Dutch organisation which ran agents into the occupied territories, but perhaps the most intriguing is the reference to a German organisation (£300 'but maybe much more'), since it is generally assumed that he was unable to spy in wartime Germany. The figure may, of course, refer to expenditure on German agents seen in and run from neutral countries such as Holland and Switzerland, although his usual practice was to ascribe such expenditure to the country concerned.

Meanwhile, Major Campbell put himself about at home with the lack of tact that had characterised and foreshortened his time in Petrograd. On 9 December he had a long talk with Cumming about office organisation. He proposed that work should be divided, with each clerk confining himself 'to one section of telegrams, i.e. Newnun – Petrograd, Garton – Rotter [Rotterdam], etc.'. Laycock, whose work Campbell thought little of, should be sent to the War Office. Cumming agreed neither with these nor other proposals – 'which would I think cause a lot of confusion, and I think our present staff enough for normal work' – but agreed that each clerk should be responsible for the filing of his own section and that they might experiment with sending customers summaries of telegrams rather than copies of originals. Busy customers would doubtless have welcomed this rather than shoals of individual, often unimportant, reports, though Cumming doubted that the Bureau was 'competent or equipped for such work'. He was probably right that they were not yet capable of properly assessing their own product, and the trial he agreed involved only the Petrograd, Stockholm and Rotterdam stations. We do not know with what results, but this was not to be the last of Campbell's criticisms.

However, the year ended with signs of progress on a number of reporting fronts, including the tactical. Cumming refers to a discussion on 16 November with the War Office about 'information supplied by us as to the preparations for a raid now being made by Tr'. Later he notes criticism 'by MO2 of our CDV[U?] reports, condemning them as a waste of their time', while in the early days of the new year he records that 'GHQ is quite satisfied with our news; but works its own area just in front of their lines'.

This is a reference to GHQ's own intelligence-gathering operations, supervised by MacDonogh who was now based there. On 12 December Cumming refers to communications with an unidentified agent on whose behalf he had apparently wrung an important concession from the Foreign Office 'to prepare copies of all his future reports on trade and commercial matters and drop them into the Legation or Consulate – forwarding the original reports to us in the usual way'. On the same day he discussed the 'aero pigeon scheme' with GHQ's Captain Bell, to whom he gave maps of landing places; for all that this seems to have referred to the release of homing pigeons in or over enemy territory, it is possible that it referred to parachutists since until 1917 Intelligence Corps officers known as 'pigeons' were parachuted in to make contact with agents.

Cumming's reporting of commercial intelligence was probably a higher priority and a more involving task than we might readily imagine, especially as the British naval blockade of

Germany intensified. All aspects of German trade, particularly in chemicals, oil and food, were as far as possible prevented, while the identification of sources of supply as well as accurate reporting on shortages in Germany were central requirements for Cumming right through to the end of the war. In fact, it is possible to get some idea of the importance of commercial intelligence by appreciating that an essential aspect of this war of stalemate was the prolonged struggle at sea between the German submarine attack on British supplies and the British blockade of Germany. Although the British won, there were periods when it was a close-run thing. Early in 1915 Cumming records the War Office as saying that 'our Commercial Intelligence is v.g.' and that they wanted a monthly estimate.

One of his most frequent War Office interlocutors was still Walter Kirke, who told him on 4 December 1914 that 'I ought to write a history of the war as far as our business took us (to Dinant) as a guide for our successors'. Dinant was one of the small towns in Belgium in which the advancing German soldiers shot and bayoneted civilians, including women and children, during the early weeks of the war. Six hundred and twelve were murdered at Dinant in late August and the mention by Kirke might suggest that the taking of the town marked the end of a stage in Cumming's operations (perhaps the end of all his pre-war preparations, which had featured Dinant). They also agreed that CMS, Cumming's nephew, was 'first-rate and will have something more done for him' and that he would have been 'the very man to carry through the aeroplane scheme'. One of the few family papers to have survived touches on this. Dated 30 November and sent by Murray Sueter, Director of the Admiralty's Air Department and usually referred to as 'Sue' in the diary, to CMS, c/o Cumming at 2 Whitehall Court, it thanks CMS for his part in obtaining a 120 h.p. Sunbeam engine Morris Farman aeroplane for the Admiralty 'at reasonable cost' and promises a cheque. This is very likely the Maurice Farman deal that Cumming referred to earlier.

The top-floor rooms he had in Whitehall Court were to be his headquarters and home for the duration of the war. Built in 1900 in the heart of Whitehall, housing the National Liberal Club, the Authors' Club and a hotel, this was (and is) a handsome mansion block of prestigious and fashionable apartments with views over the river and Embankment Gardens. It was ideally situated for Cumming, close to his customers and controllers and in a part of London where there are many official and non-official comings and goings. It was also convenient in other ways, as recorded by Frank Stagg: 'As soon as "C" got his lower limb he was in his car with the Chief Constable's number plates. Going to lunch at the RAC he generally ran up Regent Street (to have a look at the girls he said) and delighted in passing the wrong side of the "islands" with his Chief Constable's numbers.' On 22 November he got agreement from the managers of Whitehall Court to build an extra room for the typists at a cost of £50, and also agreement from the Foreign Office to spend a further £400 on buying two cars, with the suggestion that 'second hand ones might be found'.

A frequent subject of discussion with Kirke and the War Office was what Cumming called 'the Folkestone arrangements'. These caused confusion and dispute at the time, and have caused more since. In essence, part of GHQ's intelligence operation which came to be run by majors Cameron (Cameron was almost certainly the AC referred to earlier) and Wallinger had its headquarters in Folkestone from where it ran spy networks into the occupied territories through French or Belgian head agents in Holland. Folkestone was also an important screening control for refugees, selecting those deemed of use or threat. It was never part of Cumming's organisation but he had a Folkestone office which worked alongside the army, and there were demarcation disputes. After early successes, the GHQ organisation's espionage contribution declined as Cumming's increased and there are indications that, had the war lasted longer, he would have taken over.

His liaison with other Whitehall departments seems to have been by now well established (viz. his acquisition of chief constable's number plates) and he had no bureaucratic difficulty in having a couple of fraudulent agents detained and another expelled. L called and left on 15 December 'after a warm discussion of his merits'. On the same day he had another long meeting with the Russians who recommended that the proposed expedition (of technicians presumably) should be equipped as for the Arctic with furs and sleighs, advising that 'The place is very small – only 300 inhabitants and not connected with any railway.' At the bottom of this diary page, Cumming printed the word Ogenkvar. A couple of days later, he noted: 'Routine work a little falling into arrears or neglect owing to enthusiasm over Petrograd.'

Just before Christmas there was a War Office proposal involving demolitions and 'tapping wireless', which Cumming said he could not undertake without authority, and on Christmas Eve discussion of a site for a 'wireless School' featured the Lords and Oval cricket grounds and Hendon. His entry for Christmas Day reads, unsurprisingly, 'In the office – C. Major AC, LK, Kenny, Miss Moore ... McLean,' and is followed by a list of the London addresses of some staff. On 28 December, when Cumming was of course working all day and everyone at the War Office was 'out', he noted that two of his staff were visiting (wireless) school sites at Chelmsford and another in Wales. New Year's Eve finds him making arrangements for depositing currency in banks in Salonika and Corfu and covertly sending 'five hundred gallons' to a point east of the Dardanelles entrance.

For Cumming and May this was their first Christmas without Alastair. We know where Cumming spent it but we can only surmise that she was with him.

11

A WIDER REACH

The year 1914 proved fecund in the intelligence war, its successes due in gratifying measure to the institution of lunch.

The lunch in question took place in August 1914 when the then DNI, Rear Admiral Oliver (known as 'Dummy' because of his taciturnity) walked over to lunch one day at the United Services Club (now the Institute of Directors) with the Director of Naval Education, Sir Alfred Ewing. Ewing, who had been Professor of Engineering at Tokyo, Dundee and Cambridge universities, had an interest in codes and ciphers but was by no means a professional cryptographer. Nor was anyone else in Britain. Oliver was troubled by heaps of unreadable coded German signals regularly passed to him, probably because no one could think of where else to send them. Many of these intercepts were the result of the British having cut, in the first hours of war, the main North Sea cable carrying German international communications, and so compelling the use of radio.

At about the same time it was decided to mobilise naval cadets, thus substantially reducing the work of the Director of Naval Education. The lunch may have been planned with this in mind, but otherwise the happy coincidence of leaving his growing pile of unread intercepts and lunching with an intelligent, under-employed man prompted Oliver to make the obvious suggestion. Ewing agreed and set about recruiting putative cryptographers for a new department that was to become known simply as Room 40, named after the set of rooms in Old Admiralty Building that was to house it.

A good deal has been written about Room 40, particularly *The Life of Sir Alfred Ewing, the Man of Room 40* by his son, *40 OB or How the War was Won* by H. C. Hoy, *The Zimmerman Telegram* by Barbara Tuchman and Penelope Fitzgerald's account of her four famous uncles, *The Knox Brothers*. Room 40's success in code-breaking was arguably on a par with that of its Second World War successor, Bletchley Park (run and staffed by some of the same people) but it is less well known than Bletchley, in part because radio itself did not play as great a part in the First World War as in the Second.

In November 1914 Oliver was promoted and was succeeded in his post by the forty-four-year-old 'Blinker' Hall, as already noted. Hall was a successful and innovative commander of the battle-cruiser *Queen Mary*, until illness curtailed his sea-going service. It is curious that Cumming, who frequently uses nicknames in his diary, never uses Hall's; possibly he thought it cruel, since Hall's rapid blinking was also accompanied by a facial twitch. Hook-nosed and balding, Hall was often thought to resemble Punch – perhaps not only in manner – but in the opinion of Compton Mackenzie the figure he most resembled was Cumming himself: 'His nose was beakier; his chin had a more pronounced cutwater. Nevertheless, when I looked at the two men I could have fancied that each was a caricature of the other.' When fixed by Blinker's 'horn-rimmed horney eye' Mackenzie felt like 'a nut about to be cracked by a toucan'.[1]

Many felt the same. Hall was a demanding but inspiring task master, a fearless, effective and highly political bureaucrat who, in the matter of the interception of mail, talked the Home Secretary of the day into approving his illegality. He was also a formidable interrogator, quickly seeing through Margaret Zeller, better known as Mata Hari, as well as the consummate fraudster Trebitsch Lincoln, who fooled almost everyone else. Having supervised the capture, interrogation and imprisonment of the

American-based German spy and saboteur Franz von Rintelen, Hall, in best Edwardian manner, became a lifelong friend of his victim.[2]

Hall was an outstanding DNI anyway, but his great achievement was his imaginative apprehension of the potential of cryptography, to which end he gathered in Room 40 not only service officers (including at one period Trench and Brandon) but distinguished fellows of Oxford and Cambridge colleges, a director of the Bank of England, a dress designer, an art critic, a publisher, a future Lord Chancellor and a Roman Catholic priest. Unusually for the intelligence community of that period – and, again, like Cumming – he also employed women, preferably with naval connections, two foreign languages and typing. (His typists were brigaded by the formidable, cigar-smoking Lady Hambro, wife of the banker.) Until well after the Second World War women with naval connections were quite likely to find themselves in SIS.

Although ruthless in protecting the sources of cryptographic intelligence, Hall was equally determined that no opportunity to use it should be missed for the sake of source protection, and he was ingenious in finding ways of disguising it. The best-known and surely the most important example was his daring and successful use of the famous Zimmerman telegram, which in 1917 was a significant factor in bringing a reluctant US government into the war. One who worked for him, Admiral Sir William James, published a useful and affectionate biographical study in 1955, *The Eyes of the Navy*, but Hall deserves further and more contemporary attention.

He was a figure of great importance as far as Cumming was concerned. Not only was the DNI (or, now, the DID) one of the parents of the Secret Service Bureau but Cumming's own naval background and the predatory disposition of the War Office meant that it was to this parent that he most naturally looked, even if he did not always send it the majority of his business. Also, Hall expanded the role of DID to achieve a degree of political and strategic influence that is unlikely to be achieved again. It is one of the truths of espionage bureaucracy that he who controls the greatest secrets wields, or gains access to, the greatest influence. Hall's unique energy and vision made his influence greater still.

It is hard to say precisely what role Cumming and the SSB had in Hall's operations, but it is clear from the diary that they were intimately involved and that there was a substantial area of overlap. Cumming did a lot of what might now be termed Hall's legwork, carrying out operations to procure the access or other results that Hall demanded. As DID, Hall had resources of his own other than Cumming's, and when operations come to light it is not always clear whose they were, though it is sometimes plain that both were involved.

As far as is known, Cumming had no separate cryptographic responsibility. His own code section seems to have been devoted more to producing codes and ciphers than to breaking other people's. Nevertheless, he had virtually daily meetings with Hall for long periods throughout the war, and as frequent meetings with some who worked for him such as Lord Herschell, Claude Serocold (a well-known City man and successful Solent yachtsman) and the novelist, A.E.W. Mason. In at least one operation, a plan to buy Turkey out of the war, the men involved – Whittal and Eady – were selected and sent by Hall but paid and 'run' (in the operational sense) by Cumming, to whom they reported. To ask whose operation it was, therefore, is to impose a distinction not made by those involved.

A source of further confusion over cryptographers is that Cumming had on his staff a gifted cartoonist, Crowther Smith, who executed a series of cartoons of those he called the Night Code Staff of the Bureau. Included among his subjects were Sir Alfred Ewing and Dilly (Dillyon) Knox, a classicist and codebreaker who was very much a Room 40 man, and subsequently a Bletchley man. It may be that people and roles were interchanged more freely than we think and that there was, at least in Admiralty circles, something of a freemasonry among all concerned with codes and ciphers. A further source of confusion is the discretion instilled into that generation, evidenced by the fact that in William James's biography of Hall neither Cumming nor his organisation are once mentioned, despite almost daily meetings in Hall's office.

Cumming's first entry for 1915, however, concerns communications of a different sort. Under the heading, 'Secret ink shown to me by Mr J. Toye', he describes a simple method of secret writing:

To write. Squeeze down onto a piece of glass the paper on which you wish to write. This may be plain notepaper or preferably a sheet of printed matter. It must be well soaked in water.

Lay upon this a sheet of dry paper and write the message upon this with a hard pencil. On holding up the wet paper to the light the writing will appear as a watermark. On drying it will be invisible.

To read. Soak the paper in water and hold it up to the light.

To erase. Hold the wet paper before a hot fire.

On the first Saturday of the new year Cumming compiled an 'Agents pay list', a list of twenty-three names and initials which may include agents, head agents and abbreviations for operations or places. The money comes to over £6,500. At a meeting in the Foreign Office a week later he was ordered to limit himself to £5,000, with a £1,000 margin, a dramatic increase over peacetime funding.

Personnel problems in Petrograd continued to take up a lot of his time but not so much that he could not spare 8 January for seeing a man about building pontoons in Southampton. On 12 January there was good news: he was promoted captain, a more senior naval rank than is often appreciated and, since Nelson's day, the decisive one, conveying influence and status and an enhanced ability to get things done.

Throughout this period Cumming's most regular Foreign Office contact remained Ronald Campbell, Private Secretary to Sir Arthur Nicholson and, from 1916, to his successor Lord Hardinge. Although Cumming had to suffer Foreign Office restrictions, notably in his desire to use consular communications, he seems to have got on well with Campbell, some twenty years his junior, and there are indications that from early on he saw the Foreign Office as a valuable ally in battles with the War Office and Admiralty. As Frank Stagg recalled:

'C' always used to boast that as he had three masters he had not got one at all, as he could always set the other two against any objector. They were, of course, 'Blinker' Hall, Colonel French (of MI1.c) and Ronald Campbell ... it used to annoy us younger ones when 'C' called that young FO official 'Sir', but his naval training must have lasted, and we ought to have understood his reasons.

MI1(C) was the War Office section dealing with secret agents and liaison with the Bureau; at one period the War Office announced that it had subsumed Cumming's part of the Bureau into MI1(C) and that this was what the Secret Service would henceforth be known as. Although adhering to the letter of this decision, at least in some of his dealings, Cumming never fully accepted the change in nomenclature, as neither did the Foreign Office. The term continued in use well after Cumming's time, both by and within the War Office, but it never attained permanent status, nor wider Whitehall endorsement. Confusion was further confounded, however, by the fact that it was sometimes convenient for the service to adopt War Office cover, and to call itself MI1(C). (The origin of MI6, a War Office name that it does bear still, was, according to Compton Mackenzie and a contemporary War Office chart, that MI6 was a department of military intelligence which included interpreters whose services and whose cover was used by the Secret Service. The Security Service gained its other name, MI5, because it was precisely that – the fifth department of the War Office's Directorate of Military Intelligence.

An agent not mentioned in the list of payments was one referred to as J. Cumming had a long yarn about him with Hall on 24 January and met him on Sunday 31st when they drove around in a car for three-quarters of an hour. He was a double agent (one who works for two services but whose loyalty is only to one so that he all the time informs that one of what the other is doing) and had recently come from Antwerp. He reported that the Germans were 'anxious to know (1) about the sailings of transports and he is to visit Dover, Folkestone, Portsmouth, Southampton and Plymouth and report; (2) whether Spithead is defended by a BD [boom defence]; (3) our actual casualties on Jan.- th; (4) a questionnaire; (5) they paid him fifty and will pay 1/- a ton for every ship they get through his information.'

This interesting variant on payments by results refers to the submarine war, which had started with the spectacular sinking of three elderly British cruisers off Holland in September 1914. The request for casualty figures refers to a cruiser action, the Battle of Dogger Bank, fought on 23 January between Admiral Beatty's battle-cruiser squadrons and a smaller German force. It was a successful action from the British point of view with the *Blücher* sunk and the *Seydlitz* all but, although it was marred by lack of determination in pursuit. It was an important action in terms of national and naval morale because German raiders had been bombarding east coast towns. It was also important for Room 40, in that it was the first major action resulting from their cryptanalysis of German signals.

Cumming is not known to have contributed but there are suggestions in the diary that he may have done so. Following a yarn with Hall the day after the battle, he commented: 'DID told Lk. [Laycock] that our Fleet acted under orders on the assumption that every time the *Blücher* came through the Canal there was an attack on England. Vide Petrograd telegram No . . .' Unfortunately we know nothing more of this telegram. However, on 12 February Cumming remarked that Hall 'acknowledged our assistance in Admiral Beatty's fight'.

Petrograd was not the only place where there was confusion and illwill between different British departments and agencies. It also showed itself in Holland, engendering rivalry between the agent networks controlled from Folkestone and headquarters in London. The Dutch operations, whether mounted from Folkestone or Holland, centred largely on networks of train-watchers set up to monitor German troop movements in Belgium and occupied France. One particular network which became Cumming's responsibility was to provide a great deal of important tactical intelligence, but in 1915 the mainly army-controlled networks – which at one time numbered an estimated 6,000 agents – were beginning to be productive, albeit not always secure or well organised. Anthony Clayton, in his history of the Intelligence Corps, remarks on the abundance of information and the difficulty of communicating it across closed or controlled borders. As for rivalry, he notes: 'At the top the several organisations including the two military ones, one in London and one in Folkestone . . . were in rivalry, a rivalry that led to waste of effort, risk, frustration and bitterness never satisfactorily resolved.' He describes the early career of an Intelligence Corps officer, Payne-Best, who was second in command of the London organisation and began by questioning Belgian refugees at Tilbury. 'But on being sent to Holland his excellent work was handicapped by unreliable agents and the inter-organisational rivalries.' Payne-Best later worked for Cumming and played a well-known, but not enviable, part in the Second World War. (Along with another SIS officer, he was lured to the Dutch/German border at Venlo just after the start of that war, kidnapped by the Germans, interrogated and imprisoned for the duration.)

Throughout the disagreements in Holland, Cumming, for all that his bluff and straightforward manner was not that which people expected of the Chief of Secret Service, seems to have been an adroit bureaucratic operator. The diary shows him to have been more often in the role of peacemaker than participant in these internecine quarrels, standing outside and a little above them despite the fact that his own people were frequently involved. His good-willed desire for compromise in order to get on with the job was not contrived, but was at the same time a posture that found immediate favour with senior officials and frequently worked to his advantage. As early as Sunday 31 January 1915, during a conversation about other matters with Ronald Campbell, he recorded that they touched on Holland: 'He said he was of the opinion that I should control the show – through Tin [Tinsley] . . .' This was what effectively came about later in the war.

The other subject that Campbell wanted to discuss on that day was what was going on in Norway and Sweden. Cumming had for some time maintained a significant presence in Scandinavia, partly for German naval reporting but also as a channel of communication to and from the eastern front. Later, it became an important conduit for information about revolutionary Russia. As in Holland, though, rivalries were beginning to take their toll, particularly those concerning the War Office military attachés. Campbell 'took the view that they should be under me rather than under Consett. I told him I would arrange a modus vivendi with the latter. He decided to ask Sir A.N. for 150 a month extra. I reminded him that I had been allowed 1200 for Norway in peacetime and was at present allowed 70 a month for the two.' As in later decades, however, respect for neutrality was never out of the Foreign Office mind: 'He is particularly anxious that nothing whatever should be done to disturb the minds of the Swedes – especially to connect us with any of their news going to Russia. No connection is to be made between these countries.' He returned to the subject on 9 February: 'I understand that the [very distinguished] personage who I was informed at the beginning of the war was supplying DID with all the information re Denmark, has now stopped this and it behoves me to increase my organisation accordingly.'

He continued to devote a good deal of time to codes, receiving in February from Campbell the copies of 'the compromised G code'. It was probably being withdrawn as of no further use but the context almost suggests that Cumming might have been going to use it to send misleading information, provided the compromise was not known to the Germans.

Meanwhile, he was spreading through the eaves of Whitehall Court and had part of the floor lowered, which meant temporarily vacating his office and bedroom. During January and February six new staff were taken on. A note on the last day of February gives typists' hours as 9.30 a.m. to 6 p.m. with one day off a week, with clerks 'working same ... but 'til work is done'.

A more unusual addition was deployment into South America. On 9 February he was instructed by Hall 'to send a good man to Santiago and Puntas Arenas [sic] for certain purpose and he could spend up to £2,000'.

It is likely that this 'certain purpose' was the tracking of the German cruiser *Dresden*. In November 1914 a powerful German raiding squadron under Admiral von Spee had sunk two old British cruisers, the *Monmouth* and the *Good Hope*, in the Battle of Coronel, off Chile (the first British defeat at sea for a century). The following month von Spee was about to attack the Falkland Islands but ran up against the very battle-cruiser squadron under Admiral Doveton Sturdee that had been sent to hunt him. During the subsequent battle, four of his five cruisers were sunk, with only *Dresden* escaping. For the next three months she evaded pursuit among the sub-Arctic inlets and islands.

On 4 March 1915 Maurice Hankey noted in his diary that he had learned from Hall that she had been discovered in a remote Chilean bay, a discovery usually attributed to cryptographic intelligence although there is no evidence of any until the following day, 5 March. Cumming's man, meanwhile, a Mr Pam [probable], had been equipped with passports and tickets and dispatched on 11 February. He travelled via Buenos Aires and subsequently communicated through the Anglo-South America Bank in Santiago. We do not know whether it was he who found the *Dresden* in Chile but Cumming telegraphed something to him on the day of Hall's conversation with Hankey, and four days later the British cruiser *Kent* sighted and pursued her. She fled to the Juan Fernandez group of islands where, on 14 March, she scuttled after a brief engagement.

Further deployments Cumming was instructed to make at this time were those into Madrid and Barcelona, but Cumming gives no clue as to why. It is possible that he was setting up communications centres in connection with operations around the Mediterranean.

Meanwhile, the Bertrand Stewart business persisted. On 3 February he advised the War Office that they should pay Stewart's trial expenses then went off to dine and talk shop until late with Lord Herschell of Room 40. His social life is never more than suggested in the diary and when it is it is in connection with work. George MacDonogh, now a general and back in London as DMI, called on him in his office and on St Valentine's Day, a Sunday, Cumming drove down to Sittingbourne to lunch with him. This is one of a number of passages in the diary suggesting that, despite their disagreements in earlier years (and disagreements to come), they had a friendship outside of work, albeit one that arose from it. The fact that MacDonogh, like Cumming, had recently lost his only son (to illness) may well have played a part.

There were meetings and discussions concerning deployment in the Near East, particularly the question of the division of control between the army headquarters in Cairo and Greece. There were also discussions about the Dardanelles, with Cumming handing over reporting on Turkish troops and learning from Hall 'that we shall allow Russia to enter Dardanelles and we have built dummy ships and the Trs know it'. Hall was considering a suggestion to pay £3,000 to a Mr Vincent Such [probable] 'for his friend Mahmoud to go to Shakshish from Constantinople' and he instructed that all messages from Whittal and Eady, the two secret emissaries, should be sent personally to him on 'distinctive' paper, as should all reports dealing with aircraft.

Edwin Whittal and George Eady were Englishmen with a deep knowledge of Turkey. Their deployment by Cumming was, as we have seen, on instructions from Hall, but the story did not begin with him. It apparently began, as Stephen Roskill pointed out in his biography of Maurice Hankey, with a suggestion of Hankey's, whose diary entry for 4 March 1915 reads: 'Saw Captain Hall . . . who said that negotiations have been opened to bribe the Turks to oust the Germans, as I had proposed earlier.'[3]

A summary of this operation can be found in Rhodes James's *Gallipoli*.[4] Essentially, Whittal and Eady were offering the Turkish government a bribe of £4 million – authorised by Hall without informing his own superiors, the Foreign Office or the Cabinet – to play no further part in the war. The scheme was not as fantastic as it sounds and might have worked if the British government, unknown to Whittal and Eady, had not promised Constantinople to the Russians. The Turks were reasonably pro-British and were unhappy about the alliance with Germany. Negotiations proceeded some way despite the fact that the Dardanelles operation, that great disaster-in-waiting (foreseen as such by Hankey) had already begun. If Turkey had been bought out of the war it would have made a significant strategic difference as well as shortening the supply lines to Russia, which may have had an effect on subsequent political developments. It was certainly a better idea than the botched forcing of the Dardanelles.

Hankey knew Hall well, possibly from his time as a naval

intelligence officer in the Mediterranean, and admired and trusted him. Cumming, as we have seen, was involved early on and on 9 January he records that at least one of the agents, Whittal, was not optimistic: 'Mr Whittal called – sent by DID – He thinks the project a "forlorn hope" but will make enquiries out there and will call on Limpus [Admiral, in Malta, the man who had advised the Turks on the fortifications] on the way. His friend will call tomorrow and I am to have codes ready by Monday.' In fact, he saw them both off over the next couple of days, preparing codes, arranging communications, paying £500 into Eady's bank and 'suggesting a scheme for Dedeagatch', the town where they were to negotiate with the Turkish representatives. It is possible that he also sent others to support them, specifically a Major Sampson and two other men, Edmonds and Lafontaine, at least one of whom was experienced in Turkey. The coded communications included 'three new dictionaries and six new complete shifts'.

On 16 February he submitted reports from Major Sampson on Turkish troops and a few days later recorded sending telegrams to Sampson and Whittal. There were doubtless further communications before the crucial meeting took place in Dedeagatch on 15 March. When Eady returned to London on 21 April Cumming had a

long yarn with him re NE matters. He could not negotiate with Talaat [Bey] as he did not know our position with regard to Constantinople. The day he opened negotiations we bombarded the Dardanelles. The day his man landed in Smyrna we bombarded it! Money no use. Thinks we could deal if Constantinople internationalised – i.e. left in nominal Turkish possession under international control.

Thus ended one of history's myriad what-ifs, though it was not, as we shall see, the end of Cumming's activities in Turkey. Otherwise, March was taken up largely by cruises and

Russian matters. The former involved the fitting out of a number of cruising craft, ostensibly manned by wealthy Britons who played no part in the war or, in one case, by ostensible Americans. In fact, they were crewed by men working for Hall or Cumming and were on covert reconnaissance expeditions. On 2 March, after calling at Holt's Bank in Whitehall, Cumming discussed with a Captain Cullen the forthcoming Mediterranean cruise of the 1,300-ton *Beryl*. Cullen (who was actually a commander but Cumming sought captain's rank for him) was subsequently issued with a 'telephoto camera', developing equipment, two pairs of Zeiss glasses (German, in short supply since war broke out), a Ross telescope and a rifle. He might also have been issued with another craft, since on 13 March Cumming records offering his motor boat *Commander* at valuation: 'She is to be sent down by rail and Bailey is to follow and show their engineers how to drive her.'

On 25 March he took another officer, Captain Bayford, to Hall who 'authorised him to buy a certain class of vessel in collusion with Simons'. Simons was almost certainly Lieutenant F. M. Simon, RNR, and the vessel the 581-ton steam yacht *Sayonara*. She was previously owned by an American and Simon, a gifted mimic, could pass as one. Provided with a notional owner, Major Howell, and notionally American crew, the *Sayonara* cruised off the west coast of Ireland, initially in search of secret German submarine bases but later providing information about Sir Roger Casement's attempt to arm and forment the Irish nationalist uprising. Sir Basil Thompson, head of the Special Branch at Scotland Yard and another with whom Cumming records fairly frequent meetings, was involved.

In *Secret Service*, Christopher Andrew gives an amusing account of how the operation succeeded mainly in arousing suspicions that the *Sayonara* was a German rather than a British spy vessel. The extent of Cumming's involvement is, as usual, hard to estimate, but in this as in similar cruises around Spain sponsored by Hall it seems likely that he was the provider of equipment, some personnel and perhaps communications. On 24 March he mentions buying yet another vessel: 'DID gives me authority to buy tramp £4,000–£5,000 through JJB to hand over to Symonds.'

Personality clashes meanwhile raged unabated in Petrograd, culminating in a decision on 25 March to withdraw two of Cumming's people in the wake of a row during which the military and naval attachés threatened to resign if Major Campbell (who had been sent back after his stint in London) remained. This unhappiness in the British official community does not seem to have affected relations with the Russians, although twelve days before this they had caused disruption in London by rejecting all the 'technicians' who had been painstakingly recruited. They simply announced, wrote Cumming, that they 'did not want the wireless staff – of whom we have eighty waiting'. It seems likely that the British had taken the idea farther than the Russians had agreed and that only when confronted with its full embodiment did the Russians realise that it was a potential Trojan horse, helpful but at the same time giving the British unprecedented access to their communications.

In London Colonel Nicolaieff could throw no light on the matter but told Cumming he did want 'help for three of their Agents which I promised and arranged to prepare orders'. Intelligence services of allied powers commonly help each other, of course, but that help usually is limited to the provision of intelligence reports or facilities. There was already a considerable intelligence flow between Cumming and the Russians, though Hall had recently complained that he wasn't getting enough naval intelligence out of Petrograd. Help with agents, however – involving the possible revelation of their identities – is an altogether more delicate matter, and the Russian request indicates an unusual degree of inter-service intimacy.

On 12 March he achieved another breakthrough with the Foreign Office, when Campbell agreed 'that I might arrange to hand messages sealed up in an envelope to certain firms we knew, to be conveyed by hand to Consuls for transmission'. He was evidently in favour at the time, since the previous day he had recorded a Foreign Office decision that what he called the 'Norge [Norwegian?] organisation' was 'to be handed back to me'.

He spent a day at Bursledon attending to 'local affairs' and on 15 March interviewed a Swede 'who can pass in Tiaria as a tr. Talked about sacrificing his life for his country – a lot of other tosh without any point – think we ought to do what he proposes and worth risking something. Offered him pay at the rate of 400.' As a strongly patriotic man, Cumming's reference to 'tosh' may at first seem surprising. But it was probably how he viewed any posturing, especially when someone spoke of sacrificing himself for neutral Sweden.

Three days later he went into some detail about how he got permission to retain the unspent money on the 'Aero', rather than return it to the Foreign Office. The money was for 'special purposes', which to his mind included the immediate ordering of another car. He then added that Hall had 'asked for B's letter as he is to defend the SS against renewed attack'. The context might suggest that it was the Secret Service as a whole rather than Cumming's branch in particular that was under attack, though it could have been the latter. His autonomy was by no means secure and War Office threats increased as the year went on.

April began with his first trip to France since the accident. He had discussions in Folkestone on the way and reached Paris via Abbeville and Amiens on Easter Sunday. He immediately called at the 'WO' – either the British military representation or the French War Office – but, predictably to all except perhaps him, found no one available. He also called at the hospital at Neuilly where he had been treated. Easter Monday was spent making 'long calls at the French WO. All morning discussing organisation.' There was then an inevitable call on the British Military Automobile Depot before further discussions with the French on censorship.

This subject concerned him more often than might be thought, since censored mail of all sorts proved a useful check of the effectiveness of the economic blockade against Germany. In London, Hall had already involved himself in the opening of foreign mail which the Post Office was unable to cope with, successfully translating the Home Secretary's threat of imprisoning him into a prime ministerial blessing. His action led to the founding of the War Trade Intelligence Department, in temporary offices in the drained lakes of St James's Park, and for the rest of the war Cumming did considerable business with them, and with their successor organisation, the Ministry of Blockade.

On his way back from Paris he travelled via Rouen, where he again made a hospital call, and returned to more rows over Petrograd. He subsequently pleaded that Major Campbell's temporary majority should be made permanent as a sign that his second withdrawal was not to everlasting punishment, and it was possibly this sort of action that prompted Hall to complain that Cumming took too much care of his staff. Meanwhile, he had recruited for his 'Petrograd room' a Captain Thornhill whose later posting to Russia would help re-establish harmonious and productive working relations.

Among many others he interviewed at this time were lieutenants Bellairs and Brock, in the DID's room. 'They are going to play Golf and I am to supply them with codes.' Mr Calvocoressi, already listed as one of twenty-six recipients of pay the previous month, was, along with Francis Joye [probable], being prepared for Genoa, though he had first to be dissuaded from using his own complicated idea of a code based on Roget's Thesaurus and the numbers of meanings for each word.

More boats were fitted out and crewed, including the *St George* commanded by Lord Abinger, who was to make contact with the *Beryl* and place himself under her command. However, it was operations mounted from Rotterdam that engaged ever more of Cumming's attention and on 15 April he was introduced by Hall to a Miss Bennett-Burleigh 'whom I was obliged to engage for Holland at £1 a day'. This is one of a number of references to people for whom he was obliged, as he often puts it, 'to find a berth'. In Athens, meanwhile, whither George Eady had been dispatched, trouble was brewing with the military attaché and with the Foreign Office in London over British policy. But it wasn't all work, quite. Sunday 18 April was, Cumming wrote, a 'Slack day – nothing much doing. Took four hours off.'

He also noted that 'About this date Lenois [probable] – one of Oppenheim's men shot in public – his wife being present'. Oppenheim almost certainly refers to the military attaché at The Hague and the army network he was involved with, although there is plenty of scope for confusion because he later assessed and issued reports produced by Cumming's network; also, the commercial attaché at The Hague, responsible for monitoring the blockade, was called Oppenheimer. Although it never reached the heights, or depths, of Petrogradian drama, British inter-agency rivalry in Holland was to become more complicated as the year went on, and its resolution was still some way off.

Cumming pestered the Admiralty, the War Office and the GPO for a private telephone line to the Admiralty, Folkestone and Dover. The link with Folkestone was installed on 27 April but by the 29 'the instrument has gone wrong temporarily'. His enthusiasm for new technology never faded, any more than did his enthusiasm for secret inks.

On 23 April he recorded, with an exclamation mark but no explanation, the arrest 'by the Trs at Wesel' of Jonkers van Aaders [possible]. By the end of the month he was pleased to have recruited Mr Hans Vischer from the Colonial Office (which agreed to make up his pay, since Cumming could not afford enough) for Switzerland, and was trying to get hold of a Major Mouread, 'a Maltese of wide experience and many languages'.

The pattern of the next couple of months was much the same. Deployment into Romania features increasingly, yet more boats were crewed and fitted out (some with guns to be unshipped and hidden), Miss Bennett-Burleigh was seen a number of times apparently in a double-agent role (on one occasion Cumming remarks wryly that she interviewed him in a taxi) and an army officer, Valentine Williams, whom he had spent time recruiting and training, was abruptly called to the front 'so that all my plans fall through'. The liability of his military staff to sudden recall was something he had already complained of and would do so ever more vociferously through to the end of the war, and beyond.

Early in May he saw a Mr Lavery who 'thinks he can get a cinema film show into Tr – to take films of the war'. Cumming was pessimistic but didn't entirely dismiss the idea. There is an ominous reference to 'leakage', apparently from the French, with whom Cumming was to discuss it. It also appears that he was giving further operational assistance to the Russians in London: 'Called on General Yermoloff. He wants Mme Helena at Conduit Street watched, also Chursatoff.'

A Mr Gray came to see him with an alarming account of how the Germans might drop bombs of 'Cyanogen, carbon monoxide or arsenurated [probable] hydrogen' on London. It is easy now to overlook the alarm aroused by the hitherto unheard-of prospect of the mass bombing of civilians. Zeppelins were not then the cumbersome curiosities they might now seem, but terrifying weapons, and the Germans had few qualms about chemical warfare. The high priority that we know Hall gave to Cumming's aircraft reporting suggests a stream of which we now have no record and which very possibly included the monitoring of Zeppelin movements and aerodromes.

On 20 May there is a reference to office reorganisation and a 'dinner party to Staff (WO and Admiralty) in the evening'. This could be a reference to his own staff but it looks more like officers of the General Staff to which, with Hall's and MacDonogh's support, Cumming was in the process of being appointed. He refers to this a number of times and on 15 June recorded a surprising conversation about it: 'General C. spoke to me re my request for a GSO grade. He says I am equal in rank to him and the DMO and DID! And it would be a step down! He is perfectly willing to recommend me for Commodore but I declined this as it would make me senior to my superior officer the DID.' He had come a long way from Lieutenant Smith (retired), as had the Secret Service from the organisation that was born incommunicado in Victoria Street in October 1909.

The day following the staff dinner, Tinsley arrived from Rotterdam. He was an energetic, self-advertising and none too scrupulous former businessman whose later role, despite his faults, was important and beneficial. Conversations with him involved days of talks – 'Capt. Tinsley arrived at 11 and stayed until 6.30 with a short interval for lunch' – especially when his extravagant but generally successful claims for compensation for his alleged loss of earnings and business were the subject. He also earned himself a reputation with the Foreign Office for lying, which suggests that Cumming's remark on 23 May not be a misprint: 'He says he has issued to the FO three million bulletins.' There were, anyway, many competing examples of evident self-interest: 'Professor Gardner came. He is a queer nervous man (Prof. of Archaeology at Lond. Univ.). Wants to go to Athens where he has many friends and thinks he could go disguised as an officer.' We hear no more of him. A more welcome arrival, though, was Cumming's old friend TP, 'looking well and volunteered to do any work'. Some work was promptly found for him: 'Miss Bennett-Burleigh. Turned her over to TP . . .'

After a minor bureaucratic struggle, Cumming recruited and posted the multi-lingual Maltese Major Mouread and at the same time despatched another man, Gabriel, to Italy for some undisclosed role at or near the Italo-Austrian front. On 3 June he spent the day at Southampton on 'semi official business' before returning at 7 p.m. and 'working at papers nearly all night'. Papers were evidently multiplying because on 9 June he noted that four typists had called 'on appro', but he did not take on any of them. On 12 June he saw another three and on the 17th two more staff joined. On the same day he saw another foreign liaison contact, Captain Fusali 'of the Italian S. Police' about an agent code-named Litre who features fairly often during this period. On the 18th he had an hour with Sir Arthur Nicholson in the Foreign Office, whom he found 'very kind and said I might come to him whenever I was in difficulty'.

This brief remark may indicate a discussion of some consequence. The bureaucratic origins of the early Secret Service meant, as we know, that it had joint War Office and Admiralty parentage with Foreign Office funding, but no further Foreign Office tasking or operational control. As Secret Service activities increased, with the consequent likelihood of international repercussions, the Foreign Office's operational involvement naturally increased as well, but it still seemed to view the Bureau as an organisation that existed almost entirely for the sake of military and naval requirements. It did not yet consider using Cumming in support of its own foreign policies, preferring the role of benevolently inclined trustee – and occasional referee – who had to keep an eye on what the youngster was doing.

For Cumming, however, this powerful purse-holder represented both a guarantor and a nuclear umbrella (as it were) to shield him against the predatory self-interest of other departments. Getting the Foreign Office gradually to assume full guardianship, to use him for its own ends and to become the major part of his organisation's *raison d'être* was a gradual process which took years. This manoeuvring of himself into their shadow was a significant bureaucratic achievement, perhaps attributable as much to his personality as to his service's successes. It was a process that was already under way by early 1915. In fact, Hall had the vision to suggest, in August, that Cumming's organisation should be fully independent both of the Admiralty and the War Office. This was a remarkable suggestion to have come from the head of Naval Intelligence, suggestive of considerable confidence in the Secret Service. Cumming raised the idea with Campbell but Campbell, as befitted the Foreign Office, was cautious at this stage: 'Does not entirely concur with DID but would like to see me more independent.'

Later in June, Cumming crossed the Channel again to visit GHQ and the headquarters of the British First Division, from where he was taken to an observation post near the front line. He travelled, as usual, by Rolls-Royce and was probably still using two sticks. By the end of the month he was planning some scheme with the Belgian legation, who were to find him a Belgian officer. On the last day of the month he listed his staff both at home and overseas – a total of forty-seven – but, as before, it is possible that some of these were head agents controlling unlisted sub-agents.

Early in July Ronald Campbell came to him with a complaint: 'My men have evidently not obeyed instructions to send paraphrases of their reports on contraband to the Legations.' A few days later he noted that they still had not obeyed him and that he was having to repeat the instructions.

On 7 July Cumming and Campbell spent the entire day together. They were probably discussing problems in Holland which occupied an increasing amount of everyone's time throughout that summer, but Cumming still found opportunity to drive, lend or procure cars for Hall, Campbell, Lord Herschell, Lord Fisher, the First Sea Lord, and others. He doubtless found it congenial to run an unofficial transport pool for senior figures; and it was also, no doubt, very useful.

Sabotage operations were also in the air. On 14 July Campbell gave a Foreign Office ruling which Cumming summarised as: 'No action stores demolition neutral countries.' It is possible that Denmark was one of the countries concerned since he and Campbell were at the same time estimating the monthly costs of Cumming's operation there as about £860, which comprised expenditure on seven agents or operations and, interestingly, a French contribution of £120. In addition there was provision for £100 for 'Wi (Tiaria)', which may indicate an agent in the German port of Wilhelmshaven. Meanwhile, there was further expansion of London premises, with number 46 Whitehall Court dedicated to typists, 44 to codists and two additional flats in Ashley Gardens (numbers 50 and 60) taken on. On 1 August he listed home-based staff, with pay rates, showing thirty-three people of whom twelve were probably typists.

The War Office called a conference on Holland on 22 July to consider a recent GHQ proposal concerning the structure of intelligence work there. Essentially, there was need for a unified command and control structure but the situation was doubtless worsened by operational setbacks as German counterintelligence penetrated and rolled up the exising train-watching networks.[5] What the diary shows of Cumming's role is, first, his bureaucratic care in seeking advance agreement to his proposals and responses and, second, that he was very far from seeking to extend his growing empire for its own sake: 'I read my letter [to the conference], which amended the proposals to the extent that I protested against divided control and many organisations and suggested handing over the whole system in Holland to GHQ – Rotter [Rotterdam] included.' Four days later he recorded: 'GHQ declined proposal as to handing over my Dutch organisation to them and preferred to leave things as they are.' Nevertheless, he appears to have taken on at least part of one of the British-based army organisations, referring it to 'Lieutenant O'Cafferty's menage'.

Arrangements for communicating with agents in the USA also feature at this time, though that does not mean that they were Cumming's agents. He issued codes to military officers bound for America (including in one case a Colt automatic pistol and a safe) and arranged for telegrams sent from America to have unique designators, e.g. 'Car' meant anything for Colonel Agar. There must have been Foreign Office agreement because telegrams were to be sent via the British Consul in New York, who would himself hand them over to a well known American bank. The following month Cumming was considering using further commercial organisations, including an international firm of accountants of whom he notes: 'Many agencies in USA, all Scotch.' He later discussed with the War Office and TP 'a scheme for a Bureau in NY to be run jointly'.

On 29 July he was asked by Hall to 'link up with the Spanish organisation'. Hitherto, British operations in Spain at this period have been regarded as exclusively naval, but this shows the difficulty of drawing hard and fast distinctions. Cumming's first task in the new arrangement involved, typically, sending a car to Vigo. That evening he indicated that his role as provider was not limited to automobiles: 'Capt. Watts called for paper fasteners. Took him out to dinner.' August began satisfactorily with a 200-mile test run of the new Rolls-Royce.

A few days later he listed users of his 'U. code', among which were Athens, Malta, Gibraltar, Petrograd and Cairo, while individuals such as Lord Abinger (who was presumably at sea) communicated with him via Madrid. On 16 August Hall told him that 'my code was all [illegible] and my messages read by the enemy'. He does not say which code. His reaction, as is often the case with those whose codes are genuinely broken and are reluctant to face the appalling consequences, was to deny it: 'I do not believe this is possible.' Fortunately, it seems he was right. There is no evidence that any of his codes were broken (though other British codes were) and he later noted Hall as saying that the code in question – the breaking of which was known through Room 40 intercepts – seems to have contained press material, not Cumming's messages.

Cumming's writing deteriorated again at this period, but he still found time to note the greediness of a Mr Abbott, a 'half Greek author' who offered his services. Another offer of service – in fact a request for a job – was made by Lieutenant Commander Dorrien Smith, of the family who owned the Scilly Isles (and still own Tresco), and to whom Cumming was distantly related. After this he worked on a 'new idea' until two the following morning, remarking that it had been an eighteen-hour day. The next day, a Sunday, he was again 'Working all day until late', the entire morning having been taken up by a brief chat with Tinsley.

It was perhaps a refreshing start to Monday to have an hour's talk with Harold Nicolson at the Foreign Office, while waiting to see the Under Secretary, and perhaps even more cheering to get Hall's agreement to pay off Miss Bennett-Burleigh. On 27 August he noted, 'Saw Trench and Brandon re. employment of former' and the day following had a long yarn with someone called Dulac 're. his adventures and discoveries in Copenhagen'. Later, he mentions turning Dulac down and paying him off. The last days of the month were taken up entirely by the continuing Dutch disputes, about which there was to be a conference in Paris with Cumming represented by Colonel McEwen of MO6. O'Cafferty produced for him a report on the recent naval bombardment of Zeebrugge.

On 1 September he called on Trench and Brandon 'who promised – if I took on Stagg – to work with him in close co-operation and help him to render his Naval news section valuable'. A few weeks later, after a long yarn with Cumming and TP, Stagg agreed to come. This was presumably Frank Stagg whose recollections of Cumming we have quoted already. Stagg said he worked as secretary to Hall and was succeeded by Serocold after making 'a horrid botch of the job'. Hall, he said, 'sent me across to "C" with instructions to help him all I could'.

Stagg recalled Cumming's staff as totalling only five, all men, but he probably had in mind only the relatively senior in closest proximity in Whitehall Court. 'There was Cockerell, a mining engineer recently taken on, the actor Guy Standing [whom Cumming mentions as calling on him a week or two after Stagg arrived], Newnun, another mining engineer from the Colombian emerald mines and a "promoted ranker" who ran the office [Laycock] with a Sub. Lt. Jolly RNVR, who had previously worked at "The Tatler".' The annual budget, Stagg believed, was 'only about £6,000' but the amount of material that came in surprised him. He arrived shortly before further office reorganisation:

> It was difficult to get officers released unless they had been gassed or wounded, but we did get two young subalterns quickly who had no special qualifications, and then a measure of decentralisation and regionalisation was effected. Newnun gaily took over Greece and the Mediterranean; Cockerell Belgium and Holland (most important as Rotterdam was the main supply); Standing all the Americas, until William Wiseman who had been gassed at Hooge arrived to begin his startling career in Anglo-American relations. I took over all the NID liaison, Scandinavia and the Baltic, and the Russian Empire! The latter was quite a big proposition as the German bags on the Siberian mail train were being extracted and opened [his text actually has 'unopened' but this is presumably a misprint], and yielded much useful stuff which was dealt with in the Board of Education.

The opening of the German diplomatic bags was a little-known operation which might in part have accounted for the frequency and intimacy of Cumming's relations with the Russians.

Stagg also provides some further indication of inter-breeding among Whitehall code-makers and -breakers, with a suggestion that Cumming's staff were involved in both:

> Codes were gone into very thoroughly, but the old expert Bentley became a nuisance to both 'C' and 'Blinker'. He was convinced, I remember, that the personal column in the The Times was being used by the enemy using an antique Dutch–English dictionary. At last 'Blinker' put some nonsense in himself, and sure enough within 48 hours Bentley arrived with an interpretation from his old dictionary. We had to protect 'C' from Bentley's visits, for the latter was obviously wandering. In our code room there was a wizard named Hooker but Max Bonn, Tiarks and others from

Room 40 OB used to spend much time in our code room.

Purposeful leg-pulling such as Hall's, not unknown in later decades, is a small pointer to the tradition of humour and self-mockery that became one of the British Secret Service's best-kept secrets. Humour is strangely absent from most spy books, whether memoirs or novels. Perhaps it is hard to be thrilling while being funny. Even in the rare spy novel that does have it – Compton Mackenzie's *Water on the Brain*, for instance, or Graham Greene's *Our Man in Havana* – the humour arises from the absurdities of those who take themselves too seriously rather than from individual character and institutional spirit. Stagg quotes another example, drawing on Cumming's interest in secret inks:

> Secret inks were our stock-in-trade – and all were anxious to obtain some which came from a natural source of supply. I shall never forget 'C's' delight when the Chief Censor, Worthington, came one day with the announcement that one of his staff had found out that 'semen' would not respond to iodine vapour [commonly used for developing secret writing], and told the Old Man that he had had to remove the discoverer from the office immediately, as his colleagues were making life intolerable by accusations of masturbation. The Old Man at once asked Colney Hatch [normally a reference to a lunatic asylum, possibly used here as slang for a research establishment] to send female equivalent for testing – and the slogan went round 'Every man his own stylo.' We thought we had solved a great problem. Then our man in Copenhagen, Major Holme, evidently stocked it in a bottle, for his letters stank to high heaven, and we had to tell him that a fresh operation was necessary for each letter.

Economic intelligence about blockade-breaking, not the most obviously dramatic aspect of espionage but always important, also had its moments:

We had close contacts with the War Trade Intelligence Department, who had their offices in the lake in St James's Park. They were puzzled by the amount of honey passing into Sweden and our man, Savage, tapped some of the caskets on the quays at Gothenburg and sent specimens home. More than 80% of it was pure rubber. Then we asked the French to keep a watch on Swiss imports, and when the French liaison officer told 'C' that they had kept a careful watch on imports of french letters to Switzerland and had worked out that 3 months import would supply every adult male in that country with 8 per diem for a whole year, the Old Man laughed until the tears rolled down. That was a great joke of his for a long time.

Stagg's mention of William Wiseman refers to a thirty-two-year-old baronet, Cambridge boxing blue, would-be journalist, failed playwright and businessman who was interviewed by Cumming on 14th September and taken on for 'general work' the next day. Wiseman was probably one of many men to whom war came as a blessing, giving their lives a purpose which otherwise might have been dissipated in unfocused strivings after self-advancement. He was, as Christopher Andrew notes in *Secret Service*, 'just the sort of adventurous, resourceful, capable maverick who appealed to C'. His career, including his intelligence achievements, is well documented,[6] and for present purposes all we need note is that, after Cumming sent him to New York in 1916, his reporting on German activities in the USA, particularly the sabotage of munitions bound for the Allies, had a great effect on Anglo–US relations and helped bring America into the war. His winning personality was an intelligence asset and through his close friendship with 'Colonel' House, President Woodrow Wilson's confidential adviser, he exercised a significant influence on the President and on the US government's attitude towards the war.

Stagg's recollections were not concerned with the Secret Service's reporting – partly, perhaps, on the assumption that it was common knowledge and partly because it is characteristic of the profession to dwell on the fun that was had rather than on the stuff produced – but he did mention one area. This featured a Captain Walter Christmas whom he described as Dutch, although from the context it seems that he was Danish. Christmas, he recalled, had been 'NOIC [Naval Officer In Command?] at the Skaw [sic] and had given us all his navy's coast-watching reports, he stipulating only that a pretty girl was always at a Skaw hotel as go-between. One of these inadvertently gave him away, and Christmas had to leave Denmark hurriedly, and we got a flat for him in Shepherd's Market.' SIS developed something of a tradition both in pretty girls and rapid exfiltrations, and the efforts made on behalf of Christmas were probably more than justified. Knowledge of German shipping movements in the Baltic would have been of the greatest importance to the Admiralty and may well have been partly what the writer of the 1939 letter, praising First World War coverage, had in mind.

Stagg also mentioned covert listening stations in Scandinavia: 'Our listening stations could not hear Kiel, though Wilhelmshaven was within range, and of course we had their codes. So Godfrey Isaacs was asked to help, and the Norwegian NA [naval attaché] wrangled things with his own people, and three Marconi experts were sent to Horten with forged USA passports "to reorganise the Wireless system in the Norwegian Navy," and to listen to Kiel.' This is another example of the difficulty in drawing hard and fast distinctions between the work of Room 40 and the work of Cumming.

In the autumn of 1916 Stagg himself was sent under an American passport to northern Norway, describing his part in the resulting 'anthrax bacilli story' (the discovery of German preparations for using anthrax as a biological weapon) as a 'great coup for "C"'. While there he befriended the second-in-command of the local Criminal Investigation Department, Redvald-Larsen:

That good friend of Britain told me he would always help in any way he could without letting down his superiors if we passed word on to him. Savage in Stockholm then heard of the journey of Baron von Rosen and two German agents 'on a scientific visit to the Lapps' via Narvik and, as we had Harry Day and many horses taking 'precision munitions' from Lyngen into Finland [for Russia, presumably] and dodging Swedish territory, their visit looked suspicious. Redvald-Larsen was informed and, before they crossed the Norwegian frontier, had them searched. The rest is history.

He goes on to refer to a little-known aspect of the story concerning disguised carpenters' pencils that had been seized from the Germans:

Those carpenters pencils with their beautiful piece of glass blowing that made [a] perfect delay-action incendiary were being used by Hun agents all over the world, so hurriedly the Admiralty sent out to all ports 'Seize all pencils and spirit-levels.' Such a collection arrived at the Admiralty from Falmouth taken off Dutch liners en route to Buenos Aires – little stubs half eaten away and a flotsam and jetsam of Faber, Bavaria and all his lead products. Once again, 'C' was overjoyed.

Cumming's diary rarely refers to such incidents and achievements, and indeed only occasionally to product as a whole. On 2 September he wrote of some illegible organisation, either his own or a War Office network controlled by him, that it had reported 'everything is paid up to the 10th of this month. After that we may expect about 15 reports a month from four travellers in Tr and others, costing about £120 a month.' On 15 October he proudly announced: 'We sent out 90 telegrams × 20 = 1800 reports today – a record!' Hence, no doubt, his recent recruitment of more typists and his purchase of more office furniture from Maples.

Meanwhile, internecine squabbles and operational losses among agents run from Holland involved people at ever more senior levels, seeping up through Whitehall like rising damp. On 3 September Sir Arthur Nicholson asked Cumming for his suggestions and the following day Cumming learned of a new War Office proposal 'that I should hand over the whole of my military organisation to Cameron!' GHQ, meanwhile, commended the information they got from Tinsley in Rotterdam, but things had been going wrong for months with the army networks. We have already noted the agent shot in front of his wife (a War Office agent), and on 6 September Cumming learned that Major Wallinger had had 'seven or eight of his bridge watchers jugged in Switzerland'. The military network that Cumming may have controlled lost its best agent at the end of July.

On 9 September he made another trip to Paris, driving the 165 miles or so from Boulogne in six and half hours. He was there for a War Office conference on the Allied intelligence effort. He stayed at the Hôtel de Crillon, lunched with the ambassador and strolled in the Bois de Boulogne for the inevitable long yarns (he must have managed well on sticks, unless his artificial leg was already fitted). The conference comprised representatives of the French, Belgian, Russian, Italian and British intelligence services – predominantly the military services – and lasted two days, though Cumming and Colonel French of the War Office did not attend the second.

The Allied intelligence organisation in Paris was considerable. The following year, 1916, MacDonogh appointed the then Viscount Mersey to head the British part of it. The Viscount, whose memoir was quoted earlier, described the Bureau Central Interallié (BCI) as an intelligence pool or clearing house for all the allies, each of whom had separate offices under one roof (including the French Deuxième Bureau): 'Our main business was to coordinate and to some extent condense military intelligence . . . which bore directly or indirectly on the conduct of the war.'

Much of the work was connected with war trade, for which he noted that censorship produced a great deal of information, and he had some involvement with espionage and counter-espionage. He would have worked closely with Cumming's organisation, though he does not mention it by name, and was peripherally involved in some clandestine activities. He recalled the opening, photographing and re-sealing – all within thirty minutes – of a neutral diplomatic bag on the Franco-Spanish border and the arrival in the office of a young man 'of singularly unprepossessing appearance' who asked for the loan of one of his two cars. It would have an accident and be out of service for a few days – 'nothing fatal' – after which it would be repaired and returned. The 'accident' was a ploy to delay someone while his room was searched.

On 14 September Cumming interviewed a man who knew a man who could 'get Spanish anarchists to go into Tiaria, get employed at armament works there and blow them up'. The idea appealed but he must have been unhappy about some aspect because he did not, he wrote, 'close with him'.

As the arrests in Switzerland indicated, matters there were progressing little better than in Belgium, and were to get worse. A part of Cumming's operation in Switzerland was run not very successfully by Lieutenant L.G. Campbell, based over the French border near Geneva. This is probably the L G C whom Cumming mentioned on 4 December as wanting an assistant and half again as much money. Another part of the Swiss operation was run by the recently recruited Hans Vischer. He too was unsuccessful and on 18 September Cumming closed it. (Vischer was re-employed in Switzerland later, albeit with little more success.)

There were also two War Office networks in Switzerland, one of which, as we have seen, had recently suffered serious losses at the hands of the Swiss authorities who were far less willing than the Dutch to turn a blind eye to Allied efforts against the German invader. It was at about this time that John Wallinger (elder of the two Wallinger brothers involved in British military intelligence) recruited the author Somerset Maugham to his network. Maugham's fictionalised account of his activities, *The Ashenden Papers*, was published in 1928 and represents, according to Maugham, a generally accurate picture of what he did. It is a very readable collection of linked short stories and marks an important step in the development of twentieth-century espionage fiction. It is not fantasy literature, like Le Queux's novels, and is among the first spy fiction to have been written by a practitioner. It introduces the detached, sceptical, often disillusioned hero or anti-hero who was to prove the ideal observer-participant – and sometimes victim – of later spy writers. Spying, like war, is 90 per cent waiting and Ashenden's experiences are a pretty good impression of unsatisfactory espionage in the curious limbo of third countries. Maugham apparently wrote another fourteen of these stories but unfortunately heeded the advice of his friend, Winston Churchill, and burned them because they were deemed too revealing. It is important to appreciate, though, that his Swiss experiences – unlike his later Russian adventures – were gained while working for War Office intelligence, not for Cumming.

The main point about all Swiss operations at this time was that – certainly as far as Walter Kirke, who received the intelligence, was concerned – the results were disappointing and the networks inadequate. It may be that Kirke was looking only at tactical military intelligence, which was probably not to be had in great quantity or quality in Switzerland, rather than at other kinds, such as embargo- and blockade-breaking intelligence, or – a subject that grew in importance as the war went on – reporting on the activities of subversive Indians. Cumming's military intelligence effort was concentrated upon Holland, while he regarded Switzerland as primarily French operational territory.

On 20 September 1915, during a long talk with Cumming, Sir Arthur Nicholson proposed 'limiting GHQ's zones and handing over K and me our £ direct'. Although it was some time before this happened – particularly for MI5 – the fact that it was raised at this date indicates the way thinking was going, though there were battles yet to fight over War Office control.

Cumming still found time to mess about in boats. On 28 September he 'tried *Commander* off Charing Cross pier with Lk and Weston'. Six days later, however, she broke down during another trial and had to be moored off Trinity Wharf, then sent for repairs.

He began October by securing promises from Hall, Ronald Campbell and Colonel French to help him improve the position of his staff. At the same time he received a promise from the French to supply him with explosive in Paris but frustratingly he doesn't say for what. What he sought for his staff was probably something to do with status and pay – they had no pension rights, no security of tenure and sometimes had to take pay cuts when moving from other departments – though it could have been working conditions and facilities. These latter were, Stagg recalls, greatly improved when Lieutenant Colonel Freddie Browning joined from the War Trade Intelligence Department, which he headed. A director of the Savoy, Browning seems to have been everyone's idea of the ideal man-about-town; he would have been a valuable and entertaining fixer in the life of Bertie Wooster. Sir Samuel Hoare, the Conservative MP and future Foreign Secretary who worked for Cumming in Russia, described him as 'famous upon every cricket ground and in every racquets court, the friend of more people in the world than almost anyone I knew'. Stagg paints very much the same picture:

> Life must have become very much sweeter for him [Cumming], as it did for all of us, when Fred Browning joined. His amazing humanity, knowledge of men and women and 'people that mattered', put the 'C' organisation right in the picture all round. Browning's hospitality was unbounded and, being distressed at the way the female element of the staff had buns for lunch, he got a canteen built on top of Whitehall Court, extracted a chef from the army, an old Savoyard, and used the buying agencies

of the Savoy to secure cheap food in a time of food stringency. As for Browning's relations with 'C', they were inimitable. He brought happy evenings to the Old Man by having gay parties with all the stage beauties that he had at call and, in more serious ways, he was the perfect link; seldom doing anything himself, but linking up with those who knew what was what in any particular line . . . The marvellous thing about both 'C' and Fred Browning was that no field of enterprise was outside their scope. The slogan used to be, 'I have no use for the usual channels, except in the early morning.'

It wasn't all in the diary.

The Browning Way was to serve SIS well, both in his time and after it. A certain social cachet always helps in getting things done and Stagg's reference to using other than the usual channels became a valued tradition. But it was also more than that, becoming and remaining what modern military jargon might term a significant 'force multiplier'. The unrecorded nature of things fixed, acquired or carried through in this way is one reason why there could be no fully satisfactory history of SIS.

On 7 October Cumming referred again to the agent, Dulac, who was apparently employed after all. The mission had evidently not gone well and after it Cumming revealed that 'Dulac was sent out only as a blind to draw attention from the real man'. On the same day Lord Abinger called again, en route for Gibraltar, and was issued with a Lee Enfield rifle and 'best Ross glass'. A few days later Cumming got permits to visit two internment camps, something which seems to have become a minor theme in his daily life at that time. He had earlier visited Pentonville gaol and had debriefed co-operative German prisoners and turned spies. On Wednesday 13 October, in a rare reference to outside events, he mentions a Zeppelin raid. There had been a number of these on London during the summer, usually dropping incendiaries, and although casualties were not large by Second World War standards they were sufficient to engender increased anti-German feeling, some of which, unfortunately, was vented upon innocent German-born English citizens.

The wireless car he had mentioned to the French – also referred to as the 'WT Car' – features during the middle of the month, including the postponed delivery of another, a reputedly 'two kilowatt WT Car'. A few days later he discussed 'the Syrian scheme and the Spanish organisation' with Hall, and recorded meeting the author A.E.W. Mason there. He sent someone called Whittington to New York in connection with the South American scheme. By the end of the month he had secured a promise of a weekly judgement – 'praise or criticism' – on his reports, and on the 28th he spent an enjoyable day at Southampton with a lorry. On the 30th he interviewed nine typists and had a discussion with Ronald Campbell about prefixing the letters CX to his telegraphic traffic with Gibraltar, Petrograd, Athens, The Hague, New York, Flushing, Berne and Paris. This should not be taken as a list of his overseas stations but probably represents those on a particular communications loop. The CX prefix had staying power, surviving in later SIS vocabulary in a number of ways.

The debate over the division of labour between the various services continued, although Cumming's diary shows no sign of the jealousies that seem to have infected various parts of the War Office and which are said by Kirke (in the Kirke Papers) to include Cumming. It may have helped that he seemed to be getting his way. On 2 November he noted that Sir Arthur Nicholson 'had written a long minute to [Colonel] French defining my duties'. A subsequent document, dated 17 November, sets out his rights and responsibilities, referring to him by the title that became permanent – the Chief of the Secret Service – and clearly stating that, as Nicholson had earlier indicated, he was under direct Foreign Office rather than War Office financial control, was responsible for all espionage and counter-espionage agents abroad and could dispose of his staff and his funds as he chose. (There was no reference to MI1c.) A week later Nicholson wrote to MacDonogh insisting that all Secret Service work in neutral countries, such as Holland, should be under him – 'i.e. under me', Cumming adds, stressing that this includes counter-espionage work.

There exists a longer, undated document setting out these points at greater length, entitled 'Cabinet Orders with regard to this Special [sic] Intelligence Service of the British government'. It uses the abbreviation SIS that was to become permanent (with, of course, the substitution of 'secret' for 'special') and includes two important additions to the earlier document: a paragraph instructing other government departments to 'render to the Chief of the SIS every facility in the selection of suitable personnel' while ensuring that someone's service in SIS should not injure his career in his home department, and forbidding the recall of staff without Cumming's assent; the final paragraph commits the Foreign Office to 'place at the disposal of the SIS one nominal acting or supernumerary post in those countries where diplomatic representation exists', as well as providing 'semi-diplomatic immunity for SIS records' and the 'necessary means for secret communication'.

These additions represented major advances, not only operationally but in terms of Whitehall status and Foreign Office involvement. The first year or so of war, despite bringing personal tragedy, must have been a good one for Cumming.

In his own office, meanwhile, November brought complaints from a member of staff whom he identifies only as LSO:

> LSO again gave me notice. He accuses me of partiality with the typists – particularly Miss C., instanced my taking her and four others to Westminster Bridge one Sunday dinner hour: he says I chose the typists on account of their social positions – dress – that I give instructions to Miss C. behind Miss Moore's back etc. etc. and that he would like to have been Asst. Prov.

[Provost] Marshal – when he wd shake up the women in Boulogne and elsewhere!

Pleasing as it might be to explore Cumming's partiality for typists, we learn no more. His reaction showed understanding rather than irritation, and possibly implied shell-shock on the part of LSO: 'I think he is nervy.'

There was also some slight awkwardness with his Russian friends. On 6 November Laycock had lunch with the Grand Duke who promised him a letter of introduction in Petrograd. Cumming was pleased: 'This seems so good a thing for him [Laycock] that I am sending him out to carry the A to Z code etc.' Two days later, however, at a meeting in Yermoloff's room with four other Russians and Serocold:

The General [Yermoloff] spoke to me rather anxiously as to the arrangements we had made with GD to send him reports. He said that of course as regards our own reports we were free to send them to whom we liked, but with regard to War Office papers he was under bond not to show them and had never done so. He asked me to get War Office authority before sending any. He explained that his position with the GD is a difficult one. GD was under him but was socially familiar with his superiors. I promised to select carefully the reports sent, but I feel we have been a little precipitate.

This is, of course, further indication of a significant intelligence exchange, possibly, given Serocold's presence, including decrypts. (Cumming never refers to an interpreter being present during his discussions with Russians, nor to which language they used; it was probably English, or possibly French since that was the language of educated Russians.)

On 16 November Cumming made his daily call on Hall armed with 'Essen reports, bomb and pistols'. Two days later he attended a War Office meeting with Colonel French and four or five Belgians or French. Its purpose was to inquire into recent German counter-espionage successes in Brussels which had largely destroyed one of the army's networks: 'Commandant Tournay pronounced Gilson absolutely innocent and stated his moral conviction that our posts had been interfered with and the man in Brussels denounced to the Germans by rivals!'

Towards the end of the month he spent a good deal of time wining and dining, and making presents to, the Danish Captain Christmas. Following his sudden departure from Denmark, Christmas stayed at the St Ermine Hotel, St James's, and on 26 November he dined with Stagg, Holme (probably he of the suspect bottle of semen), Cumming and 'three ladies' at the RAC. One of these was possibly Mrs or Miss Christmas. Perhaps the others were the attractive female intermediaries with whom Christmas had previously dealt.

The following day Cumming listed Tinsley's staff in Rotterdam as comprising twenty-seven British, Dutch and Belgians. Again, the functions of most of these people is unclear, but for some he lists tasks and areas of responsibility, such as reports, cashier, Maastricht, translator, 'contraband political'. The month ended with further territorial disagreements with the War Office in the course of which Kirke tried to dismiss the Foreign Office as having 'nothing to say in the matter'. More co-operatively, there were arrangements for one of Cumming's military officers in Switzerland to have his reports edited by the military attaché, since much of what he had been sending made little military sense. In fact, on 30 November Cumming recorded him as asking plaintively for the Order of Battle for the German army, so far as it was known, in order to check his agents' reports.

It made understandably little sense to Cumming that he had to fight to get such information out of his own side in order to improve intelligence performance, while, as he pointed out, the French were giving it freely. Agents naturally respond better to case officers who are well briefed and can ask better questions; the case officer is also better able to see through flannel or inaccuracy. Also, the War Office's habit of posting people in and out of Cumming's control at short notice must sometimes have made for shallow or irrelevant reporting, since there was not always time for expertise to be gathered. Thus, when Stagg talked of Newnun 'gaily taking over Greece' his phrase suggests both the flexible and lively spirit of the times, and the superficiality. It takes time and application for people to learn their subjects thoroughly and both these qualities were doubtless, in some areas, lacking.

On 7 September the French proposed that they should second an officer to Folkestone (to Cumming's operation there, presumably) and that he should second one to Paris, where the man would have a room in the French Admiralty, a further indication of the closeness of liaison. The following day he had a long yarn with O'Cafferty 're. interfering with agents (very difficult to spot the really guilty ones)'. Fabrication of intelligence, or even judicious exaggeration, has probably existed for as long as the profession itself, and it is likely that it was this rather than betrayal that they discussed.

There are no diary entries for Sunday 12 September to Wednesday 15, while the pages for the 16th and 17th are missing. On Saturday 18th Cumming crossed to Boulogne, apparently returning the same day and driving back to London via Rye. The following day he wrote that he 'Walked over to DID', his first reference to walking in London since losing his leg. It is possible that he had had his artificial leg fitted during the blank days.

The following week he interviewed a number of officers, occasionally commenting on them. The first was on Monday 20 December: 'Interviewed: Captain Sassoon. Good chap. French, mother Russian, many friends in France – Jew by religion.' It is a pleasing reference, but the poet Siegfried Sassoon's diaries show him contentedly on the Somme at this period: 'December 10th. Fine and warm. Did attack on Le Quesnoy before lunch.' He is still there on the 17th, possibly on the 18th, though there is then a blank until Christmas. Sassoon was not, anyway, the only person he saw that day: 'Miss Bennett-Burleigh called and left photos.'

On Christmas Eve he had a dictaphone installed in the office, while Miss Cooke (could she have been the Miss C with regard to whom he was accused of partiality?) took on the 'transmitting machine'. This Christmas, however, he was not the only one at work. On Christmas Day there was a conference to consider recent Scandinavian troubles, which he refers to as the 'Kobj debacle', and he made calls on Ronald Campbell and Hall, who were both at work. On Boxing Day he called on Colonel French whom he found proposing 'to extend Kell's sphere to "British Empire"'.

Kell was eventually successful in getting MI5 officers into most Empire countries, arguing that in security terms the Empire was an extension of Britain itself. Cumming was uneasy about this. Although working relations seem to have been co-operative and effective, the mutual suspicion engendered in those early years lived on in both MI5 and parts of MI6 for decades. It is perhaps inevitable between intelligence and security services with their different but overlapping complementary roles; it was not always destructive, never dominant and never seems to have been as great in Britain as in other countries but it naturally lent itself to caricature, as in Mackenzie's *Water on the Brain*.

Later, when the Foreign Office allowed Cumming to post his officers to embassies as Passport Control Officers (PCOs), there was further trouble which, Stagg recalled, Cumming determined to fight: 'When the appointment of Passport Control Officers to embassies abroad was mooted, MI5 was insistent that they come under their wing. "C" fought a hard battle against General Cockerell, and won, the argument being that a division of "security authority" was bad enough in this country, but would amount to suicide abroad.' We should not forget that, from the earliest days, Cumming and Kell had both been equally enthusiastic about dividing the SSB.

12

TR/16

It is already clear that much of what went on in Cumming's life, whether it was family, lunches, office parties or work, is not found in the diary. In fact, nearly all of what was operationally important is not mentioned at all. Most of it will never now be known but, fortunately, a few other papers have survived and these, along with some published material, give us an idea of the underside of the iceberg.

There is, for instance, no mention in the diary of the case of an agent symbolised as TR/16 (TR, as we know, normally meant Germany and the number might suggest – but this is hypothetical – that there were at least fifteen other German or German-based agents of whom we know nothing). TR/16 is unusual in that some papers about him have survived along with, in the Ministry of Defence archives, one of his most significant reports. He also featured twice in public print:

> I knew him as the Dane. What his name was, or where he came from, I do not know, although I met him several times. Slight of build, fair, with blue eyes, he looked the reserved, well-bred Scandinavian of cultured and professional interests. He certainly did not look the arch-spy that he was. When I came to know him better, however, I realised why he was so successful. He was a marine engineer of exceptional quality; he was a man without nerves, always cool and collected; nothing escaped his austerely

confident eye; and he was possessed of an outstanding memory for the minutest detail of marine construction.

Thus Henry Landau, who worked under Tinsley in Cumming's Rotterdam station, in a memoir published in 1934 called *All's Fair*. The CBE granted to Tinsley in 1919 indicates that, despite his pushiness and his reputation for untrustworthiness, he ran a successful and productive station that must have had good claim to be Cumming's best. Its success was by no means dependent on TR/16 alone, but he was the kind of agent who, at pretty well any time, could make his case officer's, or the station's or even the service's, reputation.

He was not in fact Danish but German, the kind of native agent with direct access whose absence Cumming bemoaned pre-war. Born in 1875, he was a naval engineer who was court-martialled and degraded for having insulted (by striking) a relative of the Kaiser while serving at one of the North Sea ports. Embittered against Germany and the Kaiser, he made contact with Tinsley via the British legation at The Hague in November 1914. It is not known precisely how the two came into contact; the likelihood is that TR/16 walked into the legation and offered his services, but there is a reference to his having been 'suborned' by Tinsley. He could pass as Danish and seems at one time to have been known by the code-name 'Dane'. It says something for Tinsley's restrictive security practices that Landau, one of his best officers who acted as stand-in case officer, never knew TR/16's real name or nationality. Nor is it known how wartime communications with TR/16 were arranged, apart from the fact that meetings seem generally to have been in Holland.

Communications must have been good, however, because on 2 June 1916, just after the Battle of Jutland, TR/16 was sent the following message: 'Reliable information urgently required regarding German losses in North Sea action yesterday.' He set out that day on a tour of German ports: 'I went at once to Bremen, travelling from there to Danzig, Kiel, Rostock, Geestemunde, Emden and to Sande near Wilhelmshaven, in order to ascertain the exact German losses in the North Sea action of May 31st.' He completed his tour on 21 June and his detailed five-page report reached London less than a week later, with copies sent to several overseas stations, including Alexandria, Rome and Petrograd. Headed with Hall's handwritten accolade – '100%' – the report is a precise and comprehensive account of German damage, which was (unsurprisingly) greater than admitted. News of it was urgently required in London not only in order to assess the likelihood of the High Seas Fleet seeking battle again, but also because Jutland had become a significant political issue at home. The British press largely accepted the German account of their losses and were thus able to portray it as more a defeat for the Royal Navy than a victory; whereas German losses had in fact been severe enough to ensure that they never again sought major action, regarding the very idea as – in Andrew Gordon's words – an invitation to mass suicide. Nor was TR/16 the only agent reporting on the subject; there exists another report – CX183 of Sunday 19 June 1916 – sent from Copenhagen and quoting 'German agent D15', who had arrived from Wilhelmshaven. There is less detail of the damage in this report but it contains a statement of German personnel losses as 63 officers, 2,414 men killed, and 490 wounded.

There is also earlier (March 1916) reporting from TR/16 on German ship and submarine construction which shows something of why a post-war evaluation of his product described it as always accurate, up-to-date and of the 'very greatest possible value'. He seems to have been an ideal agent: able to travel freely in pursuit of a subject of great intelligence interest concerning which he was an expert, careful, discreet, accurate, well-motivated and capable of getting to a neutral country for debriefing. At the time when it most mattered, he fully answered the very requirement which Cumming's organisation had been set up to meet in 1909.

Nor did he stop there. He continued spying after the war,

providing, by the mid-1920s, practically all SIS's intelligence on German naval and aviation matters. The German revolution, or near-revolution, at the end of the war meant that he was socially reinstated and he set up in private practice, becoming director of a number of companies and expanding into aviation while retaining his extensive naval and military contacts. Case officers who succeeded Tinsley did not find him an easy agent; there were periods when he was unproductive, and one during which he dallied with the French. Nevertheless, since covert German rearmament began not long after the Treaty of Versailles there was no shortage of intelligence requirements in his field and he usually confounded criticism by coming up with something unexpected and valuable at his next meeting. He also expanded his contacts to include the police in reserve forces.

His report on 7 November 1934 on German submarine construction, dismissed at the time on grounds of 'improbability', was in fact the first concrete evidence that Germany was rebuilding her U-boat fleet.

Two years later, with another war becoming more likely, TR/ 16 was still spying but he worried that his age made him less able to take the strain, while the security climate was worsening. He looked forward to retiring in order to live out his life without worry and later passed details of two men he thought might be recruited to succeed him. Meetings were still in Holland, sometimes arranged via postcard from Luxembourg, and he never carried anything across the border in writing (though he did smuggle into Germany written questions which he disposed of after learning). The meetings were monthly, usually in hotel rooms, with the surrounding area under surveillance by an officer other than his case officer and by a trusted agent whom the station used in this role.

In April 1938 he reported that while attempting to recce a secret airfield with underground accommodation he had been stopped and questioned by a civilian foreman who reported to the Gestapo. TR/16 talked his way out of it, then immediately drove home through the night, arriving at 3 a.m. and destroying any papers he thought might be suspicious. At 8.15 a.m. the police arrived; he persuaded them that he was an innocent nature-lover who had had no idea that he was looking at an aerodrome. However, the next time he crossed the Dutch frontier he was subjected to an unprecedentedly thorough search, and his portable typewriter stripped. His case officer advised him to lie low and meetings were suspended for a couple of months.

At his next meeting, in November, he was – on London's instructions – shadowed throughout by an agent the station had used before, presumably in order to see whether the Germans were watching him or even whether he had been turned and was covertly in touch with them. The agent, a Dutchman named Van Koutrik, had never before known on whose behalf he was watching a flat, a room or an entrance, but this time he was permitted to find out, noting all movements, conversations and hotel registration details. His report confirmed that TR/16 was telling the truth about his movements when not with his case officer and London's rightly cautious mind was, presumably, eased.

It would not have been had they realised that Van Koutrik was a double agent working for the Germans, and that he copied his report to them.

Meetings continued normally for the next few months. If the German investigation seems leisurely, we should appreciate that they had no idea of TR/16's long espionage history nor, at this stage, of the largely informal and unofficial access he had contrived for his retirement. At the meeting that was to be his last, on 18 July 1939, he reported that he had been warned for barrage balloon duty in the event of war, but thought he could get out of it. The next meeting was fixed for 20 August.

This was the only meeting that TR/16 ever missed. Instead, he sent a postcard regretting that he couldn't travel and suggesting that his case officer send someone to Germany to meet him. The writing was his but the station was suspicious because

TR/16 had always refused to communicate with his case officers through third parties. London, noting that he had never previously suggested a meeting in Germany, suspected a trap and ordered that in no circumstances should anyone be sent to see him.

On 10 October, some five weeks after Britain declared war on Germany, *The Times* carried a Reuters report announcing the execution by axe of Herman Krueger (he was normally known as Karl) after he was 'found guilty of working against Germany in favour of foreign Powers'. There is, though, some reason to think that this was bluff and that he may in fact have committed suicide during interrogation.

TR/16's quarter-century espionage career was unusually though not unprecedentedly long, particularly for a wartime agent; had he survived the Second World War as an agent it might well have been unique. Not enough is known of his product to be certain about including him in the top division of spies, but he merits consideration on the basis of his First World War work. To have had a marine engineer able to tour German ports and say which ships were where, expertly describing their armaments and state of readiness, must have been of great value to the Admiralty.

At about the time of TR/16's capture an SIS officer in Holland was ordered to burn all papers held by his station, in case of invasion. Among them he found many from Tinsley's time, including a file of agents' reports and detailed drawings of the defences of the mole of Zeebrugge, obtained in advance of the storming of Zeebrugge on St George's Day, 1918. This was further indication that Cumming had sources capable of producing local tactical intelligence reporting.

Like most espionage losses, that of TR/16 was not a failure of anything sophisticated but a combination of ill-luck and neglect of elementary procedure: allowing one agent to learn the identity of another. Details of his capture were confirmed by post-war interrogations of German personnel. It is unrealistic to attempt serious comparisons at this distance but it does appear that in Cumming's day operations in Holland – certainly those concerning TR/16 – were more securely handled than was the case at the onset of the Second World War when losses included not only TR/16 but two officers in what became known as the Venlo Incident (referred to earlier). The fact that Henry Landau had not known the identity of the agent he occasionally had to see was evidence of very tight security indeed.

13

1916

The year 1916, the bloodiest so far of an unprecedentedly bloody war, began with the Austro-Hungarian offensive in the Balkans which led to the conquest and occupation of Montenegro and Albania. The railway between Germany and Turkey was reopened and in mid-January the Kaiser journeyed on it to invest his ally, King Ferdinand of Bulgaria, with the rank and insignia of a German Field Marshal. Perhaps in anticipation, on 1 January 1916 Cumming was summoned to the Foreign Office by Sir Arthur Nicholson to be told that 'he is not very keen on Albania but wants information re Bulgaria'. On 16 April the War Office wanted more information from still-neutral Romania about troop movements in and out of Bulgaria.

A week later, after working until 1.30 a.m. and being unable to sleep thereafter, Cumming was dealing with another old friend: 'Called on DID (who concurred) and on Gen. M. [Mac-Donogh] re his decision as to K doing all CE work in the British Empire as against British Islands (United Kingdom). He promises that this shall be the limit and that Malta and Egypt shall be excepted from K's area.'

February began with another staff dinner at the RAC, followed by unspecified new office arrangements, calls and information from Mr Rothschild, the recruitment of Lord Onslow into the code section and, on the 24th, a difficult six-hour drive in the snow from Boulogne to the Ritz in Paris – 'Bailey drove well.' The next day's discussions included a session with the French Minister of War (a far cry from the days when Cumming felt he had to prove his identity to the French), then the overnight train to Marseilles and the P & O steamer *Moolton*. When this sailed after dark its passengers included three generals. Their destination was Malta and their purpose an international conference, due to start on 1 March but postponed until the following day to await the arrival of the Italian admiral. When it did start, the principals included three French admirals, three other French officers, two Italians, two British vice-admirals and six other officers including Cumming. The following day Cumming was put in charge of a sub-committee of nine.

With his professionally admirable but historically frustrating discretion, Cumming does not reveal what was discussed, though the conference was widely known about (Compton Mackenzie refers to it) and it may be significant that among the senior British representatives there was considerable experience of Turkish matters. Malta was familiar to Cumming from his naval days, when it was the social hub of the Mediterranean fleet, and his hastily scrawled notes indicate a hectic social round outside conference sessions, along with frequent informal discussions. It was still in session on Saturday 4 March but thereafter the diary is blank until the 16th when he arrived at Southampton with despatches for the Foreign Office and Admiralty. The conference itself and the sea voyage back were probably a welcome break, perhaps the longest he had had since 1909, though the voyage could not have been as relaxed as in his salad days in the Mediterranean. German submarine warfare was mercilessly successful – that month the Reichstag was to vote for unrestricted submarine warfare, the Russian hospital ship *Portugal* would be torpedoed with the loss of 950 lives and the Folkestone–Dieppe ferry *Sussex* with the loss of fifty. Despite this, it would be another year before their Lordships of the Admiralty would be forced by the Prime Minister, aided by the courageously subversive actions of junior officers, into adopting the convoy system.

There are few diary entries for the rest of the month, though the start of the next finds Cumming getting Bailey to drive Admiral Limpus of Malta – now, perhaps, a useful new contact – across to Boulogne (where in fact the Admiral missed his train 'owing to carelessness of transport officer'). By the middle of the month he was discussing with the War Office a report on the possible occupation of Denmark by the Germans and persuading Campbell at the Foreign Office to agree that 'within reason I am entitled to entertain those with whom I have business and that it is a legitimate way of furthering my dept's business but I must control it myself'. This suggests that before then he might have been paying for entertainment himself, though it is possible that Campbell was simply giving official blessing to a practice already in being.

At the end of April Cumming was involved in a postponed proposal to seize a German consulate and was sending an officer to Lisbon to take charge of the military intelligence mission there. With Hall's support, he achieved the appointment (and promotion) of a Lieutenant Baring to take charge, along with agreement that the 'Military Lisbon man to be my man'. This shows yet again the difficulty of knowing precisely who was working for whom, since Cumming has generally been regarded as having no involvement in Portugal. On the last day of the month, a Sunday, he spent three and a half hours in a taxi. Presumably, he was still debriefing some agents himself.

In May he obtained Foreign Office approval for 'our working for WTID' (War Trade Intelligence Department). This may have meant approval for his being tasked by and submitting reports to the WTID, a widening of knowledge of his activities which was presumably why he needed permission. It was at this time, too, that he gained partial control of – or sometimes simply access to the services of – Permit Officers at British missions overseas. This was an important development, a precursor of SIS's future (and too long extended) tradition of using the position of Passport Control Officer at missions both as cover and for its access to persons of interest. He seems to have shared the services of Permit Officers with MI5, since on 19 May he recorded Kell as addressing them, and giving them instructions, in his (Cumming's) office. On 3 June, however, the Foreign Office instructed him to 'stop all Permit O's till further orders', but less than a fortnight later business resumed with his interviewing an officer called Fitzroy as a potential PO in New York. By the end of the month he was also deploying someone to Honolulu.

June began with a list of callers (eleven, not an unusual number), a yarn of some hours' duration at the Censor's Office, and a note – evidently of great interest and pride – to the effect that the Lancia he normally used had covered 14,020 miles since 10 May 1915. Among his callers a few days later were one D'Oyly Carte, while on Sunday 11 June he made a call himself: 'Went to Buckingham Palace by command and had a long interview with the King. He told me a lot of stories about the Naval Battle [Jutland] and I enjoyed my audience very much.' He then added, with that mixture of humility and pride which it is probably unjust to see in purely social terms, 'Cols. Wigram, Derek Keppel and Commd. Godfrey Fausset were nice to me.'

This is not the only example of Cumming's contacts with the Palace. Although he gives no indication of the purpose of this one, two days later he records his then Petrograd representative, Captain Sir Samuel Hoare, MP, as having an audience with the King; it is possible that events in Russia and the state of the Tsar and his family were the reason.

Diary entries for the summer of 1916 are brief and mainly routine. Cumming inspected possible new premises at 52 Vincent Square, took on a garage, confronted Arthur, a scout he employed, about stealing, and subsequently had several meetings with the boy's scoutmaster. He also took on four more typists, engaged a Mr Salisbury for Switzerland despite disliking him, got Sir Samuel Hoare promoted from captain to colonel and discussed with the War Office the continuing problems in Petrograd. These now centred on one of his own staff, Thornhill, whom he wished to remove but whom the War Office wished to retain 'because his identifications [of German units, presumably] are good'.

Sunday 2 July, the day after the start of the battles of the Somme, he described as a quiet day in the office but noted the following:

> I was informed by an eye witness that an application was made by the Belgian Staff to give the Belgian order to me and to Captain Burnham and that our names were scratched out and those of General Cockerill and Col. Kell substituted by someone in the War Office! I am not quite certain of the second name put forward – it might have been Col. Downing or Lieutenant O'Cafferty.

Meanwhile, Sir Arthur Nicholson had been replaced at the Foreign Office by Lord Hardinge, with whom Cumming had a session on 13 July. He asked for a further £5,000 per month for 'German organisations, Trade and Contraband' and to finance eleven Military Control Officers (MCOs – officers appointed by Cumming and responsible to him for information but to MI5 for the granting of visas) he had spread between Petrograd, Paris, Madrid, Lisbon, Rome, Athens, Alexandria, Stockholm and Christiana. His requests were granted in full and they went on to discuss the German, Russian and French Secret Services, as well as 'quasi military missions in allied capitals, rival organisations, WTID, Athens and Petrograd'. Also, interestingly, 'Bonn'. (This refers to a man rather than a place, since Max Bonn was a German translator who worked for Cumming and whose brother, remarkably, 'occupied an analogous position in the German Foreign Office'.)

Such occasional references to possible spies or networks within Germany itself are particularly interesting because

Cumming is generally regarded as not having spied within Germany. In TR/16 we saw there was at least one considerable exception and there were certainly others, but some references seem to be to organisations rather than to individual agents. From 1917, and possibly earlier, he had a Lieutenant Brickwood running a section to help British POWs escape by sending maps, compasses and other equipment into the prison camps by secret means (not long before this entry Cumming mentioned having interviewed two British officers who had escaped via the Swiss border).

Overseas stations were expanding considerably during this period. Towards the end of July Cumming listed six people and three cars in Salonica, eight (including three typists) in Athens, and no less than fourteen in Paris. Most of the latter there seem to have been engaged in registry work, so it is likely that they were employed mainly in the exchange of intelligence with the French government, and that there were certainly others more senior to them (a Captain Lygon for instance) who are not mentioned.

He also continued his unofficial role as transport officer for those in the know, frequently sending or lending cars (particularly to MacDonogh), often with brief references such as, on 1 September: 'Sir D. Brownrigg in Lancia to Kipling.' There are similar brief references to various problems, such as that of 6 September: 'Harvey retd.: He says Brutus was convicted on the evidence of instructions written out by D. on the back of a questionnaire and mentioning Brutus by name – this was found among his papers by the Police.' Questionnaires (briefing reminders) were greatly favoured by Cumming and agents were frequently given them once they became trusted. Brutus was probably a codename and he features only once more when, on 14 October, he apparently 'arrived safely'.

On 20 September Cumming increased his involvement in Spain. Major Dansey – possibly Claude Dansey, who was to become a significant figure in SIS – reported on his recent visit there and Cumming took him and Freddie Browning along to see Hall. They made a persuasive trio, proposing a 'CE Bureau for Spain' that would include 'a nucleus for recruiting men to go into Germany'. Although doubting that much good would come of this, Hall approved. Dansey, Cumming reported, 'believes he can make use of Mr Sinclair [blank]'s organisation in Spain and reports that there is a vast amount to be done'.

A few days later he was inspecting a wrecked Zeppelin, L.32, in Billericay. It had been shot down by British aircraft with the loss of all crew and from it (though unmentioned in the diary) a valuable, recently introduced German signal book was recovered intact and passed to Room 40.

In October Sir William and Lady Wiseman were much in evidence, occasioning a number of dinners and theatre outings. It has been thought that, in the more sensitive and important aspects of his work of wooing the US government to the Allied cause, Wiseman (who went about New York as Walter Wisdon, director of W. Wisdon Films, Inc.) was reporting over Cumming's head and had little to do with him. To assume this is probably to take the handling procedures of certain telegrams as indicative of the whole relationship, which is misleading. Cumming was evidently close to the Wisemans and saw a great deal of them whenever they were in this country; given, too, the way that both he and Wiseman operated, it is likely that Cumming was fully informed of everything going on on the US front.

On Sunday 8 October he compiled a list of staff and agents (numbers only, no names) that gives a clearer picture of the size of his organisation. As with other such lists, it should be viewed with caution since 'agents' remains undefined and could include regular, paid or unpaid intelligence producers, occasional providers of facilities, unknown sub-agents of head agents or even one-off contacts. Also, it is unlikely that, say, the New York station defined 'agent' exactly as did the Alexandria station. Nevertheless, its rarity and apparent comprehensiveness make it worth quoting in full:

Staff and Agents: Headquarters 60; Aviation 11; Holland 10, 240; Norway 10; Sweden 10; Denmark 80; Russia 12; Alexandria 300? Athens 100; Romania 30; Salonika 40; Malta 8; New York 8; S. America? Switzerland 15; France 20; Italy 8; S. Africa 3; Spain ab[about] 50; Portugal 2; Odds & sods? Total 1,024.

The 240 listed with the 10 for Holland must mean agents in Belgium, who were mostly run from Holland and whose large number will be explained later. At sixty, Cumming's headquarters was very much larger than hitherto, having expanded to include such people as a Lieutenant Merton, RNVR, a doctor of chemistry who worked at secret inks and bombs, and who was eventually succeeded by Dr Dawson, later a professor at Edinburgh University. 'Aviation' refers to the little-known Air Section at 11 Park Mansions in Vauxhall Bridge Road under Lieutenant O'Caffrey. Cumming frequently mentions O'Caffrey (with whom he had lately viewed the crashed Zeppelin); and although the full duties of his team are not entirely clear, an important part was to work out the courses of German bombers from intercepted radio signals. They probably dealt with spying on German airfields and possibly also with sabotage, as well as with the use of carrier pigeons.

The question mark against South America (although Cumming had recently sent another officer to Santiago) may refer to the fact that his operations there were nascent rather than active. After May 1917, however, he seems to have deputed spying in South America to a Mr Knox-Little, a businessman with South American experience who ran his own independent network of agents on Cumming's behalf.

Greek affairs had been assuming greater prominence throughout the year and a visitor who received almost daily mention during the latter part of October was Compton Mackenzie. Meanwhile, Captain Granville Barker (could this have been the playwright and director?) was appointed in charge of records, with the idea that he should actually keep a record of everything the organisation did. Whether or not the good captain did good work, virtually nothing remains.

On 7 December Cumming recorded: 'Sir William Tyrrell came and gave us a long dissertation on the Peace Terms.' It is easy to forget now that the question of whether to continue prosecuting the war or to make peace with Germany was ever present, with a vocal minority always urging peace. Tyrrell, later to be Under Secretary at the Foreign Office, may have been on secondment to the Cabinet Office at this time.

Christmas 1916 was unsatisfactory. On Christmas Eve Cumming drove down to Southampton and Bursledon where he was 'Very dissatisfied with progress'. He returned that evening by train and worked late. Christmas Day begins with a memorable entry: 'All day in the office. Rather quiet – not many staff about.' The only other entry for that day records a suggestion by Kell that Cumming should post a liaison officer into his office, but Cumming demurred: 'I don't quite see what he would do.' On Boxing Day an army officer from The Hague, 'belonging to Wallner's service', expressed concern at 'the rivalry and collision of agents in Holland ... we could not keep our men secret and the Belgian agents made a regular business of farming the information they received.' Later Cumming saw a GHQ map which showed that Colonel Cameron 'is starting six new posts in my area where he already has ten others' (these were probably train-spotting posts). Next he saw a telegram from Colonel French snubbing Compton Mackenzie 'for his suggestions on military matters and ordering him to report to the MA.' French also wanted to 'strafe' Cumming over his monthly train-watching reports, while Hall refused his request to cancel the appointment of a Major Horne whose reporting procedures were 'quite against my orders'. Ronald Campbell dismissed excuses given on behalf of someone referred to as 'FN', and a few days later Cumming was ordered by Lord Hardinge to reprimand him severely. Cumming commented: 'I do not think this quite satisfactory as if explanation is correct [the Foreign Office] Minister is wrong.'

After such a Christmas period it is perhaps not surprising that the new year passed unremarked, although he began on New Year's Day an alphabetical list of 219 names that extend into the pages headed 'Cash Account'. All have a date or dates written alongside, ranging from January 1916 to May, and they may be records of payments made by Cumming in person. Some are clearly his staff, others are military or civilian colleagues such as MacDonogh and Wallner. One unexpected name is that of General Haig who, on 26 April, Cumming had noted as: 'General Haig re Burnham [?].'

Whatever impression the diary may give, and whatever vexations may have crowded into a bad year's end, there is evidence of life and spirit in the intelligence community. The following verses were written in 1916 by Colonel the Hon. CC Bingham, later Viscount Mersey (already referred to) and are included here by kind permission of his grandson. By MI6, he surely means the War Office section rather than the Secret Service, but at least two of those mentioned worked for Cumming (Hooker and Hoare), a further indication of the fluidity of the various intelligence agencies. The verses are addressed to the Secretary of State:

Hail! S. of S! Attention fix
Upon the work of MI6
The section which, I'm free to state
Is best in this Directorate.

Now first we'll take a little look, a
Passing glance at Gibbes and Hooker.
Their work is silent and unseen,
They deal in cables (submarine)
and censor stamps and codes galore

(observe the notice on the door)
And when espionage grows rifer
They fabricate a baffling cipher.

Two learned jurists next we see
Who ornament sub-section B.
(I don't want any rude remarks
From inefficient lady clerks)
They give the most profound attention
To studying the Hague Convention,
And write sagacious dissertations
On points anent the Law of Nations.
On compensation claims they're wise
Restricting enemy supplies
And everything to do with trade
Which tends to strengthen the blockade.
Few there are who can withstand a
Score or two of memoranda
Written by the pungent pen
Wielded by these clever men.
And as they're shy, as well as great,
I'll keep their names inviolate.

Of section C I'll quickly tell
They furnish MI personnel,
Interpreters and censors too
You only need an interview,
The fees are moderate: a tenner
Extracts a job from Colonel Jenner.
A lesser sum may p'raps assuage
The Greed of avaricious Page.
While twenty shillings pressed on Eden
Ensures a job in Spain or Sweden
But if you meanly close your fist
They'll put you on the waiting list.

The vigilance of D alarms
Those worthy men who deal in arms.
And if they call, these comers get
An awful time from Somerset,
While Gifford rates them like a Hun
For breaking Section 21.
Till limp and cowed they go away
In wholesome dread of 30 A.

You ask of MI6 E? Well it
Is the home of Captain Kellett.
Who regulates with bonhomie
The interior economy.

A word or two must still be said
About our very worthy Head.
He guides with sure and skilful hand
The efforts of this noble band.
And takes them up to those on high.
(By that I mean the DSI)
You'll find him very much at ease
In dealing with the Portuguese
And organising them for War.
His name of course is Major Hoare.

And now, Lloyd George, your name affix
To orders granting MI6.
A sorely needed rise in pay,
Beginning, if you please, TODAY.

14

La Dame Blanche

Earlier in 1916 a young artillery captain called Henry Landau was stricken by German measles while on leave in London. Of Anglo-Dutch parentage, Landau had been brought up in South Africa, educated not only there but at Dulwich College (with P. G. Wodehouse), in Germany, at Caius College, Cambridge, and latterly at the London School of Mines. He was fluent in French, German and English and was a young man of some initiative, able both to cope with the orthodox and achieve the unorthodox. In 1913, for instance, he picked up and befriended an attractive prostitute in Leicester Square, made her respectable and successfully married her off to an army colonel who, after a convenient death in action, left her well provided for and socially secure.

When the war came he joined the Australian Volunteer Hospital. He dealt with casualties of the Battle of Mons and witnessed deaths from tetanus more agonising than anything he subsequently saw during considerable action with the Royal Field Artillery. As he was going on leave his adjutant gave him an introduction to his sister, who worked for what she called the Censor's Department in London. She must have taken to him because she told him that her 'Chief' was looking for someone with his sort of background, military experience and knowledge of the Continent (further evidence, in addition to that already noted, that Cumming had staff in War Office departments).

When German measles delayed his return to the front, she talked
to her Chief and Landau found himself ordered to the War Office
and given language tests. Then, while convalescing in comfort
at the Waldorf Hotel, he received instructions to report to a
Colonel Browning in Whitehall Court. There he was informed
that he had been transferred to the Intelligence Corps and
attached for special duties to the Secret Service. He was to see
the Chief immediately:

Up several flights of stairs I went until I reached the very top of
the building. Here, in a room that resembled the stateroom of a
ship, I was confronted with a kindly man who immediately put
me at my ease. It was the Chief, Captain C, a captain in the
Navy. He swung round in a swivel chair to look at me – a
grey-haired man of about 60, in naval uniform, short in stature
with a certain stiffness of movement which I later discovered to
be due to an artificial leg.

After a few preliminary remarks, he suddenly came to the
point: 'I know all about your past history. You are just the man
we want. You are to join T in Rotterdam leaving tonight via
Harwich and the Hook. Our train-watching service has broken
down completely in Belgium and in North Eastern France – we
are getting absolutely nothing through. It is up to you to reorganise the service. I can't tell you how it is to be done – that is your
job. You have carte blanche.

'Use T as "cover"; communicate with me through him. Within
reasonable limits he will supply you with all the money you need
for the organisation. You will find others in T's office in charge
of other branches of the Secret Service; cooperate with them.

'You are in complete charge of the Military Section; responsibility for its success or failure is on your shoulders. Consult with
Colonel Oppenheim, our Military Attaché at the Hague, as to the
kind of information we require. A handbook and other information
about the German Army will be given you by Colonel Oppenheim.
We will also send you questionnaires from time to time through T.

'Urgent military information you obtain about the Germans will be telegraphed in code by Colonel Oppenheim direct to GHQ. Hand T all written reports concerning less important information; he will send it to us through the diplomatic bag. Anything else you want to know, ask T. Here is his address,' said he, as he handed me a slip of paper. 'Commander Sykes, in the next room, will furnish you with your ticket and expenses and will tell you when your train leaves Victoria,' he added as he offered me his hand, wishing me good luck.

A few weeks later, Landau's battery was wiped out on the Somme.

This is taken from Landau's book, *All's Fair*, subtitled *The Story of the British Secret Service Behind the German Lines*, published in 1934. It is unlikely that Landau remembered his briefing word for word after nearly twenty years but we can be pretty sure of the gist of what he wrote and that it is an accurate description of how things worked in the Rotterdam station. In this book and its sequel, *Secrets of the White Lady* (1935), Landau's detailed description of his work for Cumming and Tinsley is based not only on his memory but on his post-war access to the records of the Belgian White Lady (La Dame Blanche) network.

Landau's publication of these matters was deeply disapproved of by SIS in the 1930s and his books banned in Britain. For some years his reference to TR/16 as 'the Dame' (noted earlier) was thought to have been responsible for TR/16's arrest and execution, though it was not. As well as disapproving of the principle of case officers writing about their agents, SIS was particularly concerned because some of the leading Belgian figures identified by Landau (albeit with their permission, and perhaps encouragement) were also active against the Germans during the Second World War when there was an offspring to La Dame Blanche, the Clarance network. It is because of this sort of eventuality that SIS remained – and remains – adamantly apposed to unauthorised disclosure.

Fortunately, no one actually seems to have suffered from anything Landau wrote and, if he had not published as he did, one of the great espionage achievements of the century would have remained largely unknown even to SIS itself, as well as to history. The Imperial War Museum archive contains a few La Dame Blanche reports and papers and there is an unpublished dissertation by P. Decock,[1] so far as is known but the remains of SIS's early archive yields not a word about what must have been one of the brightest feathers in Cumming's cap (there is a brief reference in the diary). The following, very brief, account is no substitute for reading the books (both, sadly, out of print).

As Cumming had warned, Landau arrived in Rotterdam in the wake of disaster. Both the Folkestone-based network under Wallinger and Cameron and what became known as SIS's Frankignoul Service of train-watchers had been broken by the efficient and pervasive German counter-espionage. Train-watching was already established as a major source of information about the deployment of the German army in the field. That army's dependence on the railways for movement and reinforcement meant that the monitoring of troop trains yielded intelligence about everything from the supply of rations and ammunition to preparations for an offensive or the strengthening or weakening of sections of the front. There were many patriotic Belgians willing to spy on the Germans, despite the 'Electric Curtain' – a wartime forerunner of the Soviet Iron Curtain, a combination of electrified fences, mines and guards – that sealed the frontier with Holland. They also braved the German prohibition on anyone travelling more than thirty miles without permission, the requirement for every citizen to report monthly to the local German Kommandantur and the prospect of execution if caught. The chief difficulty was in getting information out. Landau quotes a post-war study of Allied espionage which showed that nearly all betrayals and compromises involved frontier couriers, many of whom lived near the border and were by tradition and peacetime calling venal, being smugglers and poachers and so on.

Wireless transmissions were too easily identified and pigeons attracted too much attention, so reports had to be carried out or sent. Methods ranged from throwing reports over the border wire, to hiding them in barges or trams (the Frankignoul network used one of the latter very productively, until betrayed), to cutting the wire, to concealment about the person.

La Dame Blanche originated with a network set up by a Belgian engineer, Dieudonné Lanbrecht, who was recruited by Belgians working for the GHQ network and who made successful use of priests and railway employees – accurately reporting, for instance, German preparations for Verdun – until he was betrayed and shot, without revealing any of his thirty-odd agents. His example inspired five men – his engineer cousin, a professor of physics, a Roman Catholic priest, a Belgian police chief and a Liège banker – to continue his work. They at first called themselves the Service Michelin (Michelin tyre advertisements were common) and went on reporting to the GHQ service, but continued to be subject to breakdown and betrayal.

Landau, meanwhile, had been working eighteen hours a day in Rotterdam to re-establish the flow of intelligence, and had met with some success, albeit that most of his information came from individual agents rather than the networks that were needed to cover the occupied territories. It was one of these individuals, a German deserter, who was to give him what he called with excusable pride 'the biggest Secret Service scoop of the War' – the innocuous-sounding German Field Post Directory, which listed the whereabouts of all units and their designation numbers. He could now leave Tinsley to worry about the infighting with other Allied services, British and Belgian (the French having agreed with Cumming that they would take priority in Switzerland and leave Holland to him), while he got on with the crucial work of establishing secure and reliable border crossings, each isolated from the other, known to very few and, unknown even to those few, often duplicated.

Thus it was that when, in 1917, the Service Michelin was

desperately seeking reliable ways of getting their very considerable information out, Landau made contact with them and was able to offer half a dozen virgin crossing points guaranteeing the rapid transmission of intelligence. They made it a condition of their collaboration with the War Office Secret Service – which is how SIS was often known in the field – that they be regarded not as spies but as soldiers, incorporated as an independent unit of the British army with rank structures and pay. Landau said he would have to consult his Chief in London but, knowing how long it would take the War Office to be persuaded of such unorthodoxy, he wisely and courageously used his initiative, and didn't. The following day he told them that his Chief had agreed.

Promising what you know you cannot deliver is, of course, something that no good intelligence officer or any other official, civil or military, should do. It is of a piece with Landau's subsequent chequered business career. At the same time, intelligence services need people, just as armies do, who will occasionally turn Nelsonic blind eyes. If what you do works, you are congratulated; if it doesn't, you are never forgiven.

Landau's act of deception was triumphantly vindicated. The Service Michelin changed its name to La Dame Blanche – a reference to the legendary White Lady whose appearance was to herald the downfall of the Hohenzollens – and later, emphasising their view of themselves as soldiers fighting a war, rather than spies in it for gain, they changed their name again to the Corps d'Observation Anglais. Many, perhaps most, of the 904 'soldiers' and 180 'auxiliaries' (an astonishing number for a secret organisation operating behind enemy lines) were Roman Catholic and the leadership was almost entirely professional, academic and priestly, including some 80 priests and nuns, 144 graduates, 211 civil servants. Of the 904 soldiers, 626 were men, 278 women. They maintained fifty-one train-watching posts and administered themselves and produced their reports from twelve secret secretariats. Forty-five were arrested, five condemned to death, two shot and one killed on duty. The two who were executed, the brothers Louis and Anthony Collard, were caught by chance when an anonymous tip-off by someone who knew nothing of the network but was jealous of a girl led the Germans to a secretariat just as reports were being typed and prepared.

Given that the very large number of some 1,084 people were involved, it is a tribute both to their dedication and security procedures as well as to Landau's planning that so few were caught. (To put these numbers in context, Landau quotes a post-war assessment that the Allied intelligence services ran over 2,000 agents in Belgium and occupied France, most of whom were connected with train-watching, several hundred of whom were caught and imprisoned, and over 100 of whom were shot. About 220 other people were also shot on suspicion of espionage.)

It was due largely to La Dame Blanche reporting that, by the end of the war, the GHQ Brown Book was able to show the composition of every German division. Landau's own estimate was that the network provided 75 per cent of all Allied intelligence received by GHQ through neutral states, and 95 per cent of that which came from the occupied territories. Landau was obviously an interested party, but a letter from Cumming to La Dame Blanche, quoted in the unpublished Decock thesis, contains what is probably an authoritative estimate since it could have been made only by a recipient of intelligence from all sources, and not by any single producer:

> The work of your organisation accounts for 70 per cent of the intelligence obtained by all the Allied armies not merely through the Netherlands but through other neutral states as well . . . it is on you alone that the Allies depend to obtain intelligence on enemy movements in areas near the Front . . . the intelligence obtained by you is worth thousands of lives to the Allied armies.

The details of the German spring offensive of 1918 were discovered by two nuns from a German staff officer (Landau comments that priests were particularly useful in recruiting for the network since they were trusted and could make good use of the confessional). La Dame Blanche also located the long-range German gun that bombarded Paris. At £10,000 a month, it was very expensive to run, but the expense was clearly judged worthwhile.

The moment of truth for Landau came when the war ended and for the first time he could travel to meet the people whose names were known in Rotterdam only to him and Tinsley, and with whom he had been communicating so carefully. He had to tell them that they were not, as they believed, soldiers of the British army, that they had no official existence, that he had misled them. However, he had already confessed his deceit to Cumming who, far from reprimanding him, had given his word that he would get them 'militarised' and see that they got the pensions and honours they deserved. Landau believed him and assured leaders of La Dame Blanche that 'the Chief' would fix it.

It was always, Landau said, 'a pleasure and inspiration' to work for Cumming because he encouraged initiative, trusted subordinates and issued instructions that were 'at once definite and flexible – above all, liberal'. He was also a man of his word; the soldiers of La Dame Blanche were granted their longed-for military status complete with British army pensions, honours and medals. The leaders were given the CBE (military) and personally congratulated by Haig, about 200 others were also decorated and something like 1,000 qualified for war and service medals. The £30,000 secretly provided by the Liège banker to get the organisation going – long before the British had anything to do with it – was repaid by Cumming.

It was no mean feat to get such swift agreement from a War Office not renowned for bureaucratic flexibility and it may be that Cumming was able to call in a few favours; perhaps all those cars for VIPs. But it certainly would not have happened on that scale if La Dame Blanche's contribution had been anything less than as Landau describes it. Nor would it have happened without the firm endorsement of Macdonogh, and perhaps of Haig himself. The strongest opposition came from the Belgian government, which disliked the notion that its nationals should be rewarded for having spied for another power.

La Dame Blanche essentially formed itself and was not Cumming's creation. Its flowering was the result of the marriage of its potential with his facilities. Landau attributed its success to religious faith, patriotism and the bonding that came from the members believing themselves to be a military organisation. Dewé, one of their leaders, attributed it to:

> The protection of God which never failed us; the oath taken by our agents as soldiers; the precise instructions given to our agents as to their conduct in case of arrest; the vigilance and sagacity of the War Office service, who only sent us trustworthy couriers, and who warned us repeatedly against getting into contact with other Allied secret organisations; these were the principal factors which contributed to our preservation.

There is much else in Landau's books, references to procedures, incidents, cases and proposals of which little or nothing is known. For instance, remarking on the importance of not spying on the Dutch, despite German provocation, he mentions discreet Dutch assistance to the Allies and the secret provision of copies of ciphered German telegrams, passed to London. We have already noted the Zeppelin blown up in Brussels in June 1915, which he credited to British sabotage following information passed by pigeon. He also mentions intelligence on German wireless-guided motor torpedo boats, deployment of which was frustrated by countermeasures, as well as other agent reports giving the defences of Zeebrugge and Ostend.

He records an episode strikingly reminiscent of that concerning Max Schultz but this time involving a British spy called Brewer. Brewer was apparently arrested in 1912 in Hamburg while boarding a vessel with plans that Cumming had asked for, and was eventually freed by the post-war Hamburg soldiers' council or Soldatenrat in order to negotiate with the British on the revival of the old Hanseatic League. There is reference to post-war agreement by Cumming to a Belgian proposal for a secret exchange of intelligence and, surprisingly, to a German proposal to co-operate against the French (who were plotting, against agreement, to carve out part of Germany and make it 'independent'), which Cumming explored, then dropped. Landau concludes that he never knew blackmail to be used in British espionage, though he thought the Germans 'past masters' at it.

Following the war Landau was sent undercover as Passport Control Officer to Berlin, then Cumming's plum post, but found peacetime work uncongenial and resigned. He was succeeded by Frank Foley, who was to become one of SIS's most successful case officers and is now honoured for his work in saving Jews in Berlin during the 1930s (nee *Foley, The Spy Who Saved 10,000 Jews* by Michael Smith, Hodder & Stoughton).[2] Landau later rejoined and worked for Cumming for a further two years with a kind of roving commission during which, at Cumming's urging, he recruited the German inventor of a 'wireless robot-controlled aeroplane' and procured a new German light machine-gun.

He subsequently moved to America, from where he published not only the books already referred to but another, *The Enemy Within*, about German wartime sabotage in the USA. Neverthless, there is a sense about Landau that, as for so many who had successful and exciting wars, nothing in the rest of life was ever quite as good again. Given the achievement of La Dame Blanche, it is not surprising.

15

THE SZEK CASE

Among much else that must have been going on at that time is a rather sad story, some parts of which have featured occasionally in books and the press ever since. This time, however, there are archival papers from Cumming's time which give a different version.

Of the books that have featured the story, the best known are Stephen Roskill's biography of Admiral Beatty (1980) and Barbara Tuchman's *The Zimmerman Telegram* (1979), though Landau also wrote about it. In the 1950s Roskill interviewed the aged Admiral of the Fleet Sir Henry Oliver, Hall's predecessor as DNI, finding his First World War memories 'astonishing clear' (Oliver died in 1966 aged 101). Among these memories was that of Alexander Szek, an Anglo-Austrian who helped repair the powerful wireless transmitter in Brussels after the Germans captured the city. Szek, the story goes, had access to the German diplomatic cipher and, under pressure from the British, agreed to copy it piecemeal and send it to London via Holland. When it came to the last part of the code-books, however, he refused to hand it over and the British, fearing German discovery of the all-important breakthrough they were about to make, killed Szek. Roskill wrote: 'Admiral Oliver, who had been DNI at the beginning of the drama, several times said to me, "I paid £1,000 to have that man shot."'

Barbara Tuchman gives a longer account. She wrote that Szek

was born in Croydon and grew up in Britain with his parents, moved with his father to Brussels two years before the war and remained there while his father moved to Vienna. When unreadable intercepts from the repaired Brussels transmitter reached Room 40, Sir Alfred Ewing requested 'extra-mural help'. The British put the wireless station under secret surveillance and identified Szek as a code clerk who could be claimed as a British subject. His sister or mother was working in England as a governess and was persuaded to write to him urging co-operation with the British.

Szek was reluctant but, early in 1915, agreed to steal the code and escape with it to England, although 'this was worse than useless, as the Germans would then have known that the code had been taken'. He was persuaded to copy it over three months, column by column, but he refused to hand over the final part, insisting that he and the contact agent leave together. It was by then April 1915. 'What happened next no one knows for certain, but Szek was never seen alive after the war . . . some claim that the Germans captured and shot him but Szek's father, after the war, accused the English of having done away with him . . . all we know is that his life was the cost of a code which the English got.'

The official record, although incomplete and at some points confused, does not support this tendentious conclusion. Cumming makes no diary reference to Alexander Szek and there is no record of any file for him having existed. This does not prove that there wasn't one, of course, but it makes it unlikely because, had it existed, we should have expected some reference to it in the file that does exist and that bears the name of his father, Joseph. This has 'and son, Alexander Szek' added to its title. The papers in it date mainly from the 1920s and consist mostly of letters from Joseph and official reactions to them, with attempts to establish what happened to Alexander.

One of the longer papers is the report of a Passport Control interview with Joseph in Brussels in April 1920. This appears to have been conducted by a straightforward passport official rather than by Cumming's representative and it refers to Joseph's 'numerous applications' to various officials to help him find out about his son; it also gives the story as given by Joseph at that time. Alexander, he said, was his eldest son, born in 1894 in London and living with his family in Brussels at the outbreak of war. Joseph, who sometimes refers to his son as Stahl, had various business interests and it was during a wartime business visit to Frankfurt with Alexander that they were detained and questioned about a wireless apparatus they had developed. The apparatus was at their Brussels works, whither they were obliged to return in order to hand it over. Alexander was subsequently forced to work for the German military authorities as a Marconi operator. His father later showed the British a certificate signed by Captain Fulda on behalf of the German military governor of Brussels certifying Alexander's employment from November 1914 to 28 May 1915 as a wireless operator who had carried out his duties satisfactorily. During this period Alexander apparently told his father that he had deciphered the German code and intended to escape with it via Holland to England, hand it over and join the British army. Joseph advised him to travel instead via Germany and Austria to Switzerland or Italy.

In September 1915 Joseph went to Berlin to join the rest of his family, whom he had moved there, and on 17 September was detained. He was informed that Alexander had been arrested at Charleroi in Belgium and found guilty of 'attempting to sell to an enemy agent the code of the German wireless station at Brussels'. After many requests during succeeding months, Mme Szek eventually received a letter dated 1 February 1916 from the German military governor at Charleroi saying that Alexander had been sentenced both to death and to life, the former for 'attempting to communicate to an enemy state, the code of the German Wireless Station at Brussels', and the latter for 'having concealed an important message from an English ship during the time he was employed at the said wireless station'. The letter intimated that the death sentence had been carried out on 10 December 1915.

Joseph and the rest of his family were interned in Germany until released on parole in August 1917 after the Germans had, apparently made 'several attempts to have the father certified insane'. They went to Vienna, then eventually to Berne, where Joseph passed information about conditions in Germany to Major Vischer and a Captain Jump. Both were working for Cumming.

The Brussels interviewer concluded that Joseph was 'mentally affected' by his suffering and, under the illusion that Alexander was still alive, had spent considerable sums on handwriting and other experts who 'had apparently taken advantage of his mental condition'. Joseph thought that the British government should be concerned because his son had wanted to help Britain. The interviewer noted that the 'mental aberration . . . appears to have existed before the war', citing as evidence a petition to the King in 1912 (acknowledged by Lord Knollys on 23 December 1912) and to the King of the Belgians (acknowledged by Count d'Anschot) 'in the hope that endeavours would be made to prevent the Austro-German alliance'. The interviewer's report was sent to the Passport Control Department in London on 31 March 1920.[1]

Two months later, in another interview with a Captain Westmacott of Passport Control, Joseph claimed he was owed money because the British had information his son had discovered. He was by now convinced that his son was alive but concealed by the British, producing an 'enormous dossier' as proof that all papers relating to the case were fake and enthusing about a new kitchen range and fire-back he had designed. He also wanted to pass on information about international politics to Lord Curzon, the Foreign Secretary. Captain Westmacott concluded that he was 'slightly unhinged, partly as a result of anxiety and love of intrigue'. A month later Joseph wrote to Lord Curzon saying that all the information sent by the Germans to Madame

Szek, including Alexander's death certificate, was the work of a 'notorious German police forger'.

The poor man continued his quest until at least 1938, his story occasionally surfacing in newspapers such as the *Daily Graphic* which, on 9 August 1930, devoted considerable space to it. In doing so it expanded on an account of Alexander's capture mentioned by Joseph in an earlier letter to the Speaker of the House of Commons, to the effect that Alexander had been helped in his escape attempt on 14 August 1915 by 'the Belgian English spy Alexandre de Block'. They failed that time and tried again at Diest on 5 September 1915, with a party of twenty-six others, plus guide. The guide worked for German counter-espionage and they were all captured.

According to the *Graphic*, the Brussels transmitter handled messages between Berlin and the Kaiser at Spa in a code comprising two booklets, one of letter groups and figures, the other giving daily changes of figure groupings. By April 1915 Alexander was in charge every other night, an arrangement made via a staff officer with whom he was billeted. According to the Belgian General Buys, who was one of those arrested, the Germans already suspected Alexander's intentions and were planning to send him to Austria to be conscripted when he made his first escape attempt near Wachtebeke on 8 August, during which he was shot through the sleeve. When he tried again the following month, the group had papers provided by de Block and General Buys, as well as 1,000 francs with which to bribe the frontier guard. All were caught, de Block and Buys being arrested later. They were all tried on 9 December, Buys and de Block sentenced to three and two years respectively, while Alexander, who was said to have had code details wound about his person, was condemned to death.

The *Graphic* goes on to say that Joseph had his son's remains exhumed and contended that they were several centimetres too short, also that Alexander had vivid dark eyes whereas descriptions of the man about to be executed gave his as blue. Joseph believed that the Germans had shot a substitute. He also said that the Germans had reported Alexander as having hidden the codes in his pipe. The *Graphic* article concludes by pointing out that the British Admiralty in fact already had the code in question before Alexander's first escape bid, though it does not point out how this would undermine Joseph's case.

Meanwhile, official reactions are a mixture of willingness to help, puzzlement and pity, with occasional attempts to make good the patchy bureaucratic memory and no suggestion that anyone but the Germans remotely considered killing Alexander, or had any reason to. Joseph, who had worked for Armstrong Whitworth before the war, was recorded as being pro-British and as having done a 'certain amount of work for our Swiss agency at one time', while Alexander, 'who went under the name of Alexander Stahl, does not appear to have been of much use, though apparently shot by the Germans according to our records'. An early manuscript comment – 'An Admiralty affair, I take it. Would you kindly let me know anything that we can tell the bereaved parent?' – led to Tinsley being asked whether he knew anything about this from his time in Rotterdam; he replied that he had never heard of father or son. Next the question was put to Room 40. This provided a concise and conclusive response from A. G. Denniston, one of Room 40's leading lights. His reply, written in pencil on notepaper, is dated 9 March 1920: 'Nothing was known of this man in 40 OB. The story of W/T and cryptographic activity given in the letter does not correspond with the facts.'

That should have been it, but the story does not end there. Each time Joseph succeeded in getting the story to some figure of authority, or getting it into the British or foreign press, it was looked at again, usually by someone unfamiliar with what had gone before, but once or twice by someone with vague memories of Joseph from his Swiss days. A 1928 version refers to a 1919 investigation by 'the Sub-Committee appointed by the Inter-Allied Claims Commission to enquire into any claim for services rendered the Allied Armies by civilians, in such ways as Secret Service, Propaganda, etc. Unlike many claims, the full facts in this case were obtainable.' It goes on to say that the Belgian government, which was represented on the Claims Commission, did not support the case. According to another paper the commission found Alexander 'to have died of disease during the war in territory then occupied by the German forces'.

This was queried by Kell in 1930, who asked SIS whether Alexander was shot or died, quoting a foreign press cutting of 28 December 1915 which announced his sentence on 9 December and his execution on the 10th. The question was put via memo to Stewart Menzies (a well-connected former cavalry officer who moved from army intelligence to Cumming, and was Chief of SIS during the Second World War), with the reminder: 'The real original information concerning the death of Alexander TZEK [sic] is of course amongst the papers of the Commission of which you were a member, which sat in 1919 . . . there is no evidence whatever that Alexander Tzek did die of Influenza.'

False stories that contain elements of truth often have the longest legs, particularly when driven, as this was, by somebody's obsession. Joseph Szek's petitions were many and he convinced himself that his son had been seen alive in Holland after his capture. The story that he had actually been liquidated by British Intelligence seems to have grown in Joseph's mind over the years. It was not part of the accounts he gave nearer the time of the events.

There is still, however, Admiral Oliver's unequivocal statement. All we can say of that is that his mind could not have been as clear as Roskill believed, and that he was wrong. In the light of the Claims Commission and archival evidence, it would require the most determined conspiracy theorist to keep the story going. A considerable number of people would have been involved in the cover-up, including the Germans and the scholarly, priestly and professional occupants of Room 40 who were noted for their independence of mind as much as for their patriotism. Such considerations would not, of course, destroy a strong strain of conspiracy virus, since its defence against any contrary evidence is to redefine itself so as to include whatever is adduced, with those involved either conscripted into the ranks of conspirators or dismissed as unwitting dupes. Either the nonagenarian admiral was confused, or Stephen Roskill was hard of hearing.

All evidence apart, however, the story is inherently unlikely. A reputation for murdering those who helped them must be second only to a reputation for being unable to keep secrets in the list of qualities intelligence services do not want. Additionally, the picture of Cumming built up through the diary does not match that suggested by this story, which would have him, in Richard Deacon's words, as 'fearless and ruthless to the point of having no qualms about ordering an assassination, even if this meant killing one of his own agents'. Cumming would doubtless have had few qualms about killing the enemy but he almost certainly would have had qualms about ordering the death of one of his own agents; he would have been far more likely, if persuasion failed, to have suggested that Alexander hand over the last instalment and then feign illness and drop out of sight, so that he never had to return to work. A doctor's letter or certificate could easily have been provided (genuine or forged) and Alexander could have been spirited across the border to fulfil his wish of joining the British army. There, of course, his secret would have been safe from the Germans since he would be unlikely to have met any except in battle. Not only was there no need to kill him but his abrupt unexplained disappearance might well have been counterproductive, arousing German suspicions.

However unlikely the story, though, and however weighty the evidence against it, it will probably survive in some form. People believe, and read into accounts, what they want. Given which, it perhaps does no further harm to consider fancifully and briefly – and separately from this story – whether it could ever be right in war to kill someone who was helping you if you believed that by doing so you could prevent the discovery and nullification of what he had done. It is not easy when at peace to appreciate the differences made by being at war, nor is it easy for us to imagine ourselves into Cumming's time when, in their daily dealings, people were possibly franker, more direct and harder-headed (yet probably more respectful) than we. The formalities of human intercourse were more important, the sentiments, or appearance of sentiments, perhaps less so. The same might apply to the Second World War (it would be interesting to compare, say, the phrasing of army officers' annual confidential reports then and now), but that occurred in a world more accessible to many people's imaginations. If, therefore, there was a serious likelihood that the Ultra secret, which would shorten the war and save many thousands of lives, was about to be unintentionally revealed to the Germans by the actions of someone who had helped you acquire it, would you – assuming there was no other way of stopping it happen – kill him?

16

ATTRITION AND SUCCESS

Nineteen seventeen may have seen the beginning of the end of the war, though it was probably not widely apparent. Partly through Hall's bold and ingenious deployment of Room 40's decrypt of the famous Zimmerman telegram (in which Germany proposed that Mexico should join her in war against the USA), the United States entered the war, while revolutionary Russia, riven by military disaster, privation and political dissension, left it. Britain, which was paying crippling sums to keep the war going, was saved from bankruptcy only by last-minute American loans. Attrition on the western front drained all three armies, with the Germans not yet reinforced by troops released from the eastern front, the French mutinous and the British alone maintaining an offensive attitude. Haig sought a decisive breakthrough with the battle that became known as Third Ypres, or Passchendaele, a name that, linked with the word 'attrition', was to acquire in British ears, a depth and grimness undreamt of before.

For Cumming, it was a year of bureaucratic attrition during which he seems to have fallen foul of Hall and to have been all but taken over by the War Office. Nevertheless, the year heralded a fundamental redirection of the Secret Service, though this, as with the larger events, might not have been widely apparent at the time. The War Office-imposed reorganisation of his military section led to better production and distribution of intelligence in London, but it must at times have been a close-run thing.

There are large gaps in the 1917 diary, which become an increasing feature from that year on. Many of the entries are brief *aides-mémoires* simply listing people to see, or those seen. Only towards the end of the year, when the reorganisation debate is raging, does the diary become fuller and only then does Cumming rehearse with himself, and for himself, arguments and attitudes. There are, however, some surviving letters to supplement and explain diary entries.

In essence, the reorganisation of his Whitehall Court headquarters involved changing from a geographical structure to a functional, or subject-based one. So far as possible – which was not always very far – officers in charge of geographical sections were familiar with their countries and languages but often they knew little of what intelligence customers actually wanted, which meant that agents were often not asked the right questions and good or bad answers were not always recognised for what they were. This is made apparent in a later (27 February 1919) report by Captain Somerville, RN (Cumming's first Head of Naval Requirements Section) entitled, 'Report on Naval Intelligence Secret Service'. Somerville's report also echoes a refrain of the diary, to the effect that naval and military staff seconded to Cumming were too often taken from him by the Admiralty or War Office as soon as they had become more or less competent. An example of this occurred on 2 June 1917 when Cumming records learning from a lieutenant on his staff that he had already 'left my service and joined the DID at the Admiralty!' He also wearily records instances of the Admiralty and War Office deploying his officers on their own missions as by right rather than favour. Apart from this, competence in clandestine matters was further eroded by the service's rapid expansion and the employment of people with no experience. There was training in certain mainly technical skills – codes, secret writing and so on – but training in espionage as such, if it existed, was probably limited to lectures and instructions. People learned on the job how to handle and debrief agents and much information and many opportunities must have gone astray.

There exists a handwritten manuscript, drawn on by Paul Greengrass in his BBC adaptation of Maugham's *Ashenden* stories and by the BBC's *Timewatch* programme, which describes training lectures given by Cumming. It belongs to Professor John Dancy and comprises the extensive memoirs of his late father, Dr J. H. Dancy, though the parts pertaining to Cumming are a very small part of the whole. These seem to have been written after 1967 and reflect the author's recruitment and training for the purpose of reporting on military patients in Dover hospitals who were thought to be part of a conspiracy to evade service (Dr Dancy was a medical doctor). This would, of course, have been more Kell's responsibility than Cumming's and it is not in fact clear that the author ever had anything to do with Cumming other than visiting his headquarters for training purposes. Of these, however, he gives useful descriptions, including the information that Cumming ran a 'spy school' for newcomers at 5 p.m. on Tuesdays and Fridays, in Whitehall Court. He gives vignettes of Cumming and other figures, saying, for example, that Cumming always gave his lecture after finishing his cup of tea, that although he smoked he thought that officers and agents should not be dependent on smoking, that he drew his staff from a much wider social range than Hall, who was a snob and who was – interestingly, given their contrasting characters – closer to Kell than to Cumming. Dancy also attended lectures by Ewing and Melville, recalling Melville's advice on breaking and entering to the effect that doors squeak more in daytime, usually on the upper hinge. Commenting on Admiral Oliver's recruitment of Ewing, he says that Oliver was an enthusiastic amateur cryptographer, and he makes it clear that Freddie Browning was, officially or unofficially, Cumming's deputy.

There is much in the manuscript that is verifiable (such as his assessment of Browning's position), but also much that could have been garnered from the better-known memoirs and books, some that is demonstrably wrong and some that is questionable. It would help if some surprising details – such as the assertion that a copy of the Schlieffen Plan was stolen by Kell from Germany in 1908, the year before the founding of the Bureau – were capable of verification. It would also help if just one of these twice-weekly classes were mentioned in Cumming's diary. For instance, a date the author mentions as being the occasion of an introductory lecture by Cumming – Friday, 8 January 1915 – is recorded in the diary in some detail. Early in the afternoon Cumming went over to the War Office, saw the DMO, then the CIGS and later, after a further session with the DMO, Colonel Agar. Thereafter he 'Retd. to office. Writing till 8 + telegrams + all GHQ stuff after.' As we have seen, the fact that something is not in the diary does not mean it did not happen, but this entry gives the impression that there was no room for a lecture on that day.

Furthermore, the description of Cumming as 'striding towards us to greet Haldane' on 8 January 1915, less than five months after losing his leg and during a year in which we know from Frank Stagg that he was still on sticks, carries little conviction. Ditto that of the spy Sidney Reilly, later famed for his exploits in Russia, who allegedly sat in on the lectures in 1915 after having 'been with the SIS for at least twelve years', which would entail his having started six years before it was founded and having met Cumming well before 15 March 1918, which Cumming recorded as their first meeting. The manuscript also rehearses the popular version of the Szek story, with the addition that the family was detained in England by Kell at the time Joseph Szek said they were interned by the Germans.

These and a number of other contradictions, incongruities and unlikelihoods make it impossible to read the story without serious reservations. Nonetheless, the account may be essentially true, if sometimes inaccurate in detail. Professor Dancy, who is to publish the account soon, believes his father to have been at times inventive and anyway untrustworthy with regard to dates;

it would also be surprising if memories recalled half a century after the events were not occasionally confused and interwoven with recollections of what the author has read, or heard, since.

Something conveyed rather more certainly by the diary, though, is that throughout 1917 (and presumably despite successes such as TR/16) Hall was not getting from Cumming what he thought he should have had. He complained about inadequate intelligence and displayed increasing asperity in his dealings with him. For instance, on 3 September, during a dispute about the appointment of Major Thwaites as Wiseman's assistant in New York, he demanded to know whether Cumming was 'serving the Bureau or the Nation'. Cumming noted, again rather Pooterishly, 'I should have replied "the *Nation* through the *Bureau* – my only means of serving it."' On 26 September Cumming took to Hall a bunch of telegrams that had come to him under the rubric 'encode in section V' and pointed out 'this was done without my knowing it was passing through. He said I was "quite safe" and the system was to continue but if I didn't like it SS could be transferred to him.' (These might have been Washington telegrams relating to Room 40 material and Wiseman's close relations with Colonel House, President Wilson's adviser, though on 12 September Cumming was told by Campbell of the Foreign Office that 'the Secret telegrams may be decoded and dealt with by our codists but he considers I ought to see them – but no one else should do so'.)

It is not clear what intelligence Hall thought he lacked. Part of the problem may have been that Room 40 was already giving him much of what he wanted, ensuring that the German Battle Fleet could not threaten a surprise attack. The rest, such as dockyard work or the movements and intentions of individual submarines, was either well covered or very hard to obtain, beyond the limits of direction-finding. It was not until July of that year that the Admiralty reluctantly introduced the convoy system, and Hall must have been under great pressure to do more to counteract the disastrous losses to German submarines (in June alone they sank 286 Allied merchant ships for the loss of only two submarines). Yet despite this it must have been, thanks largely to Room 40 and the Zimmerman telegram, a very successful year for him; towards the end of it he was knighted.

Nevertheless, relations with Cumming and the Secret Service seem to have become pretty dire. On 4 September Cumming noted of MacDonogh (by then promoted major general and back in London as DMI – Director of Military Intelligence) that he was 'very heartening about my position and hinted definitely that if [I were] sacked by the Navy he would take me on with pleasure'. This is revealing not only of the state of relations with Hall – Cumming had, after all, always regarded the Navy as his principal parent and the War Office as an important but predatory taskmaster – but also of how each of the service departments continued to view the Bureau as its own creature, to be sustained or axed regardless of anything that the Foreign Office or Cabinet Office had written on the matter. It is possible – though there is no evidence to suggest it – that Hall resented the success of Cumming's Western Front reporting.

On Sunday 16 December Cumming was sent for by Hall and 'scolded' for lack of information on Romania. His explanation – that his best man there, Laycock, had been compelled to work for the military attaché and that two other members of staff had been taken away from him – did not satisfy Hall.

He said my organisation was not good – that I appointed the Secretaries to work strange to them and that I had no Staff. This shows plainly that someone in my office has been complaining to him behind my back. He listened to my explanation of my organisation and reasons for the appointments but was decidedly seedy and irritable.

By this time the reorganisation had just been put into effect and it was at first unpopular with some staff.

Apart from this, personal relations with Hall seem to have continued as normal. On the day following one of their spats the two of them went together with a small party to see a demonstration of tanks ('Very interesting and instructive') while on Saturday 20 October Cumming called to congratulate Hall on his knighthood. He does, though, indicate that others were aware that relations were strained and possibly that sympathies were divided: Claude Serocold (who worked closely with Hall) assured him after his call 'of his friendship and support and that of his room!' On the same day Cumming sent, or perhaps handed, Hall a fulsome handwritten letter of congratulation which survives among the Hall papers at Churchill College, Cambridge.

My Dear Chief,
Among the hundreds that will rejoice over this honour that has come to all of us there is no one who will do so more warmly and cordially than he who writes to congratulate you – in his own name and in that of everyone of his staff . . . Not only I, but many, many of those who serve you and know you are looking to the day when you will have a far greater control of our Service and a more powerful voice in the movement of the Fleet . . . I have never coveted greater talents so much since I became one of your 'lieutenants' . . . I owe you far more than I could ever repay and wish I could serve you better . . . such as it is however you have my unswerving loyalty and devotion.
Yours, very sincerely,
    M. C.

Relations may have been cordial but the central issue remained. Cumming's entry for Christmas Day reads:

Called on DID and paid my respects. I told him that I regretted very much that he was not satisfied with our

381

Naval information and that if he and my other Chiefs decided that they could do better with someone else they must not allow personal considerations to stand in the way. At the same time I could assure him that I was doing my best and believed that the new organisation would put fresh blood and energy into the work.

There is no record of Hall's response to this informal offer of resignation which, blunt and honourable, was probably typical of Cumming and of the ethos into which he was educated. Things do appear to have picked up thereafter, however. In his 1919 report Somerville wrote that in the three years up to October 1917 the Bureau had produced only 260 naval reports, while in the year from November 1917 it produced around 8,000, with an allegedly proportionate improvement in quality. While we know nothing to contradict this striking claim, it is the case that Somerville, as the first head of Cumming's Naval Requirement Section, had an interest in making it. Even if we make allowance for that by halving it, though, it remains a very significant improvement.

There is also post-war evidence of the restoration of Hall's good opinion of secret agent reporting. Among the Hall papers are notes for two lectures he was to give in the mid-1930s. In the first he makes the point that 'Agents' work *not* despicable. A nation which starves its armed forces, and also starves its Intelligence Service, deserves the fate it will get.' For a lecture on intelligence in wartime, he noted that individual agents were not good at monitoring the movement of ships because of the time-lag in getting the information back but that they were good for monitoring material and resources. By the end of the First World War, he writes, agent coverage of naval matters was effective and submarine activities remained the only serious worry. He cites as an example a case that yielded much useful intelligence on enemy materials and acquisitions. Most German insurances were reinsured in Switzerland. London therefore – whether he or Cumming or both, he doesn't say: 'Sent out there a big man in the Insurance world who lived there for some months and from whom we received lists of all war material reinsured; after a little practice, we could pretty well place what articles were being manufactured.' Agent reporting was also effective on morale behind the lines and on blockade intelligence.

> In one neutral country, a lady – English – was married to one of
> the secretaries through whom all despatches and telegrams to the
> Head of State passed. By this means we were able to read every-
> thing the Ambassadors in the enemy country were saying to the
> Head of their State and it might be mentioned that it was through
> this source that the first solid information of the coming collapse
> was received.

The reorganisation of the military section of the Bureau was the work of MacDonogh who, as DMI, was as successful and energetic back in London as he had been at GHQ in the field. Cumming records many more contacts with him than with his DMI predecessor and the reorganisation seems to have begun with the appointment of Colonel Dansey as head of MI1(C) (i.e. the War Office department of that name, not Cumming's organisation) in August 1917, with the brief to study the Bureau's military reporting and to recommend changes. On 22 October there was a War Office meeting which Cumming attended but at which he was not allowed to speak. MacDonogh, he said, wanted to

> make sure that he had absolute control over the military
> part of the SS Bureau. He proposed to do away with div-
> isions by Geographical [sic], and substitute sub-divisions,
> so that the Military would be self-contained and his Mili-
> tary staff be able to control more directly the Agents

(Head) in the field. He said we particularly lacked a good organisation section resembling that in MI5.

Following further meetings, MacDonogh summarised in two 12 November letters to Hall what he thought should be the fundamental principles of future SS Bureau operations. It was not to concern itself with policy unless instructed otherwise by the Foreign Office, the War Office or the Admiralty, nor was it to approach any members of those departments without authority, nor communicate with other departments not represented in the Bureau headquarters. The Foreign Office, War Office and Admiralty would each have representatives integrated into Cumming's staff who would be responsible for giving guidance in the field on intelligence required by their departments, under Cumming's direction. Cumming would have no deputy, since MacDonogh thought it an 'anomaly' for Cumming to have a second-in-command equal or superior to his own (MacDonogh's) representative. (Freddie Browning was keen to be Cumming's official deputy, and was supported in this by both Cumming and Hall. He probably was the de facto deputy and may even have transferred from the War Office Intelligence Department on that understanding.)

Later, a 27 November letter from Colonel French to Cumming shows that Lord Hardinge of the Foreign Office proposed strengthening Cumming's position, specifically by ensuring that military officers should not be removed at short notice and that the Bureau should have a charter agreed in writing by its three sponsoring departments. MacDonogh refused this, on the grounds that it was against Army Council practice to commit itself not to post officers and that both he and Hall were unwilling to participate in a formal written charter. Hardinge accepted this on the understanding that Cumming was given a 'fair chance' and that he was intended to be 'master in his own house'.

It seems from these and other papers that control of the

Bureau during this period, in terms of its structure and aims if not its day-to-day running, had moved decisively in favour of the War Office as against the Admiralty, with the Foreign Office in the weakest position. MacDonogh played a significant part but it was probably also a reflection of the priorities of war and of the weighting of, and demand for, the Bureau's reporting. The geographical sections were replaced by sections characterised by types of intelligence, with such titles as Economic, Air, Naval, Military, Political, while other sections were responsible for personnel, movements, cover, liaison, escape plans, communications and secret devices. The single most effective measure was the attachment of officers from customer departments to the sections responsible for acquiring the intelligence.

This is illustrative of a fundamental truth about intelligence organisations: they tend to be as good, or as bad, as the requirements placed upon them. If the requirements are precise, clear and important the response both of case officers and agents tends to be better, and failure certainly more apparent, than if the requirements are woolly, general and not obviously relevant, producing answers as unsatisfactory as the questions.

Thus, the most productive and enduring reforms of intelligence services are often those occasioned by an important customer taking a serious interest, rather than indifferently accepting whatever comes along. Elements of what might be called the MacDonogh Reforms survive in SIS to this day, though subsequent changes were not usually accompanied by the loss of autonomy apparently suffered by Cumming at this time. 'Apparently', because it is not clear that his loss was as much as appears from the papers and in one respect the Bureau made a very significant – and future life-saving – gain. This was the acceptance – the first time it had been officially acknowledged – that it should report on other than purely military requirements. As we have seen, it had until that point, officially at least, been barred from seeking or reporting political intelligence.

As for Cumming's attitude, he does not appear to have

regarded the reforms as an unwanted intrusion, though he clearly had his worries. He was more concerned that his voice should be heard than he was to oppose change. Once the decisions were made, he dutifully got on with implementing them. Indeed, it is possible that inspiration for some change came from within the Bureau itself: on 23 August he recorded a meeting with TP, Freddie Browning and MacDonogh's man, Colonel Dansey, at which 'Browning brought forward a proposal for reorganisation which we discussed and in principle approved'. On 21 October he noted:

[MacDonogh] will consider my suggestion of lumping together Dansey No. 4 and 5, in which case he thinks organisation should stand – *Air*: Smith, *Economics*: Browning, *Military*: Dansey leaving Sampson to run the special side, Somerville *Naval*, and for *Organisation* a good, strong character officer whom he will get for us. He had intended to put Drake in Dansey's place, but this was dependent on us taking over the whole of Holland.

This last suggestion, echoed by Landau, must indicate the priority accorded the Bureau's military reporting.

The day after the meeting with MacDonogh, Cumming reported it to Hall, who thought the details 'should be hammered out by subordinates and that he, I, the DMI and Lord H [Hardinge] should meet and come to a decision. I said that if I was included in a meeting all my doubts and anxieties would disappear.' He was included in further meetings but the conclusions of the process, when they arrived on 29 November, were clearly not subject to further discussion: 'Received today the batch of correspondence from MI1, which comprises instructions for the new organisation. There are many points in this that I did not understand but they may clear up later. In the meantime I am not invited to offer any remarks upon them. They are *instructions* and I am to carry them out.'

This he did, with six section heads beneath him. He still had reservations but believed that change was necessary: 'I don't quite see the way clear but if it will keep each man to his own business it ought to improve the present system which allows the agents abroad to send in anything so long as there is plenty of it – all trade stuff with a little second rate CE work.' His senior staff were not so happy, probably because they felt relegated from their previous status. They also disliked having to sign an undertaking not to talk business outside the office (the result of a recent indiscretion, apparently), with Browning objecting that it was illegal. Nevertheless, opposition faded and Cumming found himself spending Sunday 2 December 'trying to fit the new Sections and dependants into the rooms at our disposal so as to keep all the flocks around their shepherds. Trying to let every officer retain the Secretaries he is accustomed to work with and make each Section complete in itself with an adequate staff.' There were more staff grumbles a week later but MacDonogh's mind at least was by then on other matters: 'DMI sent for me to ask if he could remain in Switzerland for a few days without being shadowed and recognised. I told him he certainly could *not*.'

These issues apart, there are reassuringly familiar elements to 1917. The year begins and ends with lists of cars, a number of which were bought for stations abroad although Ronald Campbell's two-seater Lancia is a little harder to explain (it is possible that Cumming used his motor industry contacts to get cars for people). On 8 January there was an India Office conference on 'General Ridout's scheme for Pekin', and a few days later MacDonogh approved a 'China scheme'. On 13 January Cumming told Major Wallinger 'to cut out recruiting in Spain altogether as far as my work is concerned'. Three days earlier he had had a long talk with a Professor Adam on 'the new Intelligence Organisation at 10 Downing Street', while on the

20th he was seeking clearance to pass the minutes of the Enemy Exports Committee to the French, and also trying to get the Foreign Office to send him its reporting telegrams, an important resource for anyone in Whitehall who was supposed to know what was happening overseas. With the defeat and occupation of Romania, it became important to deny the Germans access to Romanian oil; towards the end of January there are several entries concerning the number of wells successfully plugged, the extent to which a refinery had been rendered useless and a call for estimates of oil in stock.

In February he noted that MacDonogh and Hall were to 'make out a new set of rules to meet altered circumstances [in Russia? the US?] setting out what I may or may not do', and later that month he listed twenty-one of his staff who had been mentioned in dispatches. In March, during a discussion with Colonel Sampson on the briefing and debriefing of the 'Turko-Swiss branch', he wrote that agents could not be summoned to London because it would put them under suspicion and 'because of their names and addresses having to be communicated to MI5 they are of no use as secret agents'.

In June there was a struggle between MacDonogh and the Foreign Office over Cumming's contacts with a Colonel Buchan. Although not certain, it seems likely that this was John Buchan, the novelist, who had been given the rank of lieutenant-colonel (see Andrew Lownie's biography) and had recently been appointed Lloyd George's Director of Information, in which capacity he oversaw the activities of the Anglo-Russian Commission. In *Buchan in his World*, Janet Adam Smith says there is clear evidence that Buchan had plenty to do with those involved in secret work. 'Correspondents and secret service agents at all hours', he noted in a letter of May 1917. This was about the time he began his Richard Hannay novel, *Mr Standfast*. MacDonogh wanted there to be no contact between Buchan and Cumming, the Foreign Office the opposite; the Foreign Office won.

In August Cumming again travelled to GHQ in Paris, during which he was taken on a tour of the Front. Apart from discussions with Brigadier-General Charteris, MacDonogh's less than adequate successor in GHQ, and with the French in Paris, part of the reason for his trip seems to have been to review the operation of his Swiss organisation, then under Major Harran in Berne. He listed fourteen staff under Harran, who travelled from Berne to meet him. The following month, after a visit from a Mr Barclay, he listed questions about the French (parts of whose army were mutinous) which he apparently had been asked to answer: '1. What French think about continuing the war. 2. What they think about the English and the part they have played. 3. Propaganda: is the Bosch doing much and how much does it amount to?' (He had earlier been asked to discover how the French had knowledge of some British reports that had not been passed to them, with the implication that there was a leak from within the intelligence community.)

In October there was a conference on intelligence arrangements in Italy, with Samuel Hoare producing a report from which it appears that Cumming had at least three staff in the country and that 'SF and CE' matters were reported to him. Apart from Hoare's published autobiographical accounts, there are papers pertaining to this in his Templewood archive at the University Library, Cambridge,[1] including a summary of those papers still withheld by the Cabinet Office. These all refer to Cumming and include correspondence about a 'Note by the Pope', about Hoare's tasking and about peace negotiations. Among the open papers is a good deal of correspondence with MacDonogh, to whom Hoare seems to have reported on military matters.

Early in November there was further evidence of the unhappiness of some staff over the reorganisations, when a man called Mertens threatened to approach the Prime Minister and the War Cabinet about the matter. Cumming ordered him not to, saying that he considered 'the proposals perfectly reasonable and intend to do my best to carry them out'. Mertens should agree or resign and 'must do nothing whatever to bring about a difference between my two chiefs as I consider this the greatest disservice he could render the country at the present time'. Near the end of the month Cumming ran into Commander Barker, Naval Assistant Provost Marshal, in White's Club and 'offered him occasional use of car for official work'. The Provost Marshal was a potential source of personnel.

The major themes of 1917 – the entry of the USA into the war and the death throes of Tsarist Russia – feature in the diary but not more prominently than matters concerning Greece, Romania and Switzerland. There survives a brief post-war summary of the Bureau's operations in all three of these countries, plus Russia, with an introductory minute that makes clear that it was part of a much larger historical archive compiled during the early 1920s from files and personal recollections, now lost. As well as being brief, the summaries are not entirely accurate, as is evident from manuscript notes on the Romanian section made some decades later by Captain Boxshall who had been involved at the time and who, as a very elderly and venerable bowler-hatted gentleman, could still be viewed in Whitehall in the 1970s.

According to the Romanian notes, Cumming had no organisation in Romania before November 1915 but he then sent an agent to Bucharest to act as a post box for messages from Constantinople (where he had an agent or agents) written in secret ink on newspaper wrappers. The agent, and his successor, transcribed the messages and telegraphed them by arrangement with the British Minister in Bucharest. The summary notes that ministers were generally not warned of the arrival of such agents or 'representatives' and that the latter were instructed to 'overcome whatever unwillingness the Minister might show'. The agents reported on the then neutral Romania's troop movements, morale and strategy, military equipment and trade with the Central Powers. They had no contact with British military attachés, nor were they asked for political intelligence.

Captain Laycock was also sent out, ostensibly to find another substitute for the first post-box agent but largely, according to the summary, because he and Major J. Baird could not get on with each other in London. A Mr Maw used paid agents such as stationmasters and Customs officials who could tell him about goods passing through while Laycock, posing as a civilian, ran his outfit from his flat with a Mr Guthrie as codist.

Laycock donned his uniform on Romania's entry into the war and declared himself a military mission, attached to the military attaché. He now ran his office openly from his flat and gathered assistants, including a *Daily Chronicle* correspondent.

When Bucharest fell in October 1916 they all moved to Galatz and Mr Maw's organisation was disbanded. Meanwhile, a member of parliament, Commander Norton Griffiths RNR, arrived with a mission to destroy the Romanian oil wells. 'It is not clear,' the summary comments, 'that he was definitely appointed to this job by C., but he knew all about C.' After another evacuation, the so-called military mission 'ceased to bear any resemblance to an SS organisation', in which form it remained until the armistice. After that Cumming re-established his representation under Captain Boxshall as PCO.

There is, however, another paragraph to this summary, a self-confessed puzzle to the authors:

One other name must be mentioned in connection with Romania, namely that of Colonel A. Boyle of the Canadian Army. At some period, believed in 1918, he got in touch with C., departed to Romania and made himself indispensable to the King and Queen, who were then living as refugees in a train. According to his own account, which is somewhat borne out by original autographed letters, signed photographs and various Romanian orders presented by the King, he appears to have acted as chief advisor to the King of Romania. He also got into touch with an organisation of Jews whom he bribed to destroy the Russian Black Sea Fleet, promising them so much per ton sunk. A number of ships of the

Russian Black Sea Fleet were sunk and Colonel Boyle wrote IOUs for £2 million as a reward. Colonel Boyle states that he had C's authority for this, but as no correspondence remains and his name is unknown as forming any part of official SS organisations operating in Romania, the matter cannot be cleared up. Most of the Bonds which Colonel Boyle admitted having given are still [1924] in circulation and have not yet been redeemed.

This illustrates how sketchy the summary notes were. In fact, Colonel Joe (Klondyke) Boyle was a well-known figure who took part in the post-war Paris peace conference and whose dashing exploits in Romania and southern Russia were admiringly described in a 1932 autobiography by George Hill (*Go Spy the Land*), one of Cumming's most successful agents in Russia. Boyle was a Canadian who as a boy had run away to sea, become amateur heavyweight boxing champion of the USA, made himself a millionaire out of the Klondyke gold rush, and on the outbreak of war had equipped a Canadian machine-gun detachment at his own expense. He was, according to Hill, sent to Romania and Russia to organise transport and railways, but he clearly had another role that was connected with Cumming.

When Hill first met him it was at his hotel in the provincial Russian town of Mohileff (or Mogilef), whither Hill had returned after the successful deployment of his swordstick against a pursuer. He was examining the blade – 'only a slight film of blood half-way up the blade and a dark stain at the tip' – when he noticed a powerfully-built man in British uniform. He was later to describe his new colleague as 'a man whose equal I have encountered neither before nor since, and to have enjoyed his friendship and to have worked under [sic] and with him will always remain one of the proudest memories of my life'.

This was presumably the Boyle who was well-enough known in the Whitehall intelligence community for further reference to him and the IOUs to be made without explanation. The record of an Admiralty meeting held on 7 April 1919 to consider secret service expenditure, and comprising the usual Admiralty and War Office representatives as well as Cumming, Kell and Lord Hardinge, refers at one point to post-war claims by those who had spent on behalf of the Secret Service or were owed money by it. Cumming estimated his liability to such claims as 'under £300,000' which he could meet without a specified grant. The record continues: 'It thus appears that apart from Colonel Boyle's claim (which is being dealt with specially), SS funds will not be called upon to meet any claims other than the £3,000 mentioned by Commodore Sinclair [Hall's successor as DNI and eventually Cumming's chosen successor].' Furthermore, there are a number of other brief post-war references in Cumming's diary to Colonel Boyle which, though they do not specify that it is he, suggest from their contexts that it is.

Cumming's operations in Switzerland were complicated and, even with the help of the Swiss summary, it is still not possible to say precisely who did what for whom and when. These complications are partly due to the fact that there were two army networks in Switzerland, as well as Cumming's, while some of the personalities involved moved from one organisation to another. Also, the Swiss authorities were – and remain – sufficiently anxious about their neutrality to take measures against any espionage detected on their territory, so there is no record of collaboration with the Swiss government to make things clearer.

According to the summary, Cumming had no station in Switzerland until May 1915, when Captain L.G. Campbell was appointed. He was relieved as PCO in Berne by Captain Harron in June 1916, by which time the Berne staff comprised Sergeant MacInroy Vibert (described as 'British Jew who actually did the passport work in Berne'), Lieutenant Cafferata, RNVR, who liaised with the French in France and recruited and trained agents (he had been trained by Tinsley in Rotterdam), Captain van den Heuvel, who assisted Cafferata in Pontarchier and, later, Major Binns who worked under civilian cover against Austria.

Additionally, the military attaché ran his own agents. The Foreign Office continued to resist Cumming's attempts to get British consuls throughout Switzerland to help, though there were 'a few notable exceptions'. In order to get round this, PCOs were appointed in order to take passport control matters out of consular hands and so assist Cumming, theoretically without the knowledge of the consuls. Among the three PCOs listed for Zurich, Basle and Lausanne was Mr Maw (presumably ex-Romania), but in March 1918 his activities 'led to a warrant for his arrest being issued by the Swiss authorities and he came home'. Mr Chaplin of Zurich was 'relieved from his post on account of drink'.

The Geneva station was opened in March 1917 by Captain Middleton Edwards and at about the same time a meteorologist, Professor N.W. Thomas, was attached to the Berne station for what sounds like a very congenial posting: 'the Professor's work consisted solely in ascending to a certain height up a mountain twice a day and telegraphing to London the direction and force of the wind. The purpose of this was intended partly to work out the possibility of gas attacks and partly for the information of the Air Force.' Also in Geneva in 1917, Mr Whittal inaugurated political reporting, seemingly off his own bat and despite local resistance although the Minister, Sir Horace Rumboldt, was 'greatly in favour of PC officers and assisted them in their work'.

The expansion of networks in Switzerland, and the lack of any central controlling authority, led GHQ and the War Office to propose that GHQ should control it, but this was vetoed following an inspection on Cumming's behalf by Colonel Rhys Sampson. Instead, it was decided that in October 1917 Cumming should send Major Hans Vischer 'to be chief of all the organisations in Switzerland in so far as military work was concerned'. Vischer was troublesome; the summary stresses that he was not 'chief of the organisation in the full sense of the word, and [had] no control over personnel' before going on to say that he had no qualifications at all to recommend him. The 'immediate friction' of his arrival provoked the retirement of Captain Harron, after which Vischer assumed complete control and 'attempted to reorganise'. The summary writer, possibly a participant and unashamedly partisan, describes the reorganisation as having made no difference to existing stations but 'merely to have increased the staff very largely at Berne, and to have raised the monthly expenditure to four times its original amount'. Among the changes detailed was the starting in Bellegarde of a 'definite school for agents'. The following year Captain Edward Knoblock, the playwright, was appointed Travelling Inspector in Switzerland. After the armistice the Swiss organisation was reduced to two men, majors Langley and Jump, the former to run western agents and the latter eastern.

Deservedly the best known description of secret service work in wartime Switzerland is that to be found in Somerset Maugham's collection of stories, *The Ashenden Papers*. Maugham is often assumed to have worked for Cumming – as he did, later, in Russia – but as we have noted in Switzerland he was working for one of the army networks, run by the elder of the Wallinger brothers (the other ran IPI – Indian Political Intelligence). Maugham's stories are lightly fictionalised accounts of actual operations and agents concerning which his role was more that of general facilitator (luring a wanted man over the French border to be executed for example) than producer of secret intelligence. The truthful feel of these stories would be immediately recognisable to anyone who has spent time in a foreign country pretending to do one thing while actually doing another. Their importance, however, extends beyond historical verity into literature. The sceptical, middle-aged hero, Ashenden, and the world-weary tone make them modern spy stories, progenitors of Eric Ambler, Graham Greene, Len Deighton and John Le Carré. Although Conrad, in *Under Western Eyes* and *The Secret Agent*, was arguably the father of the modern spy story, what Le Carré has called Maugham's 'mood of disenchantment and almost prosaic reality set the tone for much of what

followed. He was also probably joint first, with Compton Mackenzie, to have experienced espionage as an already established
novelist.

As for what was achieved by any of the Swiss networks,
Christopher Andrew gives a plausibly downbeat account in
Secret Service which there is no evidence to counter, though it
is unlikely to be the whole truth. On Cumming's side, for
instance, there was almost certainly a good deal of reporting on
German embargo-breaking (of which the condoms are the most
memorable example), while good tactical military reporting was
probably hard to come by because it was less available in
Switzerland. The most active parts of the Front, including all
British sectors, were well to the north of the Swiss border. The
problem is also that the archives contain few references to intelligence product, compared with intelligence personnel, procedures
or, occasionally, operations, which makes assessment of the utility of these various organisations always difficult and sometimes
hazardous.

There is, however, record of a possible Swiss case, indicative
of the sort of successful counter-espionage operation that might
have been undertaken without War Office or GHQ participation, or even knowledge. It is mentioned not in the Swiss
summary but in a 135-page document entitled 'Notes on Instruction and Recruiting of Agents, compiled for CSS by Staff of
M.I.1.c.' and dated 31 December 1918. We cannot be sure it
took place in Switzerland because the account refers coyly to 'a
neutral country' but reference to the border with France and
other details make it likely.

The local station knew a well-dressed Belgian woman of good
family, looks and education who also had 'good cause to hate
the Boche'. She was recruited and agreed to penetrate the local
German intelligence organisation, most of whose members were
known. She was directed towards a particular German and consented that 'nothing be shirked in order to obtain a successful
issue'. She established relations with the man, allowed herself to

be 'recruited' by him and was tasked by German intelligence with undertaking a trip into France for them.

Having by this time entered intimate relations with her German case officer, she persuaded him to accompany her to France. For this trip she was given the addresses of German head agents in France as well as communication addresses in Paris and 'several articles of underclothing impregnated with secret ink for delivery to a certain address in France and partly for her own use with full instructions as to how to use same, but they did not initiate her into the method of its development'. Once in France, her companion was promptly arrested; he confessed and the French security authorities followed up the addresses and identifications.

Meanwhile, the station set about the destruction of the German network in (presumed) Switzerland by placing with an agent they had recruited in the local secret police the handwritten instructions given to the Belgian lady by two German head agents; he pretended he had discovered the paper and the two agents were arrested. Their arrests led to eight or nine others and then to the capture of the Head District Officer who came across from his base at Freiburg in Germany. Notes including a carbon found on him led to further arrests including 'neutral officers up to the rank of Captain in charge of posts of Gendarmerie close to the French frontier and of whom one blew his brains out to avoid arrest'. The total cost of the operation was about £60, and the German intelligence network was destroyed.

Another country in which Secret Service activity became well-known as a result of an author being involved was, of course, Greece, chronicled in detail by yet another Royal Marine officer, Sir Compton Mackenzie. He wrote some ten volumes of autobiography one of which, *Greek Memories*, was banned when he tried to publish it in 1932 and led to his plea of guilty to breaching the Official Secrets Act by revealing the identities of some he had served with, the fact that Cumming was known in Whitehall as 'C', the contents of wartime telegrams, the fact that

Passport Control was used as a cover and the acronym MI1(C). He was fined £100 with £100 costs.

It was Cumming's successor, Sinclair, supported by Kell, who took exception to the book, although Mackenzie had already published a fictionalised version of the same events in his novel, *Extremes Meet*. It is, of course, easy to poke fun at the use of the sledgehammer of the courts to crack such tiny nuts, but almost any successful secret service is found to act against unauthorised disclosure of its secrets, since the reputation for keeping its secrets is an essential condition of its success. People will not work for secret services if they sense that their contributions are vulnerable to 'sell-by' dates. Mackenzie was to take a deadly revenge in his later comic novel, *Water on the Brain*, in which Sinclair and Kell are satirised as deadly rivals commanding organisations more concerned to spy on each other than on anyone else. Although the histories of both services could show grains of truth in this respect, albeit more in attitude than actions, they would be no more than that – grains among fixed strata of co-operation – but the contemporary persistence of the myth demonstrates the lasting qualities of good parody.

An unexpurgated *Greek Memories* was finally published more than half a century after the ban. It is a lively, entertaining read, and – after making due allowance for authorial bias and the imaginative component of dialogue recalled decades later – seems generally accurate. Mackenzie's task in neutral Greece was what was referred to at the time as 'B branch', which meant counter-espionage, while 'A branch' was concerned with getting intelligence. The post-war summary describes work in Greece in 1916 as 'almost entirely I(a)' corrected in manuscript to 'I(b)'.

Mackenzie was, by his own and the accounts of others, brilliant, energetic and troublesome, as well as often, and unpopularly, right. He was probably a good case officer, certainly if his description of how he handled his awkward but productive source in the German legation (the porter code-named Davy Jones) is anything to go by. He makes many references to Cumming, for whom he clearly felt great affection. He had worked for the Bureau for some time without their ever having met until Mackenzie was summoned back to London in the midst of a full-blown row with the Foreign Office over his activities. His description of this first meeting is worth reading in full. He went to it expecting to be sacked:

> In those days taxis were hard to find. So when I reached 2 Whitehall Court I told the driver to wait, for I fancied that ten minutes would probably be the extreme limit of the interview, judging by the tone of the voice at the other end of the telephone which had informed me that the Chief would see me at half-past five that afternoon. I inquired for the whereabouts of Captain Spencer's flat and was directed up the familiar staircase which led to the Authors' Club. I debated for a moment when I reached the first floor whether I would turn aside into the Club and have a strong brandy before climbing to the top of the building where C's headquarters were; the reflection that I might need one even more acutely ten minutes later dispelled the temptation.
>
> It is always possible to tell by the attitude of subordinates what is likely to be the attitude of the head man in any show, and my reception upstairs by various young lieutenants of the RNVR was ambiguous. There was that air of nervous anticipation with which schoolboys watch the attitude of a victim who has been sent for by the Head. Even pink-faced lady secretaries came fluttering one after another on some excuse into the room where I was waiting, presumably to take a quick glance at the man who had ventured to defy C for nine months. After about ten minutes of this embarrassed waiting a young man came in and announced that the Chief wished to see Captain Mackenzie immediately. I followed him into C's private room, tucked away under the roof, crowded with filing cupboards and shelves, and with the rest of the space almost entirely filled by C's big table. The dormer windows looked out across the plane-trees of the Embankment Gardens to the Thames, over which twilight was

creeping. I saw on the other side of the table a pale clean-shaven man, the most striking features of whose face were a Punch-like chin, a small and beautifully fine bow of a mouth, and a pair of very bright eyes. He was dressed in the uniform of a naval captain.

C paid no attention when I came in, but remained bent over the table, perusing through a pair of dark horn-rimmed spectacles some document. I stood watching the blue dusk and the tarnished silver of the Thames until presently C took off the glasses, leant back in his chair, and stared hard at me for a long minute without speaking. 'Well?' he said finally.

'Mackenzie, sir,' I replied. 'Reporting to you from Athens.'

'And what have you to say for yourself?' he asked, putting in an eyeglass and staring at me harder than ever.

Somehow I suppose I must have embarked on my tale in such a way as to win his attention, for after a few minutes he murmured in those faintly-slurred, immensely attractive accents of his: 'There's no need to tell me all this standing up. There's a chair beside you.'

So I sat down and went on talking until about a quarter to seven, when a pink-faced secretary with a bundle of papers put her head round the door. She conveyed an impression that she had been deputed as the least likely person to have her head bitten off if she was interrupting matters of importance. C held out his hands for the papers and signed his name on them one after another in the bright green ink he always used. Presently we were left alone again.

At half-past seven he said: 'Well, you'd better stop and have some dinner with us.'

'Thank you very much, sir,' I said. 'Would you mind if I went downstairs and sent away my taxi?'

'Have you been keeping a taxi waiting two hours?'

'Yes, sir, I thought you would probably be finished with me in a few minutes.'

'My God,' C exclaimed. 'No wonder you're always asking for another thousand pounds every month!'

I went down to pay off the taxi, and when I came back the offices were empty. C took me into the dining-room where I was introduced to his wife as the man who had given him more trouble than anybody else in his service.

After dinner C showed me various books he had been buying. They were mostly sets in bright leather bindings.

'These ought to be in your line,' he said. 'You're a writing fellow, aren't you?'

Those books and the large oil-painting of a young officer in the uniform of the Seaforth Highlanders were the chief features of the room. I remember the tale of how C had cut off his leg with a pen-knife in order to reach his dying son and put an overcoat over him, and the little room filled with that large portrait expressed how large a place the original must have held in his heart.

It must have been after eleven o'clock when I got up to leave. C came along with me to the door of the flat. 'Well, you'd better look in every day while you're in London,' he told me. 'I thought this would happen.'

'You thought what would happen, sir?'

'Why, I intended to make myself extremely unpleasant to you; but I said that when I saw you I should probably find you a man after my own heart and fall on your neck. We'll have dinner at the Savoy one night soon.'

I felt, as I walked down the marble stairs of Whitehall Court, that we should get a real move on in Athens presently.

The presence of May is made to sound normal and the placing of Alastair's portrait suggests that their bereavement was not something they were trying to hide from. Like Sykes, Cumming's paymaster, Mackenzie mentions books but unfortunately leaves no account of which they were.

Their affection was mutual. Mackenzie later recalls how he was given Cumming's swordstick, a mark of great favour: 'On November 2nd, the day before we were to leave for Greece, C presented me with the swordstick he had always carried on spying expeditions in time of peace. "That's when this business was really amusing," he said. "After the War is over we will do some amusing secret service work together. It is capital sport."'

This affection is corroborated by Frank Stagg's less well-known memoir, in which he throws an interesting light on Mackenzie's reporting:

> 'C' had a passion for Compton Mackenzie whom he was using in Athens and who got him stuff from that City's underworld. The blighter used to send reports in blank verse which pleased the Old Man, but our people loathed CM because they had to unravel the rubbish – yards and yards of stuff that could have gone on a postcard.

Stagg describes the sending to Greece of the Danish Captain Christmas, friend of the Greek royal family, a visit recalled by Mackenzie in contemptuous terms. According to Stagg, the feeling was mutual, but there was a postscript:

> What he [Christmas] had to say about Compton Mackenzie was unrepeatable, and he came home to tell us in person his view of the situation. I took that most loveable man to the Hippodrome, where Fay Compton was singing a song in which the last line of each verse was, 'I'll take a little more off'. Christmas was getting more and more excited and clapping roundly, until at last Fay Compton said, 'But I can't take any more off.' When at the height of his enthusiasm I asked him if he knew she was Compton Mackenzie's sister, he looked tragic and said, 'I take back every-thing I said about him. If only I had known he had a sister so lovely I should have made friends with him instead.'

Christmas, we may recall, was the man who had been exfil-trated hurriedly from Denmark because of a slip-up made by one of the pretty girls he insisted should be his courier.

The impression given by Mackenzie in *Greek Memories* of

the dominating role he played in the Bureau's activities in Greece is largely borne out by the post-war summary. According to that, Cumming's first head of station in Athens was Colonel Rhys Sampson, sent there in February 1915 from his attachment to the French Deuxième Bureau. He recruited Mackenzie in December 1915, finding him available as a result of ill-health after Gallipoli. A month later Rhys left Athens for Egypt, leaving Mackenzie in charge.

With the overthrow of the royalist party and the succession of Eleutherios Venizelos, the Prime Minister (whom Mackenzie strongly backed, in opposition to Foreign Office policy), Mackenzie's activities greatly increased and he 'commenced running agents very strongly', as well as being supplied by Cumming with a yacht for communicating between the islands. The summary confirms his story of seizing the German diplomatic bag (in fact, it refers to several seizures and is corrected in manuscript to the one that Mackenzie mentions) and comments: 'By August 1916 Captain Compton Mackenzie could do anything he liked in Greece, and whatever adverse comments may be passed on his services, it is certain that he did at times excellent work.'

He was joined by Edward Knoblock (whom he had himself introduced to the Secret Service) in November 1916 but when in December the royalists returned he and his office had to withdraw to Syra, which had been seized by the Royal Navy. A number of his agents were shot. While at Syra he raided the Cyclades Islands and seized the records of the German consulate. He also had a number of officers employed as control officers throughout the Aegean Islands, of whom the summary lists ten including a Lieutenant Larkin, RNVR, 'Nephew of Sir M.C. afterwards killed with Tanks in France.' (It was for Larkin's widow that Cumming acquired the second houseboat.) Mackenzie finally returned to London in August 1917 'owing to the constant representations of the Foreign Office', and Lieutenant Commander Myres reopened the Athens station with a staff of seven, plus another five in the islands.

If history disguised as fiction is to be trusted, then Mackenzie was not the only active officer in the eastern Mediterranean and Near East during 1917, nor the only writer. Among May's possessions after she died in 1938 was a copy of a story taken from the June 1923 edition of *Blackwood's Magazine* (no. mccxcii, vol. ccxiii). It is called 'A Bow with Two Strings' and is written by a pseudonymous author, calling himself Hasta – a Turkish word meaning sick or unwell, with possible connotations of the Sick Man of Europe. May's copy of the story, which is still in the family, is annotated, 'For Lady Mansfield Cumming and no-one else'.

Hasta tells the story of an Irish-Armenian doctor, George Roupin, whom he met after the war and who had, he discovered, 'been one of the principal actors in a side-show which I had helped to stage'. Hasta never says what his role was but describes how knowledge of a planned German offensive in Iraq was gained from bits and pieces of information put together by intelligence officers at GHQ and – though he never names him – in Cumming's office in London. One partly burned document, for example, was fortuitously picked up by an agent following a fire at the German headquarters at Kreuznach, and forwarded via Switzerland. Combined at GHQ with a postcard taken from a captured German soldier, it indicated that a vast supply of munitions and equipment was being secretly built up at Haidar Pasha, the western terminus of the Baghdad railway in Turkey, and that the offensive was planned for early October 1917.

Hasta, without explaining his presence, describes the entry into the room at GHQ of a naval officer, 'a thick-set man wearing an eyeglass and walking with a slight limp', whose arrival reduced the assembled army officers to respectful silence, 'for this was the man in whose hands lay the active side of the British Secret Service. Fearless and hard to a remarkable degree, he never spared himself in the service of his country.' Hasta then describes Cumming's accident, adding that it happened on the Meaux Chaussée and that when he regained consciousness he ordered that his secretaries be wired for 'and within three days was again directing his world organisation from a Paris hospital'. (Interestingly, he adds that what he calls 'the Chief of the British Intelligence Service in the field' – presumably MacDonogh – not only lost his only son, as Cumming had, but was also severely injured in an accident during the first five weeks of war and continued directing his work from a hospital bed, in his case in a village near the front line.)

Hasta next describes Cumming's assessment back in his 'quiet flat' in London of the evidence for a forthcoming German offensive, detailing some of it, and then switches to Roupin, by then an army doctor serving in France. Roupin is suddenly summoned back from London and introduced to a man called Stewart, of the British Secret Service, who establishes Roupin's suitability and willingness to undertake a secret mission. He is next introduced to the naval officer, who 'was engaged in examining some water-colour sketches' and who, after a searching glance, asked him, 'Are you quite clear that the job you will be required to undertake is a dangerous one, one that no paid agent would be likely to carry out successfully, and that we are only prepared to entrust it to one who, from patriotic motives, is prepared to risk everything?' The briefing then proceeds along lines recognisable from descriptions of Cumming's briefings in memoirs. On the way out Roupin confesses to Stewart that he thinks that trusting solely to himself is leaving rather a lot to chance. 'Stewart smiled. "The Old Man does not leave very much to chance," he said.'

After training, Roupin travels clandestinely to Turkey via a series of agents and a change of identity to that of a medical officer in the Turkish army. It is arranged that he becomes the medical officer for the Christian and Armenian labour battalions – virtual slaves – working under German control at Haidar Pasha. During the next few weeks he prepares his demolitions, planning to set them off just before the assembled supplies, enough for two armies, were to be moved, but on the very day he is badly injured in an accident. The next day, in hospital and in despair that his plans have come to nothing, he hears and feels a series of huge explosions as the depot goes up. He realises that his mission was not the only one, that there was a back-up, and he recalls Stewart's smiling assurance that the Old Man left little to chance.

What is most remarkable about this story is not so much that it was Cumming's first appearance in fiction as that it must have been written while he was still alive, since it appeared at the time of, or just before, his death. A later writer might have made it up on the basis of memoirs and stories that appeared in later years, but at the time Hasta was writing there were very few outside the intelligence community who could have said what he said about Cumming. Its reticence, as much as its detail, gives the impression of having been written from within. And the Haidar Pasha station was blown up in October 1917.

Whether or not this story happened as told, 1917, that year of attrition, ended better for Cumming than it began. Following the reorganisation there were some forty-one officers working in his various London establishments, plus secretaries and clerks and obscure South American staff under Mr Knox-Little. Staff abroad, according to a later list, had increased 'out of all bounds'. The special link with the US government in which Cumming acted as facilitator, employing Wiseman's sister and brother-in-law, was working to great effect. Russia had become an unknown quantity, seemingly as much to itself as to everyone else, but it was now possible to be confident of the defeat of Germany. Cumming was, perhaps, genuinely looking forward to the 'capital sport' he had promised Mackenzie after the war; no doubt once again with swordstick in hand.

17

Peace but no Rest

As predicted by Sir Samuel Hoare, confusion in Russia worsened. Cumming's Russian liaison contacts in London became increasingly unsure of what they should be doing and turned to their British liaison for help, handing over agents and seeking jobs. Shortage of money and the numbers fleeing Russia prompted General Yermoloff to ask Cumming, on 3 January 1918, if he could take on his cousin Mme Bartholomé as secretary. When Cumming saw her the next day to explain that he could not employ aliens she gave him a 'very interesting account of Russia's position and the entirely Boch character of the revolution'. He had that day discussed with Hall the possibility of organising an 'entirely new service' in Russia.

Meanwhile there were urgent matters closer to hand than Moscow: 'Bailey [his driver] returned with Sunbeam Car from a Mission then came straight up to report to me. In the interval (8 minutes only) the car was stolen and driven off.' It was reported to the police and the next day: 'Car was found by Police at 6am on Chelsea Embankment but stripped of Magneto, Dynamo, Lighting set, Accumulators, Claxon, Speedometer, Hydraulic Jack and Tools.' Although occasionally, the fortunate provision of such detail facilitates an easier intimacy with the past than rehearsals of greater events. Although there are gaps, the 1918 diary is fuller than the previous year's, but it is something of a hotch potch with no dominant theme, albeit there are a number of intermittently troublesome ones.

One such was the continuing conflict with the army in Holland, some of it at least occasioned by Tinsley's behaviour. Tinsley had already made difficulties with rival army services, particularly with Payne-Best who, as already noted, later worked for Cumming.[1] (See Christopher Andrew's *Secret Service* for details). Payne-Best suspected Tinsley of blackmailing Dutch firms who dealt with the Germans. A War Office investigation failed to find any evidence but Tinsley had already established an unwelcome reputation for, in the words of Captain Kirkpatrick who was to succeed Payne-Best and later became Permanent Under Secretary in the Foreign Office, 'lying and unscrupulous intriguing'. Yet at the same time Tinsley was running a very successful outfit. On 7 January Cumming asked MacDonogh to explain to his seniors 'why T is a doubtful asset and say we haven't an alternative ready'.

On Sunday 17 February he spent all morning and again from 4 p.m. to 6 p.m. in discussions with Tinsley, continued the following day. Matters rumbled on. On 29 June Landau, who, as we have seen, was running La Dame Blanche, returned to London for a long talk, prompting Cumming to observe: 'He is very nervous and won't speak but gives me the impression that there is "something rotten".' By September, however, the issue seemed to be less a question of Tinsley's integrity than of the old problem of control on the ground. During another long yarn an upset Tinsley offered to resign rather than return under a cloud, protesting that he couldn't get on unless he were in sole charge, that he would put everything in the hands of his successor and then be ready to 'do any useful work – minesweeping or anything'. Part of the problem, at least, was an army proposal to put Kirkepatrick and another officer in Tinsley's office but not under his command. After several days of discussion, MacDonogh came down decisively on Tinsley's side and Tinsley assured Cumming that he 'had no intention of having a row with Landau' and would do his best to make things work smoothly. This seemingly serious disagreement finds little reflection in Landau's accounts.

On one day in February there were two minor illustrations of the continuing difficulty of knowing who worked for whom in the intelligence world of this period. Lord Herschell told Cumming that Hall 'wants to engage a man called Korvine for work in connection with TRs going to South America by Trans Atlantic Line and to pay him £1,000 a year. I am to send the money monthly to Herschell.' An accountancy audit of such transactions might suggest that either Korvine or Herschell worked for Cumming. The same would apply to MacDonogh's secretary, Miss Ouden (?), whom MacDonogh wanted admitted to Cumming's Luncheon Club – very likely a reference to the rooftop canteen he had had built, with the Savoyard chef and food provided by Browning. This necessitated the lady being put on Cumming's pay list, and so appearing as one of his staff. There was another example towards the end of the year when, on 6 November, Hugh Whittall, one of Cumming's staff, left for Constantinople 'but in the service of the DMI'.

Additionally, Cumming's code section appears to have provided codes to other departments. At the end of January he records taking three over to Hall, and in April he mentions having sent four to Malta with another – called M2 – required there 'for communicating with Barcelona'. On Sunday 28 April, however, the code news was more sombre: 'Mr Wood from Rotterdam called and reported that Mr Mondeg de Leon [probable] had arrived from Holland – under escort. Colonel D interviewed this man who confessed to have sold our cipher to the enemy and also three days' telegrams from the Hague.' The cipher concerned might, of course, have been a military or Foreign Office one rather than Cumming's.

He might also have been involved in propaganda work, a subject he had been sniffing around for some time. On 20 February he received a reply from MacDonogh to a minute he had put up on propaganda in enemy countries. He notes that

MacDonogh's 'orders from War Cabinet apply at present only to *Turkey* and he wishes me to *prepare* for that – subversive measures only – but to hold my hand altogether for the present until Lord Northcliffe's and Lord Beaverbrook's positions are made clear'. On 16 March, however, when asked for tasking by the colonel in charge of the Cinema Lorry (probable) Detachment, he observed: 'It seems to me a matter in which we ought to work more closely with propaganda, but this also is imposs. under present circs.' Nevertheless, he had some sort of involvement because the subject continues to feature, such as on 17 April when he discussed it with Ronald Campbell at the Foreign Office and agreed to 'hand Middleton Edwards over to Lord Beaverbook'. There is an earlier reference to his having someone working in Lord Northcliffe's office.

The question of demarcation with MI5 reappeared in February 1918 when Cumming called on Campbell to show him 'DMI's letter re MI5 tasking taking over all my organisations in Allied countries. He says I ought not to accept this, but I told him I could not but obey orders.' This may have been occasioned by rearrangements in Greece and Egypt and may also be the matter of a minute MacDonogh showed him on 2 March 'addressed to War Cabinet but DID and himself protesting against any interference with their I [Intelligence] services. Also a letter from the S. of S. of the same tenor with regard to Political Section. This letter mentioned that our Service was unrivalled and said also that it was an axiom that two parallel [probable] services with the same object acted disparagingly on each other.'

It is not clear whether this welcome compliment was paid by the Secretary of State for War or for Foreign Affairs. With regard to the latter, though, Cumming refers on 6 and 8 March to the setting up of a new Foreign Office 'Intelligence Bureau' under Sir William Tyrrell, who called to discuss the distribution of Cumming's reporting: 'He will receive all our Reports and will be solely responsible for their distribution.' This sounds like a form of assessment unit, a foreshadow perhaps of the later Joint Intelligence Committee (JIC).

From 13 March to 5 April Hall was away on a trip to Italy and Malta, assiduously seen off from the station by Cumming. Meanwhile the presence in Italy of Sir Samuel Hoare had led to increased intelligence activity. On 11 April, during a visit to Cumming, he proposed 'a system of SS recruiting' which would involve an army officer, McEwen, and on the 17th Cumming records getting agreement for 'recruiting, and sending men through the Italian lines at Valona provided we were kept fully informed'. In fact, liaison with the Italians seems to have increased (though Cumming regrets having to tell one Italian visitor that he no longer had a network there) and in the Hall papers in Cambridge there is a 14 November 1918 letter from the British Ambassador to Rome, Sir Rennall Rodd, paying tribute to Hall 'organising with the Italian Naval Authorities a special secret information service . . . it has been of great value to us to obtain rapid and sure information about what was going on on the other side of the Adriatic.' Although there is no indication that Cumming was involved in this as a principal, the chances are that he would have provided facilities and training under Hall's direction.

One of the facilities he increasingly provided at this time was demolition and sabotage, primarily in Russia and Romania. The Allies took action to prevent Russian war stocks and equipment falling into enemy hands, particularly after Russia's withdrawal from the war, and on 6 April Cumming records: 'Sent for by CIGS who received me kindly and questioned me about the Kharkov demolitions. He would like to know: 1) Can the job be done? 2) Are the factory hands Bolshevists?' On 13 May he went with Captain Carrington to Croft Down Road (probable) and 'inspected lathe etc. – for bomb-making etc.', collecting it three days later in his lorry and setting it up, apparently in Whitehall Court; on 20 May he refers to the installation of the workshop and subsequently makes a couple of trips to Bursledon to fetch tools. He probably never felt comfortable being far from a lathe and finding reason for a workshop in Whitehall Court was something he doubtless pursued with zest. In that part of the building where he had his offices, now the Horse Guards Hotel, there is a large two-storey suite, known as the Egyptian suite, which was converted into accommodation from a former workshop. A rooftop addition, which might have been the canteen, is nearby. The precise location of Cumming's office and apartment is unknown and the accommodation has anyway been redesigned and altered several times since, but it is possible to get a pretty good idea of where it must have been.

Cumming's fondness for things was commented on by Edward Knoblock in his memoir, *Around the Room*:

> He had a passion for inventions of all sorts, and being a rich man, he often bought the rights to them, such as strange telescopes, mysterious mechanisms with which to signal in the dark across the front, rockets, bombs etc. But once he owned these inventions he hated the idea of parting with them, and it was an obvious struggle between his sense of possession and his sense of patriotism which of the two should win. I need hardly say that the latter always got the better of the former – but not without a certain amount of groaning and reluctance.

(The Patent Office has no record of his having taken out any patents.)

Apart, incidentally, from repeating the story of Alastair's death, Knoblock also offers a variant of the stories of Cumming stabbing his artificial leg: 'He said that when interviewing job applicants he would sometimes take his sharp paper-knife and jab it to the hilt through his trousers, concluding, if the applicant winced, "Well, I am afraid you won't do."'

Meanwhile, bombs made in another place were still falling on London. On 7 March Cumming records Major Hargreaves being blown out of bed and Miss Cresswell having a bomb fall through her room. Indeed, it seems to have been a day for happy endings, at least for some: 'A Mr Parry was brought to see me by Dansey and Knoblock – linguist, good presence and address etc. Unfortunately (for him) I recognised him as the JGP of 1911 whom I sent to Danzig but who never arrived there.'

Nor was sabotage the only fun Cumming had in mind. Perhaps partly because of frustration with his military taskers and masters, and partly because of the difficulty of running a truly clandestine operation overseas using officers who were officially military, he called on the Foreign Office on 12 April and told Ronald Campbell 'about my plan for starting a *Secret* service'. The context was possibly Switzerland because a few days later he was telling a Mr Otway that 'we wanted an independent organisation in Switzerland and Scandinavia which would keep us informed when the Armistice period commenced'. It was probably for this purpose that in late June he investigated buying a toy distribution business in Switzerland but sensibly pulled out before committing himself (albeit only after – to his annoyance – his identity with his cover-name, Captain Spencer, had been revealed to the businessman involved, whom he never met).

Changing times were reflected in changing tasking. On 2 May MacDonogh sent for Cumming 'and asked for information as to TR preparations for invasion. Informed him already in hand, but I am adding to them.' The massive German spring offensive, reinforced by divisions released from the Eastern Front, was still making progress on the central part of the Western Front near Paris, although the drive to the coast had been halted in the north. As far as is known, there were no German plans to invade Britain at this time, and it may be that MacDonogh was referring to possible British plans for diversionary landings around the North Sea or Baltic ports.

Two months later the War Office was seeking 'socialist reports from France, Italy and from Berne about both'. Sir William Tyrrel 'was satisfied with DMI's reports of internal conditions in France and we need not go forward with GB [?]'. On 28 August, following another call on Tyrrel, he notes the tasking to be given to an agent in the British press: 'To ascertain quietly and unostentatiously the attitude of the various sections of the Press in regard to the Peace Offensive.' This was an unusual assignment for an overseas-based intelligence service and it may have been simply that Cumming happened to know someone who was well placed, although the information gathered would have been overtly available. Whatever happened, on 28 December that year he was instructed by Tyrrel to close down the operation.

In April Sir William Wiseman visited from America and, as usual, Cumming saw a good deal of him, learning on 20 April that on hearing of initial German successes in their spring offensive President Wilson had remarked: 'This will mean an Anglo-American alliance.' (A considerable advance for the hitherto neutrally-inclined Wilson.) Sir William was around for over a week but it was not all high politics; when he came to bid farewell, en route for Paris on 29 April, he coincided with a Mr Turner Norris who 'came re. a Vacuum Cleaner – cost £35'. There is, sadly, no evidence to suggest that the tradition of the spy posing as vacuum-cleaner salesman began with this encounter. On 17 May Cumming records that he 'Lunched with the Churchills – Captain Spencer and a Mr Caulfield (Algy)', but there is no indication how this came about.

The year shows signs of increasing financial pressure. At the end of August Cumming noted that Ronald Campbell was 'very satisfied with our reduced total and told me to retain the £10,000 reserve on deposit in WL as hereto for'. There are also indications of rather patchy involvement in the Far East, not detailed in the diary but commented upon dryly in the post-war summary: 'No new stations were set up until June 1918, when C. determined to inaugurate work in the Far East, and sent out Captain James to that end. Business cover was provided, but he was recalled by telegram immediately on arrival in Shanghai, since it had been reported that he had been indiscreet on board ship so that his mission was known.' Another attempt was made in

October with a furniture-dealing agent code-named Orange. He, too, was recalled 'after a month's work since it was discovered that he had merely obtained a passage to the Far East for his own purposes and did not intend to work. No further efforts to start an organisation in the Far East, other than a few agents existing in Siberia, were made until April 1920, when the services of Mr Denham were obtained.'

It is possible, though no more than that, that Orange was 'the egregious Mr King' whom Cumming interviewed with Freddie Browning at Scotland Yard on 27 November. Mr King 'gave his word of honour that he would not betray any information about our FE organisation to anyone in future and Mr Basil Thomson then asked us to accept this'.

India was forbidden to him, as he told a Colonel Muspratt of MI5 on 3 October. The Colonel was 'going to start MI5 out there' and Cumming offered any help he was permitted to give. The previous month he had noted that his organisation in Palestine had been transferred to the military. Presumably this was part of the ESMIB, from which he had been keen to extricate himself.

On 23 September he received from America what he called his 'autoped', courtesy of Major Thwaites, in New York. This must have been the scooter upon which legend has him patrolling the corridors of Whitehall. His usual progression on one good leg, one artificial leg and one or two sticks must indeed have been slow; if he rode the scooter as he drove cars, he must have been a bureaucratic menace. On the same day a Conte de Lesdain bade farewell, having been mentioned a number of times without any suggestion of problems until Cumming received Mme de Lesdain. Here, for once, his gallantry got him into trouble:

She was rather excited and objected to my taking her (divorced) husband's part – also his lawful (or unlawful) wife's part on the occasion of de L. marrying her. It seems evident that my visitor was never his lawful wife at all. On her leaving and my expressing sympathy by retaining hold of her hand, whilst saying goodbye, she tried the 'unhand me monster' pose, so I could say no more. I think she is straight but very excitable, hysterical, and in love with Captain Barton. What she wants me to do is impossible, as I explained to her.

This encounter may well have coloured his view of a Miss Wale whom he met a few days later. She had been taken on by the War Office 'for Russia' and was highly recommended to Cumming but he found her 'rather highly coloured and I shall think myself lucky if she doesn't give trouble later'. He was also called on by the job-seeking Mrs Dale Long, presumably wife of the pre-war agent. There was an office wedding (Miss Caswell) and, in New York, a death (Miss Bygott).

He spent much of the first half of October planning a ten-man mission to Bulgaria and appears to have got approval for it, but it may have been overtaken by the Armistice. Large parts of October and November are blank, save for one or two frustratingly brief references such as that for 21 October: 'Gave Colonel Sampson Motor Rug and Colt Automatic.' An earlier frustrating reference was that of 9 September: 'Called on DMI by appointment and received his orders for a special job. Then to Sir Graham Greene.'

The Armistice, when it came, was no surprise, but nor was it anti-climactic. There are numerous published descriptions of the anarchic revelry and exuberant celebrations in London. Cumming announces it to himself with 'Armistice was signed at 5am today', but does not say whether the staff celebrated or worked as usual. He, it seems, did the latter, being called on by Tinsley – never a brief affair – and himself calling on MacDonogh. He had anyway been briefed on the armistice terms by Hall at the latter's house a month before. Within two days of its signing, on 13 November, he was introduced by Tinsley to Paul Stayes (also known as Robert) of La Dame Blanche to whom he paid 'pretty compliments on the Michelin organisation'. Landau does not mention this in his accounts – he may not have been aware of it – but it can be taken as an indication of the importance of La Dame Blanche that this was the first recorded post-war congratulatory act of Cumming's. Six days later he held a short informal conference in his office with the army which 'Decided to have a Committee in Brussels and elsewhere to examine claims of those who stated they had worked for us'. This could have been the origin of the committee which considered the Alexander Szek case and on which Menzies served.

There were others to be thanked, along with intimations of revolution and anarchy in Germany. On 28 November, 'Max Schultz our pre-war agent returned after 7 years imprisonment in Germany'. Schultz's brief experience of post-war Germany was remarkable and the next day Cumming took him to Mac-Donogh, Ronald Campbell and Sir William Tyrrel. On his release in Hamburg Schultz had joined the Revolutionary Party,

> eventually getting into close touch with Heiné, its leader, who consulted him frequently (in spite of M. S.'s complete ignorance of current events during the last 7 years). Heiné offers to hand over the *Vaterland* (54,000 tons) and other ships. He wants to separate Hamburg and the Kiel Canal and form a Hanseatic Colony. The Revolutionaries attacked the Town Hall but ran away after receiving one volley from its guard. After two hours they returned – practically unarmed – but with 17 sailors from Kiel, to whom the Military Governor at once handed over his sword! All the former officials retaining their offices on Heiné's orders.

Landau gives a similar account, probably referring to the same incident.

Sir William was much impressed by Schultz and, rather surprisingly, took his tale as evidence 'that Germany's revolution is controlled by authorities'. Schultz was asked to put it in writing, and Cumming to submit it as a report.

Schultz was not the only returned prisoner who is mentioned, though he was probably the most feted. Another was a man called Huss who arrived on 30 November. Cumming comments that his arrest was 'made under suspicious circs. he thinks his mother-in-law betrayed him'.

It has been said that Cumming had a hard time ensuring the continuation of his Service after the war, but this seems not to have been the case (though he did, as we shall see, have a hard fight to maintain its independence). On 25 November we find him recruiting a Captain Rogers who 'promises to act for us without pay so long as he is Harbour Master in Constantinople. I advanced him £ to work there – he says he can get agents for all Black Sea ports.' There was now a new enemy, Bolshevik Russia, and the transition from old enemy to new was apparently seamless. During a meeting about Russia on 28 December, Lord Hardinge 'agreed to my going ahead and arranging for a Peace SS on the basis of £30,000 a year which he said would be within the mark'. Nevertheless, this represented a deep cut and at the same time Cumming found that many of his military staff were discharged from their parent services without his having jobs to give them.

Yet in other respects it was business as usual. On 31 December the DMI

asked what we were doing in the way of increasing our organisation in Germany. I told him I understood that his intelligence officers were doing all that was wanted and better than we could do it. He said finally that we were to send in civilian agents to all unoccupied Germany who were to supply information to questionnaires (which Colonel Cornwall would supply) and establish themselves for a permanent service.

Cumming already had a draft 'peace estimate' allowing £2,000 for Germany and Austria together, but the DMI 'told me that we should require £30,000 for these countries alone and that he would fight for this amount'.

By then it was a new DMI, Major General Thwaites, who had succeeded MacDonogh on the latter's promotion to Adjutant General to the Forces in September. Thwaites and Cumming had not got off to a good start, prompting the latter to complain to the Foreign Office that he was being denied access to the DMI. On 21 September Cumming was called to explain himself to 'AG' – probably MacDonogh in his new post – who had received the complaint via Lord Hardinge. After this, Cumming was received 'kindly' by Thwaites who 'spoke to me about Bertrand Stewart, Rué, Gen. de Jonghe and others and said he did not believe in commencing a new job by sacking the staff. He promised to send for me whenever he contemplated changes.' On 1 October, however, he still found it necessary to call on the DMI 'by way of letting him know that I was in existence'.

Later in the month he received a letter from Thwaites calling for the amalgamation of the Bureau with MI5, with other War Office departments (MI8 and MI9) and with all the cryptographers; the clear implication was that the new service would remain under War Office control. Although neither the first nor last such attempt the scheme was probably the flavour of War Office corridors at the time because of anticipation that the imminent ending of war would bring an end also to the very large military intelligence empire that had been built up; in fact, the Intelligence Corps was more or less wound up between the two world wars. If the Bureau, with its wider-ranging foreign responsibilities and growing political intelligence role, could be satisfactorily swallowed, War Office intelligence might be less emasculated.

Thwaites's letter (drafted, an insider told Cumming, by Colonel French) was badly worded as Thwaites admitted when he told Cumming on 30 October, that he could tear it up. But the campaign continued. On 30 November, Cumming wrote:

> DMI sent for me. General Bartholomew was present. He asked why I had not replied to his minute re amalgamation and asked my opinion on the scheme. He would not let me state this however and did not appear to give consideration to what I did say. Colonel Cornwall to whom I was introduced gave us every credit for the good stuff sent in about German Battle (Order of). DMI will inspect us tomorrow at four.

The inspection was apparently satisfactory but the unmistakably military tenor of Cumming's last sentence shows the extent to which the War Office still regarded the Bureau – at least the military part of it – as its own, albeit errant, creature.

The rather different tone of Thwaites's and Cumming's New Year's Eve discussion of future work in Germany was probably due to the fact that the War Office scheme had by then been put on hold. In a judicious letter of 25 November, Lord Hardinge, while acknowledging that changes would doubtless be necessary, suggested that it would be wise to await the outcome of the peace conference before deciding. His view was echoed the following day in a letter from Hall, who was not opposed to amalgamation in principle but counselled waiting, and wanted time to think it over. Significantly, an assessment by a War Cabinet Committee, chaired by Lord Curzon and probably drafted shortly after this, describes the Bureau as 'The Foreign Office's service' and pays tribute to achievements which must have greatly aided Cumming in his fight with post-war predators:

> The conditions of war led to a large expansion of Secret Service in every direction. The main expansion took place in the Foreign Office Service in which there was an enormous growth in all kinds of secret operations abroad, involving the expenditure of

very large sums of money. The Committee had good reason for believing that heavy as this outlay has been, it has been thoroughly justified by the results and that the information thus placed at the disposal of the British Government has been equal, if not superior, to that obtained by any other country engaged in the war.

Ultimately, the Foreign Office paid and, so long as they valued the services their money bought, they had an interest in the independence and survival of the Secret Service that provided them. This battle may partly have accounted for Cumming's very brief diary entries during December, though as the month goes on meetings with the DNI become more frequent (as do Cumming's attendances at meetings of the King's Fund).

This was also the month in which the lengthy notes on instructing and recruiting agents, quoted in the last chapter, were completed. It is an interesting document with sections on the various practices and techniques of espionage – such as the use of codes, secret inks, letter boxes, cover and agents provocateur – as well as on sabotage and how to report effectively on various intelligence requirements, e.g. how to describe a new aeroplane, which bits to measure and so on. It is of course a period piece, redolent of its time, but there are elements applicable to all intelligence services at all times, such as the nine-word preface: 'Intelligence is information on which action can be taken.' The point here was that the proper concern of intelligence services to protect their sources should never be allowed to obscure this fundamental requirement forged no doubt, in the pressure of war rather than the leisure of peace.

More particularly, there are such gems as the advice to have at hand an efficient highly technical expert burglar willing to undergo imprisonment without giving the show away. As an example of the value of such assets the paper quotes 'the emptying of the safes in the Austrian Consulate and SS in Zurich'. It also notes that half-British agents recruited during the war in

Britain and sent to their other homelands 'proved anything but successful' and stresses that the first temptation to which any new agent is prone occurs when he has 'no sooner settled himself in his first class corner with his bundle of currency safe in his pocket, than he experiences a burning desire to tell some one of his fellow passengers all about his secret mission'. The section on naval intelligence written by Captain Somerville warns report-writers that Admiralty criticisms will be generally uncomplimentary and unhelpful 'except in showing what to *avoid*'. This is apparently because the assessing officers are very busy, have no time for feelings and on 'operational' reports often cannot comment without disclosing other secret information.

What the document also shows, though, is that the Secret Service Bureau, or the Secret Service, or MI6, or MI1(C), was no longer one man and his helpers, but a bureaucracy.

Christmas 1918, unlike some of those earlier Christmases, did not find Cumming lamenting the scarcity of people to work with: 'Office all day and lunched with Staff.' It should have been – probably was – rather jolly. Nevertheless, the Old Man they were all so fond of could not help observing – whether straightforwardly or ironically it is now impossible to know – 'but rather slack work'.

18

RUSSIAN ADVENTURES

There are probably more published first-hand accounts of British intelligence operations in Russia at the end of, and following, the First World War than of any other period between 1909 and the present. They include accounts by Somerset Maugham, Sir Samuel Hoare, Sir Paul Dukes, George Hill, Augustus Agar and Reginald Teague-Jones. Sidney Reilly, the best-known figure of this period, has been extensively written about, the most accurate and comprehensive account being also the most recent: *Iron Maze* by Gordon Brook-Shepherd, a book that serves also as a guide to all Allied anti-Bolshevik operations of the time.

The subject still merits further attention and, indeed, extracts of passages worth noting from the various books would add up to a full-length manuscript. Apart from the *Iron Maze*, the most vivid, colourful and generally reliable accounts are probably those of Sir Paul Dukes (*Secret Agent ST25*, 1938 and 1949), George Hill (*Go Spy the Land*, 1932) and Augustus Agar (*Baltic Episode, Showing the Flag* and *Footprints in the Sea*). Uniquely for agents of SIS, Dukes gave an oral account to the King on his return from Russia and was promptly knighted, while Agar was awarded by the King – on the spot – with the VC and DSO. Hill, whose contribution remains underrated, gives the most vivid account of a range of sabotage and intelligence operations pre-and post-revolution (at first against the Germans, then against the Russians). He also describes something Cumming might have relished, an encounter with the glamorous and predatory female bandit, Marucia (as well as, as we have noted, what it is like actually to use a swordstick in anger).

All give affectionate descriptions of Cumming and Dukes dedicates his book to him, adding that Cumming had read and approved it. Agar relates that before setting off on his mission he was given a farewell lunch by Cumming in his club, on the way to which he was astonished when Cumming 'drove past the sentries on the Horse Guards and through the entrance, explaining to me that he was one of five only who had this privilege'. They then talked of nothing but sailing boats until, after lunch, Cumming patted the young Agar on the back, said, 'Well, my boy, good luck to you,' and was gone.

Both Dukes and Hill not only performed tasks of derring-do, but produced valued intelligence about what was happening within the new Soviet government and within the Russian armed forces. Both could pass as Russian. Dukes, in various aliases, joined the Red Army, the Cheka (forerunner of the KGB) and the Communist Party, while Hill got himself appointed Inspector of Aviation by Trotsky in person. Reilly, being of Russian origin, found it relatively easy to pass as a Cheka officer. It was perhaps inevitable that he is remembered more for his part in the Lockhart conspiracy (a Russian-inspired operation that would now be described as a 'sting') and for his network of helpful mistresses, rather than for his less sensational but better quality intelligence and assessment work with George Hill in southern Russia.

Mythology, whether it helps or hinders, has a continuing effect on the work of any intelligence service. The doings of Reilly, Dukes, Hill and Agar, and of others, undoubtedly contributed to the Great Game element of SIS mythology in which the spy is not only a discreet seeker of information but also a man of adventurous action. The myth of James Bond owed much of its potency to the facts of such lives.

Another publicly available source on Russian operations of

the period is Hoare's voluminous Templewood papers in the University Library, Cambridge. From these it is clear that Hoare's 1916 tasking from Cumming on his despatch to Russia was to report on enemy trading and not to get involved in the political and diplomatic work of the embassy. However, perhaps in anticipation of Hoare's abilities and temperament, Cumming added, 'but I have no doubt you will find the subject will broaden out,' as indeed it did. The excellence of Hoare's contacts can be gauged from the fact that he was the first foreigner to report (to Cumming by telegram) the death of Rasputin – ensuring that London knew of it before the Russian government – and probably the first (perhaps only?) to be offered a sight of the body.[1] He established a relationship with the Tsar himself.

Also among the Templewood Papers is a nineteen-page typed document by Sidney Reilly entitled *The Russian Problem* and dated London, 5 December 1919.[2] Like other documents of the time, it is marred in modern eyes by the fact that what it urges – the overthrow of the Bolsheviks – did not happen, and it is thus too easily written off as unrealistic adventurism, but it nearly did happen and there was a period when even Lenin thought it likely. It is not an intelligence report but an attempt at analysis in which Reilly recognises that there will be no serious and sustained Allied intervention in order to topple the Bolsheviks, and so urges their overthrow by support for dissident Russian, Baltic and Polish forces. This is to be followed by an economic alliance with Germany, both to restore Russia and to give an outlet to legitimate German aspirations. The latter Reilly sees as essential in order to accommodate Germany, of whose determination not to fulfil the peace terms he is as sure as he is of the damage and evil inherent in Bolshevism.

Just as there is, sadly, no room to go into the operations and personalities of these well-documented times, so there is no room to look in any detail at Allied policy towards revolutionary and post-revolutionary Russia. Briefly, though, it was characterised by the desire to intervene without interfering, by calculation of

cost, national war-weariness, unease about the spread of Bolshevism, the lack of any widespread sense of vital national interests
being at stake and disagreements at home, all of which resulted
in vacillation. The operations which Cumming conducted
reflected this by being a mixture of intelligence-gathering, disruption, sabotage and assistance to British military forces. From the
first he was, thanks largely to Dukes and Hill, more successful
– given the limitations of reporting on a government that often
did not itself know what it would do next – than is generally
appreciated; for a period the only information the British government received about what was happening in Russia was from
Cumming's sources (most of the reports have not, of course,
survived).

With regard to assisting British forces deployed in Russia and
the Baltic, August Agar's almost single-handed destruction of the
Russian Baltic fleet was an act of daring and initiative generally
achieved only by young men given clear overall directions and
a loose rein. Plucked by Cumming from Osea Island in Essex,
where they were developing the navy's latest and fastest motor
torpedo boats, Agar and his two crews (all unmarried and under
twenty-one) were sent undercover to the Baltic in order to exfil-
trate a mysterious but important Englishman, of whom they
knew nothing but that it was vital that he got out. Due to
accident and enemy action, they never met him, but Cumming's
orders permitted a secondary role of helping Admiral Walter
Cowan's small British fleet lessen the threat posed by the large
Russian warships. Cumming's orders wisely permitted them to
use their torpedoes with the agreement of the senior naval officer,
and Walter Cowan – a firebrand who was decorated in the Boer
War, spent his First World War naval leaves in the trenches,
wept when the armistice was called and, as a commando in his
seventies, fought the Germans in the Second World War – was
not a man who found bold decisions difficult. Agar conducted
a series of daring torpedo attacks across minefields, with devastating effectiveness.

Meanwhile, the mysterious Englishman he had been sent to fetch found his way out overland, to be greeted on his return to King's Cross by a welcoming party from the Foreign Office, the Admiralty, the War Office and the Secret Service. He met his would-be rescuer for the first time on the threshold of Cumming's office in an encounter contrived by Cumming:

'Dukes?'
'Agar?'
'Hello.'
And the Chief, standing by, leaning on his stick, smiled happily.[3]

Cumming's diary reveals little of the bureaucratic background to these events, but what there is may supplement some of what is in the public domain. It is important to bear in mind the point made in a sketchy and unsatisfactory internal 1924 summary of Cumming's Russian operations, which is to the effect that 'no real SS work was done in Russia until the coming of the Bolshevik regime in the Autumn of 1917'. Until then, Cumming's representatives – including Hoare and the long-lasting Major Stephen Alley – had liaison and intelligence exchange functions, while Cumming's own dealings with Russian representatives in London were frequent and close enough for him to be awarded the Tsarist Orders of St Stanislas and St Vladimir.

As the events in Russia of 1917 and 1918 unfolded, the position of Russian officials abroad became uncertain and ambiguous, as did their pay. Early in 1917, on 4 March, Cumming discussed with Hoare what was needed to continue the job from which Hoare had just returned. The British Ambassador to Russia was keen that the British military mission should continue and had written to Lord Hardinge to say so, (while offering Hoare the new position of adviser on war trade to the embassy). Hoare advised Cumming that an official position and some ostensible duties were essential to successful secret work in

Russia as 'the officials are very suspicious'. (This seems to imply that, contrary to the internal history just mentioned, some sort of spying or nefarious work might have been going on.)

The October Revolution changed not only the Russian government but perceptions of where British and Allied interests lay, while access to the new and seemingly fluid centres of power was difficult. On 26 November Cumming received a Captain Bartram whom he noted 'has got leave and can go at any time but the Bolsheviks are stopping our couriers from entering or leaving Russia'. On 8 December he went to Hall's office to meet Admiral Volkov and Lieutenant Okerhand [probable] 'of the Russian Service. They want to say that their SS is worth the £15,000 monthly that it costs. If we state this, our Treasury will advance them the money.' There were, as already noted, a number of competing Russian intelligence services and the idea that the British should in effect buy one – in the absence, presumably, of continuing funding from Russia – must have seemed novel. Though a great deal of money, £15,000 a month was an insignificant amount compared with what Britain was prepared to spend to keep Russia in the war. Somerset Maugham, now working for Cumming, described in *The Ashenden Papers* how he was sent to Russia with a very large quantity of gold in order to support the Kerensky government and keep Russia fighting. He arrived too late and it probably would not have worked anyway, but it is an indication of the importance of the issue (in fact, Cumming records receiving Maugham on his return on Sunday 9 December, the day following his meetings with the Russians). Also at that meeting, perhaps typically, the Russians offered a scalp: 'They spoke also of de P whom they say is a rogue and has been taking money from them (photos of receipts shown) and supplied them with our stuff. I suggested that they should try and get him over.'

In fact, Gordon Brook-Shepherd cites the estimate for the overall cost of Britain's intervention in Russia as about £100 million, the equivalent of about £4.5 billion in today's money.

The plight of Russian officials abroad worsened during 1918. The government that had appointed them no longer existed and the new one was unrecognised by the Allies. On 8 February 1918 General Yermoloff recommended to Cumming a Russian police agent whom Cumming, finding him 'an honest looking man but quite destitute', sent to 'H. V.' (presumably Hans Vischer in Switzerland), paying him £1 a day there and £1 a day for his wife and sons in London. A few days later the DMI advised against employing Russian officers, while saying that he was not against it in principle and suggesting that Cumming consult General Knox (formerly of Moscow and later to head the British military mission in Siberia). The DMI thought that Russians divided into Bolsheviks and pro-Germans, 'the latter being better class folks who would welcome any power that would maintain order'.

Sidney Reilly is first mentioned in the diary on 15 March 1918, the date of Cumming's first meeting with him. From the start, Cumming appears to have had doubts, but the need for people who could operate in Russia was compelling. 'Major Scale introduced Mr Reilly who is willing to go to Russia for us. Very clever – very doubtful – has been everywhere and done everything. Will take out £500 in notes and £750 in diamonds which are at a premium. I must agree tho' it is a great gamble as he is to visit all our men in Vologda, Kief, Moscow etc.' Cumming went to the City with Dansey on 22 February and bought the diamonds from a Mr Schuyler (probable).

This was in preparation for Reilly's first trip on Cumming's behalf, which eventually led to his involvement in the so-called Lockhart conspiracy to topple the regime (named after Robert Bruce Lockhart, who worked for the Foreign Office, not the Secret Service as is often assumed), and from which he escaped thanks to the good offices of a few of his mistresses and a network of safe houses and couriers that Cumming had already established through such agents as Hill and Dukes. The historical note on Russia records that by the end of May 1918 (a date queried by a hand-written comment) Cumming's staff (as opposed to agent) organisation in Russia consisted of a mixture of civilians and military, with three men in Moscow, five in Vologda, two in Murmansk, two in Archangel, two in Petrograd and two in Stockholm, from where Major Scale oversaw the operation. The historical note comments that this organisation lasted only a few weeks until the expulsion of British and other Allied officials from Russia.

Another Russian scheme is mentioned in the diary on 17 March, again concerning Major Scale, Reilly's proposer. Scale, wrote Cumming, 'is sending Stevens to Canada to enlist and instruct agents for Russia'. This was presumably from among the immigrant community. Scale also suggested that Cumming should supply drugs – medical from the context – to Russian monasteries. This would be 'splendid propaganda'; the drugs could be bought in Canada and taken into Russia via Vancouver and Vladivostok.

Cumming seems also to have had people in Vladivostok at this time. On 15 April an illegibly-named lieutenant (Buins? Brims?) arrived from there to be 'strafed' by Cumming for his 'Censor-evading letters and he broke down and sobbed rather pitifully. I sent him off for a week's leave and he left me tons of papers to read! He is evidently hardworking and conscientious and his mistake was from ignorance.' When the lieutenant returned a week later Cumming found him still ill and under strain: 'I sent him away on the 3 weeks leave he asked for.' On the same day Cumming was displeased to be told by the War Office that he was still to pay Major Stephen Alley and his staff in Russia although Alley was by now, apparently, no longer under Cumming but under the War Office. He was to send £1,000 via 'V.A. Kemp'. Since Alley is one of those listed as on Cumming's staff in Murmansk in the historical notes, this is further indication of the fluidity of military appointments. To make it more confusing, on 3 June Hall complained to Cumming about the DMI sending orders to Alley and instructed Cumming to give Alley whatever help he needed: 'He said that Alley's organisation was to link up with our Petrograd one and that I was to send Alley orders through him.' Four days later Alley apparently sent a list of his staff 'of whom two Small and Calder – are ours'.

Cumming telegraphed another of his men to go to Petrograd and keep in touch with the naval attaché, Crombie, and Lieutenant Boyce. Crombie was soon to be murdered when the Cheka stormed the British embassy, while Boyce was to perform well as Cumming's major link-man in Russia. This came about following a call from a Mr Lindley who 'stated that in reply to my question: 1) That he considered Boyce the best man to put in charge of our organisation. 2) That he ought to base on Moscow. 3) That he would provide my people with money if required. He showed a very high appreciation of their value, especially Maclaren and Boyce.' Lindley was probably from the War Office or the Foreign Office and his remarks suggest that there was considerably more reporting from Russia than we are aware of.

On 18 May Cumming received another man of ambiguous status, a Mr Louden or London, whom he described as 'our new Chief of Political Service in Russia – quite good. Irish journalist – going as *Daily Chronicle* correspondent. I talked to him about communications and codes etc.' Meanwhile, the Russian assistant naval attaché brought him some papers from Scandinavia.

Conditions in Russia were now such that it was difficult even to know where people were, let alone conduct operations. On 2 June Lieutenant Reid arrived from Moscow via Murmansk and Bergen with six diplomatic bags. Cumming wrote that: 'He believes our people are stationed as follows', then lists eleven in Moscow, one in Murmansk, one in Vologda and one in Petrograd. It is not clear what he meant by 'our' but it seems not to have been only the Bureau. Among those listed in Moscow is 'Mr Lockhart (in uniform)'.

Cumming's first meeting with Paul Dukes was on 29th July 1918: 'Mr Dukes arrived from Russia unexpectedly. Long talk with him and Samson. He seems a first rate man for our job, tho' a little independent in spirit.' Cumming paid him his back pay and sent him off to see Sir Arthur Tyrrel. Two days earlier he had agreed with a Moscow-bound man named Howod to try to get him a commission, since it would help in his dealings with the Russians. Meanwhile, Howod would travel in Russia in peasant dress.

Later, on 12 October, Cumming received a Signora Pediani who had left Moscow a month previously and had 'done extremely well and hid the two Hills [George Hill was not Cumming's only Hill in Russia] during the Terror'. He engaged her as a Russian translator. He also received a General Vodar (probable) that same day and found that, far from accepting service under the Bolsheviks as Cumming had been told, the General hated them 'with a bitter hatred and his mission was from his own GS [General Staff] who remained in their offices in the War Office until turned out'. Two days later he had another long yarn about Russian affairs with the former Romanian premier, Ionescu, who urged that the Allies should join forces with the Germans to penetrate Russia from the south and drive the Bolsheviks out.

On 8 November Reilly and Boyce arrived from Russia, the latter having been 'shut up in the Fortress of Peter and Paul, but is not much the worse'. Reilly, however, was 'very indignant that his name should have been taken in vain by the American SS who accused him of betraying Lockhart. The latter has however publicly cleared him of this charge.' Later in the month Reilly – by then Major Reilly – was still demanding 'some recognition to efface the bad impression given by the American slanders'.

Officially, the American government had no secret service but it did have people who occasionally conducted secret operations on its behalf, particularly at this period in Russia. Cumming quite often refers to contact with what he calls the 'American SS' but he does not always name individuals. Some Americans suspected that Reilly was a double agent who had betrayed to the Cheka the plot to overthrow Lenin's government which – along with a coincidental assassination attempt on Lenin – resulted in the arrest of Lockhart and others, the expulsion of Allied officials and Reilly's flight. Reilly was indeed involved in the Lockhart plot but he did not betray it. In fact, throughout Reilly's espionage history there is no indication that, despite his remorseless self-interest and general untrustworthiness where women and money were concerned, he was ever disloyal to the British. One other characteristic of his brief espionage career was his ability to charm most of those he worked with. When it was decided that Boyce should be sent to Sofia to work under Dansey, setting up a separate Russian network, he asked to have Reilly with him. On the same day Cumming received another with the gift of charm: 'Mr Lockhart later Minister [sic] Petrograd called and had a long yarn.' They had a further talk on 11 December.

Boyce left on his mission to Sofia on 21 November, a day when Cumming's office was depopulated by illness – presumably 'flu – but Reilly remained a while longer, seeing Cumming on 3 December and, in farewell, on the 12th.

While continuing to send people to Russia to mount further operations and new networks, Cumming was still having to scratch around for news of those already there. On 12 November he spoke to the returned Major Alley, only to find that 'He could not tell me much about my organisation in Russia and evidently felt I had little reason to be grateful to him.' There were other worries too: on 5 December a 'Mr Kenieus [probable] reassured me as to the E. Code in the Embassy at Petrograd but threw doubts on Bourne's [probable] code in Moscow.'

These deployments into Russia were not undertaken simply to please himself or because he thought that was what he should be doing. They reflected the British government's priorities and decisions and, while those were neither constant nor unanimous (Churchill, for instance, was always arguing for more intervention; Lloyd George for less), there was a general sense that a hostile Russia was going to be around for some time, even while Britain and the Allies were making sporadic attempts to destabilise Lenin's government. Towards the end of the year Cumming sent an undated telegram to his Stockholm station which had sought guidance from him. The telegram reflects the prevailing Whitehall equivocation on the subject – intervene, if possible, but don't interfere – but concludes with a clear statement that might well have been Cumming's own: 'The only enemy now to be considered are the Bolsheviks.'

On 28 December he recorded the results of an important meeting with Lord Hardinge in the Foreign Office: 'He agreed to our continuing organisation in Russia at £3,000 a month until 31st March. He also sent CEDs telegrams re anti-Bolshevik MCOs in the different countries, working with the Govt. and Police of those countries.' This was also, as noted earlier, the meeting at which Hardinge agreed to 'Cumming arranging for a Peace SS on the basis of £30,000 a year which he said would be within the mark.'

In the 1918 diary there is a list in another hand of some thirteen minutes that Cumming apparently sent, all concerned with Russia. They begin with one on 15 March summarised as 'Mr Reilly is "willing to go to Russia for us"' and later indicate that Cumming provided Reilly with a money belt along with the diamonds. It would be an exaggeration to say that the Russian Revolution ensured the post-war survival of the Secret Service, but it must have helped.

The 1919 volume of the diary is less full than any hitherto and, although action in Russia increased, there are only about a dozen entries pertaining to it. Among these are the agreement that Cumming reached on 8 April with Sir Basil Thompson, who ran the substantial anti-Bolshevik and anti-subversion element of Scotland Yard, that the Bureau should take on all overseas anti-Bolshevik work. On 1 May he got agreement from the DMI for the use of CMBs (Coastal Motor Boats, in fact fast torpedo boats) and on 7 May inspected them with their helpful commander, Captain French, in Essex, agreeing to take two boats with two crews along with sundry equipment including searchlights. As already noted, Augustus Agar, the young officer selected to command, published his own account of this visit and its dramatic consequences. Agar is mentioned again in passing on 25 May and more substantially on 28 August when Major Scale, who was running Cumming's operations in the Baltic, complained that Agar was 'very "difficile" and he has asked Admiral Cowan to replace him'. Agar's operations were becoming ever more naval and ever less secret, having ten days before disabled two battleships and sunk a supply ship, but there was little chance that Admiral Cowan would find such an officer 'difficile'. Agar continued, anyway, to make unavailing attempts to rendezvous with Dukes (during the last of which he and his crew were virtually wrecked and were very lucky to escape). Dukes's overland escape a week later (this was not his first unexpected return from Russia) might have been more planned than is usually thought; another of Cumming's notes for 28 August reads 'ST 25 to come out next week'. He also notes Scale as estimating the Bureau's Russian financial liabilities as 'about £6,000'.

Dukes's triumphant return is mentioned in the diary on 17 November: 'ST25 arrived and gave us a moving account of the state of affairs in Russia.' The next day he spent an hour and a half with the Secretary of State for War (Churchill) as well as calling on General Bartholomew and Sir Basil Thompson. He submitted reports to Lord Curzon and on the 20th visited him at his house in Carlton House Terrace. There is reference on 5 December to a reward for Dukes, which the DMI claimed not to have known about until Cumming proved to him in writing that he did. The next mention of Dukes is on New Year's Eve, back this time from Scandinavia from where he brought news of White Russian intelligence losses and betrayals, along with the names of three recommended couriers. Cumming, meanwhile, had sought from Lord Hardinge a 'special temporary grant' of £25,000 for continuing work in Russia.

Dukes's reward was probably substantial. There was for many years a tradition in SIS whereby agents or officers who had done particularly well might, on return from a mission, be congratulated by the Chief and leave his office with an encouragingly thick envelope tucked into their pocket. Our limited knowledge of what Dukes and others actually reported during this period probably leads us to underrate their intelligence contribution, particularly that of Dukes himself. He penetrated the Bolshevik organisation at the highest levels, getting a spy into Trotsky's 'Revolutionary Council of the Northern Front' who reported their proceedings in full. A detailed six-page report of his which has survived comprises the Bolshevik assessment of where British and other forces might land and the countermeasures planned against them. The first page of this report is reprinted in Gordon Brook-Shepherd's *Iron Maze* (Appendix 3) and lists the most likely landing sites, mining and other measures to be taken, as well as the arms and materials to be issued.

Despite the extra money for Bolshevik operations, staff cuts continued. On 3 March 1920 Cumming was permitted to keep on two ladies for a further two months in order to complete a registry – this may have been his longed-for central registry, for which he had earlier been refused money – as well as another lady 'until April 1st to compile Bolshevik register'. In September 1919 he obtained agreement to spend up to £6,000 on a 'South Russian organisation'. This is probably in connection with the sending of a Colonel MacDonald to be attached to General Knox's Siberian military mission. The purpose of the mission was to back – still without fully supporting – the White Russian General Wrangel. Knox himself recruited a local assistant, Lieutenant F.B. Kirby, then *Reuters* correspondent, but Kirby seems, if the history is accurate, to have actually worked for Cumming. While MacDonald's duties were, apparently, 'in no way SS', Kirby's connections 'amounted to secret agents' and after Wrangel's collapse he went on to Vladivostok, 'commencing definitely to work up an SS there. (This is not the only use of a journalist mentioned around that time. There was also an arrangement with a correspondent in Rome.) In August of the following year, 1920, Cumming "concurred in Dukes's going to Warsaw etc. at £80 a month for 3 months".

With two exceptions, most of the remaining mentions of Russian matters in the diary are occasional budget figures and compilations of costs of trips by unnamed individuals, such as the £500 allocated on 19 April 1921 to include an agent's three months salary, travelling expenses, keep, entertainment, bribes and contingencies. The other two mentions are more significant, both occurring in the 1921 volume although it is possible that they refer to 1922. This is because the 1921 volume, which is mostly blank, has the printed dates for the earlier entries altered by hand to 1922, while the later entries are left as 1921. Cumming might have been in ill-health at this time and what may have happened is that in 1922 he began to reuse the little-used 1921 diary (it contains a typed copy of a telegram to Christiania dated 21 January 1921) but then stopped. There is no volume for 1923, the last year of his life.

However, the entry for 26 April 1921 (not amended to 1922) is significant. It reads: 'Promised Jack £750 down, £750 on his return from Moscow, £500 if his report exceptional on the understanding that he attends the conference of the 3rd International there as [illegible but possibly beginning with M or A] representative.' This suggests that Jack was the codename of an agent evidently trusted by the Russians, and was perhaps a member of the Comintern, the body charged with spreading the Soviet revolution abroad through, among other means, espionage and subversion. It was this contagion that Western governments feared most, so penetration of the Comintern would have been particularly important. Later in the inter-war years, SIS ran just such a valuable penetration, the Jonny case,[4] but the well-paid Jack obviously pre-dated this. We know nothing more of Jack than this reference, but he was clearly a case of a different order from those of the British and White Russian adventurers featured so far.

It is just possible that he was identical with BP 11, a source in Estonia who had penetrated the office of Maxim Litvinov, Soviet Deputy Commisar for Foreign Affairs, and who provided summaries of telegrams which were later doubted.[5] There was also a former source in that field whom Cumming took over from Sir Basil Thompson's organisation. Whoever Jack was, though, he sounds a more modern spy than Reilly and co., perhaps even the first of what we would now call Cold War cases. In *Iron Maze* (p. 307), Brook-Shepherd refers to Harry Carr, SIS station chief in Helsingfors (later Helsinki) as stating that one station in the area was, by 1924, producing Politburo and Comintern documents.

This, of course, was a year after Cumming's death but in her Foriegn Office monograph, *The Zinoviev Letter of 1924* (1999), Gill Bennett makes it clear that there were sources of documentary intelligence in or run from Riga at or before that time and that one at least of these sources had access to Comintern documents. Zinoviev was head of the Comintern and the famous letter was allegedly an instruction from him to the Communist Party of Great Britain to 'mobilise the wide working masses'. It was sent by SIS from Riga and was released to the press in London just before the October 1924 elections, causing a political sensation which reverberates to this day. It seems likely that the letter, though reflecting the ambitions and desires of Zinoviev and the Comintern, was a forgery, or at least was never sent as it was said to have been; the SIS agent who produced it has never been identified, and nor has the official who leaked it in London – though there are several leading suspects both within and without SIS. If the letter had an agent source, it is possible that it was Jack, though it should be stressed that we have no reason for suspecting this other than knowledge of his existence and that he seems to have participated in the Third International.

It is also possible that the source was a well-known Berlin-based fabricator and intelligence huckster, Vladimir Orlov, whom the French police (quoted by Brook-Shepherd) said supplied information to the French themselves in Berlin, to the Germans, the Poles, the Bolsheviks and others, including British intelligence; in fact, French Secret Service reports quoted by Brook-Shepherd describe him as 'a British agent'. Cumming may have been in touch with him. He mentions an 'Orlof' on the day he concurred in Dukes's going to Warsaw (19 August 1920): 'Concurred in Orloff going to Paris, Berlin, Vienna, Stockholm, Copenhagen and Rome for £500.' Orlof or Orlov is not an uncommon name but in this context it is tempting to speculate that Cumming's man might have been the forger (it is also clear from Bennett's monograph that SIS were well informed on the forging activities of his group).

It is also possible – although, again, this is entirely speculative – that Jack was the ultimate source of information about Soviet espionage and subversive intentions listed in an undated and unattributed press cutting found in the last pages of Cumming's diary. This stresses the importance of cultivating government employees, identifying intelligence officers, their houses and offices, procuring seals, stamps, forms and photographs as well as ascertaining which of 'our members' have been arrested. It could well have come from a Cold War textbook some fifty or sixty years later. To carry speculation yet further, if it was policy to get information about Soviet intentions into the public domain (as it certainly was later and as a number of concerned individuals in the 1920s were determined to do), it may have been in furtherance of this that the Zinoviev letter was leaked, perhaps as one of a series – albeit the best known – of leaks of intelligence documents. The mystery is unlikely ever to be solved, but there must be a chance that Jack played a part in it.

19

THE BIG BATTLES

Supporting the British government's keenly felt but faltering desire to fight war by proxy in Russia was one thing, but bureaucratic battles fought closer to home were more demanding, enervating and – on Cumming's part, at least – more emotional than any professional struggle. The most vital, although easier, of these was over the survival of the Secret Service in the icy wind of savage post-war austerity, while the other, linked to it, was the resurgence in virulent form of the War Office threat of amalgamation. As has often been observed at the House of Commons, the opposition is before you but your enemies are behind you.

Before considering these battles, though, we should glance at other topics mentioned in the diaries of Cumming's final years. First, in 1919, there is evidence that May and Cumming functioned as a social unit, something that does not occur elsewhere in the diary. On 12 April he attended an official dinner for what looks like the 'de Bildts', listing a number of guests such as Lady Carnarvon and Sir Eric Hambro with, at the bottom, 'Capt. and Mrs C.' This may not, of course, have referred to him and May but he did occasionally refer to himself in the third person, and the day following he drove down to Bursledon for two days. The de Bildts were evidently around for the rest of the month; 'M. de Bildt' is the only entry for Sunday 27 April, while on the following day 'M. took M. de Bildt to lunch at Windsor'. (This may of course have been Menzies, who had royal connections, but it could also have been May.)

The next reference, however, is unambiguous. It is in a rare personal letter to Cumming from an old acquaintance of his Burnford House days in the New Forest, written in September 1919. The writer commends someone for employment, remarks that Burnford has been sold, hopes that Cumming will return to that part of the world – 'Many changes among the population of the Forest' – and ends with, 'Kindest regards to Lady Cumming'. Cumming had been knighted on 26 July 1919, an event not mentioned in the diary, but, if his unfeigned joy at Hall's knighthood is anything to go by, he was doubtless deeply gratified (particularly, perhaps, as it ws an honour shared with May).

The first and last entries for 1919 were, typically, lists of cars (he had six in Switzerland alone, including a motor bike and sidecar). We get an indication of the sort of work he was still required to sustain in Germany from an inevitably long talk with Tinsley on 26 January:

the result of Colonel Cornwall's visit to Germany had been to confirm DMI's view that we are to expand our organisation in Germany in order to confirm and support the reports of the regular officers there and to present the opinions of different classes of society as to the trend of events. T. pointed out that he had 14 first class agents now in Germany but that £2 a day was the very least we could pay them for subsistence alone.

This was no flash in the pan: German political developments and rearmament remained intelligence targets. On 5 December 1919 Sinclair, the DNI, 'rang up to say that he wished to have any evidence of Tr. Naval activity. They have eight old battleships and six v.g. light cruisers. Where were these? In Baltic or in North Sea ports? Sent Commander Goff over and sent for Hilton and ordered him to leave for Tiaria tonight.'

On 2 January 1920, in early and sinister prefiguration of things to come, Cumming called on Neville Bland, Campbell's successor as Private Secretary in the Foreign Office. Cumming reported on the 'Japanese courier service – Berne–Rome and intercepts showing attempts at entente (possibly only commercial) between Japan, Italy and Germany'. On the same day he recorded further brief evidence of continuing South American interests, mentioning that a contact 'in Buenos Ayres will work for us gratis.'

The entry for 16 September 1920 indicates some of the work done in wartime Germany, albeit that it came as a surprise to Cumming. The context was justifying a pension or reward for an agent whose name resists decipherment:

Tinsley arrived: He tells me that –– was his agent and successfully burgled some safes in the German War Office to the great advantage of the Military HQ. Complimentary telegrams were frequently received from the MA in regard to these. I have heard nothing of them nor of the man nor of his methods but Capt. W— tells me that on Good Friday last he showed me a letter from the War Office giving instructions in the use of morphine – which was intended for him.

Cumming was sufficiently pleased by a compliment on his service's war record relayed by Colonel Holt-Wilson of MI5 on 27 November to record it in full:

Colonel Holt-Wilson told me that when in Köhln he interviewed a high official, the Chief of Police of the District, who said to him – 'One fatal mistake we made was the underrating of your SS. We now know that they knew 100 times more about us than we knew about them and 1,000 times more than we gave them credit for knowing. Had we not miscalculated in this matter you might well be standing before me, answering my questions in London.'

On 31 January Cumming had a meeting with Walter Long, the First Sea Lord, only to realise as their discussion went on that Long thought the Secret Service was a secret police force. Once this misunderstanding was resolved, however, 'he appeared quite sound as regards my work and the conversation was a satisfactory one to me'. On 20 February he listed twelve chemists, laboratory staff and others, including two linguists, whom he was to take on from Sir Basil Thompson's counter-subversion organisation, under a man called Worthington. Within the fortnight, however, he had to give Worthington the bad news that he was not allowed to take on the staff but that he could accept 'his gear – instruments, drugs, etc.' Meanwhile, he arranged to have his codes subjected to hostile tests by the codebreakers who had occupied Room 40. There is no mention of the results.

Cuts in funding bit deeper as the year went on. On 1 September Cumming listed eight secretaries and two clerks to whom he had to give a month's notice that day, yet at the same time activities in some areas were being expanded. On 17 September, during a discussion of the Admiralty's 'Spanish organisation', he agreed with Commander Thompson that 'the only feasible plan was for us to take over their show in the North'. On 8 October, at a War Office meeting with Kell and others on the future control of Hong Kong, Singapore, Gibraltar and Malta, 'It was decided that I have sole control in Hong Kong with possibly one officer from Kell's Dept. in my office while he retains Gibraltar, Singapore and Malta – I having similar facilities and keeping a staff in Malta . . . He is to do no collection of information.'

Three days later Cumming reached a momentous agreement with Ronald Campbell in the Foreign Office (for a period he seems to have dealt with both Campbell and Bland):

> I asked him whether those officers of my staff whose salaries were paid out of SS funds could have them paid free of Income Tax, observing that the country would lose nothing by the arrangement as the salaries were calculated on a nett basis and if Income Tax were to be deducted they would have to be proportionately increased. It was undesirable that their names and connection with SS should be known to anyone. He agreed and consented to this arrangement.

This economical and desirable practice was to continue until after the Second World War when SIS staff were reacquainted with the tax system and introduced, for the first time, to the Crown Service pension system. That the Private Secretary to the Under Secretary in the Foreign Office should be able to agree such a proposition in his master's name without apparently consulting the Treasury is perhaps a reflection of how power positions in Whitehall have changed.

1919 was also the year in which Cumming moved his home and headquarters, though that was not a distinction he would willingly have recognised. He left Whitehall Court for the fashionable but presumably unsuspecting Melbury Road in West Kensington. Sadly, his choice – no. 1 – has been replaced by a block of later flats, perhaps the result of a wartime bomb. It was a road much favoured by successful artists, two of whom – Holman Hunt and Sir Hamo Thorneycroft, the sculptor – are celebrated by blue plaques, while G.F. Watts had no. 6 built for him. The houses are large, often detached creations in the late Victorian confectionery style, roomy, with huge windows, and well-decorated tradesmens' entrances. Cumming's living quarters, according to Kathleen Murray's recollections, were upstairs, with the dining room and kitchen in the basement. The rest of the house was given over to offices. Interestingly, a 1925 Cabinet Secret Service Committee report noted that five of Britain's intelligence organisations had headquarters in and around that part of West London; the committee recommended they move back closer to central government.

For Cumming the move west was not a sudden one, forced by post-war cuts, though anticipation of those had been part of his thinking from at least 7 July 1918 when he wrote to Ronald Campbell proposing 'to take a small house on a lease not longer than 5–7 years, and to put into it such new extensions of my organisation as can be kept separate and distinct from the Main Bureau, and to work from this central office any scheme or project that requires absolute secrecy'. In fact, it was to become his home and headquarters rather than his secret annex. When discussed at a meeting of senior staff in August 1919 it was agreed that they would move as soon as the house was ready, that only heads of branches were to go there, that no one was to know the address (though a concession was considered for the DMI, who was put into brackets, with a query), that they were to reduce staff to the new post-war limits and that the office was to close from noon on Saturdays until 10 a.m. on Mondays.

One surprising point, given Cumming's usual dogged defence of the fact that he had been appointed Chief of the Secret Service, and never acknowledged need for any other name, was that the name was to be Special Intelligence Bureau. This may simply have been a suggestion by one of those at the meeting; whether or not, it did not happen. Cumming himself may have moved before this – there is a 20 April nautical-flavoured note to the effect that he 'Landed cargo of books at No. 1' – but the office move took place on 23 December. It seems to have heralded a more relaxed regime than obtained at previous Christmases: 'Staff to go on leave from Wednesday night [Christmas Eve],' noted Cumming.

Early in January 1919 he had to administer tickings-off to two errant majors, a Major G.G. who was 'very indignant at the questions raised as to his conduct in the Caucasus' and, more seriously, Major Langley from Switzerland, who was informed in the presence of Menzies 'that he was my subordinate and was to obey my orders alone. That his appointment as AMA was for cover purposes only and that in writing about office affairs to the MA and in criticising the orders issued to him by me he was committing a grave breach of decorum which I should not again condone.' Major Langley later called again, offering amends, and 'we parted friends'. Another indication of staff problems that month was the DMI's advice that 'we had better accept Noble's [probable – Knolly's?] resignation – he speaks of his Code school'.

When Ronald Campbell went off to Paris for ten days he assured Cumming that the latest War Office amalgamation proposals were not 'formidable'. Meanwhile, Sir Robert Nathan begins to appear in the diary, initially in connection with Irish work – in January, 'Sir J. Tiley [probable] promised Nathan £1,000 p.a. for the Irish work' – and later often in connection with Indian work. A senior Foreign Office official, Nathan was to feature significantly and usefully in Cumming's affairs, becoming responsible for assessing and distributing the intelligence.

'Indian work' meant, essentially, taking over the agent-finding and running capacity of Major Wallinger's Indian Political Intelligence (IPI), the organisation that spied on dissident Indians overseas on behalf of the government of India. Wallinger ran his organisation from London and he and Cumming were in frequent negotiations, particularly over work against Indian dissidents in Switzerland. On 27 March, for instance, Cumming suggested paying Wallinger £1,500 a year in Geneva, in order to 'get from him all his non-Indian stuff in exchange'. In December it was agreed, subject to Indian government approval, to put Mr Denham in charge of Cumming's Indian work, with a substantial budget of £10,000 over three years and the Indian government to pay his salary and office funds as hitherto (though there is a 3 January 1921 note to the effect that Cumming will pay him £600 a year). Possibly in this connection, a 15 December list of agent expenses shows that such work occurred in Shanghai, Japan, Hong Kong and Manila. (For the same list were twelve bank accounts, of which the seventh is described as 'Hallreward'. It was possible that the former DNI was given a substantial financial reward for his contribution to the war and that, in order that it be not known, Cumming funded it.)

Like his overseas countersubversion work on behalf of Basil Thompson, Cumming's Indian work features frequently in Whitehall correspondence during his last years and was no doubt useful in his battles for survival and independence.

A name that features once only in the diary, on 1 September 1920, is that of H. G. Wells. It is not certain that this is the author, but it looks at least possible. There was a conference on Swiss affairs – that is work conducted in Switzerland against other targets, particularly Indian – in which Cumming had included Colonel Samson and Major Morton. It was suggested that they should 'Cut down Wallinger from 1,000 to 500 for IW reports', after which Cumming notes: 'Called on J.A.W. [Wallinger] with Sam and Morton and he agreed to accept the 500 and do his best with it and to arrange that H.G. Wells's reports shd. go direct to Sam from Wallinger.'

Apart from the particular context of these reports, Wells had recently visited Russia and interviewed Lenin, and he was to remain on fairly close terms with Maxim Gorky and successive Russian ambassadors; he was a friend of Ivy Low, wife of Maxim Litvinov, the first Soviet Ambassador to London. Wells was not totalitarian but he sympathised with the aims of the communist experiment and seems to have been regarded by the Russians as an influential friend in the West, though he did not, like George Bernard Shaw, the Fabian Webbs and others described by Lenin as 'useful idiots', fall for the Russian Potemkin Village tradition. Whatever he may have been doing in this instance, it is plausible that Cumming would have sought to use someone like him to report on Soviet officials. Sympathisers do not always allow their sympathies to prevent them from reporting on whom and what they see, and anyone not sympathetic would not have had enough access to be of interest.

A warning, though, that we should not assume too much from the coincidence of names is the mention – twice – of Selwyn Lloyd, who on 20 August was given a month's notice. It would have been pleasing if this had turned out to be the later Conservative politician but at the age of fifteen it is hard to see what he would have done for Cumming, unless it was to act as a scout or errand boy. The man in question was probably one of the code room staff.

On 28 September Cumming recorded meeting a Mr Sillery (probable) who 'gave me an account of his special services'. These apparently comprised passing information in 1905 to the then British Minister at Constantinople concerning a German attempt to acquire a Red Sea coaling station: 'As a result Sir N. O'Connor visited the Sultan the same evening and insisted on these negotiations being broken off – threatening action by the Fleet and the whole transaction was closed down.' Later, in September 1914, Mr Sillery had apparently instituted his own system of passport control which led to imprisonment in Alexandria of one Kasimir (probable) Robert Mors and others who were planning to blow up the Suez Canal.

On 15 March 1920 Cumming received 'categorical instructions' from Lord Hardinge to close down his stations in Stockholm, Madrid, Helsinki, Christiana, Warsaw, Athens, Copenhagen and Trieste, to each of which he sent closing telegrams. On 24 March, however, he 'Received orders from Lord H to withdraw notices closing down,' and sent countermanding telegrams. The reason for this unusual degree of bureaucratic haste and muddle was, of course, the draconian cuts in public expenditure then enforced.

Government departments may think they have become

familiar with such cuts in recent decades, when in fact government spending has continued to rise and what are called 'cuts' are mostly reductions in the estimates of future increases. In Cumming's day, cuts meant cuts. In both letter and diary entries during the period 1920 to 1922 he refers frequently to percentage reductions and to actual sums. These vary and it is not always clear how far anticipated figures reflect what was actually spent or cut but the following illustrative figures indicate the scale of reduction. In a March 1919 letter to Ronald Campbell, Cumming refers to his expenditure at the time of the armistice as running at £80,000 per month, just under a million a year; by the time of writing it had halved; by February 1920 he was told that his total annual expenditure was to be reduced to £65,000. This seems to have been the figure that stuck – in theory, anyway – because in a letter probably written in January 1922 to Sir Eyre Crowe, Hardinge's successor as Under Secretary, Cumming says that it would cost £150,000 per annum to meet the requirements placed on him by customers (War Office requirements on Germany alone amounting, as we have seen, to some £30,000), whereas £65,000 remained the figure 'on which I am required to base my estimates'. To do this, he says, would mean closing down twenty-three overseas stations, reducing by 35 per cent in London, 40 per cent in Constantinople and the Near East, 33 per cent on Russian work, 66 per cent on German work and 90 per cent of his expenditure in Holland.

As already explained, the 1921–22 diaries are sparse and conflated. Thus, 11 and 12 January 1921 were altered by hand to 1922. They concern another troublesome major but at the same time offer a clue as to why Cumming apparently neglected his diary.

Major Morton, who was responsible for office organisation – or perhaps took it upon himself – complained to Cumming of the lack of 'office orders which he believed his military training demanded and which should be issued by himself as "adjutant"'. Cumming considered this to be his province. Morton then complained about the role of Neville Bland, Ronald Campbell's successor, claiming that he was 'Cumming's real master' and implying that Cumming should heed him less. Cumming considered this advice 'absolutely bad and pernicious, but it is only another instance of the influence constantly brought by this officer to set me against my superiors'.

Morton read out further complaints the following day, prompting Cumming to remind him

> that he had taken the opportunity when I was sick for
> and [sic] to issue 3 long memos [probable] over pro-
> cedure to the office which he had not troubled to submit
> to me for approval nor even to show me on my return to
> work. His manner though correct as to words was very
> hostile . . . I cannot but believe that he is not working
> with me or for me but against me. He is hard-working
> and zealous but has formed the unfortunate opinion that
> he is the real vital spark of the organisation . . . I think
> my illness raised a hope that he might soon be able to
> take charge of the office and this has upset his balance.

Cumming rarely mentions ill-health but it is apparent from this that he must have been off sick for some time, perhaps even for most of 1921 and a good part of 1922. There is some suggestion of this in Frank Stagg's memoir: 'As is well known, "C" later became a martyr to "angina". At a farewell dinner to him (in 1921? 1920) Blinker eulogised him magnificently for his wonderful work. In his reply "C" said: ". . . you have come to bury 'C' sir, not to praise him," and within a few weeks he was buried.'

Stagg has his years wrong – it must have been 1922 or 1923, more likely the latter – and he may not have been present because he mentions having returned to sea in 1917. But the message is clear: the Old Man, now in his early sixties, was becoming an old man. There is also, as we shall see from the Kathleen Murray letters, more specific evidence of his illnesses.

Students of the Zinoviev letter affair will also recall from Gill Bennett's account that Desmond Morton of SIS (possibly the Major Morton Cumming refers to) was one of the prime suspects for having leaked the letter to the press and to the Conservative Party. What Cumming says about him does not constitute evidence that he did, but it does convey the impression of someone willing to do what he thought his superiors ought to want whether or not they did.

Another indication that Cumming's hand might have been less firmly on the tiller by this time is the Whitehall correspondence of those years concerning money and War Office threats of amalgamation. Up to and including 1920 there are fairly frequent letters from Cumming himself, but thereafter there is a marked falling-off of papers directly written by him.

Troublesome staff seem to have been a continuing feature of early 1922, because on 17 January we find him discussing with Sir Eyre Crowe the subject of someone called Langton: 'Decided that Sparrow should interrogate Langton in presence of R.H. Campbell. He agreed with my letter to Public Prosecutor.'

He saw a lot of Sir Eyre. On 14 January (almost certainly 1921 rather than 1922) there was a Foreign Office conference concerning the distribution of SIS reports and liaison between SIS representatives and embassies. This resulted in Foreign Office instructions to heads of mission and simultaneous SIS instructions to heads of station laying down the fundamentals of a new intelligence relationship between the Foreign Office and SIS.

Sir Robert Nathan – by now head of SIS's section V – was to liaise with Foreign Office heads of department, sending summaries of reporting or verbatim reports as he saw fit and where appropriate giving oral briefings on sources. The Foreign Office, which described itself as 'assailed by a mass of information so bulky that its size is apt to frustrate intelligent examination', would advise on further Whitehall distribution of political reports. Heads of mission were told: 'Today the old type of Secret Service has disappeared and melodrama has given place to a more sober style of enquiry from which the diplomat need no longer, as he was very properly required to do before, withdraw the hem of his garment.' In parallel instructions SIS heads of station were told that 'in future your credit will largely depend on the Minister's report'. Cumming was entirely happy with these arrangements.

On the date altered to 2 February 1922 Cumming discussed the choosing of his successor with Neville Bland, the only time the subject is mentioned: 'Discussed a successor for me. He says neither DMI nor SMI [probable] would be acceptable and thinks a naval man would be preferred anyway. R a bit young and RRS too old.' We do not know who these people were but Cumming mentions the conversation in a way that suggests it was a continuous rather than urgent issue. In the next sentence Bland undertakes to discuss with Sir Eyre Crowe the issuing of SIS reports to the Treasury and the Ministry of Health. Sir Eyre 'thinks we have too much publicity already and that as a general principle all our reports – except those sent to Admiralty, War Office and AF [Air Force] should pass thro' Foreign Office.'

Either six days later or, more likely, 358 days earlier (8 February), Cumming was sent for 'by Mr Winston Churchill who spoke to me about Major Geiger [probable] for Paris. I told him all depended on his being on good terms with the S. of S. and French Staff. He telephoned for him to come over on Friday.' On the same day he discussed with Sir Robert Nathan and others a scheme for interviewing a Mrs Rasisch Nakoo (?) in Antwerp, agreeing to pay up to £100 provided arrangements were made for 'protecting the lady and not abandoning her to the vengeance of her former friends'.

In May 1921 there are cryptic references to intelligence organisations in Germany – 'German Foreign Office organisation – (Hackerman), German Police organisation (Schwarz)' – but he is more specific with figures for SIS staff and agents. Headed 'State on this Day', he lists SIS HQ as having 65 staff, with 132 overseas staff and 484 agents, making a total of 681. It appears from an added note that the figures for staff include PCOs (presumably genuine as well as those who were only SIS). The agent total is higher than might be expected, although, without knowing the criteria, we cannot say how many were intelligence-producing agents. We do, however, know from a paper of the period entitled 'An Appreciation of SIS' that sixty-five was the number of permanent HQ staff regarded as the minimum for 'the maintenance of a universal, interconnected, foreign intelligence service'. Later in the same paper there is a reference to the production of 13,000 intelligence reports per annum – which gives some force to the Foreign Office's sense of being overburdened by paper.

Towards the end of May Cumming was looking for reinforcements for what he called 'Wilberforce's Bureau' in New York, ideally a nucleus that could be expanded. The requirement, he noted, was for a Briton living in New York with no official connections, working part-time for Cumming with a salary of £1,000 plus a second £1,000 for agents and incidentals, and communicating via a mixture of commercial code and ordinary post. We have already noted the very considerable expenditure on propaganda in the USA and, though it is possible that this was an extension of that operation, it is equally possible that the reinforcement was for spying on targets other than American. However, since the proposed officer or agent would have no official connection, he would presumably have been absolved from the general prohibition then in force against SIS stations spying on their host countries.

The last pages of this, the last volume of the diary, contain the Bolshevik press cutting and the paragraph of praise from Curzon's report already noted, plus the inevitable lists of cars and registration numbers and receipts for such items as steel girders and angles, Yale locks, engine covers, gallons of varnish, as well as payments owed to a handyman called Evans. As ever, with Cumming, the demarcation between domestic and professional is unclear – and perhaps inappropriate – and it is possible that these receipts and payments pertain to the house he was building at Bursledon rather than to strictly SIS concerns.

If asked to list the dominant professional themes of his last years, Cumming would probably have named the first two as money and the War Office, there being too little of one and too much of the other. Like the early pre-war years of the Bureau, these are reflected not only in the diary but also in surviving Whitehall correspondence. Also, Cumming must have felt that the life of his beloved Bureau was coming full circle and was in grave danger of ending where it began, in a seemingly futile struggle to escape War Office control. A number of factors contributed to its survival. Early suspicions of German rearmament, the birth of Soviet Russia, an unsettled international political scene, changes in political leadership and Foreign Office attitudes – but the totality of these would not have been enough had the Secret Service not performed so well during the war. It would not have survived the chill winds of peace unless it had indicated potential for political utility.

But survival and independence were won only after a series of battles whose origins went back to the ambiguous command structure inherent in the way the Bureau was set up in 1909. A September 1916 War Office letter, almost certainly written by Colonel French, refers to the 1909 decision that the heads of the two services should be retired officers in order to ensure 'continuity of executive direction and personal knowledge of previous circumstances and procedure'. In the same letter French argues for one body to control both services and to 'carry out all negotiation with the Foreign Office'.

As we have seen, it was around 1916 that the service was increasingly referred to as MI1(C). Cumming, writing to the Foreign Office about French's letter, complained: 'Colonel French claims to control the sub-sections of MI1, of which my dept. was made one without reference to its Chief.' He continues in forthright manner, saying that ever since 1909 he had constantly been undermined by the War Office: 'the greatest defect of the present Service, is the lack of support given to its Chief by the mil. authorities', while stressing that his personal relations with both French and MacDonogh had 'always been of a most friendly nature and I have much to thank them for'.

This does indeed seem to have been the case with regard to MacDonogh, though if we had only the Whitehall correspondence to go by we might not assume so. For instance, in February 1917 MacDonogh sent Cumming a handwritten letter (in the course of a dispute over the activities of military attachés) saying he had 'never admitted at any time that you were under the Foreign Office. I have always considered that for all military intelligence you are directly under me . . . I have no intention of allowing the theory [sic] of Foreign Office control to come between myself and you.' His writ must run, unqualified by any other control, or he would tell the Foreign Office that he had no further use for 'C's branch', would withdraw all C's military officers and in future the War Office would 'conduct its own SS, War Trade, CE and identification business abroad'. He added that he had protected C's organisation from attack from all sides and concluded by hoping that Cumming 'will take this letter in the friendly spirit in which it is written'.

As an example of bureaucratic rigidity and lack of imagination it is equalled only by MacDonogh's own impositions and restrictions in the early years of the Bureau. We do not have Cumming's response but the threat of withdrawal of staff was at that time a serious matter since, as he later complained, the passing of the Military Service Act had recently made it impossible for him to engage anyone not under the Admiralty or the War Office: 'Threatened by my senior officers,' he wrote in January 1919, 'that unless I submitted they could take such steps as would completely break up my Service, I was compelled to give way.' In fact, the letter in which he wrote this makes it very plain what his feelings about MacDonogh's letter must have been:

> During the war the War Office have country by country destroyed my organisation . . . if an efficient SS is to be built up for the much severer conditions of peace the organisation must be kept clear of War Office interference . . . an examination of the orders issued to me during the War (and before) will show that they were all restrictive . . . none helpful . . . [there was] . . . constant robbery of my staff.

Again, writing to Ronald Campbell a month later, he complained that the War Office

> have constantly injured my Service. From the day of my appointment I have been disgracefully treated, my authority has been deliberately undermined and my influence even among my own staff damaged by the constant slights and humiliations . . . They have made many promises to secure my submission to their scheme of spoliation, but have never kept one of them, and in all my dealings with queer people in my strange and unique service I have met no one who was so thoroughly unscrupulous and untrustworthy as the author of the proposal [for amalgamation] put forward.

The last part of this extract presumably referred to French, but it could have been Thwaites, and it was anyway toned down before being sent to Campbell. Its heartfelt tone strikes a more emotional note than anything Cumming had written since the first days of the Bureau.

MacDonogh had been promoted to Adjutant General by the time of this 1919 exchange but both then and during the period of his earlier handwritten letter good – perhaps even close – personal relations seem to have continued despite the disagreements. Except for the very sparse final volume, the diaries of

Cumming's last years show them as fairly regular lunch companions, generally *à deux*, and on at least one occasion Cumming records MacDonogh's unofficial approval – as Adjutant General – of his tactics in the bureaucratic war with the War Office.

His pleas found a sympathetic ear in the Foreign Office. As we have seen, Lord Hardinge supported him during the 1917 reorganisation, particularly on the question of his right to be master in his own house. Hardinge remained staunchly supportive during the 1918 amalgamation skirmish, postponing further discussion until after the Peace Conference and writing, on 28 November 1918, to Thwaites: 'The present system has had the defects of every condominium; but it has worked, and all things considered has survived the test of four years of war with a fair measure of success.'

Cumming also received significant, perhaps even warwinning, support from the author of an unsigned typed note, dated 15 November 1918 and headed 'Personal for "C"'. It is an interesting document, clear, authoritative and assured, suggestive of an incisive and experienced bureaucratic mind. There are, it says, two main arguments against the change proposed (amalgamation with MI5 under War Office control); first, the methods, personnel and venue of the two services are very different; second, 'It seems to me impossible that MI5 should continue as a strictly military organisation.' (We have already noted that MI5 was in its early years entirely a creature of the War Office.) In peacetime, the author continues, most of its work will be of the nature of police work, the Home Office will be strengthened as against the War Office and will 'certainly insist' on taking over at least 75 per cent of the jobs done by MI5. But with regard to amalgamation with SIS, 'obviously the Home Office could not touch espionage'.

It was equally obvious that only the Foreign Office could be responsible for this activity: 'It involves operations abroad, and though the Foreign Office will always disavow them, for that very reason (paradoxical as it may seem) they must have full cognisance of what is being done, and power to check it, so that at the very least they may know what they are to disavow.'

These arguments hold as well now as then. It could well be that the author was some senior and well-disposed Foreign Office official, despite his use of the third person in referring to that department, yet the document gives the impression of a supremely authoritative mandarin author sitting above interdepartmental squabbles, while leaving it unsigned suggests someone who, unlike most Foreign Office officials involved, had reason not to be seen to be partial. It is tempting to speculate that it could have been Maurice Hankey.

Meanwhile, the committee on the intelligence services chaired by Lord Curzon served as a useful excuse for postponing further discussion, though it also caused problems when it came to setting financial estimates. Although, we have seen, it concluded favourably with regard to SIS, Cumming notes on one occasion that Curzon reportedly regarded foreign intelligence as unnecessary. In January and February 1919, however, Lord Hardinge, who was in Paris, learned that the Cabinet was to consider the future of 'what has been known hitherto as the FSS [Foreign Secret Service]' and wrote twice to Curzon stressing the importance of Foreign Office control and emphasising that the Secret Service's central organisation 'should be small and quite distinct from any Government Department and free from Parliamentary control'. Otherwise the first casualty would be secrecy. Hardinge also urged that there should be no personnel changes without reference to the Foreign Secretary, Balfour, particularly as the future of the Secret Service was likely to be more political and commercial than military and naval. Both the Admiralty and the War Office had been 'content to maintain the present Chief of the Secret Service during the war and for the present at all events I strongly deprecate any change'. Cumming, with his long experience, was likely to run the service more economically than 'any newer hand' and was already working on a modified peace organisation: 'I am quite convinced that his retention in office will mean a considerable saving.'

Curzon, or some about him, must have been questioning Cumming's position. In case the point had not been got across, Hardinge added in a subsequent (7 February 1919) typed note to Curzon: 'During the war the operation of the Secret Service, thanks to the most able cooperation of General MacDonogh and Admiral Hall, has been worked with very happy results. This is not merely my opinion but that of Mr Balfour ... the Foreign Office has been extremely fortunate in securing the services of the present CSS.'

Cumming could not have wished for more. Nor did he need it. It was this level of Foreign Office support, maintained by three successive under secretaries, that defeated all three (as calculated by Cumming) War Office assaults on his independence.

The forces of financial erosion meanwhile continued their remorseless work. By March 1919 Cumming had got rid of fifty-eight headquarters staff, was telling the Foreign Office that cuts would mean a reversion to the old geographical headquarters structure and in the same month set out for Lord Drogheda the consequences of a proposed budget reduction to £69,000 per annum. He used as ammunition a War Office memo saying that his was the only information they had about Russia, referring to another message (probably Foreign Office) from Paris calling his Russian information 'invaluable', and pointing out that his Russian organisation alone cost £5,000 a month. He had recently cut Holland from £20,000 to £6,000 per month, and in addition,

> The value of the reports sent from Germany by such agents as Lieutenant Thornley Gibson (I give his name as it has already been printed by the authorities in Paris) cannot be over estimated. I understand that the policy of the Supreme War Council was influenced by his last report ... the Swiss Organisation, to which he belongs, costs approximately £6,000 a month.

In an undated note to Bland he observes that secrecy in the Secret Service is 'the essence of efficiency'. This might at first sight seem a superficial remark, a thoughtless yoking of concepts which have little in common or are in practice even opposed to each other, but it speaks a deep truth. In all intelligence services the first casualties of a major breach of secrecy are reputation and efficiency of operation, and recovery of both can take years. In another undated paper containing arguments against amalgamation, Cumming calls secrecy, 'The first, last and most necessary essential of a Secret Service'.

A later undated note mentions two reductions by over 50 per cent since the war, the second in March 1920. Despite this, counter-Bolshevism work was increasing and 'inquiries' had risen by over 300 per cent during 1920–21. In 1919 SIS had three customers but, at the time of writing, this had increased to eight. British expenditure on foreign intelligence was much less than was the case with other powers, and the note cites a recent report suggesting that as at 30 October 1920 Germany was spending over £400,000 per year on foreign intelligence.

Financial adjustments are, of course, a perennial of bureaucratic life and there are few final decisions that are not later seen to have been provisional. However, if a line can be drawn after which one could say that the future of the intelligence services was secure, if not comfortable, then it should be drawn after the 27 July 1921 report of the committee that came to be known as the Prime Minister's Committee on Intelligence. This was not Curzon's committee but a smaller, less-known one composed of three officials: Sir Maurice Hankey, Sir Eyre Crowe and Sir Warren Fisher of the Treasury, with Neville Bland as its secretary.

So far as intelligence was concerned, these were the three biggest guns in Whitehall, without whose support no independent intelligence service could hope to survive. With it, survival was virtually guaranteed. The main purpose of the committee seems, initially, to have been to consider whether there was overlapping in intelligence roles and reporting; it decided there was and its report, a model of drafting at once concise and comprehensive, recommended that Sir Basil Thompson's position as Director of Intelligence (essentially a counter-subversion post) be amalgamated with the Metropolitan Police (which led eventually to the modern Special Branch). It examined the financial estimates for intelligence and for transference between the secret and open votes, touched on the idea of the single intelligence vote (as was eventually introduced in the last decades of the century), and quoted budgets as being £127,000 per annum for foreign intelligence (which probably included Cumming's budget for PCOs and, possibly, signals intelligence), £31,000 on CE (MI5 was by then a much smaller organisation), with Miscellaneous – such as the Foreign Office's own Secret Service vote which still survived – as £28,000. Of SIS, the committee noted the 'great importance' attached by the armed services to its product, the fact that Sir Basil Thompson's organisation was largely dependent on it, and its collaboration with the government of India.

Each member of the committee would have known, probably without needing to refer to it, of SIS pre-war and wartime naval reporting, of the La Dame Blanche contribution to tactical reporting on the Western Front, of the worldwide commercial and economic intelligence which helped the blockading of Germany, of the encouraging of America's entry into the war and of the intelligence from the heart of revolutionary and postrevolutionary Russia, and no doubt much else. Survival for SIS was thus assured; but life for Cumming was changing, and the night was drawing in.

20

VICTORY

He had come full circle. Large parts of these last years must have been spent at or dealing with his beloved Bursledon. As we saw at the beginning of this book, he had by then forsaken living on the water for the house he built overlooking the Hamble and the saltmarsh. This was the period from which date recollections of him with his aeroplanes, boats and his tank on the lawn. Recollections of May also date from this period; she was there, they were evidently together.

It has been surmised that he was off work for long periods with angina and was supposed to be taking life easy at Bursledon. He wouldn't, of course, have taken things easy; not only the design and building of Bursledon Lodge, but his boats, his tank and other toys, his workshop and his library, would have kept him as busy as, temperamentally, he probably had to be in order to live at all. The unceasing drive that no doubt helped kill him was also that which gave him life and made vivid what in other men might have been mundane, or sad. The wooden leg on which he scooted, hobbled and hopped for most of his last decade was less a disablement than an affirmation of character.

Thanks to the Kathleen Murray letters (described in chapter two), we now know that these surmises were broadly correct; we also have more detail of the social side of Cumming's life, of May and their domestic arrangements, and some further insight into his personality. Apart from the three pages of

Kathleen's recollections already quoted from, the twenty-three letters comprise twenty from Cumming to Kathleen, one to her father and two to Kathleen from Cumming's secretary Dorothy Henslowe, after Cumming's death. With one exception, they are dated by month and day but not year, but it is clear from internal evidence that all date from the last three or four years of his life.

They are, as earlier noted, playful and affectionate, sometimes arch, often tender, always thoughtful. Kathleen was at school in Jersey and the letters, sometimes accompanied by books and chocolates, mostly concern arrangements for her to stay during her holidays, either at Melbury Road or at Burlesdon. Cumming moves from addressing her as 'Dear Kathleen' (later, presumably by her own wish, she becomes Kathlyn) and signing himself, 'Your old friend, Mansfield Cumming', to calling her his 'sweet little niece' and himself her 'affectionate old uncle'. Age is much on his mind; he frequently refers to it, calling himself ancient or an old fossil, and worrying that she will find him and May dull company.

These days, of course, affectionate letters from a man in his sixties to a girl in her teens are not permitted the presumption of innocence. As well as the playfulness noted earlier, such open expressions of fondness as 'I was so glad to get your nice little letter & especially the big kiss at the end. I gave it to myself in a cracked looking glass but it was very chilly & not at all as nice as a real one so you must send me another & I will put the letter in my cheque book & present it for payment when you come at Christmas . . . I wish you were here to put your dear little arms around my neck . . .' have, sadly, to be defended against the charge that they might be more than they appear.

Everything is possible, of course, and the regressive nature of the charge means that no absolute defence can ever be made. We can, however, insist that it should not be entertained without evidence, of which there is none; indeed, Kathleen's implied responses, her continuing connections with other members of the Cumming household and the judgement she made in her old age, quoted earlier – 'I stayed there occasionally on vacation, Mum & Dad never worried about me, in those days of my childhood people were safe' – suggest innocence. These are the letters of an old man who had lost his only son and who probably regretted the other children he never had. If there is difficulty in interpreting actors from another age, it may be more our problem than theirs.

Apart from revealing a side of Cumming that had been mentioned in other recollections but not illustrated, the letters demonstrate that he and May continued to function as a married couple. She is often mentioned, not only as sending her love but as writing – on one occasion, at least – to Kathleen's father about a forthcoming visit, as shortly to return to Scotland, as being in France seeing a friend who needed help, as having succumbed to the post-war killer 'flu – 'My poor wife had a very bad dose of influenza & was in bed for over 4 weeks with a hospital Nurse all the time. She has been away in Burlesdon now for a month and is quite recovered. I am going down on Saturday to bring her back . . .' – and as keeping her husband waiting – 'I have a few minutes to spare as I am waiting to take May out & she hasn't yet returned from a call elsewhere & I think I can't employ this unusual leisure better than in writing to you.'

There are also frequent references to others whom they entertain or have to stay. Not only to other children, such as the three local O'Neill sisters, called the Pirates, whom Kathleen had evidently played with, but to friends to whom they let the houseboat, to a married couple from France, to un-named relations and to friends and colleagues from London. The latter included Cumming's successive secretaries, Miss Cory, who married (and probably left) and then Dorothy Henslowe who spends parts of her holidays with them. There was also David: 'My wife has bought a nice Puppy – such a funny one. He is a Bedlington terrier & belonged to a Welsh miner. I think his master can't have been very kind, for David (he is named after Lloyd George, not Goliath) was very timid & nervous when he first arrived . . .'

In all, they seem to have led the busy, gregarious sort of life that most of their acquaintance probably led. They were fans of Gilbert and Sullivan: 'We are going tonight to the last night of the Gilbert & Sullivan season. No-one knows what the opera is to be until the curtain goes up but so much does everyone wish to be present that a great many people – over 20 groups – squatted on the pavement all night in order to be the first to enter when the doors are open this evening!'

Building work on Burlesdon Lodge proceeded more slowly than planned, partly because of a post-war shortage of skilled labour, and by 1922 – not long after it was completed – they were already altering it: 'We are staying down here for a week but the house is in the hands of the Bricklayers & everything is covered with white powder, while we have no kitchen fire and no hot water! so that we are rather picknicky and uncomfortable.' They were enlarging a spare room, adding a bathroom for the servants adjacent to their bedrooms and 'A charming Servants Hall leading out of the kitchen & with a splendid great window overlooking the Solent.' He also added a tennis court 'for the benefit of the young ladies who will I hope come & see us sometimes' and a lily pond made from 'an immense ring of curved corrugated iron sheets' and covered in concrete. He planted about a hundred trees, a hundred and fifty roses and over a thousand bulbs, intending that the house should be 'one of the most comfortable I have ever been in' and hoping that friends would stay often. Along with their evident wish for company, however, came intimations of mortality: 'I hope,' he wrote, 'I shall be spared to live a good time in it . . .'

Their servants, Mary the cook – apparently suitably plump – and Ann the parlourmaid, seem to have been a perk of his post and were to be taken on by his successor as 'C' (along with Ernest Bailey, his driver) while he and May engaged a married couple to look after them. However, Ann Hannan evidently returned to work for May; described as Irish and red-haired, she was still in attendance when May died in 1938 and was left the then considerable sum of £500 in May's will.

Among his 'toys' which he offered Kathleen the chance to play with were 'the big Boatshed at Badnam Creek – full of all sorts of boats – and the gigantic mast which you can climb up inside!' (Presumably, the mast of the *Sultan*.) In the same letter, dated 8 March and probably 1920, he mentioned having just returned from two days at Burlesdon – 'the first holiday for four months' – but otherwise most of his references to work were simply in terms of his being busy or, from quite early on, of his retiring soon. In another letter, dated 2 April 1920, he anticipated a week in Burlesdon – 'the longest holiday I have had for six years' – and in October of either that year or the next he excused himself for not replying more promptly: '. . . I write 30 letters a day ordinarily on business & it is hard to find the time to make it 31.'

When Kathleen's father died Cumming immediately wrote an obviously heartfelt letter – 'I am so sorry for you for I know what an awful shock it will be to you & how lonely & miserable you will feel' – and promised to write to her mother (then in Liverpool) to 'make sure that she can take you in.' He added 'This is not a time to talk to you about your future plans & life & I will only renew to you our promises of love & care for you. You must never feel lonely or desolate while I am alive . . .'

Most revealing are Cumming's two last letters, both dated March, one almost certainly from 1923, the other possibly that or a year earlier. The first begins by explaining why he had not replied to her last but one letter before her latest arrived: 'Just before Christmas I went down to Burlesdon to stay in our new house but the night I arrived there I had a nasty heart attack & had to send for the Dr. in the middle of the night. I went back to London the next day & had another & a worse one the same night. It took 3 Doctors & Nurse to set me on my legs again & ever since then I have been quite an invalid – not allowed to eat

or drink anything nice! or to do anything jolly or interesting!
For a long time I was not allowed to write any letters & my correspondence piled itself up in a great heap . . .' He goes on to say
that every time he attempted to reply to her 'some nasty business
letter' would get in the way and that he was now writing during
office hours, 'which is very naughty as I don't allow my Staff to
do it.' He is, he says, very much better and able to get about quite
well 'but I have become an old man all of a sudden & shall not get
over *that*!' He sends love from Mary, Ann and David (May was
still recovering from 'flu in Burlesdon) and asks Kathleen her birthday 'so that I may write it down in my birthday book.'

So there we have it. The final phase had begun well before
the retirement he had obviously planned but was never actually
to reach. The second letter, dated 24 March and almost certainly
1923, begins with another apology for his silence. It was written
in bed – the handwriting is looser and less precise – but he says
he is 'really very much better & have passed through the crisis
I think though I shall always have to consider myself an invalid
& shall have to spend a good many days in bed. I am giving up
work altogether & coming to live down here quietly. I can't
leave London till the end of August as the man who is taking
my place can't be spared till then but I am not allowed to do
any work after midday & have to be up on a sofa the rest of
the time & he comes every week and helps to get through the
work.'

Most people would, of course, have taken medical retirement
a good deal earlier but, for Cumming, Service was an absolute.
He was, he continues, 'pretty bad about 2 months ago & the
Drs. thought I should not last until August but I am ever so
much better now & they tell me that if I am careful I may live
for years – so I am being very careful!' He regrets that the Pirates
– the O'Neill sisters – are moving and so 'won't be able to run
in and out as I always loved them to do.' Miss Henslowe is
coming for her holiday and May's 'great friend', Mrs. de
Crespigny, is coming for a rest.

SIS tradition always had that when his heart finally gave out in Melbury Road on 23 June 1923, he was sitting on his sofa after a farewell drink with someone about to leave for a mission abroad. We now know why this is very probably true. Death certainly did not come when, but it came probably as, he might have wished. His succession was assured in the person of Admiral Sinclair, the then DNI, and that made another complete circle as well as a measure of Cumming's achievement: fourteen years after Admiral Bethell had invited him to take charge of the infant Secret Service, Cumming had turned the post into one that was sufficiently desirable for Bethell's successor, though theoretically Cumming's superior, to be grateful for the offer of it.

Among other retirement preparations Cumming doubtless made is a series of minutes passed in 1919 between the Lords Hardinge and Curzon agreeing that, in the lack of any pension entitlement for the Chief of the Secret Service, an annuity be purchased from funds left over from anti-Bolshevik operations in Russia, sufficient to yield a pension equivalent to that of a captain, Royal Navy. The Treasury was not, of course, consulted – as it was not over the question of income tax – and would not have agreed if it had been.

As for the Service he left behind – that ever-curious creation of a passed-over fifty-year-old retired naval commander – its autonomy and survival were the mark of his achievement. He personified and embodied his creation to a degree unusual even in that arcane branch of human bureaucracy, unmatched in this respect by any except perhaps Felix Dzerzhinsky, founder of the Russian Cheka. This was probably all they had in common, for their differences were fundamental, being those of national character and national political personality. For good and ill, expression of these qualities is often found in purest form in national Secret Service.

For all the many and major differences between now and then, the service inherited by Cumming's successors still bears his imprint. Apart from the hallowed gimmicks, such as the use of the chiefly green ink and the letter C, as well as his title (CSS, Chief of the Secret Service), there are inherited organisational structures and, more importantly, attitudes. Prominent among the latter are the insistence on putting the work first and the easy informality of working relationships.

There is also still something of both the humour and the ethos of Cumming's day, an ethical inheritance that, in a world popularly supposed to be one of ruthless double-crossing, manifests itself in loyalty, decency and a sense of purpose, as well as in laughter in the corridors. Allowing for differences of expression and attitude, there are also still traces of what the early 1920s Appreciation of SIS recommends should be sought in intelligence officers:

> he should be a gentleman, and a capable one, absolutely honest with considerable tact and at the same time force of character . . . experience shows that any amount of brilliance or low cunning will not make up for lack of scrupulous personal honesty. In the long run it is only the honest man who can defeat the ruffian.

The one-legged, monocled Victorian gentleman with the cutwater jaw might have tapped his swordstick at that; then, grinning and taking your arm, he would have added that there was sometimes a drop of cunning and more than a drop of fun involved, too, which – along with a drop of something else – he would tell you all about in a long yarn over a very, very long lunch.

POSTSCRIPT

As he lived, so he died, known to those who knew. The month before he had resigned from the RAC and presumably also from his other clubs, the Naval and Military, the Garrick, the Royal Motor Yacht and the Royal Yacht Squadron. *The Times* announced his death two days after it occurred and there seems to have been no inquest.

He was buried in the churchyard at Bursledon, a few yards from the war memorial which bears Alastair's name. The tombstone, featuring a Celtic cross, names him as Mansfield G. Smith Cumming, Capt. RN, KCMG, CB. There are two lines from psalm 21: 'He asked life and Thou gavest him a/Long life even for ever and ever.' There is no mention of the funeral in either of the two main local papers.

It is a wide grave, almost square, and short. The graveyard plan marks it plainly enough but on a cold, rainy July morning it was not to be found. The war memorial was obvious and the surrounding graves all indicated, except his. There was seemingly not even the place where it might have been. After some time making out fading headstones through wet grass, I stood where I thought it should be, facing the war memorial and watching an, elderly, bare-headed man lay a Royal Naval Association wreath. A few rows away a woman knelt and tended a grave, the rain plopping into the wet earth. It seemed that Cumming would remain elusive to the end.

But something nudged my foot. I was up against an all but impenetrable growth of laurels, rhododendrons, shrubs and weeds, a central and spreading feature of the graveyard. Amidst the tangled grass and undergrowth I saw that my boot had rubbed the stone border of an invisible grave. It took both arms to part the dripping rhododendrons and there, in the green gloom, was the top of a headstone. After more pushing, pulling and peering, the first few letters of Mansfield revealed themselves.

It was, naturally, the only completely concealed grave in the churchyard. Nearby is that of a Bursledon neighbour of Cumming's, Captain Spencer Smith of the 85th King's Light Infantry. It may have been his name that Cumming discreetly borrowed when renting Whitehall Court as Captain Spencer.

It is clear from his will that there was a marriage settlement when he married May, from which he benefited, and, like her, he appointed their nephew and his former employee, Charles Molyneux Smith (by then, Carrington) as executor (his other executor was Clarence Frank Leighton, a solicitor who acted both for him and for SIS). He left some £39,276 19 s., which encompassed various bequests, mainly to family and conditional on his predeceasing May. When she died, much later, she remembered a number of the same people.

These included Ernest Bailey, whom Cumming described as 'my chauffuer and servant for many years', giving his address as 1a Melbury Road. Bailey continued for many years with Admiral Sinclair; when May remembered him in her will she gave his address as c/o the admiral. It would probably be possible to discover more of May's subsequent life than is currently known but the best account short of such research is the magazine article by Evelyn Battye of unknown provenance and date (mentioned earlier).

We know from the last two Kathleen Murray letters that by August 1923 May was in a Southampton nursing home, recovering from an operation to remove an abcess. She was there some time, and was apparently exhausted. These letters, efficient and friendly, are from Dorothy; she implies that she too is being taken on by Admiral Sinclair. The second, dated just a week after the first, in response to a prompt reply from Kathleen, ends: 'You are right about missing Sir Mansfield – we all do enormously and so I expect do you. He was a friend such as one does not expect to meet again.'

Susannah Ritchie recalls that after release from the nursing home May wintered in Florence, taking Ann Hanna with her. She had, of course, to move out of Melbury Road and when she returned to London it was to a rented flat at 22 FitzJames Avenue where, according to Evelyn Battye, she took to spiritualism, believing herself to be in touch with her dead son and husband. She became close to Kurt Hahn, later the founder of Gordonstoun, paying prolonged visits to his school at Salem in Germany during the 1920s and admiring his idealism. Battye believes she regarded him as a substitute son but mentions that there was 'a certain amount of talk linking Kurt and May in romantic vein, despite the disparity of their ages'. The family, however, regarded the relationship 'purely as one of mutual admiration between somewhat idealistic adopted mother and son'.

In 1929 she lent him, according to her will, 40,000 gold marks on mortgage of land in Germany. When he set up Gordonstoun in the 1930s, not far from Logie, she founded Cumming House as part of it and was given permanent accommodation in the school for the rest of her life. Outdoor activities were greatly favoured, particularly sailing ('intense seamanship' as an early pupil, Jocelin Winthrop Young, put it) and there were two cutters named Mansfield and May Cumming. According to Winthrop Young, no one at the school apart from Hahn knew what May's late husband had been.

When she died at Gordonstoun on 3 March 1938 she left her furniture, pictures and books to Hahn, excepting a book entitled *The Last Phase* which bore Napoleon's autograph and her 'other Napoleonic relics', which might have included a pair of Napoleon's pistols. These were all to be sold and the money distributed. She left a leasehold house in Kensington to Violet Thompson, probably a niece, and probate of some £41,980 10s. The Cummings were always comfortable. She also left the copy of the Blackwoods story about the Old Man, who never left anything to chance.

Appendix I

Hector Charles Bywater (1884–1940)

External Evidence

In 1990, William H. Honan, Bywater's biographer suggested, on the basis of certain passages in Bywater's biographer suggested, on the basis of certain passages in Bywater's own book, *Strange Intelligence: Memoirs of Naval Secret Service*, that Bywater was an agent of Cumming's in Germany before the First World War.

Honan buttresses his case with the evidence of Bywater's son, a clergyman, who said that his father had indicated that some descriptions in his book of the espionage activities of an unidentified third party referred, in fact, to himself.

Honan also suggests that references in the 1911 correspondence between Sir John Fisher, the First Sea Lord, and Winston Churchill, the First Lord, to 'our splendid spy in Germany' refer to Bywater. Honan's conclusions are based upon the similarity between the intelligence described in the correspondence and certain articles by Bywater published in the *Navy League Annual* in 1910. Bywater was, at the time and amongst other things, European naval correspondent of the *New York Herald*, resident in Dresden. The principal 'third party' passage in *Strange Intelligence* refers to visits to a number of German naval bases and dockyards, including Danzig, Kiel and Hamburg, in 1912. Honan believed that Bywater had been working for Cumming since 1909.

INTERNAL EVIDENCE

On 2 March 1910, Cumming, according to his diary (Vol I fol 49) called, with Regnart, on Luz (Adml Bethell, the DNI) who gave him leave 'to follow up the English lad in Tra.' **Bywater was 25 at the time and had been in Germany since 1907.**

On 28 June 1910, Cumming records (Vol I fol 163) a meeting in London with HC (accompanied, to Cumming's annoyance, by FK (Fred Knight?) who had travelled to meet him. Cumming briefed HC and arranged 'rates of pay and other essentials'. Cumming wrote 'HC is rather young (25) for the work, and is very quiet and shy. He may do all right and as we are to pay principally by results, the plan should work well. What will probably happen is that he will either fail in getting into one of the Works, or when there will find that he cannot see anything worth reporting.' Meeting arrangements were discussed with Regnart and Cunning turned down a suggestion from the latter, commenting 'I have no intention of crossing the Tr frontier on business'. **Bywater's initials were HC, he was 25, and he lived in Germany.**

There are no pages for Cumming's diary between 19 Jan 1911 (fol 240) and Jan 1912 (also numbered 240 in the same hand). Fol 243 is dated 8 March 1912, in pencil. Fol 247 is dated 9 March 1912 in typescript. Fol 252 is dated 10 Dec 1912 in pencil. A different typewriter is used from fol 253 on. Thus there are no entries for the summer of 1912, the period when Bywater probably made his third party tour of German naval bases, or for the period covered by the Fisher/Churchill correspondence in 1911.

On 2 Jan 1913 (Fol 255), Cumming records an account query from M (Macdonogh). 'The amount corresponded so nearly with H_2O's pay that I asked through the telephone whether they had not made a mistake as to this. I went over at once and found out that this surmise was correct, the mistake having arisen owing to H_2O having been paid two amounts during one quarter – this happens owing to the fact that he only draws his pay when he comes in person and this he can not do at regular intervals'. Cumming also handed over a report from H_2O.

H_2O is, of course, the chemical formula for water, adopted here as a probable play on Bywater's name and as a method of disguising it, particularly if he had become a productive source. It would have been more secure, also, to draw pay on visits from Germany. Maddonogh's query must refer to the Secret Service Bureau's account for December 1912 which records two payments of £125 to H_2O, one marked 'November' in brackets. Cumming's wording strongly suggests that H_2O was paid quarterly (as salaries were at the time). A quarterly payment of £125 indicates an annual salary of £500, the equivalent of Cumming's own. This would make H_2O a very highly paid agent. We know that Cumming's paymasters were tight-fisted and would have been unlikely to authorise such sums for an unproductive agent. Assuming that all agent quarterly payments of £125 are likely to refer to H_2O, then the following payments of £125 are also likely to have been to his account (all under the code '64'); June 1912, September 1913, December 1913, March 1914, June 1914. Against the latter there is the pencilled note '22/10/10'. If this date is taken as H_2O's start on the payroll and June 1914 as the end, it suggests an agent career of 44 months. Bywater's book adumbrates an operational tour in Germany of 42 months.

On 18 Feb 1913 (Fol 279) Cumming handed 'H_2O's latest report to McJ [Captain Jackson, DNI] and showed him the *Daily Mirror* of yesterday with the front page illustration of the supposed new type of Tr 'one gun battleship!!!'. Fol 299 (29 April 1913) shows that H_2O reported on naval matters. 'I handed him H_2O's report R which he said was very good and remarked that H_2O sent a lot of good stuff. In future we are not to put the numeral letters on the reports submitted and we are always to add to any French measurements their English equivalents.' In other words H_2O was reporting from at least the continent.

On 7 May 1913 (Fol 305), Cumming described a conversation, again with McJ, and says 'He told me that the two Captains had been criticising H_2O's report on Borkum and had found misleading statements in it . . . I told him that Borkum was a difficult – almost an impossible place – and that it was extremely difficult to get reliable information about it'.

Bywater records a third party reconnaissance of Borkum (*Strange Intelligence* p 154 onwards), imprecise as to year but certainly in the summer: 'there were several sentries about but they took no notice of the harmless citizen from Emden who was giving his new summer suit – price fifty marks! – an airing in the sea breeze.'

Cumming (fol 328) records for 19 Dec 1913 'called on Roland and handed in H_2O's report.' On 1 Jan 1914 (fol 332) 'Called on Tab . . . I looked through some criticisms of H_2O's reports made by the tripper, but could not remark on them without seeing him and discussing the various points.'

The high level of matches between the diary references to the 'English lad', 'HC', and H_2O, and Bywater's curriculum vitae, together with the chronological matches provided by the accounts, make it extremely likely that Hector Bywater is identical with Cumming's agent H_2O. The implications of this identification are interesting. Bywater was an expert and, later, authority on Naval matters. This and his salary suggest prolific reporting. Moreover, Bywater's own writings also become a valuable source in their own right and suggest that Cumming's early penetration of the German naval target was far more successful than historians have given him credit for. His 1914 CB begins to make better sense.

Appendix II

'Since this account of the Schultz affair was written, further information has come to light as a result of the researches of Mr. Ian Sumner of 28 Norwood Grove, Beverley, East Yorkshire HU17 9HS (*ian@sumneri.freeserve.co.uk*).

In 1999 there was discovered in Hamburg a model boat made by Schultz while he was in prison, beneath the funnel of which he had concealed a note explaining who he was and what he was doing there. Mr. Sumner has been able to examine Schultz's prison records and a hitherto unknown account, compiled by Schultz himself, of his arrest and imprisonment.

Very briefly, these show that Schultz was born in Hull, the son of an emigrant shoemaker from East Prussia, and that he married into the family of a prominent local fish merchant, named Hilton. Working out of Southampton, he bought and sold yachts on the continent and had travelled at least once in the Mediterranean before working for Cumming. His memoir not only gives further detail of his arrest and of others in the spy ring but implies that his family received Christmas presents throughout the war from Cumming, while Schultz himself seems to have been in touch with a 'Mr. Constant' in London. He died in 1924 and was buried as Max Hilton.

Mr. Sumner intends to publish his researches in full but would meanwhile be grateful for any futher information on any of those involved.

Notes

Chapter One

1. Further information about this campaign can be found in Alan Hartfield, *British Indian Armies in the East Indies*, ch. 16, Place: Publisher, 1984. Also K. Douglas Morris, *Naval Medals 1857–1880*, London: Naval and Military Publishers, 1994. This latter includes a picture.

Chapter Three

1. PRO CAB 16/8.
2. N.H. Gibbs, *The Origins of Imperial Defence*, Oxford: Clarendon Press, 1955, pp. 8ff.
3. War Office Jacket S, 527/2D, 'SS Germany', MO2 minute, 27 May 1907.
4. 'Sub-committee of the CID appointed to consider the question of Foreign Espionage in the UK', PRO CAB 16. Proceedings of First Meeting, Tuesday 30 March 1909, p. 2, 'Evidence of Colonel J. E. Edmonds'.
5. 'Sub-committee of CID', op. cit., Terms of Reference, 25 March 1909.
6. 'Sub-committee of the CID', op. cit., Report CID Paper 47a, para 7.
7. 'Sub-committee of the CID', op. cit., Report, paras 8 and 9.
8. See F.M.G. Evans, *The Principal Secretary of State*, Manchester: Manchester University Press, 1923.
9. See Howard Robinson, *Britain's Post Office*, Oxford: Oxford University Press, 1953, p. 21 et seq., and G. R. Elton, *Star Chamber Stories*, London: Methuen, 1958.

10. See Southwell Papers, British Musuem.

11. See W.S. Churchill, *Marlborough: His Life and Times*, London: Harrap, 1933–38.

12. See F.P. Reynault, *Le Secret Service de l'Amiraut Britannique 1776–83*, Paris, 1936.

13. See Treasury Notes on Civil Estimates, Class One, 22; 1927 Secret Service pp. 4–5, 'Inviolability of the Secret Service'.

14. See M. W. V. Temperley, *George Canning*, London, 1905.

15. A good account may be found in Kenneth Ellis's *The Post Office in the Eighteenth Century*, Oxford: Oxford University Press, 1958.

CHAPTER SIX

1. Donald Bittner, *Royal Marine Spies of World War One Era*, Royal Marines Historical Society, 1993.

CHAPTER SEVEN

1. A fairly full account of the affair may be found in Nicholas Hiley's 'The Failure of British Espionage Against Germany 1907–1914', *Historical Journal*, 26, 4 (1983), pp. 867–89.

CHAPTER TEN

1. Cumming refers to the agent as 'Finch', who was almost certainly Harold Wade, then living in Germany. Cumming had in fact recruited Wade's friend, Eustace Wearing (later *Daily Telegraph* correspondant in Berlin and the first British journalist to be expelled by Hitler) in 1912 but Wearing developed cold feet and his mission was taken up by Wade, who first reported to a surprised Cumming in a darkened room in London. He was a good agent who later joined SIS and was working for Cumming's successor at the outbreak of the Second World War. His concern for one of his then agents had consequences which are manifest to this day. (I am indebted to his son, Mr David Wade, for this information.

2. See Alan Bullock's *Hitler: A Study in Tyranny*, London: Penguin, 1991, p. 45.
3. See the Kirke Papers, HQ Army Intelligence Corps.

CHAPTER ELEVEN
1. Compton Mackenzie, *The Life and Times of Octave Five*, p. 113.
2. See Franz von Rintelen, *The Dark Invader*, London: Frank Cass, 1998.
3. Stephen Roskill, *The Navy at War*, vol. 1, London: Wordsworth Editions, 1998, p. 159.
4. Robert Rhodes James, *Gallipoli*, London: Weidenfeld & Nicolson, 1999, pp. 48–9.
5. The background and the negotiations over the next few months are usefully summarised in Christopher Andrews's *Secret Service*.
6. See his biography by Fowler.

CHAPTER FOURTEEN
1. P. Decock, 'La Dame Blanche', unpublished dissertation, Université Libre de Bruxelles, 1981.
2. See Michael Smith, *Foley: The Spy Who Saved 10,000 Jews*, London: Hodder & Stoughton, 1999, p. 53.

CHAPTER FIFTEEN
1. BMCRL134.

CHAPTER SIXTEEN
1. Templewood Archive, Box 2, Part III, File 1, Cambridge University Library.

CHAPTER SEVENTEEN
1. See Christopher Andrews's *Secret Service* for details.
2. Report of the Secret Service Committee, Home Office, February 1919, para 7, 'Secret Service During the War'.

CHAPTER EIGHTEEN

1. Templewood Papers, Box 2, Part II, File 4a; and Hoare's published account, *The Fourth Seal*.
2. Templewood Papers, Box 2, Part II, File 3.
3. Dukes, *Secret Agents* ST25.
4. See Michael Smith, *Foley: The Spy Who Saved 10,000 Jews*, London: Hodder and Stoughton, 1999, p. 53.
5. See Andrews's *Secret Service*, p. 398.

BIBLIOGRAPHY

M ost of these books are referred to in the text, several more than once. For background reading Christopher Andrew's *Secret Service*, despite the fact that it was published some fifteen years ago without the benefit of recent releases of material, remains the best overall guide to the development of our intelligence services and structures. Important background may also be found in Stephen Roskill's magisterial biography of Maurice Hankey, *Man of Secrets* (Collins, 1970), in Andrew Gordon's excellent account of Jutland and the Naval century that led to it in *The Rule of the Game* (John Murray, 1996); also in Charles Seymour's *The Intimate Papers of Colonel House* (Ernest Benn, 1926), in Martin Gilbert's *History of the Twentieth Century* (HarperCollins, 1997) and in John Keegan's *First World War* (Hutchinson, 1998).

Otherwise, in no particular order, books that should be read include *Strange Intelligence* by Hector C. Bywater and H.C. Ferraby (Constable, 1937), *Bywater* by H.H. Honan (Macdonald, 1990), David Stafford's *Churchill and the Secret Service* (Little, Brown, 1999); Peter Hopkirk's *The Great Game* (Oxford, 1990) and *On Secret Service East of Constantinople* (Oxford, 1995); Nigel West's *The Faber Book of Espionage* (Faber & Faber, 1994); Christopher Andrew's *For the President's Eyes Only* (HarperCollins, 1995); David Fromkin's *A Peace to End All Peace* (André Deutsch, 1989); Gordon Brook-Shepherd's *Iron Maze* (Macmillan, 1998); Samuel Hoare's *The Fourth Seal* (Heinemann, 1930); William James's *The Eyes of the Navy* (London, 1955); Penelope Fitzgerald's *The Knox Brothers*

(Harvill, 1977); Peirs Brendon's *The Motoring Century* (Bloomsbury, 1997); Montague Grahame White's *At the Wheel Ashore and Afloat* (Foulis & Co, London); Captain Von Rintelen's *The Dark Invader* (Lovat, Dickson, London, 1933); Gill Bennett's *The Zinoviev Letter of 1924* (Foreign Office History Notes); Somerset Maugham's *Ashenden* (Mandarin, 1991); Henry Landau's *Secrets of the White Lady* (Putnam, 1935), *Spreading the Spy Net* (Jarrolds, 1938) and *The Enemy Within* (Putnam, 1937); Compton Mackenzie's *Greek Memories* (Chatto & Windus, 1939) and *Water on the Brain* (Cassell, 1933); Sir Paul Dukes's *Secret Agent 'ST 25'* (Cassel, 1938), Augustus Agar's *Baltic Episode* (Conway Maritime Publications, 1983), *Showing the Flag* (Evans Brothers, 1958) and *Footprints in the Sea* (Evans Brothers, 1962); George Hill's *Go Spy the Land* (Cassell, 1932); Peggy Benton's *Baltic Countdown* (Centaur Press, 1984); G. R. Elton's *Star Chamber Stories* (Methuen, 1988); F. M. G. Evan's *The Principal Secretary of State* (Manchester University Press, 1923); Howard Robinson's *Britain's Post Office* (Oxford, 1953); Kenneth Ellis's *The Post Office in the Eighteenth Century* (Oxford, 1958); Reginald Teague-Jones's *The Spy Who Disappeared* (Gollancz, 1990) and last but certainly not the least worthwhile – nor the least entertaining – the incomparable William Le Queux's *Spies of the Kaiser* (Hurst and Blacket, 1908).

INDEX

A (agent) 150, 158, 175, 210
Abinger, Lord 309, 316
AC (agent) 242–3, 244, 246,
    251–2, 255, 263, 269, 275,
    279
Adam, Professor 387
Adam Smith, Janet 388
Admiralty
  spying missions 117
  and SSB 72, 134, 150, 173, 370
  and War Office 70
Agadir crisis (1911) 91, 222, 225
Agar, Augustus 423, 424, 426–7,
    435
agents 121, 132–4, 150–3, 196
  businessmen as 132, 153
  and case officers 96–7
  Cumming's attempts to get
    worthwhile 145–7
  first meeting of with Cumming
    119–21
  fraudsters 228
  instructing and recruiting 220,
    418
  intelligence gathering 145–7,
    158–9
  meetings with Cumming 118,
    120–1, 123–4, 126, 127–8,
    135–6, 145–7, 148, 165–8,
    185–90, 206–10, 213–17
  need for recognition 162
  organisation of system of 95–9
  payment 151, 153, 157, 158,
    168, 172, 174
  protection 116–17
  seen as 'scallywags' 98

unclear as to who they were
  working for 127
under War Office control 112,
  122
working for French and British
  Secret Service 169
see also individual names
air force 65
airships 218
Alley, Major Stephen 280, 286–7,
  427, 430, 433
Andrew, Professor Christopher
  286, 306, 320, 396
anthrax bacilli 321
Archer, Mr 255
Asquith, Prime Minister 68, 71,
  91–2
Atherton, Gertrude 43
Automobile Club (later RAC) 39,
  42

B (agent) 97, 120–1, 148, 172,
  175
  origins 209–10
  patriotism towards Austria 120
  payment 125, 156–7, 172
  and sub-agents 148, 151,
    156–7, 172
  and War Office 119, 124
Bailey, Ernest 345, 466, 472
Baird, Major J. (later Viscount
  Stonehaven) 274, 391
Ballard Committee 73
Bangs 265, 267
Baring, Lieutenant 345
Bartholomé, Mme 407

487